NEITHER FEAR NOR HOPE

NEITHER FEAR NOR HOPE

The Wartime Career of
GENERAL FRIDO VON SENGER UND ETTERLIN
Defender of Cassino

Translated from the German by George Malcolm

Foreword by Captain B. H. Liddell Hart

Presidio

This edition published 1989 by Presidio Press
31 Pamaron Way, Novato, CA 94949

Library of Congress Cataloging-in-Publication Data

Senger und Etterlin, Frido von, 1891-
  Neither fear nor hope.

  Translation of: Krieg in Europa.
  Includes index.
  1. Senger und Etterlin, Frido von, 1891-
2. World War, 1939-1945—Personal narratives, German.
3. World War, 1939-1945—Campaigns—Western. 4. Generals—
Germany—Biography. 5. Germany. Heer—Biography.
I. Title.
D811.S41413 1989   940.54'82'43   89-3511
ISBN 0-89141-350-2

Printed in the United States of America

FOREWORD

BY CAPTAIN B. H. LIDDELL HART.

General von Senger's book is one of the most interesting memoirs of the commanders in the Second World War, and in some important respects the most illuminating of all. No other has provided such an instructive picture of battlefield conditions and the tactical problems of that war. At the same time it is outstanding in the light it sheds both on the dilemma and on the mind-workings of a soldier, brought up in the atmosphere of German culture and in the traditions of the old Army, who found himself serving a Nazi regime that was profoundly repugnant to his instincts and to his education.

His book bears out what I earlier came to recognise in the course of our friendship and private argument—that he was more frank in admission of error and evil than most of his contemporaries, while suffering the more acutely, because of his awareness, from the dilemma in which he was placed and the sense of inability to find any solution that could ease his mind and conscience.

Frido von Senger differed in many ways from the "Prussian" German general of popular conception. He was a Catholic from Baden, in the south-west of Germany. He was a Rhodes scholar at Oxford just before the First World War, and that experience left a deep mark on his mind, while broadening his outlook. Returning to Germany in 1914, he was given a commission as a reserve officer soon after the outbreak of war, and saw trench-fighting on the Western Front from the close quarter view of the infantry, which helped towards acquiring a sense of tactical realism. That led on to a regular commission, and after the war he became one of the picked band who were selected for the new Reichswehr, in which he chose to transfer to the cavalry arm—a decision prompted more by his love of horses than by belief in their future as a military instrument. More remarkably, he gained an important staff post in the Army High Command before the next war, and much higher appointments during it, without taking the normal General Staff course.

5

When that war came in 1939 he was commanding one of the few remaining horsed Cavalry regiments, but in 1940 he was given charge of a brigade, now motorised, which supported Rommel's drive for Cherbourg. After the collapse of France he was sent to Italy as chief German liaison officer with the Franco-Italian Armistice Commission, and spent the next two years there. His account of Italy's situation, divergences, and weaknesses is very revealing. Then in the autumn of 1942 he was transferred to the command of the 17th Panzer Division on the Russian front, and took a leading part in the abortive effort to relieve Paulus's encircled army at Stalingrad. That enlarged his experience, and he conveys a vivid impression of it to the reader. His division had only thirty tanks, and that was more than most of the other panzer divisions then had, while it was woefully lacking in adequate transport for the infantry element, so that it was far from being an armoured division except in name. On any realistic reckoning of the German "armoured" strength at this time, the extent of their success in maintaining the struggle on the Eastern Front is more astonishing than their diminishing effect and eventual failure.

In June, 1943, Senger was sent back to the Mediterranean theatre, as chief German liaison officer with the Italian army in Sicily—to organise the defence of that island, and direct the operations of the German divisions there, in view of the imminent invasion by the Allied armies from North Africa. His is the most important and illuminating account of that campaign from "the other side of the hill."

His handling of a very awkward situation made so good an impression that, despite his known critical attitude to the Nazi and Fascist regimes, he was then sent to extricate the German troops from Sardinia and Corsica—a difficult task that he ably fulfilled. Then, in October, he was given command of the 14th Panzer Corps, which covered the western sector of the Italian "leg" and had to meet the advance of the U.S. Fifth Army under Mark Clark, which included a British and French corps. Despite heavy adverse odds, his corps succeeded in checking repeated Allied attacks during the next six months, and holding its ground in the successive battles of Cassino, until that front was at last cracked by the two-angled Allied offensive in May, 1944, from front and rear.

Senger's story of these battles is intensely interesting (and very revealing about the opportunities missed by the Allies), while its value is greatly enhanced by frequent passages of tactical reflection that have both a fullness and depth that is rare in the war memoirs of fighting commanders. His account is remarkably objective not only in dealing with the operations but also in regard to the political aspects of the war, and the personalities of the leading figures on the Axis side. His objectiveness makes his evidence about the unjustified destruction of the Abbey of Monte Cassino by bombing all the more impressive and convincing.

After the collapse of the German front south of Rome, Senger helped to check the Allies' advance on the Arno, and subsequently their autumn offensive, when his corps covered the Bologna sector on the eastern flank. His narrative of the closing stages of the war in Italy is even more fascinating, and a real contribution to history. The book finishes with two particularly valuable chapters—on the "Strategic Controversies of the Allies", and the "Causes of the Defeat of Hitler's Germany"—and a final one on his post-war experiences in "Captivity". In sum, it is a book that no one interested in war history can afford to miss.

CONTENTS

LIST OF ILLUSTRATIONS

(between pages 160 and 161)

11

LIST OF MAPS

1

THE CAMPAIGN IN THE WEST

PROLOGUE

Peace had ended, yet in this winter of 1939/40 war had still not broken out for me. I had taken no part in the Polish campaign. The 3rd Cavalry Regiment, of which I was the peace-time commander, had been split up among various separate divisions. I had then formed the new 22nd Cavalry Regiment, whose purpose was to provide reinforcements for the only existing Cavalry Division. Some weeks later I was nominated to succeed my Brigade Commander, General Count von Waldenfels, who had died in the assembly area near the Dutch Frontier.

I well knew that in modern war cavalry is an anachronism, yet I had stuck to this branch ever since I joined it after the First World War. It was like living on some island; expansion of the Army had started under the National Socialist régime and structural changes in the Wehrmacht had been introduced on June 30th, 1934. But the expansion did not extend to the cavalry, which managed to retain its specially selected officers, recruited mainly from the old Prussian officer corps. As my own roots were in southern Baden I had no traditional ties with these Prussians. Yet I was fond of them—all the more, perhaps, because they now had no real meaning; for in Germany the Prussian concept had evidently capitulated to National Socialism.

Thus it was that I passed a few more unclouded months of that severe and snow-bound winter among these younger comrades. We were still virtually at peace, in quiet country houses in the region of southern Oldenburg and Westphalia. My batman, named Feuerstak, was a good fellow. He was a mild, blond lad, the belated offspring of a peasant farmer in the Harz, and he had been with me since the Göttingen days. He was devoted to all my family and was always ornamenting P.'s picture with flowers. Among the other batmen he made little impression, for he was quiet and unassuming. Nor did he look for conversation or popularity, and this entirely suited me. Since he was not overworked, he would spend hours reading the Bible or just sitting at the window meditating.

15

The officers still had their horses as in peacetime. My own were three medium-weight chargers; for me it was a source of both pleasure and health to keep them in condition.

Warlike preparations were made for the still uncertain eventuality of a campaign in the West. There were tactical exercises during which the march into Holland was rehearsed in detail.

On Sundays we made short excursions to the near-by frontier at Strype, which we observed with some curiosity—as though it might still have trenches, as in the static fighting of the First World War. In the meadows the spring weather had brought out long stretches of hawthorn with yellow blossom decorating the hedgerows. One or two more snowstorms ushered out the winter and then came the warm sun.

Among ourselves—that is, among my older and more intimate officer acquaintances—I could discuss the situation without reserve, or to use an expression of my friend Baade, "get my bearings". We envisaged with some uncertainty the prospect of a showdown in the West, for with our instinctive aversion to the Government we had no faith in it, while the memory of the First World War was disturbing. To a certain extent we trusted Brauchitsch and Halder, for nobody could say that they were Nazis; having received a thorough military training, they would form a more sober judgment of the western opponent than Hitler and his advisers. While the officer corps of the cavalry represented only a small minority, its Prussian outlook was to some extent reflected in the other branches of the Army. Yet from the old Prussian system something more important had survived—the General Staff with its traditionally realistic appreciation of the prospects of war against the Western Powers. In Berlin, where I had worked for some years in the Army High Command, my contacts with many an officer served to strengthen in me a military scepticism that I had already felt on the political side. I now recalled a conversation I had had with the Chief of the Army High Command, General von Hammerstein, who resigned soon after Hitler came to power; he believed that our policy would make us enemies of the West and therefore lead to our defeat.

Now that war was upon us, I realised that personalities like Hammerstein and Beck were only a small élite within the General Staff; they occupied the predominant posts—those of Quartermaster-General and Heads of Departments in the great General Staff.

In Berlin as well as in the provinces there existed another type, whose thoughts were confined to strictly military affairs. These men were incapable of any higher strategic concept, being unable to think politically. They had gradually gained in numbers and influence, for they suited the régime better than highly educated General Staff officers. Politically uneducated officers had also found their way into the General Staff, the O.K.W. (Supreme Command of the Armed Forces) and the O.K.H. (Army High Command). Some of them reflected their prototype, Ludendorff, by virtue of their strictly military proficiency, while others—particularly the younger ones—were merely the sons of people who had become more or less enthusiastic for the new form of government. Under these circumstances it seemed to me that there was little prospect of the General Staff exerting its influence to prevent the outbreak of a world war. Yet I did not abandon hope.

Hence it was all the more of a shock to me when on the evening of May 9th, 1940, the executive order was issued for the invasion of neutral Holland. I was overcome by a certain weariness, such as I had experienced prior to attacks during the First World War— a feeling that at all costs I must have one last profound sleep. Early in the night I proceeded to a command post in a previously selected advanced position, from which I could expect to direct the initial movements of the main body of the cavalry division, which I led. In those last hours of slumber I experienced a great unease— a kind of stage fright or tension, as before some arduous cross-country ride or when confronted with the uncertainties of fate; maybe it was just fear.

On the morning of May 10th the reports from the front were no more favourable than during the previous night. I had an uncomfortable feeling that the regiments had come to a halt before the Dutch fortifications, which were assumed to be weak. I therefore moved up without stopping at the battalion or company commanders' posts. A company commander confirmed my misgivings. In the line of infantry I saw a light tank from the division engaging a near-by Dutch bunker. As the machine-guns from this bunker compelled the riflemen to keep to the ground, I sought cover behind our tank. This is hardly the right procedure, since a tank attracts the opponent's fire; yet it is the kind of thing one does. A young lieutenant, von Köckeritz, had also taken cover here. His runner turned to me, saying: "Sir, the Herr Leutnant has been hit, he is in a bad way." I replied: "My boy, the Herr Leutnant is about to die."

At this moment the unexpected occurred. In the small Dutch bunker a white flag was put up, the troops broke through and began their swift advance.

From the harbours of Lemmer and Stavoren the brigade was now due (according to plan) to cross the Zuyder Zee into northern Holland. The squadrons were to be embarked in numerous small fishing boats which would be towed by a few larger ones. On the latter were mounted cavalry guns and grenade-throwers to provide cover for the landing. The entrances to the harbours had been blocked with sunken ships, and these had first to be blown up. The sea was very stormy. To me it seemed out of the question to seize the far shore with these particular landing forces if there were any sort or organised defence. Success could only be achieved by a surprise attack. I had already advanced this view during the preparatory tactical exercises, and now I was decidedly against risking this operation until such time as we had achieved mastery of the air over the Zuyder Zee.

On Whit-Sunday I drove over to Stavoren to examine the preparations there. From seaward a small warship approached and at first lay off, watching us. When it fired a shell into the harbour everybody ran into the houses for shelter. I found some sort of cover in the open, where I felt safer. For an hour the shells arrived at regular intervals while I cowered behind a pile of bricks. The defensive fire from our small cavalry guns was quite ineffective although the range was only 1,000 metres. One shell from the destroyer fell among one of the gun's crews. It was a horrible Whit-Sunday. Behind that pile of bricks I had some melancholy reflections. It seemed unbearable to have to end one's life, perhaps, in this defenceless state. Before me lay the little harbour with its colourful boats in the spring sunshine. I might well have travelled to such a place with P., even have sat with her in the little public house over a morning cup of coffee. But the passenger steamer that invitingly suggested such a peaceful trip was hit by a shell.

When Holland capitulated there was no point in the landing operation, which was cancelled. Between May 16th and 18th the brigade was taken back to its old billets on the border. The local population greeted us enthusiastically as returning conquerors. But I was overtaken by a feeling of pain and compassion for the ignorance of those who had been misled. The Calvinistic inhabitants were reserved, and keeping aloof, proceeded in their national dress to the churches.

The cavalry division was now sent behind the Panzer divisions of Army Group Rundstedt on a road that was well known to me. Here the German forces had broken through, and here was the focal point. Would this, the last cavalry division, once more go into action? It seemed very doubtful.

THE ROAD (MAY 26TH TO 31ST, 1940)

It was believed that a big tank battle had taken place at Waterloo, but we saw very little evidence of this—only a couple of abandoned tanks.

While on the move to the south of Brussels the brigade for the first time reached a district from which the civil population had fled. The general effect was one of chaos and disorganisation. But an adjutant managed to find quarters for me in a villa built in the English style, standing in a huge park with gentle slopes. In the garden hydrangeas were in blossom.

The customary associations of the word "war"—foreign lands, the proximity of death, uncertainty, hostile people, violence, destruction and separation—are stern and harsh. Nevertheless for me the harshness was tempered, for I was returning to a "wartime home". During the invasion of 1914 I had marched along that some road; in 1915 and 1917 it had been the road for supplies, in 19,18 for retreat, and in 1940 it was once more *the road*. Destiny had again turned it into the road of war after a generation—the same road with the familiar places: Mons—Valenciennes—Douai—Lens—Loretto. In those distant days I had travelled along it as a lieutenant; now it was as a brigade commander. I looked up the landlady of the quarters I had then occupied. Unbelieving, she gazed on me, claiming to recognise again the Lieutenant von S., if that was indeed the man who stood before her. . . .

As the cavalry brigade moved at a leisurely pace, I could make some small detours in order to revive memories. And so it was easy to locate the house at Jenlain where I had first known P. in the last year of the First World War. In those days she wore the nurses' uniform of the Bavarian Red Cross, her hair curling over the brow beneath her cap, the face with its clear oval outline, the large eyes and lively mouth evocative of Marie Antoinette.

In the small private room of the soldiers' rest centre that was managed by P. everything had been in good taste. The few antiques gave the room an air of mellowness, while the books testified to the literary interests of its occupant. The flowers provided splashes of colour, and some large silver-framed photographs disclosed the occupant's background: there were officers wearing the elegant cuirassiers' helmet which even in those days made an oddly old-fashioned impression; and pretty women with long strings of pearls in self conscious poses.

This room, in which my life had taken a new turn, brought memories rushing in upon me. The many incompatibilities between us had seemed to preclude a conventional love-suit. For centuries our respective families had been settled in different parts of the country, hers in the Mark of Brandenburg, mine in southern Baden; not that this proved an obstacle to us. P. had "come out" in the Berlin of the Wilhelmine era and had frequented those large houses which were never the *milieu* of the Prussian military caste to which her family belonged. When the First World War broke out I had just returned from two years' study at Oxford, where I had acquired a cosmopolitan outlook on national customs and conditions. It was never in my nature to judge people either by the particular district they happened to come from or by their nationality.

The adjutant roused me from my reveries. We must get back to the great road so as not to miss any runners. During the drive I

was silent. The past had me in its clutches; the experience had been
a mixture of pleasure and pain. Now I was irrevocably separated
from P. But in a more recent past I recaptured her image—mounted
on a big Irish bay, my favourite, she was riding to hounds—side-
saddle in the English fashion and in English habit. Through many
years in the hunting-field she had acquired a firm seat, and I gave her
fast and reliable mounts which when following hounds took the
stiffest fences safely. As for P., she rode according to the Italian
school, of which I had long been a devotee. Even side-saddle, she
could adopt the forward seat to ease the load on the horse's back.
Its neck would be fully extended, and during a jump the line of its
back formed a harmonious curve from nose to tail.

Presumably all this was over and done with now. The three
horses, moving along somewhere with the column in the staff
echelon, seemed to me like luxurious toys of a declining era. Over
many years I had had a succession of them; once more I pictured
them with heads leaning out of the big loose-boxes, eyes hungry for
movement, ears pricked, coats shining: Swallow, Axel, Knightrider,
Heliotrope, Jester, Titan, Quartus, Quetta, Royal Eagle. Soon there
would be no more horses to share the fortunes of war with their masters.

It was the road which jerked me out of this dreamland at the spot
where the weary squadrons were moving forward. It was here that
in 1914 the thunder of guns on the not-so-distant front could be
heard. Then the road had been more peaceful than at this moment;
for it now offered the gruesome spectacle of an unceasing stream
of refugees—human beings linked by a common misfortune. They
were of two kinds. Some sprawled or sat in vehicles, while the others,
tired and ill-shod, dragged themselves along, pushing hand-carts or
bicycles piled with bedding. Crammed lorries were towing trailers
at walking pace. Once I saw some people crouching over a draped
hearse. To me the most distressing feature was the sight of the old
people who had been left behind and the children who did not complain. Frequently they stood shyly near the field kitchens—hungry
middle-class people with stylish hats and shoes, mothers in whose
eyes was a plea for their children.

At Hersin, a small place west of Loretto Hill, I waited two days
for the squadrons to move up. This was the hill where in 1914/15
we had been in action for month after month. Before Verdun, this
had been the millstone round our necks in the senseless war of
attrition. In those days a ruined chapel stood at the summit, but now
the area around it had become a vast cemetery. In addition to the
thousands of crosses there was a big burial ground for the bones
of those dismembered bodies that nobody could put together. Countless thousands had sacrificed their lives here to gain a few feet of
ground. Their memorial bore this inscription:

You, the wanderer treading this Mount Calvary and these paths that once were steeped in blood, harken to the cry rising from the hecatombs: People of the Earth, unite. Humanity, be human!

And on the other side:

Piles of bones once animated by the proud breath of life, now merely scattered limbs, nameless remains, human chaos, sacred agglomeration of countless relics—God shall recognise you, the dust of heroes.

According to our Army situation report, the troops had now "stormed" and captured this hill, yet there was nothing to be seen save a shot-up tank and a shell-crater which had once more disturbed the dead. There were no trenches, no artillery emplacements, no new graves, no battlefield.

On Vimy Ridge, once the scene of such bitter fighting, now stands the colossal Canadian war memorial. After the First World War an enterprising business-man had preserved part of the near-by trenches by cementing them. Here the antagonists had lain facing each other at a distance of ten to twenty meters, thus keeping out of the way of the reciprocal artillery fire. By way of attraction for tourists, one or two pieces of equipment had been left lying about—a *Pickelhaube*, an 8 mm. machine gun, and in the opposite trench, the corresponding British relics.

This time, however, the war had merely swept past Loretto Hill like a breath of wind. In those trenches, so thoroughly built for the earlier war, the Allied troops had again put up a brief resistance and again pieces of British equipment had been abandoned there.

I stayed three days in Hersin, but this time "on the other side" of Notre Dame de Loretto, so that I could at last see what in former times we had tried to spy out with our telescope. At Cambrai the new, motorised "Senger-Brigade" was formed. Here, too, I was overtaken by melancholy recollections, but of a different kind. I found the spot where on December 1st, 1917, I had disinterred my brother's body from a mass grave. As a fighter pilot he had been shot down on the previous day during the first tank battle in history. In the clear winter sunshine I had spent a long time searching for the exact spot, until after much questioning I was sure of it. With a couple of helpers I dug for hours in the mass grave while the German counter-attacks swept past us in this first tank battle of Cambrai. The English artillery fired on the advancing infantry and we had to seek shelter in the grave. On one occasion we were buried up to the thighs. We managed to free the body, which lay in the lowest of three layers of corpses. But the stretcher-bearers rightly refused to carry it back through that intense artillery fire. So I seized the legs of the body under my arms and dragged it towards my car, finally propping it up in the seat next to mine.

Not far from this battlefield of 1917 and the villages of Bourlon and Moeuvres lies the chateau of Havrincourt. It was here that after the spring offensive of 1918 I had lived as adjutant to the XIV Reserve Corps. The chateau had been razed to the ground. But now it had been completely rebuilt in the old style, and served as quarters for Army Group von Bock, from which my brigade was assembled.

THE NEW WAR (JUNE 7TH TO 16TH, 1940)

By now I had completely lost the "stage-fright" that had overtaken me in Holland. I merely wanted to get to grips. While the brigade was assembling I drove ever nearer to the front where fighting was taking place. We crossed the Somme—there at Péronne, where I had spent many months during the earlier war. In those days the guns were changed every evening, like so many tennis rackets, because each day they had been worn out in action. But now there was no thunder of guns to indicate the direction of the focal points; no sound of any fighting. We crossed the Weygand line, and for the first time saw something resembling a field of battle—the high wall of a park which served as a strongpoint had been the object of the fighting. Behind some carefully thrown-up earthworks lay a few corpses and much war booty. As sometimes happened in 1916 after the big battles, so now an endless column of prisoners drew near, tired, indifferent and sad—yet there had been no big battle. Our attempt to reach the front line failed. The villages were too blocked up and destroyed by artillery fire. At one place the soldiers rolled a wine barrel into the road and filled the mugs of the passers-by. From a neighbouring shop a man threw an umbrella into every vehicle as it passed.

My brigade was sent to operate with Panzer Corps Hoth (which had broken through to Rouen) in order to cover its left flank towards the south east, that is, towards Paris. We covered 200 kilometres in 25 hours, mostly in thick dust, frequently along roads used by the columns. The Panzer divisions had broken through, but the gap was narrow. To the right and left, the infantry divisions had not advanced so quickly. It was necessary to work one's way around occupied villages, then mop them up, incurring losses in the process. The enemy attacked the point of penetration from the air with bombers, which also caused losses.

My adjutant, the son of General Feldt, drove his tracked vehicle over a mine, killing the occupants. I had taken this young officer into my staff, and on this day had made him follow in the rear to ensure his safety. His brother had fallen in the Polish War. It was my bitter duty to write to the father, who commanded the cavalry division, that he no longer had any sons. It was only three days since I had left his command area, taking his son with me.

The news of this severe personal loss reached me in an old farmhouse in which I had hoped to pass a few restful hours. To the right the view stretched far across the pleasant landscape in the bright June sunlight; to the left stood an ancient water-tank and another cottage. There were always some hours that breathed an atmosphere of peace, even here. Happiness somehow seemed to exude from the immaculate beauty of the land, mingling with deep sorrow over the fate of friends.

The brigade had moved up into the front line on the Seine. Two bridges that I wished to capture had already been blown up. Parts of the brigade crossed the Seine. Follow-up units of the Manstein Corps took these elements with them, subordinating them to the corps, so that they were temporarily removed from my authority.

For a while I rested at a small pleasure spot which already savoured of Paris. One part of the place was in flames, and the heat was oppressive. I sent for a bottle of champagne from the cellar of a house in ruins, and while drinking watched six *poilus* plucking chickens for a field kitchen. Two others were digging a grave in a pretty garden for a dead civilian who lay on the pavement, glazed eyes staring at the passers-by.

Later I reached Rouen, where the entire left bank of the river and the old part of the town on the right bank were burning. The shops were closed; a few scared shop-keepers opened theirs again in accordance with orders, but there was nothing one could buy other than fruit and cake. On the river-bank machine-gunners were shooting at looters and at furtive wanderers in the deserted streets. The fire brigade tried to master the fires. An officer who was trying to save the cathedral shot a man alleged to have attacked him; a driver held the man by the collar. While returning I looked down upon a sea of smoke from the burning tanks. Standing out above the smoke was that Gothic wonder, the Cathedral; flames were shooting up the wooden scaffolding round one of its towers.

The next day we marched without contacting the enemy, keeping behind the Panzer Corps. It proved one of the finest days for an "outing". The countryside away from the main road was deeply peaceful, like some large park with high hedges enclosing narrow remote lanes. In some places the scene was reminiscent of those English prints of the eighteenth century: a small garden of flowers sparkling in the June sun, in the background a real cottage, heavily thatched, the open stable door revealing the croup of a white horse.

During these sporadic storming movements our daily life assumed a certain rhythm. Towards 5 p.m. the forward thrust and the urge to fight subsided. Then some fine and quiet garden was reconnoitred, and tea was served. If no orders arrived, we remained idle and behaved like happy travellers on some romantic car journey. Scouts were sent ahead to find night quarters. The days were always quiet.

In this way the scouts found Chateau Motteville, a large Norman castle belonging to Count Germiny. No soldier had yet crossed its threshold, but it was completely unoccupied. The flower-beds had been freshly watered, a light shone through the open church door. In the dozens of guests-rooms we found the beds made up; the cellar was full of Roederer champagne, the living-rooms had copies of *The Times* and the *Revue des Deux Mondes*. After a bath and fresh laundry (lent by an officer after my own had vanished in the tracked vehicle) I enjoyed a long, deep sleep. The next morning I had break-fast alone, the meadows spreading before me into the distance. Pampered guest that I was, I lingered with a cigarette and some reading matter, as if I were at the start of a long, peaceful day in the country.

The illusion was shattered as soon as I reached the hall. Many officers awaited me—on the left, French prisoners, on the right, German commanders and adjutants who wished to speak with me.

The brigade advanced downstream along the banks of the Seine towards Le Havre, so as to prevent the encircled troops from break-ing out southward across the river. The control of operations was difficult as our troops were approaching from several directions. At St. Romain there was some fighting, with slight casualties. In our rear, the village of Bolbec was still in enemy hands. The drive was rather uncanny, with the river on the left, the steep heights on the right, the columns unable to secure their flanks.

That evening we ate in a restaurant at St. Romain, with refugees sitting at other tables. We made the place secure from all directions and chose as our quarters a hospital, whose matron on the following morning said a few words of thanks to me because her worst fears had not been realised.

The brigade moved further towards Le Havre, which we were supposed to enter if this could be done "without heavy losses". As we were no longer finding any resistance, and all the troops that had broken through were already across the Seine, the brigade had only to clear the mines on the roads, and by 9 a.m. we entered the town, the last of the British having escaped just before our arrival. I made the mayor's office my command post—the mayor himself had fled, but his office preserved an air of luxury: there were flowers every-where, and the furniture was *Louis Seize*.

Now began a period of great unrest and trouble. Responsibility
weighed heavily on me; there was an atmosphere of brooding uncertainty. The oil tanks containing France's biggest stocks were
burning, and the fires could not be got under control with our own
resources. Looting was going on in the streets. The water supply
was in danger. Hundreds of English lorries blocked the streets,
having been made unserviceable at the last moment. The quantity
of captured provisions could not be estimated. On the ground floor
of the town hall prisoners were lounging about. My accommodation,
in an undamaged villa standing on a height, was most comfortable
in the *grand bourgeois* style, rich and rather cold in its splendour.
The Italian Consul joined us for meals. He had remained in hiding
until the entry of our troops, and had lost his house.

There was no peace at night. From time to time I looked out of
the window to see the light from the burning tanks reflected on the
wide surface of the sea. This went on for many hours.

The harbour district was under bombardment. Our anti-aircraft
guns took hours to bring down the barrage balloons left by the enemy.
Meanwhile the further pursuit had to be organised. The brigade was
supposed to cross the Seine and advance along the coast. But the
river was too wide here to do this with the available shipping. It was
a test of nerves to have the responsibility for the town, the salvage
of supplies, maintenance of peace and order, and relief of forces
required for the further advance.

When I allocated the duties in the office before leaving, there
was a scene. The deputy mayor, an elderly, white-haired gentleman,
had given me his ungrudging assistance throughout these days and
nights. At our departure he seemed moved, and in the presence of
the town councillors spoke hesitatingly as follows: "I am not sure,
Colonel, whether in my present position it is at all proper to say a
word of thanks. But I am anxious to do so, for in all these dreadful
hours I have had the feeling that you, sir, have wished to help this
unhappy town." The brigade started back again along the Seine,
spending a few evening hours at Ecouis, where it had halted overnight
during the advance. In the dark it crossed the newly-built Seine
bridge at Les Andelys. Next morning when the troops reached the
far bank of the river the staff moved into a luxurious villa that had
already been "plundered". Now the last orders had been issued,
and a stage was reached where it was difficult to keep awake. The
adjutant claimed to have fallen asleep while standing. Part of the
morning was spent in refreshing sleep in good beds with fresh linen.
In the afternoon we drove from Elbeuf to Vimoutiers without once
contacting the enemy.

The land became poorer. There were no more large castles as in
Normandy. At Vimoutiers the staff occupied a very attractive detached

villa. At meals in the restaurant the officers felt as if they were on manoeuvres, although the enemy had been located only ten kilometres away. The waitress was dressed in black silk with a white apron. But when they brought in the blood-stained brief-case of a French officer killed while reconnoitring the approaches, the illusion was soon shattered.

THE WAR DEGENERATES

From Vimoutiers the brigade was moved westwards towards Condé, where it was to take possession of the crossings of the river Orne. To the south of the road along which it advanced everything was reported occupied by our own troops. Up to Falaise all went well. In the market place a scene took place such as one might have witnessed in a war in the eighteenth century. Prisoners were being brought in and were piling up. They hardly gave the impression of regular troops. One soldier protested against his capture, maintaining that as the father of four children he had been erroneously called up.

The battalion forming the advance guard had met with resistance at the Orne, and there was a number of killed. Here as elsewhere, opposition developed only on the roads. Artillery was brought up, but as the brigade only had 10 cm. cannon and 15 cm. howitzers, it was doubtful whether this was worth while. Everywhere civilians were standing in the doorways of their houses as though the war were over. A battalion was sent across the Orne farther to the north, and this marked the start of those well-known bulletins: "The battalion, by dint of vigorous attacks, has captured 2,000 prisoners without suffering any loss!"

Some of our own troops approached the enemy on their own initiative, waving the white flag, which led to impossible negotiations between the outposts. Some French officers who discussed terms under the white flag with people from my brigade were declared prisoners and protested. Consequently the fighting flared up again east of Condé, with further losses.

In the evening I was constantly in demand at the front line. The French brigade commander wished to negotiate only with a person of similar rank. Because of the afternoon's experience he refused to come over, but wanted me to go to him. In the end both of us, accompanied by our respective adjutants, left our forward posts and advanced slowly and hesitantly towards one another, meeting in the middle of no-man's land.

The French colonel asserted that he had no authority and asked for a pass to allow his adjutant to proceed to his division. All this took up half the night; then Condé was evacuated. In the rear of the brigade there arose the nightmare of the transport and guarding of prisoners—thousands of them. Later I discovered that the 7th Division, advancing alongside my brigade, had done the whole of the day's march under the white flag so as not to lose time.

The question arises as to whether this degeneration in the fighting was an entirely new phenomenon, or had it been like this from the start? Were our great successes wrested from an army that had decided not to offer any serious resistance? Indeed, had there been any battles in the field, anywhere?

Possibly the German superiority in operational control and in technical resources had made the value of our infantry seem exaggerated. In view of the obvious collapse of the enemy all further sacrifice seemed pointless. Our infantry had not been able to show whether its offensive power was as great as in 1914/18. Yet in many places it had fought with heroism.

It is only by the sober, calm language of war history that the harmful results of a falsified, vainglorious reportage can be avoided.

In the language of statistics the total casualties on the German side were put at 45,000, and if this figure is divided among the divisions and the days, the resulting losses were "unbelievably small", to use the Press idiom. The enemy lost a million and a half prisoners.

Ruminating over the course of the war up to this time, I was struck by the foresight of General von Seeckt—an assessment that other military men were apt to deny him in those days. Seeckt visualised the future of war as taking the form of battles between small professional armies, in which the élite of the warring nation would be integrated: dive-bombers, Panzer troops, air-borne infantry. Compared to them, the people's army, mass-organised as infantry, would play a subordinate rôle. The course of this war proved Seeckt to be quite right. Nobody could have foreseen that a clever combination of modern weapons untried in war would achieve such speedy results.

I myself considered that the lightning defeat of France by no means signified the end of the war, as many people believed. The tactics of over-running could not be applied to the principal opponent, Great Britain, for three reasons: Great Britain had supremacy at sea, while the Axis powers did not. She was a member of a Commonwealth that covered half the world. And finally the mentality of the British was different from that of Continental Europeans, a fact that could be appreciated only by those who for years had studied them with understanding. The German idea that in other countries the ordinary man merely fights for a dominant plutocracy was not applicable to the British. They fought for an ideal that could not be understood by the Germans under the Hitler régime. Hitler had taught people to dismiss Western democracy as nothing more than "parliamentary quarrelling, the arithmetic of the majority and the corruption of crooks". In reality, however, it is the climate of democracy that enables the British to enjoy personal freedom, law and order, and to respect the dignity of man. For these things they will always fight.

On June 18th, 1940, the war appeared to be over. Without orders the westward advance was continued. Only at Vassy was there any local resistance to be overcome. Many prisoners had to be sent back. In the afternoon the brigade at last received a radio message from the 7th Panzer Division, commanded by Rommel, to which it was now subordinated: "The Division is in the process of attacking Cherbourg. The Senger Brigade is to attack Cherbourg from the direction of Valognes."

We had to set off in a quite different direction. From Vire I drove ahead northwards by car for several hours, and had the feeling that the last shot had been fired. At Carentan, when I wanted to cross the bridge, the local people maintained that it had been blown up by the British. In fact there were shell hits in the vicinity. Was the fighting flaring up again? It was no longer possible to reach Valognes that evening. I led the brigade forward up to the area St. Lo-Carentan so as to be able to commence operations at dawn along the eastern shore of the peninsula towards Cherbourg.

On June 19th at first light I reached Divisional H.Q. at Sotteville, and discovered that since the previous day parts of the 7th Panzer Division had been on the western outskirts of Cherbourg without overcoming the resistance. My brigade was to attack Cherbourg from the east.

I wanted to avoid contact with Rommel, for I could then remain freer in my decisions. So I asked that he should not be wakened. My 10-cm. batteries were moved into positions that had been agreed with the artillery of the 7th Panzer Division, and returned the fire that the outer forts were evidently directing inland, especially against the approach roads.

As they arrived the battalions were sent south round Cherbourg, then turned north towards the coast. The situation remained generally obscure. Here one could see dozens of sailors with their kit-bags running inland, because for them the war was over. Yet Cherbourg was being defended; a continuous weak artillery duel could be heard.

The battalion first into action ran into minefields and had to use its heavy weapons. Another battalion was detailed for outflanking operations further east. By using a field track bordered by high hedges it managed to keep clear of all obstructions. I decided to take my car along with the column. Things were more quiet now. There was a muffled report of a near-by shot, the bullet whistled past my ear, and I felt as if somebody had tried to assassinate me. When the surrounding area was searched, two sailors came out of their hiding-place with arms raised, but no weapon could be found.

Hugging the coast and pressing on with speed, I led the battalion along a narrow track into Cherbourg. Despite the warlike circumstances, the setting was strangely beautiful—on the right, the blue waves heaving in the sun, in the harbour, thick yellow clouds pouring skyward from the burning oil-tanks. The guns of the outer forts were silent. We could survey the whole town as well as the harbour. To the left, the higher part of the town and the inner forts stood out. For safety we kept an eye on the line of the crest, sharply defined against the blue sky. On the left and behind us there was still some minor noise of firing where the battalion that was first in action had run into the minefields.

When my car reached the centre of the town, I saw Napoleon's equestrian statue in the open square by the harbour, the Corsican pointing with his right hand towards England. Then as now!

The garrison commander came towards me and in silence surrendered the square, the harbour, and the garrison. For a moment we stood facing each other, saluting and silent. Then he invited me into the town hall, where the anxious council was assembled. I greeted them with a short speech. The customary first occupation poster was drafted. Then General Rommel appeared, evidently rather annoyed that the Senger Brigade had forestalled his division in securing the surrender of the town. A local newspaper described the capture, crediting the brigade with an "outflanking operation in the traditional manner of the German General Staff".

All that remained was to mop up. Twelve thousand prisoners had to be removed from the peninsula in wearisome stages and on foot.

On this apparently final day of fighting I wanted to have a good meal again and proceeded to an hotel, only to find that it had already been requisitioned as prisoner-of-war quarters for 120 naval officers. Greeting me politely, their senior officer invited me into a private room, appointing a very presentable sailor as my orderly officer. Thus I dined alone as the guest of my prisoners. A day or two later I called on four senior admirals and two generals. The ceremony was frigid, short and formal.

On Rommel's orders the brigade was now moved to Valognes. Here everybody wanted peace and quiet. In the little town hall I discussed with the mayor a manifesto to the populace. The negotiations were like some stage play in which I was both actor and audience. On one side of the conference table sat the mayor and two councillors, on the other side, myself with two officers. Outside all was quiet in the heat of summer; inside it was cool, and the small-town atmosphere made one drowsy. In fact there was little difference between this and the session of any town council in time of peace. The mayor gave the impression of an elderly gentleman not averse to good living. The secretary at his side was very deferential and ventured no opposition. If either of the two councillors raised some objection, the mayor became very ungracious and brusque. He fully maintained his dignity while translating the German edict into French. This was an enjoyable hour of office-work, a kind of idyll after the constant forward movement and the noise of battle. I protracted the negotiations as much as possible in order to follow the mayor's double duel—against the invaders, whom he seemed to regard as merely incidental opponents, and against his own dissentient colleagues, on whom he visited a disapproval that was all the more intense.

Owing to major difficulties in transporting prisoners we were moved for a short period to St. Lo. Then the brigade staff went to Martinsvaast.

On conclusion of the armistice we had our first hours of rest. From my quarters I drove my big car quite slowly along the lonely country tracks with their recurring bends and ups and downs. Usually the house-high hedges precluded a view of anything beyond the track itself. Here and there I passed some little house, as old as the hills and built with stones from the fields, always with a flower-filled garden. Often the house was covered with roses. The flower garden against the low frontage of the house was full of beauty. When the car reached the highest part of the road, the distant view was of white-capped waves gleaming in the sun, with far below me the yellow sands of the bay, the surf breaking in long white lines. Negotiating a few more serpentine bends, the car reached the sands and I had the wide bay all to myself. The beach was so deserted that the shadow of a gull gliding over the sands was enough to rouse me with a start. The roar of the surf heightened the feeling of solitude. The incoming rollers lifted me clear of the sand, and receding, left me firmly on my feet again, with sand and white foam washing around them.

Occasionally I drove to the north-east corner of the peninsula, to Barfleur. On the first occasion, on June 20th, the place was still not occupied by our troops. The inhabitants were timid and fearful. Frequently they stood by the walls of their houses with hands up. But they very soon thawed when I spoke with them in relaxed and colloquial French. At the harbour entrance stood an old windswept church; the harbour contained fishing craft that were not permitted to sail. The sunlight played on their coloured sails. The landlord's wife was friendly in a feminine way with her clients, whether French fishermen or German officers. There was no spit and polish here, and inside of me I was no longer wearing uniform. I was savouring to the full the pleasure of being just a person among persons.

DÉPARTEMENT ILLE-ET-VILAINE

In accordance with orders received, I eventually took over the administration of the Département at Rennes. The town was overcrowded with refugees, mostly people returning to their homes, who had to be stopped because they were not allowed into the coastal zone.

All barracks were full of prisoners. With the assistance of French officers, doctors and administrative officials everything was sorted out—for better or for worse. At an improvised camp under canvas, named Champs de Mars, there was a mixed crowd of Senegalese and Algerians.

In the railway station shortly before the German occupation an aerial bomb had hit a train loaded with high explosives; where it had stood there was now a huge furrow in the ground, measuring several hundred metres long and a hundred metres wide. Beside it, three or four trains had been twisted into a shapeless mass, and trucks had been hurled out into the open fields. It was said that many British soldiers had lost their lives in these trucks.

The forces allocated to administration of the rear areas were nothing like sufficient. The troops and the divisional staffs tackled the resulting difficulties with great reluctance. The whole brigade was employed in guarding prisoners. Strange regiments with commanders senior to me were put under my orders.

The difficulties were enhanced by disciplinary crises among the troops; from private to battalion commander they had only one wish— to return home. When they enquired how long they were expected to remain here, I invariably replied that it would be two to three years. This usually caused consternation, for they really believed that the war was over, or that they would be immediately transferred to England in order to finish it off. Nobody seemed to reckon with the possibility of a long period of occupation after the conclusion of peace.

The Département's administration was busy with problems of the movement of refugees, provision of work, currency, exchange of goods with the unoccupied territory, shortage of mineral oils, and the beginnings of food rationing.

Each morning I was in the chair for a meeting in the town hall. On my left sat the mayor, on my right the German district commandant; opposite me the representatives of the town and district officials, headed by the Prefect. He was a small and very intelligent man, but not entirely representative. At first he made several attempts to play to the gallery by opposing the sweeping German requisitions. Finding that he could get no further, he began to co-operate, until in the end there was a secret understanding between him and me

against the nonentities on both sides of the table. Before long he was
himself demanding that they should be dispensed with. The German
district commandant complained that he could not follow the proceedings, which I conducted in French. But what with the mass
of work, I had no time to spare for this elderly officer, who, although
specially appointed, was not competent to tackle economic questions.
Accompanied by the Prefect, I also travelled round sectors of the
Département such as the industrial centre at Fougères, where the
extensive shoe industry was idle. In addition to the plenary meetings
there were separate discusions with industrialists, with the Archbishop, and with the owners of the closed houses of ill repute. The
few days at Rennes involved a lot of work and little relaxation.
But once the horses had been brought up, I could at least enjoy
some riding.

At the local café Madame sat at the next table during the evening
meal. She was past fifty, not smart but pretty; with her were three
men, two older and one younger than herself. At 10 p.m. civilians
were asked by the military patrol to leave the establishment, while
the officers were allowed to stay on until 11 p.m. One of the older
men at the next table remarked to me with a smile that it was very
hard on one to be a civilian. I gave him to understand that he could
remain there until the later hour, and this was like a signal, for the
others were soon sitting at the invaders' table, inviting us to join
them in a glass of wine. Until midnight the conversation centred on
politics. Monsieur was a doctor, a specialist in radiology, while the
husband of Madame, the other older gentleman, was a merchant and
said little. The young man owned a ladies' hairdressing business, and
attended to Madame's coiffure.

As the turmoil of continuing troop movements carried me elsewhere,
quieter days began to return. Yet I was sorry to have to relinquish
the administration of the Département, which I had tackled in all its
ramifications, running it more or less autocratically.

At Lannion the brigade was disposed along a wide sector for the
defence of the coast. Lannion itself was an attractive little place. The
staff personnel were admirably housed in a hospital, while the operational staff were accommodated in a spotless little hotel. From my
room the view extended across the river to a large monastic building
made of the grey stone so characteristic of this part of the country.
On the banks of the river some old women in coifs sat basking in
the sun. When I tried to open a conversation with one of them, she
first wanted to know whether I was English or German, and on
receiving my answer she became very pensive and inarticulate.

In St. Malo, when I looked up my old friend X, the proprietor
of the Hotel de la Mer, his pleasure was unconcealed. He and his
wife enquired about P. and asked me to send her their warmest

greetings. Naturally lobster would be ordered. While the staff were having an apéritif in a small café in the town, I saw Monsieur Piet trotting round St. Malo in search of the biggest possible lobster. Before dinner there were renewed greetings at the hotel before we climbed the narrow staircase to the dining-room on the second floor. Madame herself had cooked the dinner, and when it was over she entered the room. Curtly ordering the serving-maid to disappear, she announced that a bottle of champagne would now be opened.

In addition to Madame and Monsieur, there was her ninety-five-year-old grandmother. And not for the first time this old woman told the tale of how in 1870, when the Prussians were in occupation, her first-born child died. Now, presumably, she too must soon die. She thought us "charming" and kissed our hands; her only anxiety was that "we might kill children". Monsieur was rather more enlightened. He knew Germany, and spent the whole evening talking politics. Madame, already white-haired, wore a white apron-dress. The whiteness of her face was emphasised by the ruby make-up of her lips. She was still very attractive, her hands and feet were small; she was as unhibited as a *grande dame*, and full of charm. She feared that lipstick might be forbidden, which would put an end to the small amount of coquetry that made her life worth living.

The political conversation of these bourgeoisie (as opposed to the upper strata) nearly always included something of this nature:

"Now you people are on top again, as we were in 1918. First you're up, then you're down—for us it is a great misfortune. You worked while we idled. You had an efficient government, ours was a miserable one. The chief culprit was that flabby Daladier, who neglected our armaments for the six years he was War Minister, and should be shot. As usual, the small man foots the bill, while the big man escapes the consequences".

"This has not been a real war. Seeing ourselves left in the lurch by the British, and finding that we had nothing to equal your technical methods—your dive-bombers and your tanks—we had already secretly made up our minds to give in. Hence this war has no battle-fields, no emplacements, no infantry assaults or day-long fighting. As all our refugees are only too well aware, there is nothing but ruined towns and rows of shot-up or burnt-out trucks. And in between is the peaceable, unharmed countryside, through which you were able to drive for hours on end. For us it has been a costly defeat, for you a cheap and total victory."

"We would like to know what National Socialism really is. We only know that it has made your people tremendously effective and successful. Yet nobody has been able to explain its political programme to us."

"Here, among the small fry, you will encounter but little hostility.

But do not deceive yourselves—the bourgeoisie, formerly supreme in France, will always be hostile to you, because your régime has inflicted irreparable wounds on the elements with which it is associated—the Jews, the Freemasons and the Catholic Church."

"If you experience little hostility, it is mainly because for historical reasons the English have never been liked in this region. They have let us down very badly. And now we notice this very marked difference between their troops and yours. We often wonder if we are imagining things when we see the exemplary conduct of your troops, about whom we heard such gruesome reports during the Polish campaign. It is very difficult for us to accommodate ourselves to the good impression made by these troops; for the German soldiers behave better than the English or even the French troops that were billeted here."

Thus spoke the local inhabitants, and it was more or less the same story with the ordinary French soldiers now in captivity. On the other hand the French officers maintained a very polite silence, as did the aristocrats, and also the Lord Archbishop.

French Billets

The wife of Count P. at Martinsvaast was German; her maiden name was Baroness Sch—, from the Berlin banker's family of the same name. For half a century now she had been a Frenchwoman, and her German was no longer fluent. The eighty-year-old Count, belonging to the French branch of this family, and his white-haired daughter, widow of Count D., were equally at home in French and German. They never discussed politics, and were most kind, attending to all the needs of my staff. Thus the evening meal was cooked in the kitchen of the chateau and was consumed in the magnificent hall, the food being purchased in Cherbourg.

Here were three French people who accepted their fate with equanimity, never complaining. They wasted no words on the bombardment, or the billeting of first the British and then the Germans, which had exhausted their supply of linen. They sent for workmen to replace broken window-panes. All three possessed the instinctive elegance of the true aristocracy. Their only request was the understandable one that the corpses still lying about in the park should be interred.

It was reported that one of our commanders was quartered in a chateau which possessed a pack of hounds. The officers said that the lady of the house was a sportswoman. One day she would be seen cropping a horse, the next attending to the flower-garden, and this reminded me of my wife. It is narrow-minded to think that women should not pursue all the sporting activities that attract men.

Admittedly ideas vary as to what is truly feminine. This lady's chateau was off the beaten track, standing at the end of a three-kilometre road over the fields, with woods of deciduous trees on either side. A stream wound its way through these meadows, with wooden bridges, dams and small mills, until one reached this jewel of a property, a chateau of grey stone in the Norman style, not very big, with many outhouses, stables, etc. The slope on the far side contained a huge flower garden. As one got nearer, the old cook could be seen through the kitchen window, the copper pans gleaming around her.

The officer who was billeted here happened to be out, but the servant announced my arrival to the owners, who were sitting at the dinner-table. The entrance-hall was small and ornamented with hunting trophies, brass horns and sporting prints. The countess came to meet me. She was in her fifties, a slim, sporting figure with a some-what severe, English type of face, who seemed at home in the back-ground of horses, hounds and hunting. She interrupted her dinner, and at once we found ourselves engaged in an animated discussion on the breeding of foxhounds. Her mind was exclusively on sporting matters, unprejudiced and with no trace of hostility.

When I made an attempt to establish my quarters in another equally attractive chateau with a beautiful park, belonging to the family of Count Y., I encountered the most uncompromising refusal from the lady of the house. Three days earlier her sister, the Countess, had given birth to her sixteenth child. She was awaiting the arrival on a visit of a grand-niece. Despite all this and to satisfy my curiosity, I asked very politely if I might be shown one of the guest-rooms in the huge chateau, although I had already decided not to take advan-tage of this grudging hospitality. Leading me hesitatingly up the staircase, she asked again what to do if the grand-niece should actually arrive. At this stage I boldly ventured the comment that there were such things as billeting regulations.

Of quite another type was the Marquis Z. While exploring the countryside out of curiosity and also to find a billet, I chanced upon his huge box of a house with its decrepit façade behind ageless trees. When the dog barked the Marquis came running out of the house, dressed in a blue suit with brown shoes and scruffy linen, a cigarette between his discoloured teeth. He overflowed with kindness, intro-duced himself as the Marquis, and translated this for my benefit as "Markgraf", adding: "Naturally you are a cavalryman, I can see it plainly. I too was a serving cavalry officer—we are much the same breed the world over. To be frank, I would rather have one of your kind here than anyone else."

With a generous gesture he and his wife put the entire house at our disposal. This type of billeting was rather like what must have

taken place among French colonists in North America in the eighteenth century. A ship would bring a number of young girls to the
colonists, and thereafter everything depended on the right people
finding each other.

The attitude of the beautiful Countess F., with whom I eventually
took up my quarters, was similar to that of the Marquis Z. This
final search for a billet in France began like a Tauchnitz novel of
the turn of the century. I started to look for something so remote
that I would have to ask my way to locate it. One chateau seemed
at first sight to be unoccupied. It was quite new and like a new
painting. When at last the door was opened, a well-dressed individual
turned us down, and referred us to other properties situated farther
along the hedge-bound lanes in even more remote positions. So we
moved on. At a window of the next chateau two girls could be seen,
one very pretty but rather aloof, the other, less attractive, belonging
to the house. She showed me three guest-rooms but advised me not
to stay, as her mother was consumptive. Then the pretty one made a
suggestion that I should stay at her own house. Her attitude was
similar to that of Marquis Z: since requisitioning is threatened, be
careful to choose the right people in good time.

With some hesitation she took the seat beside me in the car, and
slowly we drove along more hedge-lined lanes. On arrival, discussions were entered into with her mother, resulting in the whole
chateau being more or less put at our disposal. The head of the
family was the old Countess, widow of a cavalry colonel, living on a
modest income, who occupied the chateau only in the summer and
with inadequate domestic staff. There was no land with the property.
She had no news yet from her two sons, both cavalry officers; the
young Countess was the wife of the elder son and had her five-year-old
son with her. They shunned us, emphasising their national antagonism,
scarcely laughed, and avoided shaking hands.

This was my last campaigning billet. I had chosen it in the
expectation of remaining there for months with my adjutant, Captain
Horenburg, and my assistant adjutant, Prince Hatzfeld. It was peaceful and remote, fulfilling my requirements for a good billet. True, it
was not by the sea. The temptation to inhabit one of those chateaux
where the park runs down to a beach was great, but a suitable one
could not be found. For me hotels were out of the question. Here I
had a large bedroom and a sitting-room overlooking the old disused
entrance to a garden run completely wild with many roses along
the high wall.

Those few days at G. seemed happy, despite uncertainty as to
the immediate and more distant future. Separated from our wives
and families, this odd assortment presented certain difficulties, as
usually happens where people are thrown haphazardly together. But

all this was of secondary importance. Here we could relax after the turmoil of war; I relished my immediate surroundings—the numerous trees, the peaceful, dream-like garden of the chateau. On my frequent visits to the coast I listened to the waves and drew satisfaction from the steep thatched roofs of the stone cottages, or the little churches.

It may be that man can only find complete happiness in the past, where memory has blotted out all calamities, or in the future, to whcih he may apply his untroubled imagination. Truly happy hours leave a deep and lasting imprint.

Overdue letters began to arrive. P., never prone to tears, wrote about how she had cried when the church bells proclaimed the surrender of France. Between the lines I could read the cause of her tears. She was like me in her anxiety over this further acquisition of power by Hitler. What would be the effect of the victor's brutal impositions on the peoples of the occupied territories? The triumph of arms would merely encourage the excesses of these immoderate men, further reducing the prospect of an end to the régime. Could there be any deliverance from this shameful dictatorship short of military defeat?

After the tearing pace of the campaign the quiet hours of reflection made my own tragedy clearer. Inevitably it was the dilemma of many of Hitler's officers: they would fight bravely for victory, while at the same time hoping for defeat—because they loved their country.

My mind was troubled also when I remembered those who had fled to these parts from their brutal executioners. Long before the advent of Hitler I had regarded any form of anti-Semitism as barbaric. Among my friends were many Jews, but not one anti-Semite. I could imagine no more cultured home in Germany than that of my friends and relatives the Schwabachs—in Berlin and at their country seat at Kerzendorf. I remembered with respect my friend, Kurt Hahn, the patriot and distinguished educationalist. And I recalled with compassion the friend of my family, who had succeeded my father as Prefect of a small town in Baden, and ended his life during the war because he was allowed only half the normal rations. And I remembered the poorer Jews who possessed neither the connections nor the means to escape by fleeing across the sea. All were kindly people, kinder and more ready to help than the average run of men. It may be that for them the ageless perils of a minority status had acted like a purifying fire.

How could the German people be led along such a wrongful path? This was what all my friends were asking themselves. Here was the terrible climax of political and moral contamination. The delusion of the master race had been embraced by those whom any man of the world would regard as the very opposite of "masters", not only because of their appearance, but by reason of their lack of education and usually repellent manner. These people could now apply their narrow minds to exploiting defenceless men, veterans of earlier wars, old people, women and children. Millions of ignorant, undiscriminating people, subservient to the authority of the State, had no escape from this most dreadful aberration. Like P., one could be in two minds as to who should be the object of one's tears—the innocent victims, or the mass of complacent citizens whose conscience had been numbed.

It was in the countryide that I sought oblivion. From one of the lesser hills the plain beneath had the appearance of an extensive forest, but in reality these were thousands of trees that bordered the green pastures and the fields under cultivation. Winding their way across this landscape were the narrow hedged-in tracks, the roads and the streams. The small thatched cottages could only be discovered at close quarters, as in England. Their windows framed the peasant women in their picturesque white bonnets.

Occasionally I used some pretext to enter one of these cottages, accompanied by my friend Rohr. An open fire burned under the chimney, and over the fire hung the big pot with the simmering soup. The flagstones were kept spotlessly clean, the brass fittings on the boxes sparkled as if the sun were on them. The many brass-bound wall cupboards were not just part of the household furniture; behind some of them were the family's beds. The room, serving as kitchen, living-room and bedroom, was like a jewel-box in which the peasant woman, untouched by war, lived the unchanging rhythm of her daily life, eating, sleeping and bearing her children.

In the chateaux, too, the kitchens reminded one of pictures of bygone centuries. The wooden walls, the dark wooden furniture and the immense uptakes of the chimneys were blackened with age and smoke, contrasting with the polished brass on the walls. The meal was brought to the table in earthenware pots, the dark wine sparkled in the firelight. On the black face of the huge fireplace hung the only ornament—an ivory crucifix.

I became interested in the calvaries—those large Golgotha groups carved in stone that portrayed entire stories from the scriptures. There they stood, in the graveyard by the church, open to the sky, the pride of the village. These monuments round the low, wind-swept churches gave their stamp to the countryside, so remote from the bustle of the outside world, so far from war and industry, so devout. It is a quite distinctive district with its own language and its links with the sea.

REFLECTIONS ON THE FALL OF FRANCE

The campaign in France added a new chapter to the science of military operations. The successful invasion and occupation of the country were attributable to the new tactical use of armour. When the German Army High Command transferred the main weight of the attack from Army Group North (which had originally been earmarked for this purpose) to the adjacent and more southerly Army Group Centre, the conditions were created for a break-through. In the north the network of canals would have precluded the rapid eruption of the Panzer divisions. The French High Command squandered its forces because it considered that the entire front line should be occupied in accordance with the Maginot formula. Consequently it possessed no adequate mobile forces to throw against the spearhead of the German armour.

But this was not the sole explanation. Here, too, strategy was affected by political considerations. On the one side was the autocratic dictator, disdaining all counsel, not fully alive to the further possibilities of this western offensive, which in any case he was not bound to pursue. Thus among the German people he gained the reputation of a highly gifted strategist whose skilled diplomacy had obviated the necessity for a war on two fronts and atoned for the defeat of 1918. On the other hand the Allies were led by men determined to avoid at all costs a repetition of a blood-bath like that of the First World War. Hence the Allies' plans and their execution of them suffered from the scruples of their leaders.

Finding itself in a desperate position, the British Expeditionary Force had acted independently and had escaped. For some time its successful embarkation seemed inexplicable, but this was only a symptom of the half-hearted way in which even the Germans themselves were conducting their war. For their operational supremacy should have enabled them to prevent the embarkation. They treated the matter as of secondary importance because the extent of their victory was not fully appreciated and because they feared a possible reverse, as in 1914 on the Marne. They felt that the liquidation of the B.E.F. could be left to Army Group North, whose infantry divisions with their right shoulder on the coast were advancing more slowly. Guderian, the exponent of modern armoured warfare, apparently advised on the spot against attacking the B.E.F. with the very adequate Panzer forces at his disposal, because in the rainsodden marshy terrain such an attack "was useless and would entail unnecessary sacrifices"[1]; also because half the tanks were in urgent

---

[1] History of the Second World War—The War in France and Flanders, by Major L. F. Ellis, Appendix II, p. 389 (H.M.S.O., 1953).

need of repairs in order to be "available for other operations within a short period". In the prevailing situation this was also the impression of other higher officers, many of whom firmly believed that the German Air Force would prevent the embarkation of the B.E.F. On the German side, hardly anybody thought that the occupation of all France might involve major defence problems for a country like Germany that lacked sea power. The Germans remained blind to the numerous mistakes in the British conduct of the Norwegian campaign, because the gamble of the German landings had been successful. It is true that Hitler's Supreme Command did not reckon with a long war; clearly in such a war the German naval forces would not be able to guarantee protection for the French coasts. But this situation forced the adoption of Maginot tactics, involving defensive measures along the entire coastline, the employment of large forces for this purpose, shortage of reserves, and the risk that the general defensive system might be invalidated through a single successful enemy landing under cover of superior naval forces.

The Korean war in 1950 was to provide a further example of the problems created by invasion operations such as the German occupation of France. The North Korean armoured forces made a surprise southward penetration, occupying nearly all of South Korea. But here the counter-blow occurred much sooner than in France, for MacArthur's troops, which were covered by some 260 warships, landed at five points immediately behind the invaders, thereby turning the enemy's victory into a defeat.

Thus the campaign in France not only afforded an example of bold and energetic use of armour for the swift occupation of a country and the defeat of the armed forces of a great power, but also gave rise to problems—unrecognised in 1940—resulting from a purely land invasion without the means of safeguarding and holding the conquered territory against invaders from the sea.

The theory that Hitler himself wanted to let the B.E.F. escape cannot be confirmed, but it is quite plausible, since he immediately agreed to the relevant decision by the C.-in-C. of Army Group Centre. Hitler had never thought that Great Britain would declare war; when this happened despite Ribbentrop's forecast Hitler was dismayed and perplexed. It is therefore within the bounds of possibility that he still hoped to reach an agreement with Great Britain. But the dictator had over-reached himself, and it was now too late. He had not reckoned with a normal democratic government, which scrupulously explores all the circumstances, where the Prime Minister is constantly in conference with his Cabinet, and where the ultimate decisions are those of a Parliament reflecting the will of a majority of the people. Dictators often make a poor showing at foreign policy, because in their dealings with other peoples they tend to use the same primitive methods as they apply to their own population, which has been divested of all political rights.

The French armament industry was made to work at full pressure for German armaments. The subjugated French government had to provide workers for German factories, since nearly all Germans capable of bearing arms had been called up. Without France's industrial potential Hitler could not have kept the war going for so long. This was the big advantage that he derived from the fall of France.

2

THE ITALIAN ALLY

The Façade

In July 1940 I was ordered to establish a liaison between the Franco-German and the Franco-Italian armistice commissions at the headquarters of the latter in Turin. While travelling by car to my home in Göttingen I suddenly came upon the mounted squadron of the brigade, which was being moved up to join the main body. I could not resist leaving my car to greet these fine big horses with a final pat on the neck. Henceforth I would be completely separated from them. I could never again be the same person, and this was a painful thought. I cast my mind back over my military career and the part that horses had played in it. I had became a career officer by a mere chance. At the start of the First World War I was in my seventh half year as a student, but at no time had I made any preparations for a future career. My two years at Oxford between 1912 and 1914 had completely changed my mental outlook. This was no preparation for gaining a livelihood. The system of residing in college at the classical English universities had strongly attracted me even before I actually experienced it. I grew fond of the regulated life in the old buildings. I lived in an atmosphere of the humanities, adorned by an element of luxury in the beautiful, centuries-old gardens. The lofty dining-halls contained oak tables with silver on them. Twice a day we assembled in the chapel for prayers, attendance being obligatory for Anglicans and Non-Conformists alike.

Before the war I had done some military service and training exercises. When it broke out I was soon made a reserve officer in my peace-time regiment, the Freiburger Field Artillery, and later I became a regular service officer. The defeat of 1918 was followed by a two years' transition period akin to civil war, during which on December 2, 1919, I married P. Then came two years at the Cavalry School in Hanover, my transfer to the cavalry, and eleven peaceful years of service with the Canstatter Cavalry Regiment. During this time a son and a daughter were born to us. There followed an interlude at Hanover, where as adjutant of the Cavalry Brigade I had so little to occupy me that we lived in the country under the same roof as our horses, in the heart of the hunting district. I was then transferred to Berlin, where I spent four busy years in the Cavalry Inspectorate, until in the autumn of 1938 I took command of the Cavalry Regiment at Göttingen.

Thus I never completed a course at any military school. On passing the required examination, I was considered too old to take up the career of a General Staff officer. How glad I was to escape the misery of repeated changes of domicile, and to be able to remain with my horses! I had bought a house on the outskirts of Canstatt, where I enjoyed life for many a peaceful year.

It is rare to find good instructors among serving officers; one such was my squadron chief, Baron Geyr von Schweppenburg, another was my regimental commander, Baron Weichs. Both men had qualities far above the average. Geyr was in all respects a modern and unorthodox leader. Many regarded him as the Army's best authority on training. His custom was to plan even the smallest exercise on a realistic war basis; he trained his troops mainly at night, and made a special point after exercises of letting his subordinates criticise the arrangements. As Military Attaché in London before the Second World War he gave timely warning against under-estimating the British. In the Polish campaign he particularly distinguished himself as commander of an armoured division.

Baron Weichs was a quiet man who inspired confidence and generated the greatest respect. Like Geyr, he was a born leader. Both men despised Hitler's entourage and were fully alive to the dangers threatening the nation.

The Reichswehr that Seeckt had created was a good body of troops consisting almost entirely of dedicated soldiers who had remained on the active list. Officers were no longer advanced because of their high social position, which had so often been the criterion in the days of the monarchy. The Reichswehr is reproached with having formed a state within the state, just as the Prussian military men were said to have created their own state, or at least to have dominated it. The isolation of the Reichswehr is said to have undermined the democratic basis of the Weimar State. The Army had not become integrated with the state.

Much of this is true. The Weimar State, like the Reichswehr, was subject to presure from the extreme Right and Left. Between these millstones no genuine democracy could prosper. The Reichswehr remained loyal to the government coalitions of the Centre. True, many officers were reactionary and inclined towards a monarchy, but they did not favour a coup d'état or association with parties or sectors hostile to the state. They took their cue from Seeckt. He was a kind of paragon whom others could not equal—a *Grand*

Seigneur, reserved, cultured, elegant, well-to-do, and because of his position, not exposed to military criticism. His attitude towards the apparently simple but intelligent War Minister, Gessler, was rather too cool and unaccommodating to provide an example to the officer corps of subordinating military affairs to the primacy of political power.

My transfer to the Army High Command—the equivalent of the earlier War Ministry—ocurred almost simultaneously with Hitler's accession to power. On June 30th, 1934, I was standing with my schoolboy son at the window of our pleasant house at Dahlem. The boy wanted to know the meaning of the continuous explosions. I explained that some of the people—those who, if they were running Germany, would do her no good—were exterminating each other.

Yet this massacre involved the fate of the armed forces. Hitler had opted for the Reichwehr, sacrificing in the process some hundreds of persons, most of whom were innocent. In the impending expansion of the Army the S.A. had insisted on securing positions as officers for its adherents. This was natural, for it was their loyalty to the Führer that had created the new state, and in consequence they wanted their old campaigners to be in the new Wehrmacht. Hitler doubtless realised that if he delivered the Army into the hands of the S.A., he would be dependant on that organisation. It was never actually proved that the S.A. wished to enter this conspiracy. But Hitler would be facilitating his own acquisition of power if he silenced and eliminated opponents in the party who wanted to settle their account with him. The evil ran its course.

I had as yet no regrets for belonging to the Army. Only a few senior officers of the High Command had gone over boldly to the Nazi camp, either because they lacked political discrimination, or due to personal ambition. There was still a strong element of generals possessing integrity, who appreciated the worthlessness of a dictatorship as such, and in particular that of Hitler himself. Among these were Beck, Fritsch, Heinrich von Stülpnagel, Erwin von Witzleben, Fellgiebel, Olbricht and dozens more. As for the others, they could claim the excuse of "blindness", as indeed was the case with many sons of the German people, and never more so than after the campaign in France. In all its history this unfortunate German people had never been given the opportunity to appreciate democratic processes, or to act according to them. Already in the First World War I had been struck by the political blindness of many officers. Instead of controversy, the Germans had political security through faith in the executive. It had been so during the monarchy, and so it remained, especially in regard to the distinctive position of the Army within the framework of the state. There was no political control of the General Staff—that famed organisation which in the opinion of so many had the qualities needed for victorious wars and had been the saviour of the nation in the nineteenth century. Under Hitler this situation was to repeat itself. There was the day at Potsdam, marking the reconciliation between Field Marshal von Hindenburg, President of the Reich, and Hitler. Had not the black, white and red colours been resurrected? Had not the "party brawls" been silenced? And so the politically inarticulate people regarded them all as united— the Führer and the monarchists, the Wehrmacht and the party!

We who despaired over all this harboured no illusions, for we appreciated the psychopathically criminal character of the tribune. Although only a "grade one" staff officer, I was occasionally able to talk openly with Hammerstein and Fritsch. The tradition of the General Staff was too deeply rooted in the soil of Prussia for the many officers from old Prusian families to be rendered suddenly incapable of making decisions. Among other things they had kept their Christianity, and were conscious of this recrudescence of the anti-Christ involving persecution of the innocent, disregard of the law, despotism, personal insecurity and National Socialist delusions. I knew only too well why P. had wept at the pealing of the bells for "victory" over France.

Arriving in Turin at the end of July 1940 to establish a liaison between the Franco-German Armistice Commission in Wiesbaden and the Franco-Italian Commission, I did not feel a stranger. I had already travelled across Italy privately, and had visited it again in 1938 with a military mission. The fleeting impressions I had then acquired were now confirmed through the chance of war. Italy became my second home.

To form a true judgment of Germany's southern partner, one had to take into consideration a multitude of factors, such as political tendencies, events and traditions; one had to distinguish between the façade and the various internal compartments of the Italian régime.

The façade showed the Fascist régime as linked with the monarchy. When Fascism seized power eighteen years earlier, it had left the monarchy apparently inviolate, knowing that it was too deeply rooted in the people, especially here in Piedmont, where the ruling house had been on the throne for the past eight centuries. The Sovereign could claim not merely a historical prestige, but also a personal one. He had built up this prestige over a reign of nearly forty years. In the First World War he had at first kept his country neutral, then led it into war on the side of the victors.

Ostensibly Fascism had merely strengthened the monarch's posi-tion. It had opted for the monarchy, and could violently suppress the anti-monarchic movements that had always existed in Italy. Hence Fascism could enlist support from various conservative circles, and the consequent cessation of party strife was gratifying to many a citizen. Yet this public truce was deceptive. A state cannot have both a monarch and a dictator at its head. There would be competition between them even if the monarch should forswear all political attitudes and influences. Victor Emmanuel III did the opposite.

The more thoughtful elements gave the monarchy the bigger chance of survival; for the succession was secure, whereas the power of the Fascist dictator was such as to imperil his own succession. It was the same in Germany. The man who through a coup d'état or a political landslide succeeds in wielding power over a period of time gains so much influence that there can be no question of a normal succession. The longer the dictator rules, the younger the successor will have to be. But in Italy and Germany alike this cut across the custom of rewarding "old campaigners" and appeasing opponents. Consequently if a dictatorship wanted to perpetuate itself in a new and lasting dictatorship, the old campaigners and many other live political forces would have to be passed over in favour of a new candidate for the succession. Any change would necessarily involve violence. Thus the apparent strength of a government without a legal basis proved to be a weakness—a fact that was foresen by very few.

Many Italians also regarded the monarchy as a guarantee against upheavals in the event of the death or fall of the dictator. They pinned their hopes to the age-old tradition that the monarchy would prove a steady rock against political storms that were now in abeyance or just below the surface of events. Many believed that in supporting the monarchy they were opting against Fascism, and this was particularly true of the intellectuals. In Italy too they not only abhorred the lawless basis of a dictatorship as such, but despised those people who had helped to establish it, or who submitted to it. This is only natural. The intellectual—be he a man of action, a scientist or just a well-educated and politically conscious citizen—may understand the historical phenomenon of a dictatorship, but will never accept the mass of subservient, undiscriminating and culturally limited followers of the dictator. An attitude of servile devotion to the dictator disqualifies the citizen from membership of a politically responsible stratum of society. Hence a dictatorship cannot hope to feature any aristocratic principles, as represented by that select group of people who are capable of independent judgment and are prepared to play a part in the political life of their country.

In Italy this responsible element was not so radically minded as in Germany. Fascism had become a parasite of the monarchy. It made use of the very persons who were ready to serve the state by virtue of their trust in the authority and integrity of the monarchy. Such persons were to be found especially in the administration and among the diplomats and the officer corps. Supporters were not only royalists, but liberals of all shades, the clerical party, and those without party affiliations. Fascism was directed more sharply against its rival, Socialism, than against the ordinary citizen. It needed the favour of the masses all the more because it could not fully rely on the educated élite.

FASCISM

Alongside the orthodox bureaucracy of the government officers there was a Fascist party bureaucracy, which was also charged with administrative tasks unrelated to the party apparatus. But its activities were mainly concerned with meetings, indoctrination in foreign affairs, and maintenance of order. Its influence on politics, administration and diplomacy was less than in Germany, since the orthodox bureaucracy was still intact. This party bureaucracy was accepted but also despised.

Fascism showed signs of exhaustion, not because it had failed, but rather because it proved the rule that political life dies away if there is no struggle. The only incentive came from arguments behind the scenes and from foreign influences. Morally Fascism was not as tainted as the Nazi régime. There had been no June 30th, 1934. The murder of the Socialist deputy Matteotti had been enough to provoke a serious crisis. Hence the opposition in Italy was not actuated by conscience to the same extent as in Germany.

Italians not directly involved in party activities merely lent formal support, but were reluctant to devote their spare time to the cause. Once a year they paraded in black shirts ornamented with the party insignia. Neither the party nor the non-members took offence at this fortuitous participation. It was accepted that membership of the party could benefit one's profession. There was nothing very prejudicial in belonging to it, whereas in Nazi Germany the upper strata soon got to know of Hitler's frightful crimes.

The Lateran Treaties had more or less legalised Fascism for the average Italian citizen. Many Italians had been worried over the rift between the Holy See and a Royal House that had been accepted throughout the land ever since 1870. The mass of the people were faithful alike to the King and to the Catholic Church. Only those who have associated with the lower classes and speak their language can assess the influence of the Church—an influence that draws strength from the structure of the family, which can be described as semi-matriarchal. To Italians the *mamma* is a more significant being than to northerners, possibly because she remains aloof from political life. It is she who decides the destiny of her children, holds them in her sway, dominates the dauhters-inlaw, and is steadfast in her religion.

On the other hand the majority of men are tinged with anti-clericalism, through which they can indulge their craving for independence, their liberal instincts and their Garibaldian concepts. In Italy the youthful nationalism of 1870 had also contained an anti-religious element—a complex which in Germany became more pronounced with the call for "severance from Rome". By eliminating this complex, Fascism acquired considerable buoyancy, and this distinguished it from National Socialism.

In 1938, as officers of the mission in Rome, we were officially taken to the Chapel of Remembrance for the "Sacrifices of the Blackshirts". We Germans were astounded to learn that this chapel was dedicated to the Virgin Mary. The difference between the two movements became even more apparent on seeing the priests in their robes with military badges of rank, who were the regimental clergy of the Blackshirts, or the nuns escorting young children dressed in *Balilla* uniforms.

It was evidence of this nature that again reminded me of the difference between the two régimes. I had been hunting with a Lombardy friend and was having tea with him in his house in Milan. In the exquisitely furnished rooms I met a circle of women from the wealthy Milan aristocracy, all wearing party uniforms and pledged to various party welfare activities. Such a thing could hardly have been imagined in equivalent German circles. While driving back from a country estate I witnessed another small incident that was typical. In a certain village there seemed to be an uproar, and I expressed the desire to have a closer look. But my Italian chauffeur suggested that "it was hardly worth while, as they were probably beating up the local group leader, quite a usual event on a Sunday evening".

This independence is probably the key to the position that Fascism had attained in Italy, and it also accounts for the adaptability of Fascism in the face of a continuous evolution. Desire for freedom lies at the root of the Italian's preference for independence from the power of state and Church. With him there is a need to grumble at the state and the priests. His criticism of authority involves him in no serious risk. For this reason there were fewer informers in Italy than in Germany, where denunciation was regarded as a good deed in support of the authority of the party and hence of the Fatherland. Moreover, in Italy an excessive number of eavesdroppers would have been needed in order to report all the malcontents.

Disillusion contributed to the symptoms of tiredness in the older form of Fascism. Under the impetus of a young and energetic dictatorship, Fascism in its earlier days achieved many good things. The trains were punctual, dirt vanished from public places, marshes were drained and made habitable, and so on. Yet it could not be concealed that all this was not enough to solve the real problems of the state. In southern Italy in particular the vast contrast persisted between the rich latifundian landowners and the desperately poor agricultural workers. The dearth of raw materials made the agricultural economy dependent on the invisible export of tourism. The contrast between the expenditure of even moderately well-to-do tourists and the dire needs of the southern proletariat was hardly an incentive to the national pride that totalitarian systems try to foster. Similar was the experience of those seasoned workers from Italy who could find no work at home and earned their living abroad, separated from their families for months or even years on end. In short, the promised paradise seemed to many to be as far off as ever it was before the March on Rome.

ITALY AND THE WAR

Italian soldiers are neither better nor worse than the soldiers of any other nation. All men are by nature fond of the family, of life and peace. To enjoy war is surely degenerate; it appeals more to the single, adventure-seeking man than to the father of a family. Yet in the life of a nation the father, as head of the smallest unit, is more important than the adventurous youth, who in war is the first to be sacrificed. This fact was even more significant to the Italian, who lives so much within the family, than to the German. If the father of a large and young family is killed in action, the only result is bitterness and woe.

Before the days of Mussolini Italy was not averse to war. How otherwise could it have successfully borne the heavy and protracted battles of the Isonzo during the First World War? Piedmont is the cradle of Italy's military prowess. With the exception of Prussia, no dynasty was ever as militant as the House of Savoy. It was the campaigns of the Piedmontese battalions that unified Italy, thereby fulfilling the dreams of many generations. Everywhere the memorials bore witness to this fact.

At Turin and in that neighbourhood were a number of military schools. The Piedmontese nobility, like the Prussian one, put service in the army on a higher plane than any other service to the state. The discipline was good. In Piedmont there were also many alpine units, the best that the Italian Army could produce—proud, quiet, outwardly not very disciplined troops, but reliable types, brought up the hard way, accustomed to camping in the eternal snows with only the barest supplies. They were magnificent soldiers, to whose pride and modesty I paid tribute whenever I happened to encounter an *Alpino*. The Navy, too, was good, though I had few contacts with it.

My activities on the Armistice Commission gave me an insight into the mentality and qualities of the Italian General Staff officers. More especially in the early days the Italian Armistice Commission was manned by selected men. Its head, General Pintor, was regarded as second only to Badoglio. The war college in Turin went in for serious studies in the science of war, and especially in military history. Many Italian officers were specialists in particular periods, and wrote about them. They had to pass examinations prior to promotion.

In Turin the German delegation and the Italian officers of the rank of colonel and above occupied the Hotel Principe di Piedmonte, a skyscraper in the centre of the city. From the eleventh floor on which we lived, one looked out upon the lonely silvery chain of summits towering above the rest of the world and sparkling in the eternal snow.

In contrast to the German Armistice Commission at Wiesbaden, the Italian commission had not requisitioned this hotel, and it was still mainly occupied by the ordinary public, which made life more interesting. The Italian officers lived in the hotel with their wives. The German delegation had the same privileges of residing here as were reciprocally given to the Italian delegation in Wiesbaden. But for a long time P. was unable to start on the long journey, because like thousands of Germans wishing to travel for pleasure, she failed to get permission from the party. She could not prove that her visit would "further the National Socialist philosophy of life in foreign countries". However, thanks to the intervention of the O.K.H. she managed to arrive in the autumn of 1940.

The attitude of the Italian generals and political personalities towards their German ally underwent an unmistakable change between pre-war days and now, when the campaign in France was over. Before the war Italy was sitting on her high horse. The successful Abyssinian War of 1935/36 had added to her conceit. The organisation of the conquest had been well prepared and had involved only minor losses. The campaign had provided no real test for the troops, for the enemy was too weak.

The deficiencies of the Italian Army had not escaped the notice of our military mission of 1938. It possessed no effective modern tanks, and was therefore quite unequipped for a modern campaign. Hence the Italian government wanted to avoid war, and impressed this upon the German partner. It was characteristic of the difference between the two systems that of all people Count Ciano, Mussolini's son-in-law, was working for peace. It is true that the General Staff under Badoglio was doing likewise, for he was only too conscious of the Army's weaknesses. Reliable friends were saying that Fascism had even neglected armaments, as it wanted to maintain its popularity by giving priority to social reforms. Those in the know actually regretted the conquest of Abyssinia, which had caused enmity between Italy and Great Britain, and had given the undiscerning mass a false idea of Italy's military might.

Apart from this critical attitude towards Mussolini's foreign policy, the Italian General Staff had looked askance at Hitler's successes in Poland; it had long been worried at the prospect of being drawn into the conflict. Yet if Italy avoided the war, she would have to reckon with being treated by her partner as a second-class power.

Those in favour of restraint had the upper hand for the time being. Italy had stayed neutral in the war with Poland. When I arrived in Turin there were two different facets to the Italian partner's attitude. The undiscriminating mass of the people were enthusiastic over the German success in France, and gave credit to Fascist leaders for having on this occasion been "on the right side", that is, on the side of the victors. In Italy, as in Germany, the Army and the Foreign Ministry contained a number of short-sighted adherents of the party who despised scepticism as a sign of weakness and lack of confidence in the superiority of the totalitarian systems. It was these people who had combined with the party to urge involvement in the war. Naturally the Germans in the liaison staff could not openly discuss such matters with the others. But they saw the rift that even in Italy separated the credulous optimists from the experts in the armed forces, who judged the situation much more seriously. Anybody who failed to bestow the usual praises on the German Army was regarded as one of the sceptics. The heads of the Italian Armistice Commission, namely its president, General Pintor, and his Chief of Staff, Count Gelich, were so regarded.

It was due to General Heinrich von Stülpnagel, head of the German Armistice Commission, that I had been appointed leader of the liaison delegation. Fortunately this highly gifted man and his competent Chief of Staff, Colonel Böhme, appreciated our objective reports of the situation. These reports were produced quite independently of the Embassy in Rome.

General von Stülpnagel felt, however, that he should not accept a "political reportage" from the liaison delegation, for this seemed to him to be a function of the Ambassador. Presumably the German Foreign Ministry, which had a representative on the Armistice Commission, had given him a directive on this point. It was very soon apparent that a "non-political" reportage on so political a question was not possible. The Armistice Commission in Wiesbaden was grateful for all reports and made its own decision as to what part of them should be passed on to the O.K.W., to whom it was subordinate.

At first I used to visit the Embassy in Rome once a month; later

I kept in touch mainly with the Military Attaché, General von Rintelin, and occasionally with other members of the embassy. Over a period of two years I was thus able to witness historic developments of the greatest significance.

THE DECLINE OF THE AXIS

The advent of Hitler and of National Socialism spelt the beginning of the end for Mussolini's Fascism. The mass of the people in both countries evidently believed the opposite. The two totalitarian systems seemed to be closely linked; their victories would lead to a new world order. Yet behind the scenes the Axis was disintegrating. Italy had become implicated in the victory of National Socialism and it was now too late to withdraw. The process occurred on three different levels: the defeat of both powers in the theatres of war, the growing influence of the party on the state, and Mussolini's increasing dependence on Hitler.

Against the advice of his military experts Mussolini had yielded to the counsels whispered in his ear by the Fascist party and had renounced the opportunity offered him to remain neutral during the French campaign. For it was the Italian government that had tried to restrain Hitler from going to war with Poland.

It was not only the General Staff that was against the policy of war, but also the King and even the more far-seeing Fascists. Shortly after I had reached Turin an Italian senior officer conducted me to the scene of the alpine war against France, where I readily admired the adaptability of the troops to mountain warfare. Yet it was best to avoid speaking of "successes", for these could hardly be impressive in those few days of hostilities. The French had capitulated because they had already been outflanked by the Germans in their rear. The more responsible military men regarded this as a loss of prestige. Later events proved the validity of the General Staff's warnings that Italy was insufficiently equipped for a major war.

Yet the German "victory" still overshadowed all else. People were anticipating the invasion and defeat of England. So the Italian Press began a clamour for "Corsica, Tunisia, Djibouti" and even Nice to become Italian. The Italian Armistice Commission had to supervise the difficult Mediterranean area, while the German commission dealt with metropolitan France.

Italy's prestige which had declined in France was restored by the conquest of British Somaliland. But communications with Abyssinia could only be maintained if the Italian Fleet dominated the Mediterranean and if Egypt were to fall. Hence the order was given to launch an attack from Libya in the direction of the Suez

Canal. Before long this attack was held up, resulting in a fresh disappointment.

In the autumn of 1940 Italy attacked Greece without the prior agreement of Germany and suffered a considerable reverse. At the end of the year came the setback against Great Britain in Egypt, when Italy appealed for support in Africa. This marked the end of her independent conduct of the war.

The failure of the totalitarian powers to co-ordinate their war plans marks precisely the characteristic defects on their régimes. Usually a common basis for planning requires the weaker partner to yield to the stronger, while the stronger must respect the weaker. National war aims must be subordinated to mutual war aims, which can only be attained by pooling the General Staffs, and this in turn requires a democratic approach to higher strategic planning. But this method was incompatible with the nature of totalitarian states. Consequently Italy's attempt to conduct her own war in her own way resulted in the gradual loss of her independence. Hitler had to come to her aid in Africa, and was reluctantly compelled to clean up the Balkan situation. This proved a severe strain on his own war policy, which at this time was already envisaging an attack on Russia.

It was soon clear there would be difficulties in arranging supplies for the African venture under Rommel. The German General Staff was too exclusively occupied with the concept of a continental army, in which its traditions were rooted. Unlike the British, it was not brought up to appreciate the significance of sea communications. The two opponents did not divide the Mediterranean basin into an eastern and western zone; instead there was a north-south route which the Axis powers had to use, and an intersecting west-east route that was equally vital to the Allies. The opponents avoided naval batles, for it was in their respective interest to maintain supplies along these routes by means of convoys. The Allies' route was much longer, and they sent their convoys in two stages from Gibraltar to Alexandria and vice-versa, with Malta as the half-way point. The Italians refused to capture the island because it was too "difficult". Yet from Malta and Alexandria the north-south Axis route was not only kept under observation, but repeatedly atacked with success, so that supplies became difficult and losses heavy.

In 1940 the British naval air attack on Taranto resulted in the loss of Italian battleships, and later the Italian one-man torpedoes succeeded in damaging British warships in the harbours of Gibraltar and Alexandria. But these were acts of bravery rather than evidence of control of the sea. Both cases afforded an example of the vulnerability of battleships, whose usefulness was coming to an end.

After the defeat in Africa in 1940 and Mussolini's appeal to Hitler for help, the war in the Mediterranean area developed into a conflict between the Germans and the Allies. Rommel became a sort of idol not only to the German people, but also to the majority of Italian soldiers. He was frequently in the front line, which always produces a psychological effect. At the same time he used to intervene in the fighting over the heads of his divisional commanders, which is a mistake, though it turned him into a legendary figure with his own troops as well as with the enemy. His bravery, initiative and flair for the tactical situation were in the best German military tradition. It is often forgotten that he and Montgomery alike had the good fortune to control an almost private theatre of war. Here they were free from that close interdependence that was later imposed on commanders up to the level of army groups and above on the eastern and the western fronts. The two leaders in North Africa conducted operations in their own area without having to bother about neighbours. To the north they had the sea, to the south, the desert.

Since Libya itself is characterised by large desert tracts a breakthrough often compelled the opponent to fall back a thousand kilometres or more; he would then launch a counter-attack and after a successful breakthrough, reconquer the lost territory. The Italian advance of 1940 collapsed due to supply difficulties; this was also the ultimate cause of the failure of the German advances on Egypt. For a long time Rommel's fighting with the British was the only German war activity in the west, where it naturally attracted popular attention.

The command set-up in North Africa was a contributory cause of the degeneration of the Axis partnership. Rommel gave offence to the Italian high commanders. Contrary to agreements reached by the Axis powers he received his instructions direct from the O.K.W., the Italian Commander-in-Chief in Africa being more or less short-circuited. It is to the credit of General von Rintelen that major difficulties were avoided. Since 1940 he had been given plenipotentiary status as "German general in the headquarters of the Italian armed forces", and was always a tactful mediator. Italian officers and friends did not disguise the extent to which Italian prestige had suffered through the fact that Italy was no longer in a position to defend her colonies, not only because of her defeats, but also because of the German ascendancy in her own zone of North Africa. They foresaw that for them the war would be over once they lost their African possessions.

The atmosphere in the Armistice Commission reflected the military situation of the Axis. The German Commission showed more interest in France than in Italy. The Axis powers tried to formulate their relationship with France. Yet Italy's interest in that country by no means corresponded to that of Germany. There was a glaring discrepancy between Italy's claims and the part she had actually played in the victory. She laid claim to a number of French territories, while Germany ostensibly had no claims beyond the return of Alsace-Lorraine. Hitler was aiming at other things. In the Europe of the new order, as conceived by him, all other countries would be relegated to a mere semblance of sovereignty. They would have a say in negotiations only if their systems of government were subservient to Germany. The French government under the aged and paternal Pétain raised but few difficulties, and relied on known politicians. Consequently France established a *modus vivendi* with Germany. She not only retained her Fleet (which however had to be disarmed) but was allowed to establish an interim army of 100,000 men. Italy had to arrange for the reduction of the French forces overseas, a task for which she proved too weak.

Italy's loss of prestige in the Mediterranean made Hitler realise that in this situation he needed new helpers in Europe. Consequently Franco-German relations were increasingly consolidated, and Germany made a number of minor concessions to Pétain's government. Some warships were permitted to re-arm. France's claim to do this was based on her defence against the British attack on French ships at Oran and on the repulse of De Gaulle's attack on Dakar. She also pointed to the need to protect merchant shipping running between the homeland and the North African colonies.

The general policy was settled at the meeting between Hitler and Pétain at Montoire on October 24th, 1940. General Weygand proceeded to North Africa with full authority. The interim Army in North Africa was increased to 120,000 men. Germany began to look on France as a weak but willing ally. There was concern over the defence of North Africa against a possible Allied landing. Rome and Berlin held widely differing views on the reliability of the men around Pétain. The Italians regarded Generals Weygand and Noguès in Morocco as particularly unreliable, while the Germans were rather less suspicious of these men.

Under these conditions one can hardly blame the German government for hoping to normalise relations with France. French industry constituted an effective addition to the German war economy. On the other hand Italy, with her lack of raw materials, proved a liability. She frequently complained that she was not even supplied with the oil fuel required for her Fleet.

At the end of May, 1941, the so-called Paris Protocols were signed, Italy being presented with this as a *fait accompli*. They not only concerned France's economic production, but contained reciprocal political concessions. Thus deliveries of French arms were to be sent from Syria to Iraq. It was all the more humiliating to Italy that she was left out of this deal, for Syria was in the Italian zone of control, and France was gaining prestige at Italy's expense. Italy even began to suspect that certain German clauses in the Paris Protocols had written off Italian war claims. All that was known, however, was that French naval forces and the defences along the Algerian-Moroccan coast had been strengthened. Yet France had more important interests at stake than the early establishment of conditions of peace. She was more interested in the release of war prisoners, the easing of the barrier between the occupied and unoccupied zones, and a reduction in the costs of occupation.

On June 8th Free French and British troops marched into Syria. By mid-July Vichy had to recognise the "armistice" that had been arranged in Syria between the generals of *both* French governments and the commander of the British occupation forces, General Wilson.

THE TURNING POINT

The start of the Russian campaign at once provoked a crisis in Italy. At first the advance into Russia also revived hopes in Italy among the misguided masses that were always looking to Germany. They followed the initial German successes with interest and sympathy, attributing them to the anti-Bolshevik policy of Fascism. But those who knew the real circumstances had no such optimism. They appreciated that the German strength, like the Italian, had been greatly over-estimated, and that this new commitment would leave little hope of German help in the Mediterranean theatre of war. Yet since Italy had long been too weak to remedy her own difficulties, a favourable turning-point could only occur if Russia collapsed quickly, thereby releasing some of the German forces. Very few reflected that even if this should happen, a very large force would be needed to occupy the vast Russian territory.

To me and my friends in the delegation it was fairly obvious that December 7th, 1941, marked a turning point for the German fortunes in Russia. (Better and more objective sources were available to us than to the readers of German Newspapers). On that day the attack on Moscow petered out. Under Stalin's leadership Russia had revived. The Russian western front received the first reinforcements from the Far East. The German Army was not equipped for the winter, with the result that (even without fighting) it became weaker almost every hour. The tragedy of the bitter winter of 1812 was repeating itself.

Also on December 7th Japan launched the attack on Pearl Harbour. Evidently she was still unaware of the German setback on the eastern front. The United States joined the war on the side of the Allies—an event whose significance only fools could ignore.

Shortly before this, Field Marshal Kesselring had arrived in Rome. Hitler intended to move a new Fliegerkorps to Southern Italy in order to safeguard the supply route to Cyrenaica by subduing Malta. The German Field Marshal was also to assume supreme command over all the forces engaged in the protection of the convoys —a measure that Italy had consistently refused to undertake. The operations of the new Fliegerkorps proved so effective that in 1942 Rommel could switch over to a counter-offensive even without the capture of Malta. It took him as far as Alamein.

The British offensive had forced Italy to apply through diplomatic channels to be allowed to use the harbours of Tunisia for her supplies to Libya. The value of these ports was questionable, since land communications between them and Libya were poor. But Hitler also refused the request on political grounds, for he wished to avoid the possibility of American intervention. France was to be kept out of the war, whether for or against Germany. At all costs Hitler had to avoid an extension of the war in the west.

The estrangement between Germany and France at once produced a *rapprochement* between France and Italy. Already in November, 1941, Italy in direct negotiations with France had given her an irredeemable credit of 2.5 milliards of francs. Now Italy was pressing for Tunisian ports for the supplies to her own troops and those of Rommel in Afria. She feared that Germany might give up the African venture. But this did not happen, for the intervention of German air units had reduced losses in the supplies for Rommel's offensive.

Vichy France meanwhile came increasingly under the influence of the United States, with whom she maintained diplomatic relations.

The Germans were deeply committed to the eastern theatre of war. Italian divisions were also engaged there in accordance with Mussolini's wish. By this move he hoped to dispel the impresion of Italian dependence on Germany that was so much in evidence in Africa. But his people were becoming increasingly weary of the war. I felt it my duty to report on this when General Cadorna, son of the Italian C.-in-C. of the First World War, gave me a vivid account of the feelings of Italian womenfolk bidding farewell to their sons and husbands departing for the icy Russian steppes, for which they were ill-equiped.

My report resulted in a comment from the O.K.W. that Cadorna had talked so openly with me only because I had listened to him without contradicting—a not inaccurate surmise!

During the brief period of the Franco-Italian "entente", Darlan had a meeting with Ciano in Turin. Before it took place Ciano called on me in my capacity as head of the German delegation and assured me that he would discuss nothing with the French Minister that had not already been covered between himself and Ambassador Mackensen; also that he would inform the German delegation of the result of his talk with Darlan. But he never did.

I seized the opportunity to make a report pointing out that a *rapprochement* between France and Italy might well be expected by reason of the considerable loss of face that both countries had suffered through the rise of Hitler's Germany—France as a defeated nation, Italy as an ally. Darlan and Ciano alike seemed the kind of men who would exploit every opportunity—even a change of front— to improve the prospects of their countries. Weak and dependent powers readily form alliances against a stronger oppressor. The German Ambassador in Rome heard about my report from the Foreign Office and invited me to discuss it with him. I was told that by reason of the common ideology of the two countries, relations between Italy and Germany would always remain unclouded and that Italy would not act independently.

In contrast to this appreciation by the ambassador, I remained convinced that the foreign policy of any country would always strive for power and security, regardless of ideological affinities. It was these ideological systems in particular that I regarded as transient. I sensed that shrewd politicians in France and Italy were already anticipating the end of them.

Consequently I could not deny a certain respect for the men of the Vichy government, whoever they might be. Even if they had played false with Hitler, they were playing a part that destiny had prescribed for them, and were acting for the good of their native land. During my two years' work in Turin I had come to realise the advantages that a government can obtain for its people through calculated reticence, ostensible compliance—and deception. Active resistance cannot produce bread or move people to action, or ensure the rule of law. Rather does the sad history of this war demonstrate how many innocent people became the victims of active resistance.

It was the same with the exiled French government in London. Its call for resistance could only be justified on the basis of the independence of the motherland and the North African colonies. From a foreign land it is not possible fully to appreciate the condition of constraint of those who were left behind to live under the statute of occupation. The French collaborators were not like those quislings who were ready to accept the conqueror's ideology in return for his favours. With but a few exeptions they remained true to their convictions and the traditions of their country.

The Italian people could only wish for an early release from dependence on an ally whose conduct was so often inconsiderate. True, Italy had the same kind of totalitarian régime and restraints.

But so long as these were of her own making, she at least remained free from the deterioration, the contempt for the law, and the atrocities which had besmirched the Hitler régime ever since its inception. The more dependent Mussolini became on Hitler, the more he undermined his own handiwork. For better or for worse he had thrown in his lot with Hitler, and could no longer withdraw. The tragedy of Italy was that the absence of a living constitution had rendered inarticulate and powerless those who had the capacity for leadership and reforms.

This development was all the more painful to me since I had come to love this people and now found myself having to act as an agent of its criminal alliance with Hitler.

3

THE EASTERN FRONT

CHANGE OF SCENE

The start of the Russian campaign meant a complete break in the pattern of my wartime existence. I will not deny that I was impatient to be "in the fray". There is something that compels the military man to "stick to his guns", something that impels him into the adventure of war, with all its perils and privations. I also had an urge to test those qualities in me that appertain to leadership in war, of whose importance I was well aware.

A number of names now began to crop up in connection with the campaign in the east, names that had already won fame. Some of these caused me some surprise, for in the long inter-war years and before the First World War I had grown accustomed to high standards. In time of peace there was no falling-off in these standards. Now, when face to face with the enemy, other criteria were evidently being applied. Formerly a general education as well as a specialised one in the War Academy were essential for any appointment to the higher posts; it is possible that these assets were rated too highly. In the trench warfare of the west, strategic ability never had the same significance as in the wars of the nineteenth century, with their quick, operational decisions.

Yet something in the new principles of selection made me suspicious and somewhat damped my ardour for advancement. I suspected that despite the re-introduction of the war of movement, which had been made possible by motorisation, too low a value had been set on the operational qualities of the higher commanders. Indeed, it was in the first winter of the war in Russia that another type had already emerged—the officer with a faith in the régime, ever optimistic, enthusiastic and free of political cares. These untroubled officers were more successful than the others; they made a good impression and therefore reached the higher ranks more quickly. The school of Beck was still accepted here and there, and was represented among the top leaders of the General Staff. Yet in the category of divisional and corps commanders such men were becoming ever more scarce.

Before being swallowed up in the big movement towards the east, I was allowed a short respite. I spent a few days at the school for armoured troops near Berlin. Here I noticed that the instructional staff were in two minds. Those who had been in the fighting were evidently still affected by the Russian T-34 tanks and the withdrawals on the central front during the bitter winter of 1941/2. But they were now taking heart again at the successful summer offensive of 1942. The officers of the instructional staff seemed not at all concerned that the eccentric direction of these attacks, which had been determined by economic considerations, bore but little relation to the original strategic plans. The victorious advance in the direction of Voronesch of a Panzer division that I knew well was represented to the class as a model operation, whereas (I discovered later) it had met with no serious resistance from the enemy. I felt embarrassed at the unjustifiable confidence of these officers—so different from the scepticism of my previous surroundings.

My impressions were of quite another kind when I assumed command of a brigade—my third—which formed part of of a Panzer division in Artois. The divisional commander was a fighting man with war experience. I was told that after an evening in the mess he would expound his uninhibited views on the government that the German people had chosen for itself. This seemed to promise a closer—if not a more personal—understanding between us. We both knew that I was merely a bird of passage. Yet the time was not wasted. Sooner or later I would be given a Panzer division, since I had qualified for such a command during the western campaign. But I had never in peace or war commanded armoured forces, though I had paid close attention to their tactics and the discussions about them in the O.K.W. Now I conducted an exercise of the division at full strength—that is, with two hundred tanks. The progress of the exercise and the subsequent analysis gave me the self-confidence that is essential in war.

However, I could have no influence on the brigade, since the divisional commander regarded my appointment as transitory, and so I spent many days in complete idleness. The first autumn mists were already enveloping the yellow plains of lovely Artois. I lived in a small chateau. There was no need to worry about the staff officers. In such conditions I began the hermit-like existence that I preferred. I spent the afternoons with a gun wandering over hill and dale, usually returning with a pheasant or a hare.

When I was finally posted to Russia, I fitted myself out in my old garrison town of Göttingen, then drove to Berlin accompanied by P. and the faithful batman, Feuerstak. That evening I took leave of P. at the Zoo railway station. As the train drew out of the station it seemed to me that I was falling into a huge dark chasm.

THE 17TH PANZER DIVISION IN THE EAST

The journey via Smolensk to the headquarters of the 2nd Panzer Army at Orel took nearly a week. The Army Commander, Colonel-General Schmidt, invited me to lunch as his only guest. It is possible that his staff officers had given him a hint of my political attitude. If that were so, they must have shared my views. I was surprised and reassured to find my superior officer, whom I had not met before, talking with me in a way that took for granted our mutual abhorrence and criticism of the régime. It was quite obvious that even his officers of high rank, though continuing the fight, were convinced that victory was unattainable. Many hoped for the speedy establishment of a second front in the west, because this alone could bring Germany's hopeless war to a rapid ending.

As I was taking leave of the C.-in-C. after the two-hour luncheon, he asked me "to forget all he had said during this time". Knowing what he meant, I took up my task in a more cheerful frame of mind.

I was now able to "feel my way" into the 17th Panzer Division in its quiet position to the south-east of Orel. It struck me as being of good quality. In peace-time it had been the Augsburg Division, and on the outbreak of war was converted into an armoured unit. I soon warmed to the job and my visits to the front occupied several weeks. The regimental commanding officers seemed to have anticipated a change in the divisional command, and were prepared for it. The staff was another matter. Some of them seemed to be firmly rooted in the past and averse to any change. The newly arrived G.S.O.1, Krass, was not one of these. He was a professional man with a sound peace-time training and came from the Austrian Bundeswehr.

Shortly before the war I had travelled by train to the Far East when the Sino-Japanese war was in progress. It was difficult then to take in the great breadth of the land with its endless snow-clad pine trees and infrequent human habitations. The fur-clad travellers lounged about in sleighs and in the railway stations waiting for the Trans-Siberian Express. I remembered the sad melodies of the Russian songs which the loud-speakers in the trains blared forth almost without intermission. My spirit accommodated itself to the landscape and to its patient, long-suffering, fatalistic inhabitants. They were typified by the tall bearded old man in my lodgings, who would greet me in silence by inclining his bared head and smiling— a smile of contentment rather than devotion.

COULD THE ARMY AT STALINGRAD BE RELIEVED?

The idyll of these "honeymoon weeks" with my division during the static war was soon to end. Before long we were entrained and rolling towards the south. In twenty degrees (Centigrade) of frost the unheated carriages with their hard seats were uninviting as sleeping accommodation. I reflected on my many railway journeys of the First World War. In those days one could still find oneself a bundle of straw in a horse-truck, where it was warm and one's rest was disturbed only by the pawing of hooves. But these nights would soon be over; for a few days one would have to make do with a handful or two of snow for the symbolic morning toilet, followed by a hot breakfast and a cigarette.

The division which I now took into the turbulent and fateful war of movement to assist in the relief of the Stalingrad army was weak in material. It had only thirty tanks in the armoured element. There were no armoured cars, only one or two reconnaissance vehicles; thirty to forty per cent of the trucks were undergoing major overhauls. Hence in each battalion one company could move only on foot. These companies were formed into a single battalion which followed up behind the division. A repair company and even the workshops remained behind in the Orel area. Every truck driver will appreciate the significance of this. Was it all due to the sudden, frantic hurry or could it be ascribed to corruption?

The hurry certainly seemed essential. It was mid-December, and nearly three weeks had elapsed since the Russians at Stalingrad had fought the decisive battle of the eastern front. It was before this that we had detrained in order to assemble at Millerovo. We did not know whether the relieving operation east of the Don would still take place. Instead there was an exploration of the operational possiblities to the west of the Don against the advancing enemy. It was here that the front of our weak Hungarian ally had collapsed. During a solitary drive eastwards across seemingly endless fields of snow my car was approached by another one, and out stepped the commander of the Rumanian Division—a tall, haggard figure. After a formal and rather stiff introduction we continued in French, as I wished to make myself acquainted with the situation of the Rumanians. The bearing of the Rumanian general showed an unmistakable reserve, and a weariness of the alliance, in consequence of the defeat of his army.

Instead of being deployed westwards we now marched farther to the south. In muddy conditions the division crossed the Don at Tsymlianskaya. Despite twelve hours of driving, I myself failed to reach the headquarters of the 4th Panzer Army. Its commander was Colonel-General Hoth, whom I knew; so I spoke with him over the telephone: C.-in-C.: "You must realise that we must get on with this business of Stalingrad?" Myself: "The mission is clear to me, sir; but I trust that you are aware of the lamentable state of equipment of my division." C.-in-C.: "At the front some divisions are in an even worse state. Yours has an excellent reputation. I rely on you."

In the last comfortable quarters of the move I tried to clear my mind over a theoretical divergence between my strategic conscience and my tactical mission. I was struck by the inadequate strength of the forces detailed for the attempt to relieve Stalingrad. Not so far ahead of me, yet ninety kilometres away from the encircled army of Stalingrad, two divisions were engaged in a battle. One of them, the 6th Panzer Division, was fortunate in having been recently brought up to full strength while still in France, while the other, the 23rd Panzer Division, was said to be even shorter of equipment than my own 17th Division. One complete and two half divisions were expected to undertake an offensive to a depth of 100 kilometres as far as Stalingrad! The initial so-called surprise had already evaporated; for a fortnight the two engaged divisions had been pinned down by their more powerful Russian opponents. But even if they had achieved surprise, they would not have been able to maintain themselves in depth in this still unconquered area. Nobody could assume that the enemy would not do his utmost with all his forces to prevent the relief of the encircled 6th Army, thereby consolidating his great victory. The weakness of the German attacking forces indicated that no reserves were available. Moreover, it was out of the question that Paulus's army, which still numbered 100,000 men, should break out to establish a junction with the 4th Panzer Army.

December 15th and 16th, 1942 (Map 1). On December 15th units of the Russian 65th Panzer Brigade and 81st Cavalry Division had been identified in the region of Verch Kurmoiarskaya. The commander of the German 4th Panzer Army evidently intended to move my division with its left shoulder along the Don in a north-easterly direction. Accordingly Panzer Group Büsing (he was commander of the regiment) was ordered to proceed via Topolev towards Verch Kurmoiarskaya, which it reached without contacting the enemy. The motorised groups of the Panzer Grenadier Regiments did not reach the region of Shikovskaya until the 16th because of delays at the bridge at Zymlianskaya.

Meanwhile an order had arrived from LVII Army Corps that my division should make a surprise advance on Generalov on the river Yessaulovskii Aksai, and establish a bridgehead there to relieve the pressure on the 6th Panzer Division which was engaged to the eastward of it. The enemy was reported to have withdrawn at least some units of his forces at Verch Kirmoiarskaya and Nish Yablotchnii and taken them to the north-west, presumably with the object of attacking the flank and rear of the bridgehead at Salivskii, which was already under heavy frontal pressure.

The advancing Panzer Group had not been able to establish the

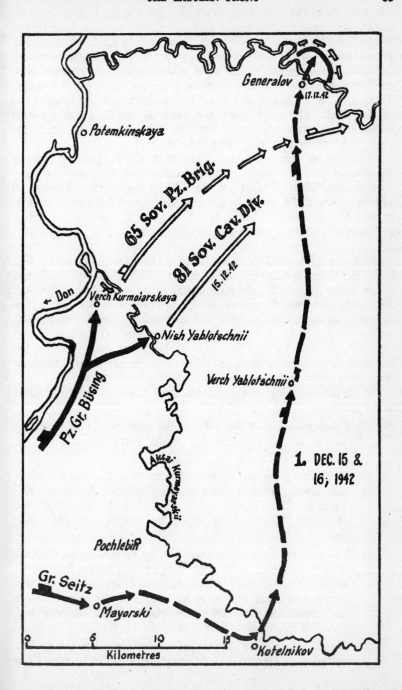

o Potemkinskaya

Generalov o
17.12.42

65 Sov. Pz. Brig.

81 Sov. Cav. Div.

15.12.42

← Don

Verch Kurmoiarskaya o

Nish Yablotschnii o

Verch Yablotschnii o

Pz. Gr. Büsing

Aksai Kurmojarskii

1. DEC. 15 & 16; 1942

Pochlebiñ

Gr. Seitz

o Mayorski

0   5   10   15

Kilometres

Kotelnikov o

whereabouts of the enemy forces on the Don. On the previous day his forces had moved northwards from Nagavskaya. The localities of Verch Yablotschnii, Nish Yablotschnii and Verch Kurmoiraskaya had been reported by the tanks to be free of the enemy but heavily mined; the bridge to the north of the latter place was in enemy hands. Now the German armour could not move from the area it had reached. There was no fuel, and the thaw had undermined the foundations of the roads. The road along the bank of the Don was reported impassible, likewise the track through Pochlebin, along which the corps commander wished to move my division.

That evening the longed-for hard frost set in. During the day the division had completed its reconnaissance of the roads for every weather condition, so that on the 17th it could start moving its wheeled units, if not its tanks, towards Generalov. I hoped to be able to move the Panzer Group from its present position to Verch Yablotschnii, where it would join up with the division.

December 17th, 1942 (Map 1). Leaving the assembly area at 5 a.m. I led the Seitz Group—consisting of Pz. Gren. Regt. 63 reinforced by Pz. Jäger Section 27, the Regimental Staff and Section III of Art. Regt. 27, and one Company of Pz. Pioneer Bat. 27—along the reconnoitred track through Maiorski, Kotelnikov, Verch Yablotschnii (where we halted from 10.15 to 11 a.m.) towards Generalov, which was captured, and by 2.15 p.m. a bridgehead was established on the far bank in the face of weak opposition. The enemy's only resistance came from multiple rocket mountings and low-level aircraft.

The surprise employment of unarmoured motorised group resulted in the following: —

(1) Confirmation that the area to the west of the battle group as far as the Yessaulovskii Aksai sector was clear of the enemy.

(2) The cutting of any commnications that the enemy might still intend between those units of his 65th Armoured Brigade, his 81st Cavalry Division (which had remained on the Don) and his main body, which had moved off to the north-east.

(3) The creation of a springboard for the launching, on the next day, of an attack on the right wing of the Russian front north of the Yessaulovskii Aksai, against which the 4th Panzer Army had been unable to gain any further ground. Here the attacks on the enemy's established line of armour had failed, with considerable losses.

(4) The forestalling of a parallel action that the enemy had intended to launch; he was intending to advance across the

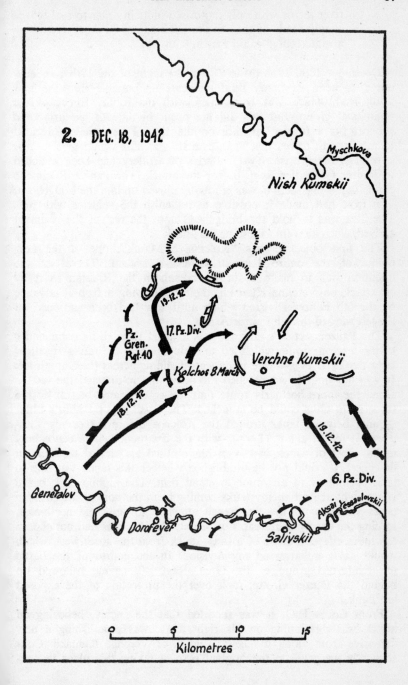

2. DEC. 18, 1942

Myschkova

Nish Kumskii

19.12.42

17. Pz. Div.

Pz.
Gren.
Rgt. 40

Kolchos 8 March

Verchne Kumskii

18.12.42

19.12.42

6. Pz. Div.

Generalov

Dorofeyev

Aksai

Tessaulovskii

Salivskii

0   5   10   15
Kilometres

river sector with only motorised units in order to seal off the
supply roads of the 6th Pz. Division, as we discovered from
an intercepted radio message.

December 18th, 1942 (Map 2). On the night of the 17th I endeavoured to send as many reinforcements as possible into the new
bridgehead, which was being held with inadequate forces of the
regimental group. But this did not occur in time to use armoured
support for a further advance on the 18th. I nevertheless decided
to attack with forces that were available, as this would give me the
advantage of surprise. Two batteries of artillery had been attached
to Panzer Grenadier Regt. 63 for the attack. The Panzer Regiment,
consisting of one section, was gradually moved up into the bridgehead.
The frost had made it possible to replenish the vehicles with fuel.
The idea was to hold the bridgehead until the rest of the regiment
arrived, when all were to resume the attack.

The first objective was "Kolchos 8 March", one of the key-
points of the entire Russian defensive system. Thereafter the
intention was to make a further breach in the Russian front by
an attack on Verchne Kumskii, thereby allowing a frontal advance
by the 6th Panzer Division which until now had been stationed on
the left wing of the 4th Panzer Army.

The Panzer section's advance was delayed through its commander
taking a wrong route which led to a slope where the tanks—particularly the Type IV's—were in danger of sliding across the smooth ice.
It was not until I had reached the scene and re-directed the section
along the more northerly route that the co-ordinated attack by the
three main units could be launched. There was a good hour's bitter
fighting between tanks around the Kolchos before the enemy withdrew. It fell at about 11 a.m., with the destruction of fifteen enemy
tanks, most of which had been immobilised as part of the built-in
defences! It could not be established whether this tactic was due to
lack of fuel or to an order to stand firm. The mobile tank battle
was fought against enemy tanks coming from the north. The German
tanks withdrew to the west, then attacked towards the north-east,
forcing the enemy to retreat. Fortunately the Russians had not chosen
the more effective tactic of a tank attack from the north-west, which
would have embarrassed my division. In the course of the battle
the reinforced group of Pz. Gren. Regt. 40, having followed up
behind the Panzer Group, took over the protection of the exposed
left flank.

From Corps H.Q. it was reported that the enemy, believing an
attack was developing on his right flank, was establishing a new
defensive front along the heights north of Verchne Kumskii. Consequently we gave up the original plan of taking this place in con-

junction with the frontal attack by the 6th Panzer Division, and instead an attack was started against the heights to the north-east of it. But as darkness set in as early as 3 p.m., the attack could not be completed. That afternoon the enemy's further attempts to attack with tanks from the north could be repulsed without much trouble.

On this day the 6th Panzer Division too, was unable to win sufficient ground to the north for the capture of Verchne Kumskii, for the resistance here was still very tough. A contributory cause may have been that the tanks of the 85th Russian Panzer Brigade, which on December 15th had been reported moving towards Dorofeyev, had evacuated the south bank of the river under the impact of the German division's attack. During the German attack on "Kolchos 8 March", the Russian tanks had been seen south of the Kolchos, falling back on Verchne Kumskii. Thereafter the 6th Pz. Div. could again occupy Dorofeyev.

On this day it had been possible not only to ward off the threat to the 6th Pz. Div. in the bridgehead, but also to provide a threat deep in the enemy's right flank. The tables had been turned. My division had not only fought well, but in this flexibly conducted attack—the first for some considerable time—it had soon accommodated itself to my ways, so that while sending the leading battle group into action, I was able to bring all three weapon groups of the division into effective support—a satisfactory result.

My division suffered fifty casualties while the enemy lost twenty-one tanks and 150 prisoners. His casualties in men were not established.

December 19th, 1942 (Map 3). This day and the succeeding night there was uninterrupted fighting. It was the culminating point of the operation in so far as the attempt to relieve the 6th Army reached its most northerly point, after which the reverse set in. The fighting occurred in several phases. At 5 a.m. the assault troops resumed their attack with the object of capturing the base at Verchne Kumskii, which was still being stubbornly defended. A corps directive had earmarked the 17th Pz. Div. to advance eastwards to the north-west of this place, and to occupy the heights to the north of it. The enemy, who had been forced to withdraw from it, must not be allowed to gain a foothold on these heights. At the same time the 6th Pz. Div. and my own division were to link up through an attack on the heights, thereby completing the encirclement of Verchne Kumskii.

By 6.20 a.m. the heights had been reached by Assault Group 63 from the south and by the Panzer Group from the north. But before the ring could be closed by the 6th Pz. Div., our front line reported rapid enemy movements along the remaining road between Verchne Kumskii and Nish Kumskii. Fire was opened at a few hundred metres, and at the same time our front line was subjected to bomber attacks by our own aircraft, whose pilots were still ignorant of the position attained by the spearhead of the division. To the south, Assault Group 63 had the task of repelling the sortie of tanks from Verchne Kumskii. Towards 9 a.m. the 6th Pz. Div. had penetrated it from the south.

I had the impression that the ring round Verchne Kumskii was bound to close very soon. On the other hand weak detachments had managed to escape from the place. As the situation was changing rapidly, I decided without awaiting superior orders to break off the action here of my Panzer Group, and to send it in pursuit of forces fleeing along the road from Verchne Kumskii to Nish Kumskii, also with the object of reaching the Myshkova sector before the enemy could establish himself there, and before he could bring up reinforcements from the north. Group 63 received orders to establish contact with the 6th Pz. Div. and to block the last northern exit from Verchne Kumskii.

As enemy tanks were sighted to the north-west, I spread the Type IV tanks out along a line to the left, for flank protection during the advance. They went into action, causing the enemy's tanks to flee, and shooting up several of them. The spearhead of the tanks was attacked more than once by our own dive-bombers.

By about 11 a.m. the ring had been closed around Verchne Kumskii, the place was occupied and cleaned up. The remaining Russian forces took advantage of the many depressions in the terrain to escape in a south-west direction.

Meanwhile the Panzer Group was advancing boldly towards Nish Kumskii, with myself in direct control. I considered it important to capture the place as it would provide flank protection for the 4th Army, and I also hoped to form a bridgehead over the Myschkova sector in order to turn in from there to the east and resume the attack together with the adjacent 6th Pz. Div. At 12.45 p.m. we reached Nish Kumskii, part of which we occupied against resistance, while our tanks surrounded the place. The north bank had been occupied by fresh enemy troops coming from the north, and these were able to gather in those falling back from Verchne Kumskii.

The battalion of Group 40 that had been detailed to move up behind the armoured section to provide infantry protection found itself unable to reach the place in daylight; its progress was considerably delayed by darkness and difficulties in finding the way, and it did not arrive until 5.30 p.m.

An earlier reconnaissance on the division's left flank had established strong enemy forces again advancing southwards. Their progress was repulsed partly by the battalion of Group 40 that was operating west of "Kolchos 8 March", and partly by the artillery in that sector. These Russian forces had evidently been drawn from the units

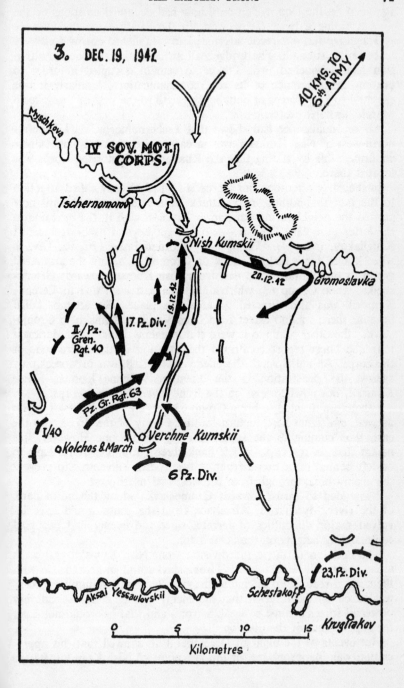

3. DEC. 19, 1942

40 KMS. TO 6ᵗʰ ARMY

Myschkova

IV SOV. MOT. CORPS.

Tschernomorov

Nish Kumskii

20.12.42

Gromoslavka

19.12.42

17. Pz. Div.

II./Pz. Gren. Rgt. 40

Pz. Gr. Rgt. 63

I/40

Kolchos 8. March

Verchne Kumskii

6 Pz. Div.

23. Pz. Div.

Aksai Yessaulovskii

Schestakoff

Kruglíakov

0   5   10   15
Kilometres

stationed on the Don, which until now had occupied positions on the river, forming a front facing west. In the localities on the Don, as at Tshaussovski, our reconnaissance had established enemy forces up to battalion strength. The bridgehead at Generalov, whence my division had debouched, would have to remain occupied in order to prevent the severance of its rear communications. Similarly it was essential to keep forces of battalion strength to the west of "Kolchos 8 March" as flank protection.

Air reconnaissance had shown that Tschernomorov, six kilometres north-west of Nish Kumskii, was in enemy occupation, and prisoners confirmed this by stating that the Russian 4th Motorised Corps was located there.

In the early afternoon our Corps H.Q. had already called attention to the fact that although the attack by my division had until now carried the neighbouring 6th Panzer Division with it, the next one to the latter—the 23rd Pz. Div.—had not got beyond its bridgehead at Krugliakov. (Map 4). Consequently I ordered the 17th Pz. Div. to wheel round for a further attack on Gromoslavka, and the armoured group to turn inwards and east from Nish Kumskii towards Gromoslavka, while Group 63, which until then had been tied to Verchne Kumskii, was also directed towards this place. The attempt failed because there was no direct road from Verchne Kumskii to Gromoslavka; the other roads to it were still in enemy hands when darkness fell. The latest report confirmed the situation in the entire zone of the corps. As anticipated, the enemy had withdrawn his forces only against the penetration in the direction Verchne Kumskii—Nish Kumskii, but nowhere else on the front covered by our corps.

I therefore decided to bring Group 63 into the Nish Kumskii region as well, and from here to turn the main body of the division to the east, thus coming to the support of my neighbours. However, this meant that on the exposed left flank three battalions would have to be left behind on a broad front of twenty-five kilometres to prevent the enemy breakthrough from the west and north-west.

I intended to thrust towards Gromoslavka along the north bank of the river Myschkova. An attack from the south would have involved major difficulties of terrain, since the enemy had occupied commanding heights on the north bank.

The decision to move the division from Nish Kumskii eastwards along the north bank towards Gromoslavka and in accordance with the corps directive "to safeguard the west flank with minimum forces" was based on the forecast that the enemy was unlikely to send very powerful forces against so weak a front, and that he would not sever the supply lines of the division.

But events of the night of December 19th showed that this appreciation was inappropriate for the key point of Nish Kumskii. Before

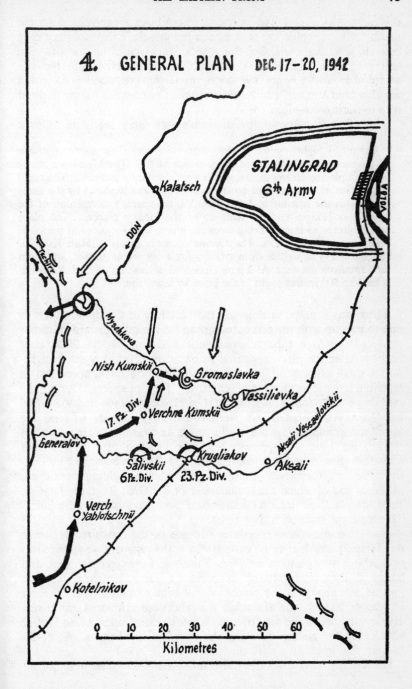

4. GENERAL PLAN DEC. 17-20, 1942

STALINGRAD
6th Army

VOLGA

Kalatsch

DON

Tschir

Myschkova

Nish Kumskii

Gromoslavka

Vassilievka

17. Pz. Div.

Verchne Kumskii

Aksaii Yessaulovskii

Generalov

Salivskii
6 Pz. Div.

Krugliakov

23. Pz. Div.

Aksaii

Verch
Yablotschnü

Kotelnikov

0   10   20   30   40   50   60

Kilometres

the night was over I had intended to establish a bridgehead on the north bank to enable me to continue the attack. This would not only provide a springboard, but the attack would clear up the situation and safeguard Nish Kumskii. Radio messages arriving in the late afternon from the Army and the Army Group contained good wishes for this bold venture and an injunction to pursue the enemy without respite during the night.

The relevant entry in the division's war diary reads as follows:

> Pursuit by night was out of the question in view of the sudden increase in the enemy's resistance and the shortage of fuel. The Myshkova sector was occupied by strong forces, which were constantly increased. The rapid acquisition of a bridgehead on the north bank was hindered by the fierce house-to-house fighting in Nish Kumskii, the enemy's destruction of the Myshkova bridges and the icing-up of the fording places. . . The place was subjected to intense firing from the enemy's DO-equipment (multiple rockets) and from tanks. The German assault group at Nish Kumskii suffered heavy casualties from artillery fire from the north-east, and from tank fire from the west. At 8 p.m. Group 63, advancing on Nish Kumskii, is held up 500 metres south of the place by heavy fire.

There was a delay in relieving the battalion of Group 40 that was due to join up with the armoured group for the push towards Gromoslavka. It could not be relieved until 2.30 a.m. on the 20th. Half an hour later the place appeared to be mopped up after costly fighting; a small bridgehead, established on the north bank, succeeded in repelling counter-attacks and capturing fifty prisoners. During the previous twenty-four hours the total of prisoners amounted to several hundreds. At 4.30 a.m. we were considering whether to send the armoured group along the south bank eastwards towards Gromoslavka, for time was pressing and the position at Nish Kumskii uncertain. But now the enemy penetrated the place backed by considerable reinforcements. Fierce house-to-house fighting developed, in the course of which the commander of Pz. Gren Regt. 63, Lt.-Col. Beitz, one of the battalion commanders, and many others were killed. The regiment suffered heavy losses.

Under these circumstances the advance of the armoured regiment on Gromoslavka had to be cancelled, for the regiment was needed to re-establish the position in Nish Kumskii. I was on the spot and launched the counter-attack at break of dawn. Progress over the ground was slow and the place was not firmly secured until noon on December 20th. In the afternoon the reinforced armoured group was able to advance in the direction of Gromoslavka. There was no further attack, for the enemy occupied the commanding heights and could prevent any aggressive movement.

During the next two days the 6th Panzer Division was pulled

back. It had barely maintained its position against heavy attacks in a small bridgehead north of the river sector. The corps was forced on the defensive and took up positions farther back. This alone could ensure keeping contact with the surviving units.

This was really a complete defeat. The enemy had evidently brought up strong forces. What I had feared at the start of the relief operations had now come to pass. The Russians had no intention of allowing one weak corps to rob them of their great victory at Stalingrad, especially after our attack had brought us 30 kilometres nearer to the great city. The attempt to relieve the 6th Army had to be abandoned. My division had suffered heavily. A loss of 300 may seem a small percentage of the total strength of some 10,000 men in the division. As the castualties were mainly from a weak Panzer Grenadier regiment however, they were relatively high. This regiment was now under the command of a lieutenant. But apart from casualties, all the fighting units were exhausted through sleepless nights in twenty degrees (Centigrade) of frost. While on the march they were no longer susceptible to "pep talks". Any word of encouragement would have sounded hollow.

I suggested to the corps commander that the defensive lines should be chosen in such a way as to have places close behind the front where the troops could get themselves warmed up.

I spent the evening of December 22nd with the less depleted Panzer Regiment, which still had twenty-three serviceable tanks. As these had to be kept well up in front, they had entrenched themselves in a circular formation. The crews were at least able to find shelter in the tanks from the cruel, biting wind. The officers had lit a small fire to warm their frozen limbs; all around was desolation and uncertainty.

The operations section and the divisional battle headquarters were now kept so near the front line that they were in danger from the enemy for hours on end. However, this kind of thing gives the troops moral confidence. The battle headquarters were still in the northern bridgehead of the southern river sector, from which, four days earlier, my division had led the whole corps forward. The bridgehead now had a perimeter of thirty kilometres and was held by four worn-out divisions! I trembled at the prospect of another well-known "last man, last round" order from the highest quarter; it would spell the end of the division.

Christmas Eve was a bad night, with the enemy seeping in everywhere between the seams of the battalions. Now there was no longer a co-ordinated defence, nor any dependable link between the individual nests of resistance. An isolated battalion was over-run by enemy tanks. In the early hours of the 25th the divisional staff crossed to the south bank. A pontoon bridge was being set up over the broken-up ice. The rescue of the battalions still north of the river depended on this bridge, for it had to carry northwards the newly arrived assault infantry unit, the only one that was still fresh and in fighting trim. Its counter-blows would relieve the enemy's pressure on the troops, failing which the withdrawal could not succeed.

But the general operational situation had also deteriorated. The corps was threatened by encirclement of its eastern flank, which had been guarded by quite weak forces ever since the eccentric summer attack towards the Caucasus. It was therefore decided to use the 17th Pz. Div. the following night as a mobile reserve assault force, placing it behind the 23rd Pz. Div. which was due to be relieved. This relief, while under enemy pressure, of battle-worn battalions by others that were just as weary could only be instigated by so-called "orders from the saddle". Each regiment of the division had shrunk to some 180 or 200 men carrying rifles, and the temperature had dropped to thirty degrees (Centigrade) below zero.

After dark on the 25th I moved a short distance away from the river and occupied an advanced command post while the staff was arranging a battle headquarters farther back for the operations control unit. I remained in this forward position for the first few hours of darkness, using a spirit lamp to brew myself some tea from a supply that was always at hand. The victualling officer managed to produce a Christmas cake.

In the clear cold atmosphere the steppes seemed to spread out endlessly towards the horizon. The wide spaces absorbed the sound of battle which seemed muffled. The sky was ablaze with bright stars.

CAUSES OF THE REVERSE

The failure of the relief operation can be ascribed to several causes. The Army General Staff must have been aware of the extent of the catastrophe at Stalingrad. Bitter discussions had taken place between the Army Chief of Staff and Hitler over the question of the retreat of the 6th Army and the attempt to break out. There is no need to waste words on Hitler's senseless decision to keep the 6th Army where it was.

More debatable is the question whether the relevant officers in the O.K.W. and in the General Staff properly appreciated the effect of the defeat on the outcome of the war. Here, as in some analogous events of the Second World War, there is a danger of obscuring historical truth. Blame for the defeat is ascribed solely to Hitler's decision. But this overlooks the inherent gravity of the defeat, already apparent at the time of the encirclement of the 6th Army, which could probably not have been made good. It was a stroke of genius on the part of Stalin to order the encirclement of Paulus's army by means of frontal attacks on both its wings, where the weak Rumanian and Italian allies could be easily penetrated.

After the encirclement, the German High Command had to accept the fact that the enemy had gained the initiative. The Russians now had two alternatives. Either they could let a considerable proportion of their attacking troops, which had encircled Stalingrad from north and east, remain in position to complete the destruction of the 6th Army, which would still allow them to use their growing forces for offensive operations on other parts of the front. Or they could adopt the bolder and "classic" method of keeping the 6th Army in check with quite small forces, and at once use the mass of the now available troops for an attack west of the Don against the beaten and defenceless Italian and Rumanian forces, throwing them back to the south-west, occupying the Don crossings and thereby also cutting off both the 1st Panzer Army in the Caucasus and the 4th Panzer Army which was fighting east of the river.

The attempted relief operation by the 4th Panzer Army between the Don and the Volga held no promise against either of those alternatives. If the Russians decided (as in fact they did) to keep major elements of their forces around Stalingrad, these would have to be strong enough to contain the 6th Army, which would become daily less dangerous as the siege proceeded. But if the Russians decided to use all available forces for a thrust towards Rostov, and if they should gain ground in this direction (which also occurred, albeit slowly) then the relief thrust by the 4th Panzer Army would in any case come to a standstill. Its rear communications were under continuous threat.

It was characteristic of the Russians in the Second World War that their successful battles did not here result in clear-cut decisions that should have settled the isue, but ended in one of their compromises that had become so familiar. And so it proved over Stalingrad. The second of these plans evidently seemed too risky to the Russian High Command, for despite the victory, Russian forces would still have to protect their lengthy flanks during the pursuit. The Russian High Command was in a position not only to throw superior forces against the 4th Panzer Army, but also to threaten its now inevitable withdrawal by launching an offensive west of the Don. And it would need relatively small forces for the Russians to achieve a superiority over the 4th Panzer Army, which now consisted only of a weak corps with 17 Pz. Div. and 23 Pz. Div., both very low in fighting capacity after their prolonged operations.

That was why the corps had been unable to participate in the advance of LVII Corps after the arrival of 17 Pz. Div.

But even if one were sufficiently misguided to believe that the corps, strengthened by 17 Pz. Div., could have pushed ahead to reach the encircled army, the question remained as to how the hungry and not very mobile mass of the 6th Army could have been brought back along a narrow strip of 100 kilometres while exposed to the fiercest attacks. It was obvious that no further forces were available for protecting its extended flanks. The difficulties of such protection have already been shown in the foregoing account of the operations of 17 Pz. Div., when three battalions had to be detached to safeguard the threatened left flank.

The final decision by the commander of LVII Pz. Corps was to place 17 Pz. Div. behind 6 Pz. Div. (which had only a very small bridgehead, threatened from all sides) and then to let the latter advance as the spearhead on a very narrow front towards the 6th Army. I had myself witnessed what happened at the spearhead, and I was sure that at this stage it was no longer possible for the 6th Army to break out for a junction with the 4th Panzer Army, since it possessed only sufficient fuel for thirty kilometres.

Moreover, the 4th Pz. Army itself was daily losing fighting power. By the night of December 19th the batallions of 17 Pz. Div. had experienced three days and nights of intense fighting in temperatures below fifteen degrees Centigrade, and on that night alone they suffered 275 casualties, equivalent to the fighting strength of one battalion. At this rate of casualties one could work out how many more days and nights the two divisions would last. It was shown once more how wrong it is to ignore battle exhaustion when assessing a situation. Only those who have seen the facial expressions of men grown apathetic through exhaustion—even among troops whose morale is high—can form any idea of the loss of fighting power and physical strength involved.

The decision to discontinue the relief operation was imposed—as always in war—by the victorious side. For weeks the 17th and 23rd Panzer Divisions fought their way back east of the Don, often themselves near to dissolution or encirclement, while the 6th Army was left to its fate.

My appreciation of the situation, as given here, was shared by a number of officers. What at that time was not fully understood was the fact that the battle of Stalingrad was one of the few decisive batles of the Second World War, not merely because it marked the loss of an army under the saddest circumstances, but because it represented a culminating point, after which the Axis Powers were forced on to the defensive. The war potential of the Allies had clearly proved itself superior.

Such a turning-point was not sufficient, however, to finish the war, which dragged on for years. This shows, among other things, how powerful the means of defence have become through the mobility of motorised armies and through their equipment with armour, which can prevent the full exploitation by the enemy of his armoured breakthrough. But it does *not* show that the defeated side, which has lost the initiative, has any chance of reversing the fortunes of war. After a battle such as Stalingrad a point in time is reached when strategy must be conducted by the politicians—if only to put an end to the war. It has been suggested in retrospect that the downfall of the 6th Army enabled the 1st Panzer Army to be extricated from the Caucasus. It is true that prolonged resistance by the 6th Army was one factor making it possible for the 4th and 1st Panzer Armies to effect a junction. But it is poor consolation to lose one army in order to save another!

To end a war one must have a politically viable government, not, however, a government that has already resolved in case of defeat to go under—in other words to remain politically passive—and that denies Clausewitz's principle of the subordination of the military to the political viewpoint.

EXPERIENCES IN COMMAND—I

Of the fighting days here described, December 17th, 18th and 19th all had certain features which at that time were typical of many a Panzer division: the divisional commander himself led the front wave of a strong yet mobile assault group. This method involved the following principles:

1. Control of the operation at the point of main effort by the divisional commander using his battle experience and exercising personal authority.

2. Smooth battle co-operation between the three main arms (tanks, infantry, artillery) under his supervision.

3. Division of the work between the divisional commander with his forward assault units and the G.S.O.1, who is static in the divisional battle H.Q.

The practice of "tactical control from the forward position" was a legacy from the cavalry, which continued in these original German armoured divisions. Meanwhile, however, the conditions had fundamentally changed. During the advances into Poland and France, and to a smaller extent in Russia in 1941/42, the armoured divisions were so plentifully equipped with tanks that the focal point of the batle centred entirely on this weapon. Since these tank squadrons were launched in the manner of the old cavalry attack—thrusting far into the enemy's defensive system against his artillery—the divisional commander could only hope to maintain authority over his constantly moving division if he travelled with one of the several waves of tanks, controlling the division by means of short radio messages. This was the method adopted in the initial stages of any campaign where the opponent was either taken by surprise, or hopelessly inferior, or irresolute in his defence.

Since then, however, the nature of war itself had imposed changes in the form of attack as well as the organisation of the division. In the decisive battles it was no longer a question of meeting an inferior opponent; rather did it seem that the balance was maintained for a while between the two sides. The armour no longer encountered weak defensive positions, but came up against other and often considerable armoured forces. In the hither and thither of the fronts there could be no penetration to depths of hundreds of kilometres, and the old queen of the battlefield—the infrantry—came into her own in the fierce detailed fighting. Yet the infantry could no longer fight in isolation. As of old, it needed the artillery, and now also the armour, if it was to stand up to the enemy in attack and defence. Motorisation and close-linking with armour enabled the infantry to become as mobile or even faster than the tanks. Thus the battle was characterised by quick changes and ever new situations. The artillery, moreover, was as indispensable as before. By means of tractors or motorised mountings it had to be made as mobile as the armour and the infantry.

At this stage of the war the German Army High Command made a virtue out of lack of material. It left armoured divisions such as my own 17th Panzer Division in the state that I have already described, making no attempt to bring them up to full strength again. These weaker armoured divisions met the operational needs of the moment; more of them were available where required than if the new material had been used for making good losses among those that had been in action. Tanks were used in all sectors of the front, but no longer in the massed quantity that was needed for the initial invasion phase.

While in many respects the tactics had undergone a basic change, one feature remained unaltered in the fighting that I have described. The mobility of the command was still an important factor. But the controller of a mobile battle must be able to cast his eye over the scene, to appreciate the terrain and to count on rapid execution of his orders. It is immaterial whether the battle group is led by the divisional commander in person or, as originally provided for, by a brigade commander. But preferably he should not *at the same time* be commander of one of the three main weapon formations that must co-operate in the action. In my own division there were no longer any brigade commanders, and therefore it was more than ever necessary for the divisional commander to concern himself with the advanced and more important fighting group.

The hard core of the division's armour was small and had to be handled on a tight rein. As the outcome of the battle depended, as always, on the use of this armour, the divisional commander had to be on the spot.

Tank tactics had also changed considerably. The tanks were no longer sent in a fixed direction deep into the enemy's rear areas, but like cavalry troops, were used flexibly to round off a success that had already been half gained by the infantry. If while so employed they came up against a defensive front that was not yet ripe for assault, they would usually be recalled and sent off in some other direction where there was a better prospect of less costly success.

In order to be able to control the armoured battle, the divisional commander usually moved about close behind the second wave of tanks during the decisive attack, where he would not become directly involved in the action. The forward tanks must fight a rapid duel at short range with a limited range of vision, and this is no place from which to supervise the whole battlefield. By keeping a few hundred metres behind the line of engaged tanks, however, it is possible to do so. Here the commander is exposed, it is true, to the enemy artillery fire, but he is not within the field of fire of the opposing tanks, where he would be exposed to the total force of the attack.

Depending on the battle situation, the divisional commander will change his position frequently between the armoured battle group and the infantry battle group. With the latter he is stationary and can better and more quietly survey the battle. Sometimes he will move into a forward command post between the armour and the infantry. He uses a command tank or an armoured vehicle equipped with two transmitters to keep him in continuous radio touch with his battle groups. He does not need a forward observation officer for the artillery. Before the battle has started the individual batteries have been allocated to work with the different battle groups. Each battery has its own observation officer with the battle group. The commander of the artillery regiment, who, as before, has to control the mass of the regiment, is in contact with the divisional commander through the latter's G.S.O.1., who is farther back at the static battle H.Q.

From the infantry attack the divisional commander will have obtained an impression of the enemy's strength, order of battle, and intentions. Artillery fire will lift the veil from the enemy's anti-tank screens. The enemy's artillery fire provides a sure indication of his strength and of the point of main effort that he has chosen. The general picture is filled in if there is prolonged and indecisive fighting, when the divisional commander will not expose his infantry to unnecessary losses.

The time is now ripe for the divisional commander (who with the commander of the armour has been watching the progress of the fighting) to order the attack by the tanks.

If at one point the attack meets with unexpected resistance, it is diverted to another, or else the artillery must first soften up the anti-tank line until it is ripe for assault.

The commander of the armour, who will be moving forward with or within sight of his divisional commander, knows that he need not press the attack to the utmost limit. Depending on his own choice of tactics he may break it off and resume it again at a point that seems to him to offer better prospects.

Once the armoured attack is under way, however, the divisional commander, being in control of the battle groups, must allocate the necessary infantry protection to the armour, and this must be followed at once by the artillery, whose protective fire is just as vital to the tanks as it is to the infantry.

At the static battle H.Q. of the division are the G.S.O.1., the operations control staff, the chief communications officer and the commander of the artillery regiment. Being in radio communication with the divisional commander forward, they work hand in glove with him. The G.S.O.1 has a large measure of independence. In an emergency he gives orders to all units of the division that have not been subordinated to the divisional commander. He arranges for the remainder of the division to follow up behind the battle group, details the flank protection (which usually demands numerous forces) and holds the reserves in hand. He is in communication with Corps H.Q., from which are issued the results of the reconnaissance; he is also in touch with neighbouring corps, and with the G.O.S.2. for supplies. Thus the G.S.O.1.'s work continues as if in the presence of the divisional commander, except that his responsibility is increased.

Experience showed that the G.S.O.1.'s static battle H.Q. obtains a better picture of the battle through continuous radio contact with the divisional commander than through the collection of reports from the units in the field. For he gets the picture direct from the most experienced commander, whose authority covers all the weapons. But the reports from the field units are not thereby rendered superfluous. They fill in details in the divisional commander's picture, which thus reflects the general impression with the greatest objectivity and in a form ready for evaluation.

It goes without saying that the forward position of the divisional commander also has a psychological effect on the troops. He is able to watch his men and see that his orders are swiftly executed—and this can be of decisive importance. The knowledge that the divisional commander himself is near at hand has been shown by experience to speed up events at critical moments. Subordinate commanders who fall short of requirements can be relieved on the spot, but usually a brief word of encouragement suffices. Above all, the divisional commander has the indispensable contact with those who carry the burden of battle—the battalion commanders. (In this phase of the war they were like commanders of battle groups on a small scale.) If their example is to inspire the troops, they must themselves become leaders of assault units, corresponding to the divisional commander's own forward activity. They must also know that they will receive recognition when their operations bring success.

At night the divisional commander proceeds to his static battle H.Q., which has been moved up close to the front during the advance. Here he discusses the next day's attack with his G.S.O.I. From here he also speaks with his corps commander and reports his impressions of the fighting These are very important, being a distillation of his own experiences and reports from the units under his command. They give him added authority in opposing any senseless demands from above, and in making counter proposals. Unfortunately the Hitler-inspired wishful tactical thinking was too readily adopted by the Army, and became all too common in the Second World War.

The principles of operational control already outlined were applied as follows:

December 17th: Attack by motorised infantry battle group into unexplored territory (no tanks being available on that day) for the purpose of creating a springboard and maintaining local superiority. Exploitation of the infantry's mobility on wheels. (Map 1.)

December 18th: Attack by the same battle group, even before the tanks became available, in order to open up the fighting without delay. Relief for the infantry at the height of the crisis by sending in the tanks, which by an outflanking movement and while engaging enemy tanks, launch an attack on the first strongpoint of the enemy's front and capture it. Continuation of the outflanking attack by all arms to invest the important second key strongpoint in order to bring the neighbouring division into the section. (See Map 2.)

December 19th: Continuation of the planned enveloping movement as ordered, the tanks attacking and disengaging before being shot up; then making use of their mobility and fighting power, they alone would move forward on the general axis of advance—Stalingrad. (Map 3.)

December 20th: Independent decision, contrary to corps orders, to recapture Nish Kumskii, thereby obtaining a better evaluation of the enemy's position with a view to the protection of the corps' left flank.

These three successive fighting days were critical for the battle of Stalingrad. They illustrate the procedure of operational control that I have described. The circumstances were ineluctable, since the division had to fight its way forward into a situation that could not be foreseen. Other circumstances, especially when on the defensive, call for a different technique of operational control. The form of control as well as the nature of the decisions by the divisional commander, can always be contested. In my case both were governed by the changing conditions of the fighting and were devised more or less instinctively. Such methods are essential if one is to act quickly on decisions derived from battle impressions. No two days of fighting are alike.

FIGHT FOR SELF-PRESERVATION

From December 26th onwards my Division, together with the even weaker 23 Pz. Div., were fighting for survival. Already the latter was outflanked from the east, while in the west my own still had contact with Rumanian forces. But Rumanian resistance soon collapsed, so that the west flank of the corps was now also threatened.

After a Russian breakthrough into the 23rd Pz. Div. on December 26th, the higher command decided on a withdrawal to a bridgehead in the region of Kotelnikovo. In this critical situation I remained for the time being at an advanced battle H.Q. on the arterial road, where I had hopes of establishing contact with the battalions. If I had occupied the new rearward divisional battle H.Q. south of Kotelnikovo, I would have been cut off from the troops and not competent to give the required directions. Even so, at first I was almost idle in the advanced position. Remnants of Rumanian troops filed past me, men who had suffered defeat when the Russians had first outflanked Stalingrad. These Rumanian soldiers, without officers and in no proper marching order gave an impression of fatigue and apathy. What else could one expect?

I now felt confident that the enemy had not managed to penetrate our positions before darkness fell. Our withdrawal would be more successful if it took place at night. I therefore moved back to the new battle H.Q., which for a few hours afforded me a semblance of personal security. In the stillness of the night the noise of battle faded, and I had a few hours of deep sleep. During that night the divisions were told: "The holding of the bridgehead at Kotelnikovo is vital for further operations".

While it was still dark I returned to the front line. Once again the weak battalions had their frozen and exhausted troops out on the steppes that afforded no cover. My division still possessed one anti-tank gun and eight tanks! All the battalion commanders had been killed, and the adjutants had taken their places.

I drove along my own front, which gave little impression of cohesion, as was now usually the case. But the front was still quiet. At a distance of two to three kilometres to my left I could see single Russian tanks deploying into battle formation ready for their attack. My own eight tanks were now joined by the much fresher motorised assault gun battery. It was thanks to this battery that in the last few days we had been able to disengage ourselves from the enemy. I launched the mobile battle group, composed of tanks and assault guns, against the approaching Russian armour, with the result that the attack was repulsed in the forward area. But already other tanks were probing far into our left flank. A bridge that we had previously wired for demolition blew up prematurely, killing twelve pioneers. How was this bridge, essential to our withdrawal, to be restored? All through the night the fighting raged around Kotelnikovo. Some units of the division, acting on incorrect orders, disengaged sooner than intended, and had to be sent up to the front again despite the general withdrawal.

There was an air of crisis in the divisional battle H.Q. at Nadolny. Arriving there, I hurried into the building with the pennant of the operations section, only to be greeted by strange faces. The staffs of both divisions were in the same place, as the withdrawal had to take place through a single remaining bottleneck. I had entered the battle H.Q. of the 23rd Pz. Div., alongside my own H.Q., and thus met its commander, General Count von Boineburg, an old cavalry man like myself.

The road along which we were withdrawing was under fire from the enemy's tanks. To counter the prevailing tense atmosphere I ordered my baggage, which was ready for moving, to be unpacked again. The withdrawal that had been ordered did not begin until the night of December 28th.

On the following morning new positions were occupied. The villages shown on the map did not exist. Now the exhausted troops were once more in the open, in a temperature of minus twenty-five degrees Centigrade. I had slept in a room occupied by two dozen other sleepers, some German, others Russian. Soldiers came and went in order to warm themselves.

On December 31st Pz. Gren. Regt. 63, finding itself surrounded, had to be relieved by means of an armoured attack. Its withdrawal during the night involved severe close-range fighting, in which a further eighty men, or ten per cent of its infantry strength, were lost.

Nor was the disengaging movement entirely successful. One battle group could not rejoin the main body of the division until the following night, when it fought its way back.

Fourteen days earlier we had launched an important operation to relieve the Stalingrad army, and although we had pressed forward up to thirty kilometres, I had no illusions about our prospects. If the Russian control of operations had been more flexible, our two hard-pressed divisions would probably have been captured, for the area to the east and west of the axis of withdrawal was entirely exposed.

The continuous suffering of the troops affected me physically. The cold was visibly sapping their strength, especially the infantry. All other arms could arrange matters so that at least a proportion had some rest at night, if only for an hour or two. This deep sleep of unconsciousness is sufficient to produce a remarkable revival of spirits. The sleeper can be easily awakened; his sub-conscious mind retains an awareness of danger from raids or from being left behind if there is a sudden withdrawal.

So great was the reduction in infantry strength that there was no further need to organise the motor transport in shuttle relays for moving the companies. While this made things more normal, the rearguards bore a heavy burden. With inadequate numbers and incapable of serious resistance, they had nevertheless to hold out and be prepared to sacrifice themselves if necessary.

At the battle H.Q. of the battalions the picture was grim. All around lay the bodies that should have been brought back for burial. Then there were the wounded prisoners, who suffered agonies when their open wounds remained unprotected against the cold. How readily these poor Russians would return a smile from those at whose mercy they believed themselves to be. How brave were the women whose houses had been set on fire by the artillery! With the fighting continuing all around, they could occasionally be seen trying to extinguish the flames. With a grin they suffered the soldiers to occupy their houses, while they spent the nights squatting in their potato sheds. Nor did they seem to hate in the manner of the peoples of those western countries that had suffered invasion. Maybe these Russian women were too unpolitical to hate. And they still had sufficient piety to hope, finding consolation in their icons.

In the first ten days of 1943 I changed the location of my main battle H.Q. only once, for the front was now more stable. Coming from the 1st Panzer Army in the Caucasus, an S.S. division had arrived as reinforcement, and there was also the 16th (Mot.) Infantry Division under Count Schwerin. For a long time this division had been keeping at least a reconnoitring watch over the big gap between the left wing of the Caucasus Army and the 6th Army at Stalingrad.

These big gaps were characteristic of the campaign—the wide Russian spaces that consumed so many men. All the "occupied" positions also had their gaps.

The 17th Pz. Div. gained new strength not only through the reinforcements sent up by the corps, but also from its own resources. The defensive lines could now again be drawn in the near proximity of the inhabited localities, which at once improved the situation. On January 3rd the division received its first new allocation of fifty tanks.

The fighting between January 2nd and 7th on the Mal Kuberle and from January 7th to 10th round Kutenikovskaya and north-west of it, along the Sal, resolved itself into a series of isolated engagements. Here again the battle groups of the division were anything up to thirty kilometres apart, which greatly complicated the unified conduct of operations. Success could not be achieved without constant re-grouping of the forces and the concentrated use of armour. Moreover, the light artillery batteries, the flak batteries (used in a ground rôle), the motorised gun companies and the assault gun batteries usually had to be subordinated to the individual battle groups, since the infantry itself possessed no effective anti-tank weapons.

The character of the fighting changed. The division was no longer alone. Above all, the fear was receding that the High Command would order the division to hold some prescribed line to the death. Indeed there was a growing feeling that the corps would be instructed to avoid encirclement—a danger that nevertheless persisted. In the area between the Sal and the Don, which was not defended by German troops, the enemy was pressing ever farther west, thereby outflanking the corps from the north.

Yet the frontal assault was growing weaker. In their offensive the Russians had won ground so rapidly that they now began to suffer from the same supply difficulties as all quickly advancing troops had experienced in the Russian theatre of war. Before launching their attacks the Russian infantrymen, with no nearby villages to lean upon, had to spend the nights in prepared positions, which cost them some of their strength. Supplies of fuel and of spare parts for their tanks broke down, for they depended on motor trucks. They were not short of victualling supplies, since they had captured numerous German depots.

In the type of fighting that now developed I was no longer able to spend each day at the focal point of the division's activity. Usually the control of operations required my presence at the battle H.Q., but each day I managed to visit one or another focal point.

Although the troops seemed to be fighting without interruption, in

order to fight at all they actually had to spend hours relaxing in some
house, or in their trucks on the move, or on a peaceful sector of the
front. Similarly their commanders had somehow to find the essential
hours of relaxation. At Kotelnikovo I and my adjutant lived in a
rather uncomfortable house belonging to a State-owned model settlement, where the housekeeping was done by an old Kalmuk woman.
We were in the region of the Kalmuk Steppes. At Yermakov I again
had a little house to myself, when I was able to enjoy two or three
consecutive nights of rest. The G.S.O.1 was in the habit of waking me
for any important decision. I had no difficulty in shaking off my
somnolence and becoming as alert as in the day. On lying down
again I at once fell asleep. How small are the needs of a man
constantly faced with death or with moral disintegration! He
needs sleep, protection from the cold, nourishment—and nothing
more.

I found sleep in those little huts that nearly always contained the
so-called Stalin bed, an iron bedstead. Most mornings, even if I had
been out during the night, I took my bath in the rubber tub with a
cold douche, followed by breakfast with strong tea. On those few
occasions when I was compelled to abandon my battle H.Q. precipitately, I never left any of my baggage behind.

As I usually returned to the batle H.Q., I could always spend an
hour or two of the day or the night there getting myself warm. Anyone can bear severe cold as long as he knows that he can get warmed
up again. But if there is no such prospect, as with the troops in this
stage of the war, then the cold can be terrible.

In these little huts of the steppes I found not only warmth and a
bed. Frequently I experienced the cosiness of a small primitive
dwelling, satisfaction in the simplicity of the few pieces of peasant
furniture, pleasure in a certain cleanliness—the white-washed wall,
the iron bed, the unpolished table, chair and chest. The dim light of
the candle was reflected in the deep gold of an old icon, while the hot
tea steamed in the bowl. Often there was also the smile of some
hospitable Russian peasant woman. We never lacked food, for our
rations were the full amount for active survice, and there were the
iron rations that had been surrendered. True, we had no potatoes or
vegetables, and naturally there was no fruit. Four or five of us had
our evening meal in the G.S.O.1.'s quarters, nearly always under
great stress and to the continuous accompaniment of ringing telephones, which usually gave unwelcome tidings. Here was the
meeting point for the assistant adjutants after their adventurous
journeys across the length and breadth of the battlefield. They were
stiff with cold, bringing a wave of cold, clean air into the stuffy
room.

On January 3rd the point at which our defensive line turned from an eastern to a northern front was Vessely Gaj. It was here at 5 a.m. that the second attack was repulsed. This extended village was defended on three sides by the weak battalions of Pz. Gren. Regt. 40. The division had retained as a mobile operational reserve all the tanks and assault guns. About 9 a.m. the enemy started his next powerful thrust. He succeeded in penetrating the locality with tanks and infantry despite resistance from the exhausted and greatly weakened companies, and one of his armoured groups reached the stream to the north of it. In the end I managed to relieve the pressure on the troops by throwing in the tanks and the assault guns.

When I entered the locality the only force still there was a small group under Lieutenant Fink, who as adjutant of a battalion held the place against superior forces. In the steppes the Russian DO-equipment (rocket launchers) flared up, and almost simultaneously their missiles exploded in this area. Fink had gathered his men about him. The dead lay about in front of the house, while inside his troops warmed themselves. Fink gave me an account of the fighting round the house. The Russian T-34's had quite recently been circling round it, but now our tanks had driven them off. That afternoon a further attack on the place was repulsed.

Despite our ground reconnaissance the situation north of the Sal had remained very obscure in the days preceding these events. By January 3rd strong enemy concentrations had been reported in the villages along the Sal north-east of its confluence with the Mal Kuberle, and this was confirmed by air reconnaisance. At the same time there were reports of movements by strong motorised forces out of the forest of Sukhosoleny in a south-west direction, and Prostorny was reported in enemy occupation. On January 4th one enemy battalion was reported moving towards Salovskii from the north. On the same day our reconnaissance, reaching as far as the Don, had located motorised infantry and armoured cars at Romanov-skaya proceeding in a south-west direction. Consequently my division had to extend its north-facing defensive front westwards along the south bank of the Sal up to Sementinskaya. As these developments threatened the supply services, a strong detachment was sent to their assistance at Martinovskaya, 40 kilometres west of the division's left wing where it touched the Sal.

Already on January 3rd the division had planned an offensive with the limited objective of dealing with the triple threat—frontal pressure at two different points, threat to the exposed left flank, and wide-ranging outflanking of the rearward communications. The plan could not be carried out before January 5th, as we had been forced on the defensive at every part of our front.

The corps wanted above all to thrust across the Sal north-west-wards as far as the Don. For this purpose the newly attached Gren.

Regt. 156 was on January 4th taken out of the right wing, assembled
near Kutenikovskaya, and sent into the bridgehead at Verch Serebriakovka before daylight. Its task was to hold the bridgehead, which
was indispensable for further movement, and to form a flanking
screen to the north and (if needed) the north-west for the thrust
by the armour, reinforced by Assault Gun Battery 203. The commanding officer of Gren. Regt. 156 was put in charge of the battle
group.

At 5 a.m. on January 5th the battle group began to move out of
the bridgehead (map 5). The movement was hindered by the thaw that
had set in. The fire-power of the tanks and artillery was weakened
through shortage of ammunition. The divisional artillery, disposed
south of the Sal, gave supporting fire. Shortly after crossing to the
north bank the battle group was attacked from the direction of
Petuchov in the north-east. Its commander sent assault guns and units
of his regiment against this opponent. In its further thrust northwards the battle group encountered the enemy in strength, but
managed to repulse him. The group had thus broken through the
forward part of the enemy's forces which had evidently been ready to
strike at the division's front from the north and north-west. This
surprised the enemy, who had not reckoned with an attack from an
opponent who had been so completely forced on to the defensive.
True that the battle group had made its sortie from the bridgehead
through a quite small gap. Its reconnaissance established the enemy
in occupation of villages on the Sal to the west of this gap, namely
at Salovskii, Ternovoj and Semenkinskaya.

All now depended on the battle group exploiting its successful
surprise operation by gaining ground rapidly to the north and north-
west. The group pushed ahead—still protected by the high terrain—
so far into enemy territory that it could deploy fully before making
any further attacks. It then debouched from the crest of the high
ground in order to open a surprise fire from the south-west against
the enemy who was moving in that direction under cover of the
heights. The effect on his moving tanks and motorised infantry was
destructive, for he had not anticipated a major attack by German
armour on the north banks of the Sal. He was thrown back to
Prostorny, and by 10 a.m. we had reached the road between Semenkinskaya and Romanovskaya.

The enemy reacted quickly by sending reinforcements from the
north to the units that had been driven back. From this it could be
concluded that he had already launched those units against the
left wing of the division, which was also the left flank of the
army.

Towards 10.30 a.m. the armoured group was again threatened by
the Russians, who had assembled in the Sukhosoleny forest and were

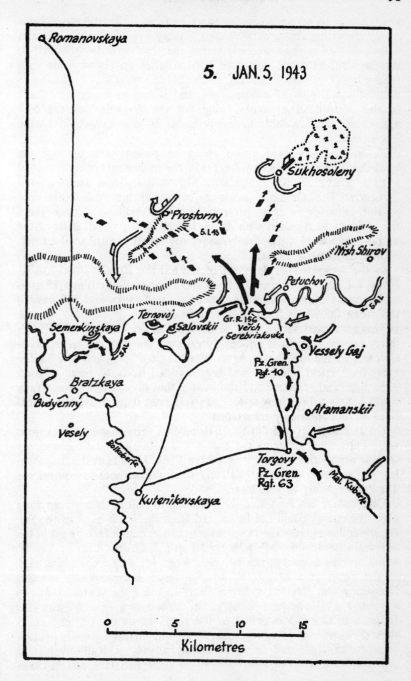

Romanovskaya

5. JAN. 5, 1943

Sukhosoleny

Prostorny

5.1.43

Nish Shirov

Petuchov

Semenkinskaya

Ternovoj

Salovskii

Gr. R. 156
Verch
Serebriakovka

SAL

Vessely Gaj

Pz. Gren.
Rgt. 40

Bratzkaya

Atamanskii

Budyenny

Vesely

Bolkuberle

Torgovy
Pz. Gren.
Rgt. 63

Mal. Kuberle

Kutenikovskaya

0   5   10   15

Kilometres

again trying to advance south-westwards from it. To the west of our battle group the Russians were also gaining strength from north and and south, using their westerly forces that had already advanced to the Sal. Our tank fire destroyed two batteries and twenty-two anti-tank guns. The ceaseless firing of the battle group was beginning to exhaust the supply of ammunition, and it had to be ordered back to the bridgehead to avoid being cut off. As this was the only armoured force available to the division, its existence could not be jeopardised.

Before the armoured group could be pulled back through the bridgehead defences of Gren. Regt. 156, the reinforced enemy launched a fresh attack on the bridgehead with infantry and armour from Petuchov. The Germans made a counter-thrust with tanks and assault batteries so as to protect their other units, and once again the enemy was repulsed with heavy losses. By 5 p.m. all units of the battle group were again firmly under divisional control to the south of the Sal-Kuberle sector.

In the armoured battle north of the Sal the Russians had lost 31 tanks, (of which 15 were burnt out and six immobilised) and 25 anti-tank guns. German losses amounted to three tanks and 129 casualties along the whole front of the Division.

This armoured thrust and the destruction on January 5th of over thirty enemy tanks had noticeably relieved the pressure on the division and on the 4th Panzer Army. For the time being and in a limited area, the tactical initiative had been wrested from the enemy. Moreover, this local offensive had shown him that my division, at any rate, could secure a breathing-space for itself even if its rear communications were increasingly threatened.

On January 6th and 7th the division was thus holding its previous main battle line, although the enemy was constantly and theateningly seeping across the Sal into its northern flank. He was evidently pursuing his intention of using relatively weak forces here to compel the 4th Panzer Army to withdraw.

On January 6th Pz. Gren. Regt. 40 had to pull in its northern wing since the enemy could not be cleared from the south bank of the Sal. On the following day the regiment was still in action facing east in the old main battle line. My advanced battle H.Q. was then at Vesely, and I ordered a local attack by Gren. Regt. 156 on a front facing east, at the same time letting the armour thrust independently towards Budyenny and Bratzkaya in an effort to clear the south bank. My advanced H.Q. became involved in close-range fighting with the Russian infantry. Meanwhile to the north of us the German tanks moved eastwards, extending their thrust still farther by order of their commander, until they met the enemy advancing south-west from Nowaja Serebriakovka. Our tanks made a surprise flank attack, there-

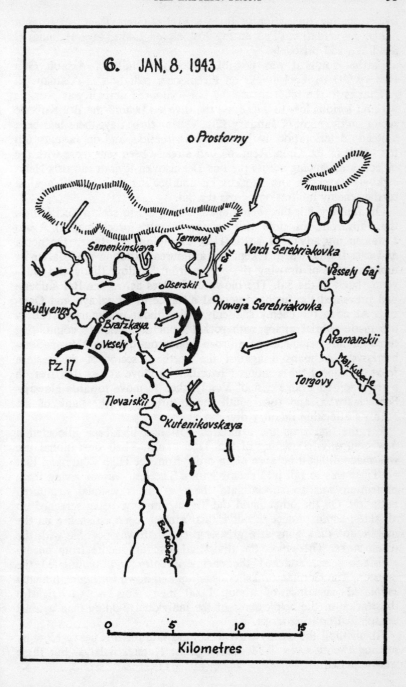

6. JAN. 8, 1943

Prostorny

Semenkinskaya

Ternovej

SAL

Verch Serebriakovka

Vessely Gaj

Dserskii

Nowaja Serebriakovka

Budyenny

Bratzkaya

Vesely

Atamanskii

Pz. 17

Torgovy

Mal Kuber le

Tlovaiskii

Kutenikovskaya

Bal Kuber

0   5   10   15

Kilometres

by extricating the seriously threatened Pz. Gren. Regt. 40 from a dangerous situation. The enemy lost eleven tanks, several hundred dead and 153 prisoners.

Farther south it was possible to employ units of Assault Gun Battery 203 to repel atacks on the pioneer battalion at Atamanskii.

Thanks to the relief thrusts by our armoured units it was possible without serious loss to withdraw the division behind the Bol Kuberle sector on the night of January 17th. During these days there had been a steady deterioration in the rearward situation, and on January 6th the whole of Pz. Gren. Regt. 63 had already been sent there with the object of advancing across the line Dennisovkii-Ryiska towards Nemetzkov-Potavskoye and Moskovskii and sealing the area off against further enemy infiltration across the Sal.

On January 8th the enemy again attempted to seek a decision on the main front, this time with stronger infantry forces (map 6). Again I was in my advanced battle H.Q. at the angle between the north and east fronts, where I kept the armoured battalion ready after its morning task of drawing the enemy from Sundov, Ilinov and Budyenny back to the Sal. The blown-up bridges across the Bol Kuberle had prevented the further intended advance to Bratzkaya and Oserskii. At noon the enemy suddenly and without preliminary artillery fire made a brief attack with rocket launchers, prior to committing three infantry regiments on a broad front from the area Nowaja-Serebriakovska-Atamanskii against the northern sector of the eastern front. I ordered the armoured battalion to move across the river on a reconnoitred bridge east of Vesely, then to move towards Nowaja-Serebriakovka, and turn south for a thrust into the flank of the enemy's attacking infantry division.

For the first time the armoured battalion had been allocated a new company, consisting of ten Tiger tanks. Their operational use was made difficult because of an order from the High Command that no Tiger was to fall into enemy hands. The best way of giving them protection was to subordinate them to the divisional armoured battalion. On the other hand the Tiger company, being screened on all sides, could protect the divisional armour by opening fire on the mobile anti-tank guns at a greater range than was possible with the older tanks. Thereupon the divisional armour, secure from enemy anti-tank guns, attacked the enemy infantry and annihilated the division. The German tanks, cruising up and down for hours, inflicted estimated casualties of about 1,000 men. This was a frightful illustration of the helplessness of the individual fighting man against unmolested cruising tanks.

At nightfall the enemy tried to compensate for this heavy blow by sending twenty-seven T-34 tanks against Kutenikovskaya, but these were repulsed.

The attack by our armour, which had lasted only an hour or two, allowed the division, exhausted though it was, to be withdrawn to the new defensive line in good order and with but minor losses. The armoured force was still intact. The artillery had participated in the action, its observation officers riding with the tanks. But it had no rewarding tasks because of the peculiarities of the fight between armour and infantry.

EXPERIENCES IN COMMAND—II

These two examples of battle groups are characteristic of the principle that the armour is kept together in defence but is used offensively at the right moment. Commanders less familiar with armoured tactics, and those who were conscious only of the endless front, thinly occupied and under threat from the enemy's armour, would under these conditions have been tempted to fritter away their own armour.

At no point of the front was the divisional infantry in a position to repel armoured attacks relying solely on its own resources. In those days it possessed neither the Panzerfaust nor the Panzerschreck.*

On the main front, which covered about forty kilometres, the following weapons were available for anti-tank defence: eight self-propelled mountings (7.5 cm.), four self-propelled mountings (7.62 cm.), and one anti-tank gun (7.5 cm.). Some of these weapons were detailed for the threatened supply area. The so-called heavy anti-tank weapons were useless during the greater part of the operations described above because they had been supplied with dud ammunition.

In both cases the rearward communications were so seriously threatened that from the tactical point of view it might have been best to send back the armour, for the division could have been cut off. Yet I rejected this step. It was only through concentrating all available tanks at a single point that worth-while results could be achieved, albeit of short duration.

These two examples illustrate the fact that in such situations it is not possible to provide effective artillery suport. On January 5th the front could not be denuded of its sparse artillery to support the armour that had gone far ahead to attack the enemy, and in any case none of the division's artillery was self-propelled. In the second example, when the Russian infantry division attacked the main front, the artillery was capable (through its observation officer) of fire direction, but it could not be effective because the battle resolved itself into individual combats between tanks and infantry.

* *Panzerfaust*: Recoil-less anti-tank grenade discharger.
  Panzerschreck. anti-tank rocket launcher.

During attacks the main battle group was almost always under my personal direction, but this did not apply to the armoured battle group, which for the general purpose of defence was used offensively. In view of the threat to the attenuated front I always had to be available in the centre, for I could not relegate the decisions that had to be made here to the G.1. But in both cases I chose a forward battle H.Q., where I could directly intervene at the northward bend of the main front and also at the focal point of the attack, and could watch the progress of the fighting and arrange co-operation between arms as the necessity arose. Here I had the shortest radio link with the armoured group, and kept it available for any incident. On January 8th the group more or less gyrated in a semi-circle round my battle H.Q. while I remained there to direct the operation.

Usually the mass of assault guns was allocated to the armoured group. Whenever it was essential to detach single companies for anti-tank defence—as happened in both cases on the remote right wing—the company was subordinated to the assault gun battery, but tanks were not sent from the armoured section. In such a situation the assault guns proved an excellent weapon; they were not in turrets and could not be swung through a full circle, so that the only way their own crews could avoid exposure to the enemy's weapons was by using their mobility on the battlefield. Without turrets the crews were unprotected, but their all-round view gave them a better idea of the situation. Thus they were less in danger of remaining stationary during an armoured battle—a tendency to which the tanks themselves were always liable because of their restricted angle of vision while on the move.

The ten Tiger tanks considerably enhanced the offensive power of the armoured troops. Their armour and their effective weapons made these tanks far superior to the T-34's, so that they could dominate the local battlefield and also provide protection for all kinds of weaker tanks. They fostered the offensive spirit but did not justify the hopes that the German High Command had placed in them, for their numbers were quite inadequate. Moreover it soon became evident that these heavy Tigers were too ungainly for the usual mobile tactics of the division. They had the tonnage but not the horse-power, and could not accommodate themselves to a running fight. The order that they must not fall into enemy hands restricted their employment.

The frequent enquiries from the O.K.W. led to the conclusion that Hitler had expected too much from the Tiger companies. Their numbers were insufficient to turn the scale in any big battle. In severe frost their great weight made them liable to slide down frozen slopes. When this happened or if they were immobilised through hits, it required two other Tigers to tow them away. Had the Russians only slightly increased their air superiority (which they never did) then nothing less than large masses of fast-moving armour could have survived in this coverless country.

THE CHANGING PATTERN OF WARFARE

According to the classical precepts of war the Russian Army High Command should have followed up their breakthrough and simultaneous outflanking movement at Stalingrad by relentlessly pursuing the Germans with powerful forces astride the Don in a south-west direction, thereby also cutting off the 1st and 4th German Panzer Armies.

The identified Russian movements north of the Sal and their occupation of places like Matikovka behind the German front led to the conclusion that these were indeed their intentions. Yet here too it was evident that their penetrations into gaps of the front—big as they might be—could not be regarded as the pursuit of a still mobile though defeated army. Since the entire German southern front had begun to totter, it was no longer a question of a parallel pursuit, but of a frontal one on a very broad front. But such a front needed to be filled in, for which purpose even a victorious pursuer must find additional forces. He must always strive to keep his pursuing columns in touch with each other and avoid any wide gap in his advancing line.

The rules of war stipulate a relentless pursuit "to the last breath of man and beast". This means nocturnal preparations and perpetual day and night marches in order to keep on the heels of the retreating opponent. The destruction that the latter leaves in his wake adds to the pursuer's supply difficulties. In the end shortage of fuel compels the pursuer to turn the job over to his cavalry, which requires fewer supplies and is more mobile over the terrain, though not so effective in action.

The activity that has been outlined occurred in alternating conditions of frost and thaw, the latter particularly trying to the fighting man, whose damp clothing became ice-encrusted as soon as the frost set in. At night-time the Russian pursuers laid siege to the villages we were using to rest and refresh our troops. The sheer necessity of self-preservation compelled us to defend these villages to the last. It is therefore hardly surprising that the momentum of the Russian pursuit could not be maintained as in former wars. It was vitiated through lack of forces.

If the defeated side possesses a more or less skilled leadership and a continuing war production for its armoured units, it can keep itself in being, since the pursuer cannot simply over-run it in the manner of the old tactics of attack cavalry against an enemy taken by surprise and possessing no armour.

When forced on to the defensive it was the practice of the German operational commands to keep in readiness behind every front a so-called "fire brigade" of one or two armoured companies. Frequently they were detached from their own divisional units to operate against penetrating enemy armour, which they attacked in the flank by surprise, destroying it or holding it up until further and more powerful reserves could be brought on the scene. But in frontal defence also the tanks proved superior to all other anti-tank weapons. Whenever they could get themselves into a prepared, concealed position, they were the defensive weapon that the enemy feared most of all. The mobility and fighting power of single tanks enabled them to take full advantage of the contours of the terrain.

Thus the armoured divisions, originally organised as purely offensive formations, had become the most effective in defensive operations. Modern defence is always organised in areas and zones, never in lines. But mobile defence requires mobile—meaning motorised—formations. Motorised reserves can be changed over quickly form one wing to the other or be moved forward from depth. The infantry, being an integral part of the armoured force, is trained to fight in collaboration with the armour. Armoured rearguards alone are able to hold advanced positions up to the last moment, when they can suddenly and without warning disengage and withdraw.

Thus large-scale operations assumed a different complexion from those of the First World War or the early part of the Second. It was now possible to hold temporarily a front such as that of the 4th Panzer Army in the episodes already described, although the enemy in his parallel pursuit had already overtaken this front. Hence the enemy's passing threats to our rearward units and supplies could be ignored, and this is what we did.

There is always a chance that somewhere the front will be able to hold. As it turned out, the 1st and 4th Panzer Armies were able to fall back across the Don, but unable to halt the enemy pursuing them across and beyond the river. While on the march towards the Dneiper, however, these Panzer Armies began a counter-offensive on the Donetz, through which they not only defeated the enemy but themselves became the pursuers.

Out of this changed pattern of warfare arose the misconception that the tilting of the scales, recognisable in war by the loss of strategic power to one side and a corresponding gain to the other, is irreversible and admits of no further hope for the loser. This misconception proved disastrous to the German side. A government that clearly recognises the situation and tries to end a war while it still has some bargaining power is not a weak but a strong one. Such a government must be conscious of its responsibility to the people for policy and strategy. If that condition does not exist, there can be no sound basis for strategy.

SOLITARY REFLECTIONS

I had personally conducted most of these last battles, and being at the focal point, had witnessed this form of close-range fighting and tank actions against helpless enemy infantry. In the armoured attack on January 8th I was among those who saw hundreds of Russian infantrymen without cohesion or leadership who refused to surrender and were slaughtered. At the height of the battle a sixteen-year-old Kalmuk youth, mounted on a Panjep pony, arrived unwittingly from the rear, hoping somehow to get back to his home. He came up to the hole in the ground where I happened to be standing with one of my battalion commanders. I was moved by the innocence of the lad. The intense cold and the wide open space of the steppes almost stilled the dull sound of the tank guns and the explosions of their shells. This was his sudden introduction to the grim drama of battle, and he burst into tears.

War demands toughness. I could forgive many a failure due to the intense cold, but I was not prepared to accept that a heavily engaged division with a fine reputation should suffer from any weaknesses in its leaders. The severe measures I was compelled to take against individual shortcomings and the mounting number of killed, wounded and prisoners proved a heavy personal burden. Other things worried me even more. On one occasion I was awakened during the night to acknowledge the receipt of "an important order" from Hitler to the effect that he would protect every officer who in the fight against partisans did not scruple to kill women and children. Hitler went on to explain that his order had been prompted by a court-martial sentence on an officer of which he disapproved because it was too lenient.

Orders of this nature were most worrying and burdened one's conscience. In such cases I would hold a brief conference—in this case with my G.1.—ending with my instruction that the order was not to be circulated. Yet the uneasy conscience persisted; inevitably the order would be promulgated throughout the Army. The fighting against partisans was always bitter, for they were regarded as illegal and treacherous. Frequently they were in control of entire towns and villages, where they terrorised the inhabitants by forcing them to provide assistance. Hence there often seemed to be extenuating circumstances for the excesses of our troops against them—including the women and children, as in Hitler's order.

In this problem I could only hope that I would never be called upon to sponsor such excesses by troops under my command. The hope was justified in as much as the southern part of the eastern front saw very little partisan activity as compared with the central part.

Occasionally I occupied quarters in some secluded spot away from the arterial road. Then I would enjoy a few hours of complete relaxation by sending for the dark green box containing the service radio receiver. These were memorable hours, when from some country far behind the front the set picked up works by notable German composers. I pondered over the fact that as one grew older, one was more and more attracted to the earlier masters of German music. And the programmes seemed to cater for this taste more than before, so that I had little difficulty in finding what I liked.

If perchance I could get the set to pick up a Brandenburg Concerto, or a Bach Cantata or Handel's *Messiah*, my joy would be accompanied by profound emotion. At first it was just pleasure in the tones and the beat of the music with its crescendo of cadences. Then I was overtaken by a feeling of pain at all the senseless sacrifices of war. My thoughts would travel back to my family, alone in their home, exposed maybe to greater stresses than I was experiencing as a serving officer. Would I ever again see my son, who was facing the enemy somewhere on the same front, or like so many others, had perhaps been flown back into the Stalingrad pocket only to end his days in pain and suffering?

Then the triumphal closing bars of the music would generate in me a renewed feeling of great happiness, of confidence and hope. Would the inevitable and rapid retreat soon restore me to my own country? When would there be peace again? Would the terror of National Socialism vanish, and the Germans, though defeated, resume normal relations with other nations? A profound peace pervaded my spirit, filling me with elation. The mysterious waves in the ether had transported me for a while into a happier view of humanity.

VORTEX OF THE WAR OF MOVEMENT

The period from January 8th to the end of that month resolved itself into one frantic struggle to gain time for pulling back the Army of the Caucasus. The distances seemed endless. Our forces were too weak to fill the area. My division could barely cover its own operational zone.

Here again the classic teachings of war stipulate that one should never be without reserves, unless of course they have to be thrown in to ease the pressure on the defensive front by means of flank or frontal attacks. It was possible to fight in this manner only because the opponent too was attenuated by the size of the territory and unable to build up any strong centres of pressure. Yet during the whole of the period he was striving to cut off the 4th Panzer Army by means of a northerly push towards Rostov.

There was now no need for the Russians to attack the division and suffer heavy losses, as they had done on January 8th. But if we attacked them they would throw in whole battalions. In general they could march forward whenever there was no resistance, with the result that our front—now only nominal—was constantly being outflanked.

Often the battalions would fight in isolation without armour, weak in artillery, and shrinking in strength. The other division of the corps was rapidly dissolving and was no longer capable of heavy fighting. Consequently my 17th Pz. Div. had to be sent into action first to the south-west, then to the north to prevent the encirclement of the corps.

As long as the divisional artillery still had two light and two heavy batteries, it was best to provide one light battery for each Pz. Gren. Regiment at battalion strength, and to keep the heavy batteries together under divisional command. Sometimes the battle groups were so far apart that the heavy batteries too had to be detailed for temporary direct co-operation with a specified battle group commander. Hence the artillery positions adjoined those of the infantry to ensure effective communications and anti-tank defences. Additionally, anti-aircraft groups were sent to the front line to work with the battle groups in ground fighting. Thus the commanders of the battle groups had a large measure of independence in the use of their infantry and the attached artillery and anti-aircraft units. The divisional command endeavoured to keep a controlling hand on the course of the battle by creating reserves independently of the front line troops, by a flexible regrouping of the available forces and by direct tactical control of the armoured groups.

Whenever possible, we avoided allocating the available tanks and assault guns to the battle groups. The medium and light anti-tank guns were of too small calibre to be effective against tanks. The heavy anti-tank guns ("motorised Z") had to be written off, as all their ammunition was defective. Only the self-propelled guns remained as effective anti-tank weapons, and they were usually distributed among the battle groups. If such a gun became defective or destroyed, a tank had to be sent into action to take its place. But in general the tanks were kept together as before, for use by the divisional command. This principle was applied to such an extent that the infantry would often find itself without anti-tank defences when exposed to armoured attacks, while the German armour was kept assembled in readiness for an assault in the right place and direction.

At no stage in the fighting did the division's strength in weapons even remotely approximate to that of the enemy. For this reason alone the defence had to be conducted on a mobile basis within the framework prescribed by the higher military authorities. The resources for doing so grew ever weaker due to reduced maintenance facilities for the overworked motor transport, which had suffered losses from enemy action. Consequently replacements for the infantry could not be sent up to their units for lack of transport. Tracked vehicles were impeded by frozen ground. In this respect the assualt guns were more mobile. They were used a great deal with great success as substitutes for tanks, and they had very few losses. They needed commanders fully conversant with the mobile tactics of self-propelled guns.

During these strenuous weeks there was a growing understanding between the divisional commander and the troops. Confidence is a magical source of power! The brave battalions knew that nothing superhuman would be demanded of them. If threatened with being overwhelmed, they were withdrawn. The division could afford this kind of evasion. Its successful armoured counter-blows had achieved results that were evidently denied to many another division. After some setback the troops always regained their steadfastness, for I made it a practice to appear at the front not only when leading a battle group, but also whenever the situation became critical.

On such occasions I invariably spent some time with the battalions, where I spoke with officers and other ranks, avoiding any show of familiarity. I was only too conscious of the paucity of my contribution. I had no difficulty in mastering my nature when exposed to danger. If a situation seemed perilous due to the enemy's breakthrough or when under fire, I could resist the temptation to return to my divisional battle H.Q., and stood fast until the crisis was over. I reasoned that a shot could hit me equally as well while returning as at the advanced position. A commander who scurries away from the front line whenever there is danger soon loses the confidence of his troops.

In times of stress there is, too, an unspoken understanding between senior officers and troops that is more eloquent than any words. When, for instance, I visited a company that had suffered particularly severe losses and its comanding officer reported: "The company still has twenty men; the morale is good", I would encourage his subordinates to talk by quietly listening to their experiences, and this was sufficient to alleviate the strain and help to dispel their gruesome memories.

Once we had crossed the river Manytch there was no more of that gnawing anxiety that at any moment we should be cut off from our retreat across the Don. One division was brought up across the river to render assistance, while the first divisions from the Army of the Caucasus began to arrive from the south.

The tanks presented a grim enough picture as they came out of battle. On the outside were riflemen, including some wounded, as well as corpses being brought back for burial. One tank had a slaughtered calf hanging over the side. In the villages fighting developed betwen our infantry taking cover in the houses and the Russian tanks patrolling the village street. Count Castell, the commander of Pz. Gren. Regt. 63, found plenty of targets for his carbine until he had to abandon the place under cover of darkness.

In the melting-pot of the defeat the barriers between nationalities seemed to break down. One day when, with my carbine, I joined up with an attacking battalion, I was amazed to see two Rumanians wearing tall white fur caps marching along as riflemen with each group. After the dissolution of their army at Stalingrad these soldiers had found refuge with the German battalions. A squadron of Cossacks had attached themselves to the divisional staff and taken over protection of the staff quarters, thereby releasing German troops for the front. These Cossacks were good men and first class at tending horses. They enjoyed the respect of the population who accepted them as fellow-countrymen despite the fact that they were now fighting on the wrong side!

Could this mark the overall decline of nationalism? That is how I regarded these little episodes. Nationalism had become the flail of humanity. In Hitler's Germany it had grown into something particularly repellent, but it also flourished in other nations, where words like "chauvinism" and "jingoism" were coined to characterise it.

The nearer we got to Rostov, the wearier we all became of the fighting. Through my daily contacts with corps H.Q. I could see that my division inspired confidence. In recent days it had held on to positions that were like fingers pointing eastwards deep into enemy-occupied territory. Now that the division was being gradually relieved by other units, I reported to the corps commander that I had started investigating three incidents concerning places abandoned without orders. My only purpose was to vindicate the conduct of the commanders concerned. But the corps commander strongly disapproved of my plan; he considered an enquiry inappropriate in a division where all officers and men had fought like heroes for days and nights on end. My G.1., who had gone to corps H.Q.

to receive orders, told me that the commander of the 4th Panzer Army happened to be there and had spoken with emotion about the operations by my division.

On the evening of February 2nd, 1943, the commander of Pz. Gren. Regt. 63 reported to me, accompanied by his adjutant, Lieutenant Lindenburg. Since the first push towards Stalingrad this young Lieutenant had been in turn a regimental adjutant, a battalion commander and commander of the regiment. I decorated him at a ceremony in a small dark room—in silence, for no words of mine could be appropriate. I went up to him, unbuttoned his ragged battle tunic and placed the band of the Knight's Cross around his neck.

That same evening the divisional staff crossed the Don. After a thaw the severe frost had returned, turning the ground into a crust of ice. The motor vehicles could do no more than ten kilometres per hour. The blood-red sun sank in the pale blue evening sky. The roads were marked with signs showing "Rostov". For a while the Cossacks kept pace with us, trotting along some hundreds of yards to one side, stirring in me memories of a long life in the saddle, of an epoch that had vanished. Wrapping myself in the thick rug, I was soon asleep despite the twenty degrees of frost. I noticed nothing when my car slid off the road and had to be extricated by a truck. I saw neither the frozen Don as we crossed it nor the towers of Rostov, a sight that I had keenly anticipated. Never in my life had I slept so profoundly as on that night. Since December 17th, 1942, it was the very first night when my division had not a single grenadier battling in the snow and ice against an all-too-powerful foe.

The next day I promulgated the following order of the day to the division—

| 17th Panzer Division | Divisional Battle H.Q. |
| Commander | 3rd February, 1943. |

Soldiers of the 17th Panzer Division!

For this division the severe fighting between the Don and the Volga, which lasted several weeks, has now come to an end.

What I would have liked to say personally to every soldier of the division can only be promulgated in cold print.

To you, the commanding officers, I give thanks for your leadership in battle. First you applied your energy to pushing forward the front of the Panzer Army. Then the enemy, realising the menace, pitted his great strength against us. Your fire and enthusiasm enabled you through offensive action and mobile operations to retain the initiative against a far more powerful opponent.

You, the younger officers, were quick to fill the gaps left by your fallen and wounded commanders. You assumed command of regiments, battalions, companies and batteries. You stood calmly and resolutely by your men, your tanks and your guns whenever the divisional commander ordered you to hold out to the limit of human endurance in the bitter cold of the nights. In armoured battles and bloody hand-to-hand fighting you inflicted on the enemy ten times your own losses.

You, the soldiers of the division, have achieved more than can be humanly expected in your uninterrupted day and night fighting for weeks on end, often while threatened from the rear and at the same time exposed to frontal attacks by armour. You had no rest between battles during those rushes from one focal point of the fighting to another.

It does not suit your Swabian traditions to make much of your deeds. But you should know that you have stood up to the severest test. The fame that your weak battalions have earned in their successful battles against divisions will go down in history.

We reverse our arms and salute the graves we have left behind us of the twenty-two officers and the 388 N.C.O.'s and men who were killed in action. For them the relentless battles in the wide open steppes are over. Though they have found eternal peace, yet do they still belong to us. Marching at the head of their ghostly column is the commander of Panzer Grenadier Regiment 63, bearer of the Oak Leaves, Lieutenant-Colonel Seitz. For all of us he was the paragon, for he combined the chivalrous virtues of the soldier with great zeal and personal modesty.

Soldiers of the 17th Panzer Division!

Here is the precept for this day and hour: you will do all in your power to strengthen and improve the fighting value of our sadly depleted ranks for the struggle that lies ahead. I too will do my utmost to provide personnel replacements and new and plentiful weapons of war. Tighten your chin-straps!

Long live the 17th Panzer Division!
(Signed) v. Senger-Etterlin.

In addition to the commander of Pz. Gren. Regt. 63 I must here pay tribute to the regimental commanders of the division when I assumed command of it, and who now, alas, rest for ever on foreign soil:

Lieut.-Colonel Heinrich, commander of Pz. Gren. Regt. 40, with whom I was on very close terms.

Colonel Elster, commander of the division's artillery regiment, who always showed eagerness for battle.

Lt.-Colonel Büsing, commander of the division's Panzer regiment, a highly experienced battle group commander.

THE AGONY OF STALINGRAD

It was at this period that the fate of the Stalingrad army was sealed. Very little information was available on this subject at the time, but these are the facts— On November 26th, 1942, a week after the

Stalingrad army had been encircled, it had half rations for only twelve days, and no more than ten to twelve per cent of the ammunition that would normally be stocked by an army. In other words, it had sufficient ammunition for one day's fighting.

Fuel stocks were sufficient for small movements within the besieged zone, but not for bigger tactical movements, let alone the strategic movements for breaking out of the pocket. This was when Göring promised to assemble sufficient air transport to provide full suplies to the Paulus Army—550 tons per day. Although 225 Junkers aircraft were available and others were being collected, his promise was Utopian.

The difficulties of the air-lift increased in proportion as the situation outside the pocket deteriorated. As long as the airstrips used for loading supplies lay within 180 kilometres of the pocket, entailing only 50 kilometers of flying over enemy-held territory, each aircraft could achieve two or three lifts per day, which illustrates the weakness of the Russian air forces. By the end of January, 1943 however, the flight distance had increased to 360 kilometres most of which was over enemy-held territory. As the fighting power of the Paulus Army declined, so the Russian anti-aircraft defences outside the pocket increased.

On December 19th, 1942, the day on which my division had got nearest to the pocket, the Army Group had in readiness 3,000 tons of transport capacity for supplies that were to be sent to the beseiged army through the land corridor. On that day the C.-in-C. suggested to Hitler that the Paulus Army be ordered to break out. This proposal was turned down on the grounds that Paulus had reported only enough fuel for thirty kilometres, while the 4th Panzer Army (which means the the 17th Pz. Div. at the time of its setback) was still some forty to fifty kilometres from the pocket.

Paulus had estimated that he would need 4,000 tons of supplies for the breakout. By December 26th the supplies reaching the pocket by air amounted to seventy tons per day instead of the essential minimum of 550 tons.

On January 9th the Russian High Command called on Paulus to surrender. On the 12th the weather deteriorated. A general, returned from a flight into the pocket, reported that the Paulus Army could hold out for another two to four days. One of two airstrips in the pocket was lost to the enemy, followed on the 16th by the second. This meant the end of supplies by air. On January 31st Paulus surrendered with 90,000 men (of the 265,000 who were presumed to have been in the pocket). Losses could not be established with any certainty. During the siege some 30,000 wounded had been flown out. In the course of the air-lift operations the Luftwaffe lost 488 aircraft and 1,000 men.

THE ENCOUNTER

After that night of deep sleep on February 2nd when I was driven across the Don, I remember coming back to consciousness in the early morning in a homely white-washed cottage. An adjoining room was occupied by an old woman, smiling hospitably in the manner of Russians, and her orphaned grandson who was drawing melancholy notes from his balalaika.

The temperature outside was still twenty degrees below zero. An easterly gale whirled the snow off the ground high into the air, whence it fell for a second time. The higher snowflakes scintillated in the sunlight. The cloudless blue sky encompassed the wide fields that were in constant agitation. In view of the cold and the cutting wind I gave up the the idea of a long walk—something I had looked forward to for the past three months.

On January 23rd I had received news from my son that he was at Stalino; it was comforting to know that he was no longer with his division in Stalingrad.

My division was dispatched farther into the district of Stalino. I was sorry to leave the open countryside for new quarters in the town, where the dirty house in which I lived was ugly as no peasant's cottage could ever be.

When the division started moving west, I tried in vain to press on ahead of it. The roads were jammed with troops streaming back through the snowdrifts. The reason for my hurry was that I hoped to meet my son, who was adjutant to the commander of the unit that would be our neighbour in our new area—the rear H.Q. of the 24th Panzer Division, commanded by a friend from the days of my old cavalry regiment, Major von Heyden.

On February 7th I thought that without too many diversions I would be able to reach this H.Q., located in a village oddly named New York. The drive as far as Stalino was good, but thereafter progress was delayed by snowdrifts and more especially by the disordered retreating Italian troops. After some difficulty I at last reached a lonely road, and for a time all went well. But within ten kilometres of my goal the car had its first breakdown of that winter. I stopped for lunch with a smoke regiment* After two hours the breakdown was rectified and we drove off, only to get stuck in a snowdrift within one kilometre. I walked back to fetch a tractor, which pulled the car clear. Then a tyre lost its pressure and the spare wheel had to be pumped up after removing the rim from the wheel frame. This delayed us for another two hours until at last we resumed the journey along a road that became ever more lonely and deserted.

---

* *Nebelwerfer—Regiment*, which fired multiple rockets.

Would this road lead me to my goal, and would the rear H.Q. of the 24th Pz. Div. (which was due to move on) still be there? As we came to each snowdrift I explored it on foot to avoid failure so near the end. We got to the first houses and I was relieved to find the H.Q. had not moved on. But my son had gone out and it took some time to find him. Then he stood before me and we embraced. At the evening meal with him and Heyden I learnt that my son had sent me a card on January 10th saying that he was about to be flown into the Stalingrad pocket. The card did not reach me until three months later. I did not know at the time that officers were still being flown into the pocket, and assumed that the air-lift was being used exclusively to send provisions to the starving 6th Army troops. My son had had to go to Göttingen for hospital treatment, and when he returned it was too late—the last aircraft had departed.

I spent the night in his quarters and departed after breakfast. The parting was painful to both of us. The rear H.Q. of the 24th Pz. Div. was understandably eager to get away from this place, for the 6th Army was due to be "newly constituted" in France. Meanwhile the Russian offensive, sweeping in a south-west direction from Kharkov, had already cut off a section of the withdrawal road between Stalino and Dniepropetrovsk. Once again the enemy was in our rear. Fully loaded trains of the 24th Pz. Div. rear H.Q. had been standing idle for days, unable to move.

I gave them petrol to enable them to move by motor trucks, and in return I received a number of vehicles, so that the 17th Pz. Div. again became fully mobile. Owing to the urgency of the retreat this transaction had to be effected in an unorthodox manner.

Acquiring these vehicles from the 24th Pz. Div., I noticed that they displayed the emblem—so familiar to me—of the prancing horse. It had originated with Baade and Cavalry Regiment 3. In Holland it had stayed with me as emblem of the I./Cavalry 22, which was part of the old Cavalry Regiment 3. Then I had left the cavalrymen, who kept the same emblem when they formed the 24th Pz. Div. At that time my wish to assume command of that division was unfortunately denied me. Now, whenever I saw individual vehicles in my division sporting the emblem, I was reminded that it stood for the old mounted cavalry division so many of whose men had perished in the ruins of Stalingrad.

DANCE OF DEATH

During the first half of February 1943 there was more marching than fighting. My division was now directly subordinated to the 1st Panzer Army. To the north-east the enemy had broken through in the zone of the 19th Pz. Div., and my division was given the task of throwing him back. The enemy had got as far as Niktorovka.

On February 9th I had launched an outflanking attack on this place with three infantry battalions—the division's entire infantry stength. The troops had to go through deep snow and got stuck at the southern exit to the place, suffering considerable losses. It had to be captured on the following day.

From my staff H.Q. I went up to the front. It was a cold, clear wintry day. As so often happens, the noise of battle was absorbed by the icy cold and deep snow. At one spot I was told that I could not drive any farther, so I had to cross a hill on foot. Niktorovka lay at a distance of two kilometres, occupying a commanding position on another flat-topped hill. I saw smoke and shell-hits. As I moved forward the explosions of the shells became louder. Pioneers were clearing mines near a bridge. For a while I walked along a narrow cleared passage through the minefield. Convoys of low, narrow sledges filed silently past us, loaded with apathetic wounded men.

I climbed the hill to reach that part of the perimeter of the place that was in our hands. The battle H.Q. of two battalions had been set up in one of the houses captured on the previous day. Corpses that had been brought here lay in front of it. In the morning sunlight they seemed puffed up. I stepped over them and entered a low dark room filled with people. The sole furniture consisted of two wall telephones at which officers were busy. From the dark corners came low moans from the wounded who had been carried in. A reservist was ladling soup out of a large container.

The most forward battalion was fighting its way ahead into the place accompanied by three tanks and seemed to have gained a few hundred metres. I followed close on its heels, taking another battalion with me in order to send it beyond Niktorovka as soon as the place was captured. The third battalion provided the screening force to the south-east. For the attack I had enlisted the fire-power of several batteries from the 19th Pz. Div., in whose sector we were fighting. There were some passing difficulties when the point of aim had to be laid further forward to conform to the progress of the attack.

The attack was directly carried forward by the three tanks which proceeded from house to house along the usual dead straight village street. The artillery itself was silent. We heard the muffled shell explosions from the tank guns and anti-tank guns. Whistling bullets came from odd directions.

The village street presented a strange sight. In front of every house lay five or ten Russians, who had only just been killed, some with bodies partly ripped open, others with brains spilling out of their cracked skulls. As their blood was still warm the bodies steamed in the cool morning sun. One Russian fired so wildly in all directions that he could not be approached. Eventually he was killed by a tracer bullet and lay on his back. His clothes were on fire, and the tongues of flame reached his ammunition pouches, whose contents were exploding on all sides. Another who had pressed himself against the wall of a house received a direct hit from a tank gun, and was stuck to the wall like a squashed fly. In the middle of the street lay a forearm. No cut and no blood could be seen on it; the hand was small and grey.

Some of the dead had been lying there since the previous day, stiff with cold. Some lay face downwards, their limbs oddly dislocated. One rigid leg pointed straight into the air. Other men had settled on their backs to die, spreading themselves out as for a sunbath.

The grenadiers were clearing up house by house, and rounding up prisoners, some of whom were unable to walk because of injuries received in the close fighting. The dead Russians were left where they lay. The prisoners were collected at the batle H.Q. and rested there alongside the German corpses. A woman appeared from nowhere—as so often happened with the Russians—and proceeded to bandage the wounded regardless of the fact that they were prisoners. For a moment I rested my eyes on the scene. One Russian had been shot through both eyelids, and his head was nothing but a large bloody lump. He moaned because his wounds were freezing. The others grinned. Here and there I exchanged a smile. They were tucking in to the soup, which steamed in the bitter cold as did the open wounds of the living and the dead.

TCHERNUCHINO

From pleasant, rural Karlovka the division was moved east to the ugly town of Artemovsk in the industrial zone. It was here that the Russian VIII Cavalry Corps had broken through; it must be halted and destroyed, for which purpose I was vested with wide powers by the 1st Panzer Army, to whom I was by then well known.

The divisional staff H.Q. moved into the industrial district of Debaltsevo, where I was accommodated in a clean little workman's dwelling. During the whole of the day I would be up forward with the fighting troops, returning each evening to these quarters. We were constantly bothered with the difficulties of the terrain. Every day I tried to close the ring round the Russian cavalry corps. If we managed to beat him, the enemy would have to fall back in a southeasterly direction; but the deep snow prevented us from making any progress in that direction. The main body of the enemy's forces was believed to be in the villages of Gorodishtche and Tchernuchino. To the north of these places the road to Voroshilovsk was in emeny hands, so that we had no communication with the German forces stationed there. First we would have to fight to free the road; then I intended to wheel south from it.

I myself accompanied the outflanking attack by Pz. Gren. Regt. 63, now organised as a strong battalion. We laboured through the deep snow, which the wind was piling up all the time, and made our way southwards from the big road with the so-called convalescent home as our objective.

Before long our spearhead came under fire. In the deep snow we had to establish an advanced casualty station. It became more and more difficult to deploy for action. The convalescent home was captured at 3 p.m. Our losses amounted to twenty-four dead and 121 wounded. The main dressing station at Debaltsevo was working at full pressure.

On February 16th I had the choice of attempting to outflank the enemy either by a wide movement or by a shorter one leading to Tchernuchino. Since the 6th Pz. Div. was gradually advancing from the east on Gorodishtche, I tried to form a centre of pressure just west of Tchernuchino, and again I moved up to the front.

In the deep snow single companies of Regiment 63 were sent so far ahead to the south of the convalescent home that they could wheel in to the Tchernuchino-Gorodishtche road. These battle groups encountered great difficulties with trucks and supplies. On their left flank the Sovchos Demetshenko was held by the enemy. I ordered one company to attack it and myself accompanied it. We were held up in front of the Sovchos, which stood on a dominating hill.

On the 17th I went along with Motor-cycle Rifle Battalion 17 in order personally to supervise its attack in Tchernuchino. There was tough fighting for every house. The village covered an extensive area, and as usual the enemy had placed strong anti-tank defences at all elevated positions. Together with the attacking company I pressed forward slowly from one hole in a wall to the next. Our artillery fire, directed by radio, was showing excellent results ahead of us, always keeping the enemy down in the next group of houses. On each side of the road we were accompanied by single anti-tank guns and tanks, which kept the flank clear for us. At one place I had difficulty in crawling through a hole in a wall and was effectively assisted by a service boot from the rear. Then I heard a startled voice: "Good heavens, that's the General!"

Since Tchernuchino had not been captured either by the motor-cycle riflemen or by Regiment 63, I tried a further out-flanking movement on the next day against Gorodishtche. I wanted the tanks to compel the enemy to shift his line of withdrawal to the south-east.

Next I hurried over to Pz. Gren. Regt. 40, and found that between the two villages it had encountered enemy defences in deep snow, and had been held up. I therefore decided to drive over to a newly arrived battalion working with the battle group operating farthest to the east. Just as I arrived it was entering Gorodishtche from the north, while at the same time the first tanks of the 6th Pz. Div. were entering from the east. The place was pleasantly situated on a steep slope of the valley with a large wooden church in the centre. It was quite empty!

The Russian VIII Cavalry Corps, under pressure from west and north, had fallen back to the south-east. On the morning of the 19th we entered Tchernuchino almost without fighting, and proceeded to mop up the surrounding countryside. Our losses on this day were small, but contrary to my expectations we captured neither booty nor prisoners, and I was disappointed and rather annoyed.

When the C.-in-C. proposed to visit my battle H.Q., I had a feeling that he would want to know why the destruction of the Russian corps had not materialised. My fears were unfounded. The C.-in-C. was full of praise for the achievements and the bearing of the division— and he was an authority on morale in battle.

I inspected the booty at Tchernuchino. It included German road trucks—again bearing the emblem of the prancing horse from the 24th Panzer Division, the unit that had gone under at Stalingrad and had once been the military home of myself and my son.

CHANGE-OVER FROM RETREAT TO PURSUIT

The 17th Panzer Division formed a small and isolated part of a 1,200 kilometre long front which had begun to waver in consequence of the outflanking and breakthrough battle of Stalingrad. After February 19th the division retreated westwards without contacting the enemy, and on the 23rd reached the district of Petropavlovska, where a bridgehead facing north was formed.

The position of the division in relation to other forces was obscure. It marched without any contact with neighbouring groups, and its only communication with XLVIII Panzer Corps, under whose command it now stood, was by radio. All we knew was that the Russian thrust towards Dniepropetrovsk persisted, thereby threatening our line of retreat from the north.

As the division was entering Petropavlovska that evening— cautiously, since it had been reported in enemy hands—the place seemed dead, the inhabitants having fled or gone to ground. In the uncanny silence each house was a potential nest of resistance. Reports from what was left of the 24th Pz. Div., which had previously moved west, showed that already on 11th February the enemy had reached and cut the railway line from Kharkov to Dniepropetrovsk. On the

15th enemy reconnaissance had advanced as far as the bridgehead to the north-east of this place and had been repulsed. Soon we learned that the enemy had also pressed forward in a south-westerly direction to Vassilovka.

On the night of 23rd February the division received orders to move north-west towards Verch Samara, which was reported occupied. At the same time the bridgehead was to be held. I formed an advance detachment consisting of Motor-cycle Rifle Battalion 17, the armoured company (the remains of the Panzer regiment), one company of the anti-tank battalion, and a light battery. The rest of the division was to function as the second wave and take over the entire bridgehead, where it would hold itself in readiness for a sudden pursuit of the enemy when ordered.

The Russians appeared to be moving back towards the north-east. At 9 a.m. the advanced detachment captured Verch Samara from the enemy who was taken by surprise. Among the prisoners were officers from the Russian III Armoured Corps and from an armoured brigade, both of which had been assembling in the region of Dobrovolye.

At 1 p.m. the advanced detachment penetrated this place. Simultaneously the enemy used his tanks coming from the south-east to attack Verch Samara from the rear. As I was approaching Dobrovolye at 2 p.m., another armoured reconnaissance car entered it, coming from a position in rear and to the right of me. There was something odd about this vehicle; when it was shot up by one of our anti-tank guns I realised that it was Russian. They clearly wished to continue their attack from the rear.

The battle lasted one hour. The enemy's attack, launched from a distance of one kilometre in battalion strength, was gaining ground, and I had only one light battery with which to repel it. This did not perturb the enemy, who was moving in closer all the time. Just as he was about to launch an assault on the battery four of our tanks arrived from the rear, having come straight from the repair depot. I directed them to thrust into the enemy's flank, but the attack was halted. That night we lost Verch Samara again, and it had to be retaken by the advanced detachment.

The day had shown that the pursuit by the enemy had lost its momentum. The Russians seemed to have no plan, and my division had taken 166 prisoners with but slight losses. The neighbouring German division, twenty kilometres to my right, had advanced to a hill. The division on my left was held back at Bogdanovka, which was being strongly defended. Direct communication with this place could not be established. As the road conditions precluded any forward deployment, I kept the divisional order of the battle unchanged for the following day. I also took into consideration that if my plan for a rapid advance should succeed, my neighbours on our flanks would be behind me. I would then be able to use the two battalions of the second wave as protection for the exposed long flank. One of the battalions was to follow by rushes close behind the advanced detachment, so as to be available in the event of a setback or encountering strongly defended enemy positions.

In accordance with corps orders to push forward on February 25th along the high ground east of Staryia Blisnezy, the second wave was moved up from its bridgehead positions to Novopavlovka, near Drobovolye. It started off at 2 a.m. with instructions to cover and screen the entire eastern flank of the advance.

These dispositions ushered in the rhythm of pursuit tactics. The advanced detachment pressing forward did not have to worry about the situation in its rear (Map 7). In order to lead the thrust I drove forward to Staryia Blisnezy. On the previous day the advanced detachment had been thrown out of Dobrovolye at nightfall and was still exposed to enemy fire. I directed it to make a westward outflanking movement which started at 8.30 a.m. At 9.15 Dobrovolye was captured, the enemy evading northwards.

Ground and air reconnaissance had established a considerable enemy concentration east of the axis of attack, in the region of Tchervonii-Sofievka, and this force was preparing to attack westwards. However, I decided not to wheel towards it, but to press on to the north, even though I could have only weak forces to screen my eastern flank.

Having been driven out of Dobrovolye, the enemy thus had no prospect of defending himself effectively in the villages to the north of the place. My advanced detachment over-ran his attempt to stand at Galtchov, Berestovii and Odaneski. On the road from this last place to Staryia Blisnezy the bridge had been destroyed, so our advance was continued in a north-easterly direction via Alexandrovka, which was taken at 11 a.m. with the capture of two 18 cm. guns. Ordering a company from the second wave to move to this place to protect the road of advance, I continued my attack towards the north-east, into the sector of the division on my right. Then the advanced detachment wheeled west again towards Staryia Blisnezy, in the sector of the division on my left, for that division was still lagging far behind, being in action south of Dimitrievka. The axis of maintenance for both divisions had been cut by Russian cavalry.

The tension increased hourly. The way now led straight into the retreating enemy. Our dive-bombers attacked one of his long columns; then the few tanks of the division swept over the wreckage. A fierce engagement developed between Barbalatova and Staryia

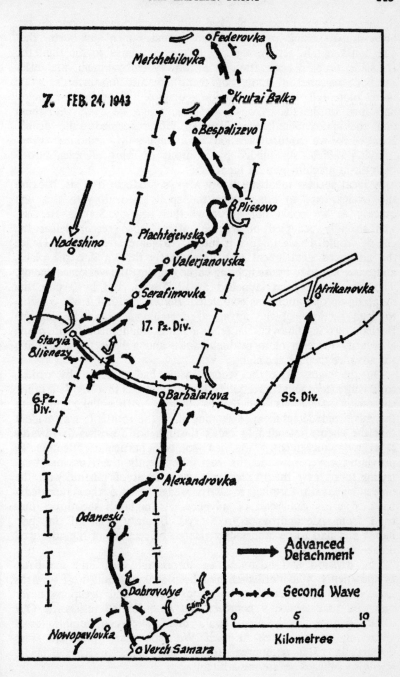

7. FEB. 24, 1943

Federovka

Metchebilovka

Krutai Balka

Bespalizevo

Plissovo

Nodeshino

Plachtejewska

Valerjanovska

Serafimovka

Afrikanovka

17. Pz. Div.

Staryia Blisnezy

6. Pz. Div.

Barbalatova

SS. Div.

Alexandrovka

Odaneski

Dobrovolye

Samara

Nowopavlovka

Verch Samara

Advanced Detachment

Second Wave

0   5   10

Kilometres

Blisnezy. The road was so blocked with broken-down armoured cars, horse-drawn vehicles and dead and wounded men and horses that one could barely get through. Only twenty metres to the right the Russians were in occupation of a railway embankment, and after we had captured it hordes of them streamed northwards, while many more fell under our machine-gun fire. To the left the enemy had men in the undergrowth; at close range we dealt with them and they surrendered. One Russian officer seemed quite drunk. Everywhere we captured weapons and supplies. My armoured troop-carrying vehicle, surrounded by a throng of firing riflemen, turned its built-in machine-gun on them.

A local success involving booty always produces a crisis, because the troops tend to linger over the spoils. I dealt with this one quickly as we could not know whether near-by Staryia Blisnezy was strongly occupied or whether after his so recent defeat the enemy would decide to turn it into a rearguard strong-point. Hence the advanced detachment was immediately thrown into the place, and bitter house-to-house fighting ensued against the weakened enemy. The attack had been launched at 12.45 p.m. and by 3 p.m. the mopping-up operation was completed. Before nightfall it was possible to send sections of the advanced detachment ahead to the line Barbalatova-Serafimovka-Nadeshdino, thus simultaneously providing a security force, a close reconnaissance and a basis for continuing the advance through the night.

On the right flank the second wave had attacked by rushes, following after the advanced detachment, and was involved in a quick succession of actions. Finally its covering parties linked up with the advanced detachment, extending it to the south. It was evident that the enemy intended to break through north-westwards towards Kharkov; consequently we had to pay particular attention to providing cover towards the east. Apparently the Russians were trying to narrow their excessively wide front of pursuit with the object of again forming a sharp wedge. Hence they repeatedly tried to cross our road of advance. At nightfall the direct link road from Alexandrovska to Staryia Blisnezy was still in their hands and had to be laboriously cleared by sections of the advanced detachment.

The division had advanced so surprisingly fast into the flank of the enemy, who until then had been striking south-west towards Dniepropetrovsk, that his numerous forces and weapons never managed to establish a compact and co-ordinated resistance. Our weak advanced detachment could thus inflict considerable losses with only minor losses to itself. We took many prisoners from the Russian 51st Armoured Brigade and the 10th Rifle Brigade, who also suffered severe casualties.

On the evening of February 25th no contact existed with the division's neighbours. The one on the right was behind us, while on the left 6 Pz. Div., though it had moved small forces into Staryia Blisnezy (already captured by my division), also had its main body behind us, and some of its units were still tied to the rear of the corps.

At 1.45 a.m. on February 26th on receipt of a corps order the advanced detachment was given Metchebilovka as its new objective. The mass of the second wave was to move to Staryia Blisnezy to take over there as covering force. The scarcity of fuel that now began could only be rectified by exchanges within the batle groups. The advanced detachment started off at 4.30 a.m. At 5.45 the second wave had taken over as covering force at Staryia Blisnezy. After mine clearance and some short, sharp fighting the advanced detachment captured Serafimovka and at once pushed on with tanks to Valerjanovka, whence the 500 men of the enemy's force withdrew to the north-east. At 7.30 a.m. Plachtejewska was taken.

In a similar attempt to enter Plissovo the armoured company lost two tanks, and the enemy toughly defended the place with newly arrived forces which replaced those we had driven back.

These events led me to a decision there and then to commence an outflanking manoeuvre by means of a fairly wide sweep to the west, using the remaining ten tanks. In order to tie down the enemy the infantry of the advanced detachment continued its frontal attack. The outflanking operation met with success. By 9.15 a.m. the tanks had reached the hill two kilometres north of Plissovo, whence they drove southwards into the rear of the enemy's defensive front. At the same time the riflemen worked their way forward from the south-west. The place was occupied at 9.30; the spoil included two 12.2 cm. guns.

Despite its losses, I ordered the weak armoured company of the advanced detachment to push northward, without taking part in the the mopping up of Plissovo. By 10 a.m. its spearhead had reached Bespalizevo, which the Russians held strongly with artillery and anti-tank guns. Meanwhile the infantry mopped up in Plissovo, defeated a weak force of fresh Russian troops coming from the northeast, then followed in the wake of the armour. Prisoners reported that the defenders of Plissovo had consisted of freshly arrived troops.

Consequently I now kept the sections of the second wave closer together. The Russians had at last evacuated Sofievka, leaving behind numerous tanks, guns and lorries.

The commander of the second wave had by now advanced to Plachtejewska and the main body was available as reserves. The villages on the lengthy supply road were occupied by us to provide a covering force. Some other villages lying off the road were also occupied, and our reconnaissance was pushed ahead to the east.

Reports showed that my neighbours were still lagging behind. On the right the S.S. Division was fighting for Afrikanovka while on the left 6 Pz. Div., having meanwhile pressed through Staryia Blisnezy, was in action at Nadeshino.

As I wanted to spare my own weak forces at Bespalizevo, that is, avoid committing them to a frontal attack, I launched an out-flanking one here also—the tanks going westwards, the riflemen taking advantage of a depression that led into the place from the east. The new half-tracked lorries (which were good over the ground) permitted a rapid and simultaneous execution of both outflanking movements. Hence the enemy's artillery fire against the road south of Bespalizeo had no effect. At 12.30 p.m. the two groups joined up in that place, and thereafter it was easy to ward off enemy forces approaching from the east from Andreyjevka.

With the additional forces that he had brought up the enemy could now at least keep the approach road, which was so familiar to him, under fire, and this caused undesirable delays. My troops had been taught to avoid moving along roads exposed to enemy fire, and to get out of their vehicles and fight on foot. Consequently a slow and long-drawn-out fight was to be expected.

But from Bespalizevo we also at once sent to the north a new battle group in order to forestall the enemy if he should try to install his rearguard or any freshly arrived units in favourable defensive positions. This battle group was able to dodge artillery fire directed against the approach road, and at 1.30 p.m. it captured Krutaj Balka.

The advance was exposed to artillery fire from the east, while only three kilometres to the west columns were seen marching in the same direction. Had I not known that my neighbouring division was a long way behind, I would have been doubtful whether these columns were friendly or hostile. This sort of dilemma was characteristic of the pursuit. We opened fire on the columns.

By 2 p.m. twilight was beginning. Before us lay the day's objective, Metshebilovka, an extended village situated along an east-west river valley, all of which could be easily overlooked. Here there could be no outflanking tactics or cavalry-type raid. It was in the balance whether nightfall would rob us of our objective, after the half-dozen skirmishes of all kinds in the fleeting hours of daylight which had enabled us to seize so many places.

A frontal attack by our armour after nightfall might cost the division its few remaining tanks, since the hills on the far side were in enemy hands. I sent forward a Mule Company*. Its commander was wounded, and the company continued its advance on foot. When darkness sets in there is always a temptation to seize a village because of the prospect of finding good accommodation for the night, and this place was no exception. Yet if the enemy should decide to put up a stiff defence, the break-in could not now succeed. After some anxious waiting, the first star-shells were fired, showing that there, at any rate, the company had penetrated on a very narrow front, evidently without encountering serious resistance. I decided to let the tanks in single file roll into the place along the road, although wheeled traffic could still be observed moving about in the village. The tanks advanced very slowly and hesitantly, keeping a sharp eye on the outskirts. A T-34 tank stood across the road, blocking it, but it was a good sign that this barrier was not under fire. Then the enemy evaded to the east and north. There was no noise of battle, only the hum of the tank motors as they slowly advanced. We penetrated into the village. But the situation was far from reassuring, for the enemy had the place and its eastern and western access roads under fire—an indication of the narrowness of the wedge that the division had driven into it. I therefore summoned up a battalion of the near-at-hand second wave in order to form a bridgehead towards west, north and east. Reconnaissance established the enemy to be in all the adjacent villages. We managed to take Fedorovka, just north of Matchepilovka.

From February 27th the division was on the move between this last place and the Donetz, meeting almost no enemy forces. I had decided independently to press forward north-eastwards to Petroskaja. Here the division cut off and captured some hundreds of retreating Russians; it was then sent north-westwards to within thirty kilometres of Kharkov, that is, back to the Donetz again. Access to the river was everywhere achieved without difficulty, but nowhere could it be crossed; nor did the higher command intend us to do so.

The main body of the division, working with the advanced detachment, took Petrovsaya on the 27th, while the outer wings of the division were still harassing routed enemy units falling back to the north.

Early on that day a Russian cavalry regiment tried to break out of the area south-east of Staryia Blisnezy between Malerjovka and Plachtejewska and move north-westwards. The two latter places were occupied by my divisional staff. I had driven back to spend a few hours of the night at the last-named. At 4 a.m., when I got up in order to return to the forward positions, there was continuous firing from the 2 cm. anti-aircraft battery that was always kept

* Mule: an unarmoured, tracked or half-tracked vehicle.

in position for the defence of the H.Q. operations section. I climbed on to a wall, only half-dressed. In the pale morning light the Russian cavalry could be seen at about 300 metres dragging themselves off to the north-west. They did not hesitate to surrender to our very small garrison force, consisting only of the operations section of the divisional staff. The battery had found its mark. Some of the mounted Russians managed to escape, but others on foot got stuck in the snow. They brought a cavalry gun into position and bombarded the village. Our anti-aircraft battery, using star-shell, could pick out individual targets. The unequal fight lasted half-an-hour. On my drive northwards I had to pass the bloody scene of action—so gruesome that I shall not easily forget it. An assortment of dead and wounded men and horses were scattered over a stretch of 300 metres. Attempts were made with inadequate means to help the wounded. On a limber sat a gunner with his head torn from the body by a direct hit. His face still hung upside down on his chest, held there only by shreds of skin.

EXPERIENCES IN COMMAND—III

In the pursuit fighting it was the advanced detachment that bore the brunt. Since mobility is mandatory in such operations, the fighting unit must not be too big. If the troops are too numerous they will block the only road, make deployment more difficult and impede the arrival of fresh forces from the rear; areas under fire cannot be quickly circumvented, and local break-away movements become unwieldy.

The division was not equipped with armoured troop-carrying vehicles, and this was its main need. Only these vehicles can give the infantry mobility over the terrain, thus transforming it into modern cavalry.

When the terrain precluded a compact attack by armour, the action invariably started with an infantry attack, which usually served to clarify the situation, since the enemy's defensive fire revealed his position, and frequently also his point of main effort.

When the commander of the attack had gained a clear picture the action was continued with artillery fire, which compelled the enemy to reveal his intentions—either to give way or stubbornly to defend himself. In the latter case the situation is ripe for sending in the armour—provided always that the terrain is suitable. The tanks are then used in cavalry fashion, i.e., in thrusts towards the enemy's flank and rear by means of wide turning movements so as to avoid his anti-tank nests. If the enemy has no tanks, self-propelled guns of the advanced detachment are brought up and used like armour. They follow the tanks in echelon, providing cover for their exposed flanks.

The commander of the battle group will personally intervene as necessary to direct the movements. He will be in the second line of the first wave or will have his battle H.Q. near at hand. He must always be in a position to halt the armour, turn it in another direction or withdraw it.

The essence of pursuit tactics is that the pursuer never allows himself to stop. He must retain the initiative and never let the enemy rest. As soon as any local resistance is overcome the next attack must begin. It is best to ignore strong defensive positions by passing round them. Every hold-up will have to be paid for later. For the enemy it is easier to break up and organise a new resistance. Threatened flanks are no justification for easing the pace. Relatively strong forces can be ordered to protect the flank, marching along with the second wave, where they also provide a readily available reserve.

In pursuit operations it is wrong to wait for the results of reconnaissance or to wait until neighbouring divisions have closed up or until supply roads have been cleared of the enemy. The need is always for hurry and still more hurry.

SYMPTOMS OF THE CHANGING PATTERN OF WARFARE

The fighting described in the preceding pages differs from the classic ideas of how to fight a war. True that these allow for the pursuit of even an unbeaten foe, provided he decides to retreat. But the classic lessons of operations, based on the experience of many centuries, did not admit that the side hitherto pursued could itself become the pursuer, as in the events just described. In the twentieth century there had been fewer and fewer pursuit actions. The single decisive batle, which in the nineteenth century still led to encirclement, no longer has a place in the pattern of warfare that has to-day become the rule. It is no longer possible to annihilate the mass of the opponent's army by means of a battle of encirclement. Consequently the pursuit assumes another form. Advancing armies fill entire continents. They can easily keep contact with and mutually assist each other if threatened with encirclement. The static fighting of both world wars started when the advance came to a halt. The attempt to get rid of static warfare then took the form of the breakthrough followed by the pursuit.

The breakthrough forces are deployed in breadth and depth. Of necessity they have long and vulnerable flanks, which attract the opponent's reserves, drawn from other and quieter sectors of his front. In both wars there were thus many cases where the breakthrough forces exhausted themselves in the attempt to go over to pursuit operations. The protracted movements and the attrition of forces gradually brought them to a standstill long before they achieved the object of the breakthrough and subsequent pursuit—the annihilation of the main body of the opponent's army*.

Stalingrad was the decisive big battle of the eastern theatre of war. The Russian front of penetration was 400 kilometres wide, the two breakthrough wedges were four to six times superior in strength to the Axis forces. The German front that yielded in face of the outflanking breakthrough covered in all some 1,200 kilometres, while the enemy's advanced pursuit forces and spearheads gained 700 kilometres in the course of the operations already described.

In accordance with its prevailing operational principles the Russian High Command decided to employ considerable forces for the destruction of the besieged German 6th Army, and it had no difficulty in frustrating the relief attempts by the 4th Panzer Army.

The Russians ignored the operational principles that in such a situation would be mandatory in the German Army. Only weak forces should have contained the besieged German army until the inevitable capitulation, while correspondingly strong forces should have been set free for the pursuit and its many alluring strategical prospects. Nor did the Russians set up large, fast mechanised formations which could have quickly reached the lower Don, thereby cutting off the 4th Panzer Army, still fighting defensively to the east of the river, as well as the 1st Panzer Army, which was later recalled from the Caucasus.

On the other hand the Russian High Command decided to push their pursuing spearheads (which owing to supply difficulties finally consisted of cavalry only as far west as possible with the object of causing the collapse of many parts of the former German front. The Russians would then form a new line farther west to serve as a starting point for their new summer offensive. After capturing Kharkov, these pursuit spearheads eventually reached the district of Poltava and the Dnieper. As the wedge-shaped pursuit that the Russians started from their breakthrough base-line took place in a westerly direction only, it was possible for the German 4th and 1st Panzer Armies to effect a junction (late as it was) north of the Sea of Azov, then by means of a northward offensive to rout the southern Russian pursuit forces, and finally to go over to pursuit without first having to fight a battle.

This German counter-offensive, carried out in the form of a

---

* The classic example of this in the First World War was Gorlice, where the breakthrough succeeded, but the pursuit petered out in its own tracks.

counter-pursuit, led to the temporary stabilisation of the German front along a line that was held until the start of the Russian summer offensive. This line ran along the Donetz, then turned back southwards towards the northern point of the Sea of Azov. Kharkov was recaptured at the beginning of March. But this was a much longer front than that along the Dnieper which we had originally intended to occupy after the Stalingrad defeat. Thus the advantage of a shorter defensive line through withdrawal to the west was not achieved.

FIGHT FOR THE BRIDGEHEADS

March and April were marked by numerous battles for the bridgeheads south of the Donetz, which the enemy was trying to hold. It is understandable that the German command wished to be in firm occupation of the south bank of the river, for this would enable it for operational reasons to build up a front facing north.

These circumstances gave me the rare opportunity of carefully preparing the individual operations against the bridgeheads and then supervising the actual fighting. I seized the occasion to give the commanders further training by letting every staff officer take charge at the front. The more senior ones were given comand of battle groups on individual days, while the younger ones were given battalions. To avoid the risk of mistakes or losses due to their inexperience, I arranged for them to be supervised by experienced commanders. Afterwards I held a discusion on the course of the battle, as in manoeuvres.

A feature of this fighting was the resolute way in which the Russians defended the bridgeheads. They were handicapped in having no tanks at their disposal. On the other hand they had an advantage in that their batteries on the north bank were presented with easy targets whenever the German troops pushed forward to the river itself or to villages near the river bank. Consequently the apparently successful attacks by our troops were often followed by setbacks in the attainment of the objective. In such cases it was very tempting to commit the available tanks prematurely.

The enemy's conduct was unpredictable. Sometimes his subordinate leaders strictly complied with orders to hold on. If the Russian infantry was over-run, the soldiers would lie face downwards in the snow, rigid and feigning death. This deception usually failed, if only because the men all assumed an identical attitude. Of course the "dead" were in the habit of disappearing at night whenever we had insufficient forces to round them up.

Other subordinate commanders on the Russian side evidently acted contrary to the orders they had been given. This was especially noticeable at the beginning of the year, with the Don still frozen over, when they escaped over the ice, being pursued by fire from their own side. Some units repeated the attempt to cross the river as late as the spring, when the ice had melted. Many lost their lives in the effort to swim through the icy water. Others, unable to stand the cold water, could be seen clambering up the trees standing out of the river.

These encounters showed up the inadequacy of those infantry divisions that had no armour with them. The division that stood east of us, newly arrived from France, was performing the same kind of operations against bridgeheads as my own division; lacking armour, it had no success.

I was now again subordinated to LVII Corps, which I knew of old. Consequently I was listened to when I refused to help out my neighbouring divisions by supplying tanks. My own experience had been that commanders not accustomed to armour can easily misuse it. So I lent them not only tanks, but infantry seasoned in tank warfare, all under my own command. I accompanied these battle groups and suggested the use of the assault companies in collaboration with tanks, being myself on the spot to supervise the operation.

The enthusiastic reception of my proposals at corps H.Q. had its effect in other directions also. I was able, for instance, to postpone the launching of certain attacks on the grounds that the proportion of replacement troops taking part was too high. I had noticed more than once that casualties could be much reduced if these young troops were allowed to acclimatise themselves gradually to the impact of battle and behaviour under fire. I had seen how in a line of riflemen under machine-gun fire a well-meaning youth had wanted to go to the immediate assistance of a wounded comrade, which could only have resulted in a further casualty.

After one of the bloodiest actions I spoke appreciatively to a battalion adjutant who had taken charge when his commander was wounded. Later on the same day I discovered that this young officer had also been wounded without this being visible to others, and that he had refrained from leaving the battlefield as his wounds entitled him to do. On visiting the dressing-station I met two medical officers who were fully occupied with him, one bandaging his arm, the other his head. Both doctors also had wounds. That was the spirit of the division—this unpretentious, poorly equipped Bavarian-Swabian 17th Panzer Division. I was so intimately bound up with it that I was loth to think of ever having to hand over the command. Yet the time was nearer than I knew. I was then enjoying the few weeks of recuperation that are given to all units withdrawn into the reserve—weeks free from daily casualties, when one could live in more spacious quarters and in clean suroundings with maybe a little sport thrown in. Some kindly officer had arranged for my horse to be brought along. Alone with my thoughts, I rode over the heath, occasionally casting an eye towards the already distant eastern front.

4

ISLAND WARFARE

The Battle for Sicily—Audience with Hitler

In June 1943 I was summoned to the Führer's headquarters. It was on the 22nd that Hitler received me at the Obersalzberg at his daily situation conference. Field-Marshal Keitel, General Warlimont and several adjutants were in attendance. Keitel introduced me to my new task—responsibility for the defence of Sicily in the capacity of liaison officer to the Italian 6th Army Command.

The assignment that Hitler gave me was imprecise. Discoursing on the possibilities of defending Sicily, his great knowledge of detail was, as always, impressive. He deliberated whether or not the island could be defended by the two German divisions without calling on Italian forces. One of these divisions was already established there, the other on its way; he also wondered whether the remaining 30,000 German troops stationed on the island—A.A. personnel, Luftwaffe ground staff, supply units, etc.—could be used in active defence.

Hitler was already reckoning with the early defection of Italy, blaming it on the "machinations of the Court, Society, the General Staff, et cetera." Turning a mistrustful eye on me, he added: "You, of course, know the Italians." Then he held forth on the strategy of the Allies, who "through failing to leap across to Sicily immediately after their landings in North Africa, had already lost the struggle in the Mediterranean".

The personal sway that Hitler was alleged to hold over so many people made absolutely no impression on me. It could hardly be otherwise, since I detested him for all the misfortune he had brought upon my country.

After the conference General Warlimont had a talk with me when we lunched together in his house. His was a clear appreciation of the situation; he felt that in the event of a major Allied attack it would be best to transfer the mass of the troops from Sicily to the mainland, but thought that most of their equipment would probably have to be left behind. This appreciation and definition of my task were not in line with those of Hitler.

Keitel also spoke with me after the general conference. Through

General Hube, stationed in Italy, he was in touch with local conditions in Sicily, and was evidently as sceptical as Warlimont over the prospect of defending the island. He held the view, confirmed by later events, that it would not be possible to keep the scanty German forces together as a mobile reserve in the interior of the island or in its eastern sector. The nature of the mountain roads and the enemy's air superiority would preclude all movement of troops during daylight.

CONFERENCE IN ROME

On June 25th I had a meeting with Field-Marshal Kesselring in Rome, the tone of the conference being somewhat different from that on the Obersalzberg.

Kesselring had risen to high command out of the Army General Staff, having gone over to the Luftwaffe in the early stage of its development. His last command had been Luftflotte 2 in the Mediterranean area, where he had earned a big reputation. Yet there were many officers among those fighting in North Africa who disapproved of his over-optimistic view of the situation, for this restricted the influence of Rommel, who was in a better position to judge. To me also it seemed that Kesselring rated the possibility of defending Sicily too favourably, and to that extent I found the strictures by these officers justified.

General Warlimont had given a clear estimate of the prospect of defending the island. Kesselring was evidently still impressed by our successful repulse of the small landing operation at Dieppe in 1942. Commanders of German land forces were usually prone to under-estimate the chances of a landing by an opponent possessing naval and air superiority. Such an opponent will always enjoy the dual advantages of surprise and superior mobility. Kesselring, moreover, was like certain other optimistic German higher commanders in failing to recognise the Allied invasion of North Africa as the first example of a major landing that must open an entirely new phase of the war. Not wanting to believe in the danger, they consoled themselves with the fact that the landing was made against an opponent reluctant to defend himself.

During the entire Italian campaign the Field-Marshal never changed his optimistic outlook; at least that is how he chose to present his views to a senior officer such as myself, but only when such officers won his complete confidence. This made it all the more difficult to have an objective discussion with him on any given situation.

On the other hand I was far more ready to accept the attitude of Kesselring towards our Italian ally than that of the O.K.W. or of Hitler. Whatever might be the behaviour of the Italians in the event of a landing, Kesselring realised that the Germans could not fight two opponents—the Allies *and* the defecting Italians. He was all for co-operating with our ally in war; politically and militarily there was in fact no possible alternative. The alliance continued. A specific agreement had been reached between the two governments that the defence of the Italian mainland and of the off-shore islands should be under the sole command of the Italian military authorities. Kesselring knew that to disregard this Italian primacy in the control of operations would lead to a catastrophe. He also realised that he had no more right to make operational decisions than one of his own liaison officers (such as myself) serving with an Italian Army Command. In this respect I was quite satisfied with the further discussion I had with the Field-Marshal about my own functions and responsibilities.

My discussion with Field-Marshal von Richthofen, C.-in-C. of Luftflotte 2, developed along less positive lines. It was significant that Kesselring was not present. Richthofen spoke to me alone, and what he said led me to conclude that the German Air Force was going its own way, as it had so often done before. Believing the Allies would choose Sardinia rather than Sicily for their landings, he had moved the main concentration of air defences to Sardinia. Richthofen's surmise was by no means irrelevant. Marshal Badoglio himself maintained in his memoirs that to attack Sardinia rather than Sicily would have been operationally more correct. Yet all this revealed a regrettable divergence of views as between the two C.-in-C.'s most concerned.

THE SITUATION IN SICILY

On June 26th in the Italian G.H.Q. at Enna a discussion took place between Kesselring, General Guzzoni (C.-in-C. of the Italian 6th Army) and myself on the control of operations in the event of an Allied landing in Sicily.

Guzzoni was in overall command in the island. The coast was manned by quite inadequately armed, immobile Italian Coastal Divisions. They were incapable of effective defence, and at best could provide only a security service. Situated in the eastern part of the island was the only German division then available—the 15th Panzer Grenadier Division, reconstituted from the remains of the Africa Corps. A second was on its way—the "Hermann Göring" Division. Also in the eastern part of the island were the Italian XVI Corps with its two divisions, "Livorno" and "Napoli", and in the western part the XII Corps also with two divisions, "Assietta" and "Aosta". Guzzoni was probably right in assessing each German division as possessing only half the fighting power of one Allied division, and he credited one of these four mobile divisions with only a quarter of the strength of an Allied division.

There were no clues to the enemy's intentions. He might land in the flat country of the western part of the island; more probably he would choose the plain of Catania on the east coast as well as the plain of Gela on the south coast. Using these two starting points for his attack, he could push rapidly inland to effect a junction of his forces and thus prevent the return to the mainland of the Axis troops stationed in the western part of the island.

The coast of Sicily was not fortified. German pioneer and artillery staffs applied themselves to the problem of the improvised Italian coastal batteries. As always happens in questions of coastal defence, agreement could not be reached on the best sites for the batteries. The Italians wanted to keep them intact and out of range of the big ships' main armament, and not use them until the enemy had landed. On the other hand the German naval experts maintained that the batteries should be kept sufficiently far forward to engage the enemy landing parties while they were still water-borne. The resulting controversy was still raging when the invasion commenced.

For some weeks now the enemy had enjoyed complete mastery of the air. The greater part of our air forces stationed in Sicily had been destroyed on the ground, and their aircraft were more or less unserviceable. In the Luftwaffe, then, it was chiefly the units of the ground organisation that remained intact; the very powerful anti-aircraft defences were an important asset in the conduct of operations. The three tasks of the A.A. forces were to repel air attacks, oppose the landings and safeguard supplies, especially in the Messina Strait.

Prior to the landing the problem of transport was particularly difficult. The German divisions, particularly the 15th Pz. Gren. Div., were not fully mobile. For operational movements they had to resort to a shuttle service. One regimental group of the Hermann Göring Division was also not mobile. In the event of operations it was to be motorised by using supply columns, but for the time being these were fully engaged in their own tasks.

It is true that the island was well stocked, although the supply depots were wrongly situated in the western part, where they had originally provided supplies for the army in North Africa. To fit our operational intentions we had to establish new depots in the region of Etna. These were stocked partly from the mainland and partly from the western depots.

On the Obersalzberg I had been told that in addition to the two divisions I would have at my disposal more than 30,000 men of the Luftwaffe ground organisation, the supply units and the administrative depots. On matters relating to the conduct of operations specialists were always available, and when an expert on rearward services appeared on the scene, I at once enlightened him as to the inadequate fighting power of these 30,000 troops. The so-called alarm units into which they were to be formed could not be regarded as fit for operations, for they were not mobile. During the fighting the supply troops could not be disregarded; in their own district they would be confronted with a twofold task, since they would have to hand over part of their transport capacity to motorise the fighting troops. The backbone for the local fixed defences of strong-points was provided by the A.A. batteries, whose commanders were therefore appointed by me as "battle commanders" of their respective districts. Subordinated to them were the inactive sections of the Luftwaffe's ground units and the alarm units of the army.

To these problems of operational control, contact with the Italian High Command, transport capacity and supplies was added the problem of signal communications, still unsolved when the landings occurred. I had at my disposal a small, inadequate staff with only one G.S.O. and no signals unit of its own. I had no reliable communications link with the C.-in-C. South, *i.e.*, Kesselring. Although in the formal sense neither he nor I was in charge of operations, the German Supreme Command (O.K.W.) had to use this official link if it wanted to issue operational directives. Telephone communications existed only on a Luftwaffe network along the coast and from the north-east corner of the island by cable to the mainland. At Enna, centre of the island and H.Q. of the Italian 6th Army, I had neither radio nor land-line communications with Rome. My only links with the divisions were the Italian land-line network and a radio station supplied by one of the divisions. My task obviously called for a fully equipped corps headquarters. I had not only to control two widely separated German divisions, but to collaborate with the Italian units, which though weak in weapons were strong in numbers. Moreover, the geographical circumstances of this theatre of war imposed on me, as on the enemy, the need to think in terms of all three branches of the armed forces. If on the Italo-German side the ground forces were the main factor, the defence had nevertheless to cope with an enemy at sea, on land and in the air. To ignore this truism is to commit one of the worst blunders.

In the discussion at Enna on June 26th, Kesselring had offered advice that, on the whole, was tactful. He recognised that the control of operations must rest with Guzzoni, and unlike Hitler, believed that the chances of defending Italy without Italian participation were very slight. Yet the difference between Guzzoni and Kesselring could be bridged only outwardly. The latter was or at least appeared to be optimistic, whereas the former made no secret of his sceptical outlook; coming events were to prove him right.

In regard to the operational employment of the German forces Guzzoni nevertheless went against his better judgment in respecting the wishes of Kesselring. He regarded the German divisions as the backbone of his forces. After all that had ocurred in North Africa he realised that to oppose the German Field-Marshal could only lead to an unbearable situation in the chain of command, making a farce of the Italian primacy.

This ineluctable compliance resulted in Kesselring making a decision that both Guzzoni and I and the commander of the 15 Pz. Gren. Div. considered wrong, and about which not even the Field-Marshal himself was happy. For his hands were tied.

Guzzoni had intended to keep the two German divisions together at the eastern end of the island as a mobile and battle-worthy reserve. In his plan the weak Italian divisions—Napoli and Livorno—were to fight a delaying action while the German forces were held in readiness to concentrate their counter-attack against that part of the invasion forces which seemed to promise the best results. From the German angle this plan had two objections. Firstly, it went counter to the theory that an enemy landing force should be repulsed at its moment of greatest weakness, namely by concentrating the available fire against it while still in the landing craft. It was right to assume that forces as inferior in strength as the defenders could not throw the invader back into the sea once he had acheived a number of simultaneous landings.

Yet this theory implied renouncing mobility in the conduct of the defence as well as exposing German troops on the coast to destructive fire from the enemy's big ships, against which the Axis forces were powerless because of their lack of sea and air power.

The second objection lay in the excessive concentration of the two German divisions so far inland—in the district of Caltanissetta— where in the narrow mountain roads and with no air cover they would be so exposed to air attacks that they could only be moved by night.

Here then was the discord that in the later Normandy landings was again to vitiate unity in the conduct of the defenders' operations. This discord could not be overcome and from the very start it sealed their fate. The only alternatives now were either defence on the coast with a rigid front, a method that transgressed all the rules of war, and would probably end in annihilation by bombardment from the ships, or the holding back of the main reserve, which, however, would be too weak to throw the invader back into the sea once he had secured a foothold.

Contrary to Guzzoni's wishes, Field-Marshal Kesselring arranged for the German main forces to be divided, one division being stationed in the east, the other in the west, both ready for use as strong mobile reserves. The 15 Pz. Gren. Div. was accordingly moved by slow marches to the district of Salemi, while the paratroop infantry division Hermann Göring, then in transit from the mainland, was being assembled near Caltagirone.

Should the eastern Axis forces be the first to come under attack, then Kesselring considered it necessary to prevent their operational encirclement by sending over reserves from the west, and in this I agreed with him. Even to-day, after a study of the campaign and of the accounts by other German commanders. I cannot endorse Field-Marshal Lord Montgomery's statement that the defeat of the Axis forces was due to their piecemeal dispersal. The course of events showed that the invaders were in a position to land superior forces simultaneously at the south-east corner of the island and in the western part. But an advance by the German western force along the north coast would certainly not have led to the rapid annihilation of the invading troops fighting in the south-east corner.

I could not agree with the choice of divisions for these two different tasks. The 15 Pz. Gren. Div. had been on the island for a considerable time and was familiar with local conditions. It had well-organised coastal reconnaissance and possessed sufficient infantry and armour at least to fight a delaying battle with some prospect of success. The division had kept its three regiments, each with three battalions, together in the eastern part of the island. For the indispensable flank protection in the west it had detached one regimental detachment. These measures fitted the situation and conformed to the German ideas of tactical control. General Roth, the commander of this division, was an experienced leader with a General Staff background. The division should therefore have been given the main task of defending the eastern part of the island.

The Hermann Göring Division (which was given this task) had some notable weaknesses. With only two battalions its infantry strength was inconsiderable. I could not discover whether further battalions were being constituted or even on the way. It had one armoured regiment. The Tiger company that had been sent to the island as G.H.Q. troops had for some considerable time been attached for supplies and tactically to the 15 Pz. Gren. Div.—an added reason for leaving that division in the eastern part. In personnel the Hermann Göring Division had certain defects, but at that time the higher authorities were unaware of this. Two of its principal commanding officers were unfit to lead in action. The first, commander of the infantry regiment, was removed by the divisional commander, while the second, commanding the armoured regiment, was replaced on my personal orders immediately after the fighting had started. Similar shortcomings appeared among other officers. The division enjoyed an unmerited prestige on all sides and especially among our Italian allies. This could probably be attributed to the high regard which paratroopers enjoyed in wartime.

The assignment of the H.G. Division to the crucial task of defending the eastern part of the island was a mistake whose magnitude I myself did not realise at the time, for I was then unaware of its deficiencies in personnel. I have not been able to discover whether it was due to Göring's personal intervention, or whether Kesselring felt that he should comply with the wishes of his superior officer in the Luftwaffe. The fact is that things were being arranged behind the scenes. Undoubtedly the erroneous disposition provides a classic example of the predominance of personal over professional motives, as mentioned in General Westphal's book *Fettered Army**. Had the newly constituted Paratroop Division Hermann Göring been a standard division of the Army, its infantry strength would have been normal and the quality of its personnel better. Even so, it would not have been given this difficult task in preference to a division that knew its job. The decision was all the more unfortunate in that the 15 Pz. Gren. Div. had to surrender a regimental group to the H.G. Division's "Schmalz Group" in the district of Catania in order to compensate for its lamentable shortage of infantry.

The Allied Landing

The landing on July 10th did not come as a surprise. The following is an extract from the war diary of the German liaison staff with the Italian 6th Army:

> July 9th, 6.20 p.m.: Radio message from 2nd Fliegerkorps indicates the presence of six convoys totalling 150 to 200 vessels in the waters north of Malta and Gozo.
> 8.05 p.m.: Radio from C.-in-C. south: 150 landing-craft at 4.30 p.m. in a position north of Malta, steering north.
> 11.15 p.m. Chief of Staff of Italian 6th Army to General Senger: We anticipate an attack at dawn against Catania and Gela.

At 5 a.m. on the 10th we got the first reports of paratroop landings in the region of Comiso and San Pietro, between Caltagirone and the coast. Enemy gliders had landed near Augusta. The H.G. Division reported the enemy to be unloading twenty transports at Gela. By 10 a.m. the situation had developed as shown in the war diary:

> Enemy has landed infantry and a few tanks at Gela, followed by disembarkations from 20 to 30 ships. The main body of H.G. Division is attacking them across the line Nescemi-Biscari. In the region round Caltagirone, local fighting against paratroop infantry. Italian C.-in-C. fears increased pressure on Syracuse and Augusta. The Schmalz battle group, north-west of Catania, still remains in reserve for the Catania plain. In the west of the island, nothing to report.
> 12.25 p.m.:
> Enemy has landed in many places between Syracuse and Licata. His main effort concentrated at Avola and Gela. The H.G. Div. is in action round Gela, details not yet available. Schmalz battle group is being moved

---

* German title: *Heer in Fesseln*, English title: *The German Army in the West*.

south towards Scordia-Lentini. The 15 Pz. Gren. Div. is moving into the region east of Enna. The Italian Livorno Div. has orders to attack towards Gela.

The H.G. Division was sent into action on this day according to plan, but failed to throw the enemy back into the sea (Map 8). The reasons for this were firstly that enemy paratroops had landed in its area and although they made no concentrated attack, wrought much destruction; secondly, the terraced landscape, dotted with olive trees, presented such difficulties to the tanks that neither side could think of using them in a co-ordinated attack. The Tiger company had its own special difficulties, due to poor mobility.

The situation that evening is revealed by the war diary: —

> July 10th, 11.45 p.m. Enemy has advanced some 10 km. through Licata northwards. He is in possession of hills for 6 km. round Gela. In the south-eastern sector his landing force has not penetrated beyond the coastal sector. It was confirmed at 6 p.m. by General v. Senger himself that H.G. Division had reached the road between Gela and Vittoria in the early hours of the morning in the face of frontal attacks and the fire of heavy guns, the division's armoured group being south of Niscemi, and the grenadier group south-west of Biscari. Between the two groups there has been fighting against paratroops. Early on July 11th, after mopping up the intervening ground, both groups will attack in a south-westerly direction to win back Gela and the coastal strip.

About noon, when the extent of the operations became clearer, Guzzoni, after consulting with me, decided to draw in 15 Pz. Div. from the west. The risk was justified by the situation and I agreed with him. This accounts for the entry in the diary: — "15 Pz. Div. is moved into the district east of Enna."

> 6.21 p.m. In a radio message C.-in-C. South warns against completely denuding the western part of the island of German troops.

> 11.45 p.m. C.-in-C. of Italian 6th Army feels that he cannot alter his decision to draw 15 Pz. Div. back into the centre. The division has accordingly begun its move to the area of Caltanisetta-Barrafranca-Piatta Armerina-Valguarnera.

These entries in the diary show that there is no foundation for Kesselring's complaint that the division was drawn in too late. Indeed, Guzzoni and I both insisted on this movement despite Kesselring's objection from Rome. Perhaps Kesselring wished to leave part of the division in the west. However, once the decision had been made he accommodated himself, the more so since the situation on July 11th developed as follows:

> 9.05 a.m. Report to C.-in-C. South that H.G. Division has started to attack and its right wing has reached Tenda, 6 km. north-east of Gela.

This report led Kesselring to the conclusion (Map 9) that vigorous

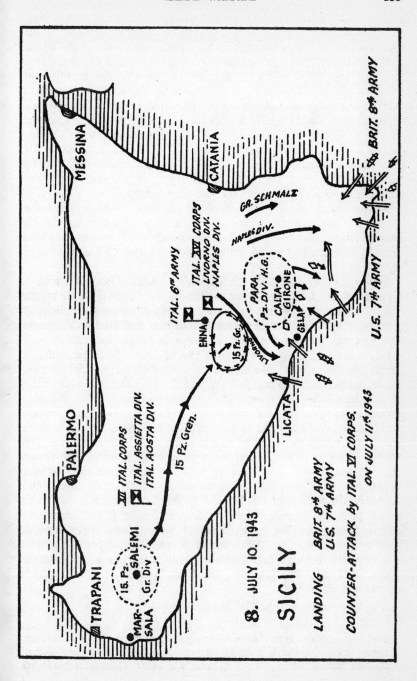

8. JULY 10. 1943

SICILY

LANDING BRIT 8th ARMY
U.S. 7th ARMY

COUNTER-ATTACK by ITAL. VI CORPS.
ON JULY 11th 1943

attacks could at least overthrow the enemy at Gela and that a concentrated attack by both German divisions against the flank of the enemy advancing northward from the south-eastern tip of the island could succeed. The commanders of both German divisions also favoured this idea, which conformed to the German tradition of offensive action. The radio message from the C.-in-C. South showed that he was by no means agreeable to a withdrawal of the front, but expected that the evidently successful attack by the H.G. Division should be followed up, and above all that the aerodrome at Comiso should be held. This last requirement was quite understandable, for the German command feared that if the aerodrome were used by the enemy, he would have such superiority in the air that Axis troop movements in daylight would become very restricted.

Meanwhile events in other parts of the front were bringing the crisis to a head. At no place did Italian troops participate in the counter-attack of the H.G. Division, which in consequence found itself in a difficult situation, with open flanks and no contacts to its right or left.

It was now evident that the Italian 6th Army Command took a different view of the prospects to that of the C.-in-C. South or the O.K.W. Guzzoni thought the available forces far too weak for offensive operations against the two enemy armies that had landed. That was also General Warlimont's view, as given to me on June 22nd.

From the beginning it was clear to the Italian Command that a thrust by the isolated German divisions, wherever it might occur, would never throw the enemy back into the sea along the entire front of 160 kilometres. This view of the situation necessarily led to thoughts about evacuation, to achieve which the so-called Etna position would have to be occupied as soon as possible. There, in a far smaller area, the Axis forces would be in a position to defend themselves, and behind a system of defensive lines commence their withdrawal across the Messina Strait. This concept was far more realistic than the orders to attack that had been issued by the C.-in-C. South and probably also by Hitler's O.K.W. Any resolute defence in the south would place the German forces in danger of destruction through an enemy landing on the north coast or through the appearance of hostile naval forces in the Messina Strait. This appreciation was supported by fresh reports indicating that in the course of the forenoon the enemy had gained ground northwards at several points of the extended front.

The war diary for July 11th states:—

Situation report to C.-in-C. South at 1.15 p.m.: "Enemy has again advanced at Naro up to Campobello. He has received no further reinforcements at Gela, but he is pressing forward from the south in the region of Ragusa. Strong enemy pressure from the south-east, where Noto has fallen.

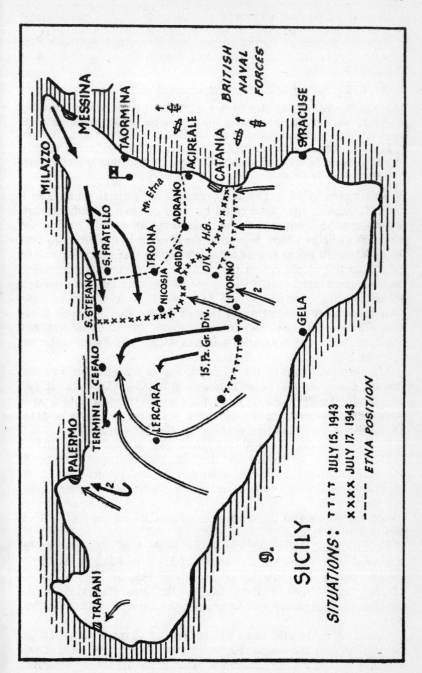

SICILY

SITUATIONS: ττττ JULY 15, 1943
xxxx JULY 17, 1943
----- ETNA POSITION

Italians consider that their own forces in the south-east have been grauadlly used up. Because of this, and in order to clear the area north-east of Vittoria of paratroops, General Guzzoni ordered the attack by H.G. Division to be stopped and the division to be moved to the region south-east of Caltagirone."

At 4.10 p.m. the H.G. Division reported as follows: —

Attack according to plan by one battalion of the left-hand marching-group, reaching the area between the river Acate and the sea to the north of it. Flank protection towards the south-east, from Point 60 to the fork in the road 8 km. south of Biscara, provided by one reinforced battalion. Strong enemy forces in the region of Vittoria-Comiso. Enemy is apparently turning away to the east.

This report by H.G. Division presented the general situation in a more favourable light than could be deduced from its hitherto slow movements. So I returned to the front to see for myself. Finding the situation to be as stated, I directed the division to exploit its success by an eastward thrust towards Comiso, hoping that under favourable conditions this would cut off those more easterly enemy forces which had advanced northwards; if this should not succeed, the division's thrust into the enemy's exposed flank would at least facilitate our own break-away movements, in view of the locally favourable situation. Despite its very forward disposition, the division was not attacked, while the counter-attack had forced the enemy either to re-embark or at least to fall back.

My directive, based on a local impression of the situation, was also prompted by various radio messages from C-in-C. South. It ran counter to the intention of Guzzoni, who nevertheless agreed to it with certain reservations. In the event, the offensive action by H.G. Division was overtaken that evening by other developments.

On the morning of July 12th, Kesselring arrived at the Italian G.H.Q. at Enna to discuss the situation with Guzzoni and myself. It transpired that the 2nd Fliegerkorps, stationed in Sicily, had been supplying Kesselring with a series of inaccurate reports, some alarming, others too optimistic. On the strength of these he had issued the orders and directives that encroached on the authority of the Italian Command.

Kesselring did not evade the urgent realities of the situation; he approved the orders already issued to H.G. Division to withdraw to the region of Caltagirone-Vizzini, as well as the orders to 15 Pz. Gren. Div. to stand fast in the area Piazza Amerina-Barafranca-Pietraperzia and to prevent the enemy's advance northwards.

Kesselring deliberated as to whether further German troops should be sent over to the island. He wanted to send 29 Pz. Gren. Div., evidently hoping thus to change the situation and regain the initiative.

In his optimistic fashion he was toying with the idea of a fresh counter-attack, doubtless still thinking of Dieppe.

Guzzoni and I opposed the idea of this reinforcement, which hardly conformed to our intended plan for a delaying action and evacuation to the mainland of the main body of the fighting troops. If we could manage to achieve this without heavy losses in either men or equipment, the operation would rank as highly successful. It was still on the cards that the enemy would land on the quite undefended north coast, thereby cutting off all our forces in Sicily. Guzzoni feared that if the enemy should break through, there would be overcrowding of Axis troops on the road to Messina, making their transfer to the mainland even more difficult.

The Fighting Between 12th and 17th July, 1943

On July 12th the Italian 6th Army Commander issued the following order to the Italian XVI Army Corps: —

"In view of situation resulting from the enemy's known advances, it is considered inadvisable for the time being to undertake any further offensive operations. In anticipation of the arrival from the mainland of the further units already detailed, the following action is to be taken:

(1) The H.G. Division is to move to the area Caltagirone-Granmichele-Vizzini as a protective force against the enemy advancing from the south. In this area it is not to launch any counter-attacks, but to delay the enemy's advance by means of thrusts towards the south.

(2) The Napoli Division—except for those forces operating against Syracuse, which are to remain where they are—will hold at all costs Pazzolo Acreide, so as to cover the left wing of the H.G. Division.

(3) The Schmalz battle group will maintain its present position in order to repel enemy attacks coming from Syracuse-Augusta.

(4) The Livorno Division will move to the area between Mazzarino and S. Michele Ganzeria to take over protective action against forces advancing from the south and west and to cover the right flank of H.G. Division."

At the same time Guzzoni informed me that he had issued the following orders to the Italian XII Army Corps: —

"The Assietta Division is to move to the area Bisayuino-Prizzi-Lercara. (These places are 40 km. south of Palermo.)

"The 15 Pz. Gren. Div. is to remain as Army Reserve in its present central position at Pietraperzia-Valguarnera, whence it is in a position to attack in the following directions:—Caltanissetta-Canicatti; Piazza Armerina-Caltagirone; Barafranca-Mazzarino-Gela."

At 2.36 p.m. the H.G. Division reported the line south of Niscemi and the Acate stream and the sector north of Riscari-Vizzini as firmly held by means of group defences covering the road leading north, but the Italian 6th Army H.Q. had the impression that this division's movements were occurring very slowly and under some difficulty. At 4.30 p.m. I reported to the C.-in-C. South in Rome that the division's disengaging movements were proceeding according to plan and without appreciable interference from the enemy.

To speed the retreat of the division, it received a further order at 9.40 p.m. to withdraw urgently to the region of Caltagirone. Guzzoni's insistence on this withdrawal was entirely justified, firstly because the more rapid withdrawal and partial disappearance of the Italian divisions left the German one in a dangerous position, and secondly because the German division itself had at 11.01 a.m. reported an enemy landing at Augusta. This imperilled its timely withdrawal to the Etna position and even endangered the planned evacuation of the island. In any case there was no sense now in keeping the division south of a line Caltagirone-Vizzini where there was no appreciable pressure from the enemy.

Yet the war diary of the German liaison staff contains an entry timed 10.40 p.m. that the Schmalz group had moved forward again to the line Solarino-Priolo. At 11.10 p.m. I reported to C.-in-C. South as follows: —

"Enemy pressure strongest at Canicatti. 15 Pz. Gren. Div. has been detailed to protect the army's right flank. From Gela northward there is no enemy interference. H.G. Division's movements proceeding as planned. The battalion that had become separated during the morning is now back with the Schmalz Group on the line Sortino-Villamundo-Augusta peninsula."

During July 12th the first reinforcements of any importance reached the island, when the second battalion of Pz. Gren. Regt. 382 joined up with the H.G. Division at Vizzini. Parachute-Rifle Regt. 3 from the Parachute Rifle Division on the mainland and the Reggio Battalion were allocated to the Schmalz group.

On July 13th Guzzoni's H.Q. at Enna was put temporarily out of action through a heavy air attack at midnight, which interrupted all land-line communication, but not the radio link. The H.Q. had to be moved. Guzzoni wanted to stay in Enna to share the fate of his personnel, but his Chief of Staff and I dissuaded him.

We now no longer expected a large-scale landing in the west, but a smaller one on the north coast. From both the Italian and the German operational viewpoint it seemed probable that the enemy would soon try to capture Catania. He had evidently renounced the idea of an outflanking movement from the sea, and his point of main effort was now on the east coast, nearest to the road leading to Messina; and again at Catania, whence he could turn the main battle line along the southern slope of Etna, the line that the Italian command had provided for.

In the early hours the enemy had already gained some ground on the front of 15 Pz. Gren. Div. and by 11 a.m. he stood on the line Serradifalco-S. Cataldo. On this front there was now a danger of outflanking the H.G. Division. Although not yet imminent, the danger grew by reason of the increasingly noticeable slowness and unwieldiness of that division on the field of battle. Once again—for the third time—it received orders by radio to assemble rapidly under cover of night in the region of Vizzini. I had to reckon with the possibility that Göring was sending the division direct orders that conflicted with those of the local commander. Guzzoni's concern was to get the division into the Etna position as soon as possible. Already on July 12th I had given the 15 Pz. Div. a general directive, in the event of strong enemy pressure, and subject to special approval of the individual rush movements by the Italian 6th Army Commander, to withdraw to the general line Gangi-Leonforte-Agira.

Here the H.G. Division, reinforced by the Parachute Rifle Regiment, was to link up with its right wing, while its left wing would touch the sea to the south of Catania. It seemed all the more urgent to move sections of the H.G. Division into the latter region, where there were no longer any reserves worth mentioning. The enemy's landing at Augusta, phased in relation to his main landing, led to the conclusion that he would repeat this type of tactical outflanking movement from the coast. At 2.30 p.m. on the 13th, Guzzoni ordered the Italian XVI Army Corps to move sections of the H.G. Division as soon as possible to the Catania area "in order to consolidate the position there".

C.-in-C. South held a similar view of the situation. His concern over this extreme left wing led him to order the drop on the afternoon of the 13th at the mouth of the Simeto river of the Machine-Gun Battalion of 1 Parachute Rifle Division. Here the battalion was subordinated to the Schmalz group.

The German war diary described the situation that evening as follows: —

"15 Pz. Gren. Div. holds the line Serradifalco-Pietraperzia-Barafranca-Piazza Armerina. Enemy is probing with reconnaissance, especially opposite the centre and right wing of the division's sector. Enemy artillery becoming more active; frequent air attacks on positions and road traffic. H.G. Division has been withdrawn to the line Caltagirone-Vizzini. The latter place is under strong artillery fire. No fresh reports from Schmalz group.

"Generally the enemy appears to be opening up along the whole front preparatory to continuing his attack.

"Late on the evening of July 13th the Italian 6th Army H.Q. and the German liaison staff moved to Passo Pisciero (east of Randazzo), as the previous H.Q. was no longer tenable.

"July 14th, 10.25 a.m.: Schmalz group holds out on the line Francoforte-Lentini-Agnone, but yesterday was in places subjected to fierce infantry and tank attacks. After nightfall enemy paratroops of undetermined strength were dropped north of Lentini. Strong enemy attacks expected in the region of Vizzini."

The nocturnal paratroop landings at the most threatened part of the new front increased Guzzoni's anxiety to assemble sections of the H.G. Division there for action. But the division considered itself too much committed to disengage, although it was not under severe enemy pressure. The situation became easier through the air-landing, twelve hours earlier, of the M.-G. Battalion of the 1 Parachute Rifle Division near Lentini, where it had relatively little difficulty in wiping out the enemy's paratroops. At 1 p.m. H.G. Division again received orders to get forces moving towards Catania.

Kesselring in Rome continued to be served with misleading reports by the 2nd Fliegerkorps at Taormina. He sent a directive by radio, which was logged at 3.15 p.m. in the war diary of the German liaison staff: —

> "C.-in-C. South considers it vitally important further to strengthen the left wing, which should be done at the cost of denuding the centre. He directs that the withdrawal of all forces to the general line S. Stefano-Adrana-Catania is to be prepared in such a way that it can be started during this night if the situation on the eastern wing should become more acute."

> At 3.45 p.m. I replied: "That pressure on the left wing was being eased through the move of the H.G. Division to Catania, but that the consequent weakening of the centre would not allow it or the Schmalz group to resist further powerful attacks from the south, and that the western wing was liable to be outflanked. Consequently a withdrawal to the Etna position had been prepared and would seem to be necessary before long."

That evening 15 Pz Gren. Div. was still occupying the line Serradifalco-S. Cataldo. At 11.30 p.m. I sent the following situation report to C.-in-C. South: —

> "In view of the danger to the right wing and flank of the German front, the danger at Vizzini, the weak position at Francoforte and the lack of mobility of the latest reinforcements it is not possible to effect a rapid strengthening of the eastern wing. I have therefore ordered the withdrawal of the entire H.G. Division with destruction of the enemy forces in Catania. The 15 Pz. Gren. Div. will be brought back to the line Nicosia-Leonforte, as it would otherwise be exposed to a double outflanking."

July 15th marked a new turn in the crisis that had existed in the Italo-German control of operations ever since the Allied landings five days earlier. It could now be assumed that the enemy would make no further landings in the west or north of the island. Had he intended to land there in order to save his forces advancing slowly into the interior from costly Axis attacks, such additional landings would have had to be made by July 15th at the latest.

For the time being we were also free from the anxiety lest the enemy should decide to move the main body or a part of the United States Patton army in a westerly sweep across the line Lercara-Termini with its left shoulder on the north coast and so attack the unprotected right flank of the Axis forces.

The pressure on the left wing—the Schmalz group and the H.G. Division—had increased, which indicated that Montgomery's army would there seek a decision in contradiction of the German operational concepts.

As was frequently the case when a crisis had been surmounted, the German operational command now became more nervous: could even better results have been achieved by adopting other measures? Relations between the commands, already difficult enough in the politico-military situation of this coalition war, occasionally became quite chaotic. Being an officer of the Luftwaffe, Kesselring felt a particular responsibility towards the H.G. Division. He had to cope with special orders not only from the O.K.W., but probably also from Göring. On one occasion the Reichsmarschall personally intervened in the control of operations by sending a direct order to the division. Kesselring, moreover, had better signals communications and personal contact with the 2nd Fliegerkorps, which was quite useless on the island since it possessed no operational aircraft and persisted in sending reports and even operational proposals to him.

Kesselring intervened more and more in the conduct of operations and even short-circuited the Italian 6th Army Commander, presumably at the instigation of the O.K.W. It became clearer every day that our Italian ally would soon give up, and the German Command had to face the prospect of continuing the fight alone. This became possible in the Etna position with the arrival of further German reinforcements.

Meanwhile the Italian 6th Army Command continued to control operations, since it was nominally the only responsible command. I moved my advanced battle H.Q. to the district north of Catania, where I at last had land-line communication with Kesselring and could establish direct contact with the Schmalz group and the H.G. Division. I could also personally supervise the battlefield south of Catania. In the forenoon the division repelled attacks on Caltagirone and Granmichele, but as the day wore on it was driven progressively northwards.

That evening the division stood on a line Ragusa-Castel di Judica-Fiume Dittainio-Corna Lunga river to its estuary. At midnight the war diary recorded: —

"Enemy pressure specially strong against the east wing, where he evidently intends to break through towards Messina. This probably accounts for the fresh air landings of small paratroop units near Acireale and westwards, as well as continuing support from ships' guns. South of the Catania plain our Parachute Rifle Regt. 3, with individual battalions enveloped, is resisting stoutly, but with heavy losses."

Until the evening of this day 15 Pz. Gren. Div. still stood on the line Serradifalco—south of Caltasinetta-Barrafranca-Piazza Amerina. It was rightly anxious about its left wing, which had become increasingly exposed through the withdrawal and deployment left-wards of the H.G. Division. The attempt to establish contact with this division or with the Livorno Division (presumed to be between the two) did not succeed. My order to the H.G. Division at 8.30 p.m. to establish contact with the left wing of 15 Pz. Gren. Div. could apparently not be fulfilled. I deliberately refused to allow the latter division to conform to the disengaging movement of the former. Ever since July 10th both divisions had had to fight in isolation from each other, but they would soon be united in the Etna position in a co-ordinated front. The longer 15 Pz. Gren. Div. remained in its present positions, the less was the danger of the retreating H.G. Division being overrun from the west. This danger gave me more concern than a possible threat to the eastern flank of 15 Pz. Gren. Div. from the gap that had developed between the two divisions.

From entries in the war diary it can be seen that on July 16th an argument developed between the German command posts concerning the withdrawal of 15 Pz. Gren. Div. That evening I asked for the division to be given freedom of movement. (It is no longer possible to establish whether an order to this effect was issued. According to General Rodt's account the division disengaged itself on its own initiative.)

War diary, 4.45 p.m.: =

"From his advanced battle H.Q. at Trecastagni (on the south slope of Etna) the German Chief of Liaison Staff has a telephone conversation with Field-Marshal Kesselring, emphasizing that in the present situation the centre of pressure still lies on the right wing of H.G. Division, and that the disengagement of this division's right wing and the gradual dis-engagement of 15 Pz. Gren. Div. conforms to the general conduct of operations. At present H.G. Division's front can be considered as stable; outflanking of the western wing has been avoided. Thereupon General v. Senger proceeds to the battle H.Q. of H.G. Division where he issues the directive to hold the advanced position."

July 16th was full of directives from C.-in-C. South that were in line with the O.K.W.'s order to stand firm. The effect of these orders was to delay as long as possible the withdrawal of the H.G. Division from its position on the Corna Lunga river and of 15 Pz. Gren. Div. to the premeditated first Etna position. So ended the phase of proper tactical movement; the new phase was dictated by the "order to halt".

On July 17th it became essential to establish cohesion between the two divisions even before they occupied the main battle line. At 12.40 a.m. 15 Pz. Gren. Div was informed by radio that the right wing of H.G. Division was not at Catenanuova, as the former supposed, but at Ragusa. All further withdrawal was forbidden, and the order was given to make another stand. This order became necessary as 15 Pz. Gren. Div. had lost confidence owing to the "halt order" issued through Kesselring on the previous day. The H.G. Division had already practically reached the new main battle line south of Catania. It took 15 Pz. Gren. Div. a little time to collect itself; it always remained a well led and reliable unit. Now it continued to fight for another full week with its advanced sections in the immediate front, and even before the arrival of 29 Pz. Gren. Div. it prolonged its front northwards up to the coast. In the later battles of XIV Panzer Corps it constituted the most reliable part of the entire front.

On July 17th Kesselring himself ordered the withdrawal of H.G. Division while he was with me at the battle H.Q. of the Schmalz group. Previously he had passed an order through 2 Fliegerkorps that the division should halt on the Corna Lunga river. But from this battle H.Q. at Misterbianco he could see for himself how these positions were exposed to heavy fire. The Allied naval forces that had entered the Messina Strait fired their broadsides at them almost continuously.

While Kesselring was there, the commander of Parachute Rifle Regt. 3 arrived. He and over 900 of his men had managed to escape from their encircled position at Lentini and had found their way back through the enemy lines. The regiment had been out of the picture since July 14th and took no part in the fighting up to the 17th. Even then it could not at once be sent into action, for it had lost all its heavy weapons. Its losses in men had been small, giving the lie to the earlier reports of severe casualties.

The front of the new main battle line ran from a position five kilometres west of S. Stefano in the general direction of Nicosia, thence south-eastwards up to a point about five kilometres west of Agira, bending eastwards along the road to Regalbuto; five kilometres west of this place it turned south-east again to Catenanuova, thence south-east along the railway to Catania up to a point ten kilometres south-west of Catania, then directly eastward to the sea.

At that time, however, the mass of the two divisions was not yet in this pre-planned main battle line, but in forward positions, where it put up a gradually weakening resistance.

HANDING OVER TO THE XIV PANZER CORPS

On July 15th the corps H.Q. of XIV Panzer Corps arrived in the island. It was to take command of the two German divisions at the moment of their junction. For the time being this H.Q. staff was exploring the actual Etna position that would be taken up by the divisions in the second phase following their junction in the main battle line already outlined above. This Etna position ran from S. Fratello due south to a point five kilometres south-west of Troina, then turned off to the south-east to a point two kilometres south of Adrano and continued due east until it touched the sea north of Acireale.

At 10.30 p.m. on July 16th, the C.-in-C. South ordered General Hube, the commander of XIV Panzer Corps, to take over command of all German troops in Sicily. The time of the transfer was to be arranged with me and reported. It took place on the 17th, shortly after midnight, in the main H.Q. of the German liaison staff when I happened to be at the advanced battle H.Q. at Trecastagni. An actual handing over of command could not take place, for the O.K.W. had made me responsible for the conduct of operations in Sicily, although I was still only the liaison officer with the Italian 6th Army Command. For the time being I retained this responsibility.

Since Kesselring had announced the subordination to XIV Panzer Corps of all German troops and consequently of virtually the entire front, he had to clear up some awkward incidents. The arrival of German battalions without their own means of transport had led to serious clashes with the Italian units. The German battalion commanders had been ordered to motorise themselves by taking over the vehicles of those Italian troops that were no longer in the fighting. This led to some shooting, with fatal casualties on both sides.

Difficulties of another kind arose later because the Italian 6th Army commander continued to be in charge of all Italian armed forces still on the western front, including those in the front line. The Italians were understandably anxious to maintain their own command posts, on whose functioning depended the orderly withdrawal of their troops across the Messina Strait. On July 22nd XIV Panzer Corps vainly attempted to dispense with the Italian XII Army Corps. On the 25th the respective corps commanders came to an agreement that the Italian Army Corps would retain the sector S. Stefano-Nicosia while the advanced detachment of 29 Pz. Gren. Div. would later be brought back, passing through the Italian positions and moving into the main position at S. Fratello-Troina, where they. would then come under the command of XIV Panzer Corps.

It was clearly the intention of the German High Command gradually to eliminate all Italian command posts on the island, and this arrangement conformed to the actual conditions that had meanwhile developed. Since these realities could not be changed, the Italian 6th Army Command had to comply, and henceforth it played only a token rôle. It still issued orders and received reports, but stopped making alterations or counter-proposals to the increasing flood of orders that C.-in-C. South was now sending to XIV Panzer Corps.

On July 31st General Guzzoni informed me that he had received a directive from the Commando Supremo to comply in future with German wishes and to hand over to XIV Panzer Corps the command over all German and Italian troops in the fighting zone. Guzzoni asked me whether at this juncture the directive really represented the German wishes. If so, he was ready to subordinate to XIV Panzer Corps all Italian troops still in the fighting zone that were considered of value to the corps.

Having received confirmation from Kesselring, Guzzoni on August 1st ordered that as from noon on the following day all Italian fighting troops still at the front should come under the command of the German XIV Panzer Corps. At the same time he instructed the Italian XVI Corps to take over the entire coastal defences. The Italian XII Corps was put at the disposal of the Italian 6th Army Command.

On August 5th General Hube suggested to Guzzoni that the Italian 6th Army H.Q. should be moved to Calabria in order to make room for his own Corps H.Q., but the Italian general was not prepared to propose such a thing to the Commando Supremo, and left it to Hube to apply to the C.-in-C. South for this to be done.

On August 8th I was recalled from my mission and handed over the duties of liaison officer with the 6th Army Command, which was still in the island, to my G.S.O.1a, Lieut.-Colonel Meier-Welcker.

EXPERIENCES IN DEFENCE AGAINST SICILIAN LANDINGS

Looking back on the situation after the landings, I can find little wrong with the appreciation that was made at the time of these operations. Then it was possible to distinguish two general trends. The first was expressed in the view that any defence against a major landing was hopeless from the start; the second, that tactical measures could deal the enemy a crippling blow at the moment of his greatest weakness.

It has already been related how Hitler's directive of June 22nd gave no indication as to which of these two views he held. But from the fact that both Keitel and particularly Warlimont issued directives concerned only with evacuation it can be deduced that Hitler too rejected the prospect of permanently holding the island.

On the other hand it must be assumed that Kesselring was hoping to achieve on the island his first eye-catching defensive success as Commander-in-Chief, and believed that, after landing, the enemy could be "thrown back into the sea". Since this thesis had considerable currency in the Wehrmacht generally, and more particularly in subordinate circles, it is worth examining it in the light of actual experience.

The thesis reflected a deep-rooted weakness in the German military intellectual tradition, which had evolved almost exclusively from land warfare. A large part of the stratum of German political and military leaders could think only in terms of land operations, not in the three-dimensional terms of forces of all arms. This limitation was responsible not only for over-estimating the value of coastal defences, but for an exaggerated idea of the difficulties of landing by an enemy possessing air and sea superiority.

The modern form of attack by integrated forces of all arms against an opponent armed only for land warfare who is inferior at sea and in the air is actually easier and more promising than a purely land attack against fixed positions. An attacker coming from seaward has the advantage of surprise. Those captured Italian generals who told Eisenhower that the landings came as a complete surprise were wrong. But what will always achieve surprise is the choice and extent of the landing places and the immediate tactics of the invader. Even in Sicily it was a long time before we could know whether the landing on July 10th would be followed by further landings in other places. Indeed, all the later landings in Italy came by surprise—Salerno, Corsica and Anzio—although we knew that the landing fleets were at sea. Surprise is easily secured if the final movements of the invader's convoys are concealed by means of night steaming, deceptive courses and artificial fog. In this respect the landing between Syracuse and Licata was a surprise, as was the omission of further landings in the western or northern part of Sicily.

Even more important than the element of surprise is the opportunity presented to the invader of keeping down the enemy on land by means of ships' gunfire. The calibre of ships' guns is always heavier than that of an army in the field which has taken up temporary positions for the defence of a coastal sector; above all, the ships' artillery is more mobile than that of the defenders. If a ship is surprised by fire from a land battery, it can always withdraw under the cover of its own smoke-screen. The defender is incapable of effective action against the ship's guns, which in the case of Sicily were barely inconvenienced by the land batteries.

During the actual landing, moreover, the attacking infantry is not nearly so exposed to counter-action as the land-bound tactician might suppose, for he is unfamiliar with this kind of attack across the water. In any properly organised landing the order to the ship's artillery to open fire is almost equivalent to pinning down the defender before ever the invading force wades ashore. Later, when the invader's infantry has moved inland, it may find itself in a critical situation if its rear communications are still unorganised, especially if it encounters enemy thrusts or major counter-attacks.

In Sicily the invader's infantry when attacked by the H.G. Division could re-embark or abandon its attack in the restricted sector of the defender's counter-attack. The great success of the landing is also attributable to the fact that the Allied Command was able to set tanks ashore almost simultaneously with the landing of the infantry. That the tanks could not be effective was due to the unsuitability of the terrain for armoured warfare.

The Allied air forces were able to destroy the German aircraft on the ground. But the attempt to precipitate a decision by means of air-borne landings failed. The destruction of the grounded aircraft was achieved by experienced bomber pilots, whereas the employment of air-borne troops was a new venture. Those that were dropped at divisional strength in the south-east of the island for seizing the areodromes could not gain their objective; they suffered considerable losses from the German A.A. batteries, which were still very strong. They did, however, delay the thrust by the H.G. Division.

The defenders had no difficulty in dealing with the British paratroops that were dropped at the mouth of the Simeto. According to General Marshall's report to the Secretary of State for War these paratroops and the 82nd U.S. Division that was dropped two days later as a reserve force were both fired on by their own troops and suffered considerable losses. General Eisenhower commented on these losses, which were all the more painful because of the Allies' complete air superiority.

These setbacks make it clear that the participation of air-landing troops and paratroops in the invasion was basically a failure, as indeed were many other such attempts in the course of the war. Nor is it easy to extract lessons from these experiences for future use. After air landings there will always be some element of danger, even if mistakes while air-borne can be reduced or eliminated by better training.

In another sphere of air activity it would, however, be most misleading to draw lessons from the landings in Sicily. In all the landings made by the Allies in Italy the objectives were chosen so as to lie within the radius of action of their land-based fighters. This explains the omission of a landing on the north coast of Sicily and, later, the choice of Salerno for a landing. In any future war this limitation will not exist. Fighter squadrons will have their bases at sea or on board the carriers that provide the actual air cover for the landings. This widens the choice of attainable landing objectives to such an extent that every defended coastal target will have to be prepared for surprise.

To round off these conclusions it should also be mentioned that for a newly landed force the rear communications are a source of weakness. Nevertheless the sea-borne supply commnications of an invader enjoying naval and air supremacy can be more easily kept free from enemy interference than land communications, for they can at any time be changed or evasively routed. Moreover they always possess their own integrated air defences.

In order properly to understand this ubiquitous superiority of a sea-borne invading force one must observe it with one's own eyes. On July 12th, 1943, I was only a few kilometres along the coast from Eisenhower, and having witnessed the same spectacle I can completely endorse the words he then spoke to the United States Chief of Staff: "I must say that the sight of hundreds of vessels, with landing craft everywhere, operating along the shoreline from Licata, on the east-ward, was unforgettable." Unforgettable it was, but differently so for me than for Eisenhower!

I have here described the prospects for the attacker in a major landing operation, and it is from this starting point that the defender's situation can best be judged. First of all it is necessary to refute allegations that the Sicilian landings could not be prevented for various reasons, including "treachery in Italian official quarters", "well known difficulties of command on the Axis side", or merely the disproportion between the opposing land forces. The failure of the defence is attributable to the tactical, material and strategical superiority of the sea-borne invader who knew how to exploit his air and naval superiority. Coasts are always long and their defence ties down many men. It was the same in Sicily as on the Italian main-land, the same in Normandy as in Korea, when on September 15th, 1950, MacArthur had no difficulty in setting his troops ashore in the rear of the opponent who had thrust southwards from North Korea.

Sicily had no continuous coastal fortifications, and the few batteries were quite unequal to the opponent's powerful ships' artillery. Then there was the difference of opinion about the location of those batteries that had been brought up. Naval experts wanted them placed in exposed forward positions where they could be effective against the enemy before he had landed. But a landing had never been tried against undamaged batteries. The Army authorities therefore sponsored the setting up of inland batteries, out of sight of the enemy's naval force, which would come into action after the landings. The strongest part of the defences were the numerous 88 mm. A.A. guns of the Luftwaffe. Some of them had to be recalled for the defence of the Messina Strait, but unfortunately the Luftwaffe never let the Army Command know about this.

There was never any question of defence in depth. The actual coastal front to be defended was 800 kilometres long. Even if there had been no Italian "Coastal Divisions"—and in any case they could be written off—the four available Italian Army divisions and the two German divisions could never have been disposed in linear formation along the coast.

The argument that was later resuscitated in France between Rommel, an advocate of rigid coastal defence, and Rundstedt, who wanted to operate with strong mobile reserves, had already been settled in this curtain-raiser invasion of Sicily. Fortunately Kesselring and Guzzoni saw eye to eye in this question, and I had no differences with the Italian general. Consequently the six mobile divisions were kept together as mobile reserves in two large groups near the coast— one in the west, the other in the east.

Since there was unanimity about these dispositions it is impossible to understand Kesselring's statement that he believed the German divisions "had their marching orders in their pockets and knew how to act", and that the mobile defence should have succeeded on its own initiative. I remember on a later occasion noticing that Kesselring was very dejected after the vain attempts to throw the invader back into the sea at Anzio, and that he was similarly depressed at the news of the Allied landings in Normandy. On these occasions his remarks made me feel that he never shared my sceptical outlook on the chances of repelling a landing by an enemy with air and naval superiority, and that his judgment must therefore be at fault.

Guzzoni and I never doubted that the most we could do was to fight for time. There was no point in giving the mobile forces a kind of mobilisation order. Orders and operations had to conform to the changing circumstances of the struggle.

I was sure of support from Keitel and Warlimont. As for Hitler, it seems that on the occasions when he was influenced by the optimistic Kesselring he was liable to change his previous estimate of the situation. It was only too well known that he preferred people and views that were prompted by emotion to those that relied on professional judgment.

Yet it must be admitted that the majority of the German war leaders shared Kesselring's outlook. They evidently failed to grasp the developments that had taken place in the conduct of the war, the evolution from purely land warfare to the integrated land, sea and air operations that alone could be decisive. Among the more junior ranks there was a kind of sea-fright—a fear that on leaving the landing boats or while still in the boats the infantry would come under annihilating fire. This mentality was understandable in a continental people. Yet the issue could no longer be in doubt when one side possessed virtually only one branch of the armed forces, while the other could employ all three branches in sufficient strength to gain the objective.

END OF COALITION WAR

Since all future conflicts will be wars of coalition, the experiences of the Axis in this field might have some significance. Through all the German accounts of the Sicilian campaign that have reached me there runs as it were a red thread of mistrust, disappointment and even hatred against the Italian ally. These sentiments were not warranted. It is true that in Sicily the Italian armed forces were barely fighting any more, but they were not treacherous. The Germans did not understand the Italian mentality or their tongue. I was familiar with their language and could therefore better understand their mentality. My two years' diplomatic activity with the Franco-Italian Armistice Commission had given me an insight into Italian military policy and into the minds of the Italian General Staff.

Italy's decision to enter the war was no doubt mainly attributable to that optimistic and more susceptible stratum of Italians whose outlook on life was nearer to that of the Germans, but their attitude changed as the war progressed. The realisation that the situation held no hope had spread among the people. The growing loss of prestige had undermined the self-confidence of the nation. The numerous humiliations imposed by the German ally had increased the weariness of war.

There was too a basic difference in the national mentality of the two nations. The Italian is by nature more critical and therefore politically more mature than the German. The idea that the war could be won by optimism and trustful resolution did not register with the Italians; the intellectuals already realised that it was lost when the offensive in Russia came to a standstill. When this conviction percolated to the man in the street, it was bound to lead to defeatism. After her humiliating experience in North Africa, Italy's insistence on keeping the supreme command of the forces defending her native soil in her own hands can hardly be designated as a sign of intended treachery. It was the Fascists themselves who pressed for the energetic conduct of the war, who rejected the proposed sacrifice of Italian soil up to the Gothic line and who wanted to continue the fight by the side of their ally. The only way to prevent the defection of Italy was to make the defence of her own soil the sacred cause of her people. To achieve this it was essential to eliminate any humiliation of the Italian Army leadership, and to avoid giving the impression that the continuance of the war was now exclusively a German interest.

Hitler, who had ordered this command set-up or had agreed to it, might well have pondered over how the Italian leadership could be more or less blatantly brushed aside. Before the discussion on June 22nd he had allowed me to see the report from a German general who had acted as a kind of liaison officer after Rommel's recall from North

Africa. Blowing his own trumpet, this general described how he had short-circuited and offended the Italian commander. Yet Rommel's position in North Africa had long ago persuaded the Italians that the war had become a German affair, and now they wanted to be rid of this system.

Even after Mussolini had fallen from power and Italy's defection was being prepared in Rome, the Italian 6th Army Command in Sicily continued to co-operate loyally with the Germans, because it was ordered to do so. Later, when the German-sponsored puppet Republican-Fascist Government wanted to execute General Guzzoni as a traitor, I was able with a clear conscience to bear witness to his loyalty to the Axis in Sicily.

It is amazing how little even the more important German leaders foresaw the consequences of the Italian collapse. They could not see that the two allies were like climbers on a precipice; if one should fall, he would so strain the rope that the other could make no further progress. Many German military men seemed to be aiming at cutting away the Italian ballast, and were loud in advocating this course.

To this political and military concept was added another factor. Like most of my Italian and German political friends I had long realised that the war was lost. The O.K.W. had directed that the close ties with our Italian ally should be maintained. This engendered the hope that the fall of Mussolini would also bring down Hitler's Nazi Government and thus spare the German people the last agony. Yet that people not only lacked the political instinct to produce such a result, but it possessed no sovereign state organisation comparable to the Italian monarchy that would be capable of winding up the war. Historically speaking, and ignoring the resentful viewpoint of the German ally, Victor Emmanuel III rendered his country as great a service in the Second World War by his timely ending of it as he did in the first war by his determination to stand fast after Caporetto. That he could not openly take this step in agreement with his Nazi ally was due to the latter's peculiar relations with other powers.

But even if one disregards all the political aspects—which should never be done when considering strategy—there were purely military reasons for ensuring the closest possible co-operation with the remaining Italian forces.

In Sicily such a policy was needed if only because the large number of Italian troops still in the island had to be puposefully controlled within the framework of the operations. Only in this way could the roads be kept clear for important movements and the troops of both countries be brought back across the Messina Strait without incurring damaging disputes or friction.

It is wrong to write off Italian participation in the fighting as though it did not exist. When the decision to evacuate the island was finally made and the German commanders were asked whether they wanted to retain any Italian units instead of sending them straight back to the mainland, a considerable number was assembled, particularly the artillery.

The course of the fighting confirmed the correctness of the operational decisions. The task involved the use of the two German and four Italian divisions to delay the assault by two large Allied armies sufficiently for an orderly withdrawal to be made into suitable defensive positions in the north-east corner of the island. Moreover the four Italian divisions had to be sandwiched in between the two German ones in such a way as to deceive the enemy's air reconnaissance into believing that there was a coherent front. By this means it was possible, contrary to expectations, to prevent an operational outflanking movement along the north coast by Patton's army.

Since British military writers tend to represent the fighting as if it had developed entirely according to the original Allied plan, it is appropriate here to refer to an American history* published even before the war was over, in which the plan of campaign is described as follows:

> The final plan of attack envisaged an American landing on the south coast to clear the western half of the island and then turn back along the north coast, where the British were to join up with them after landing on the south coast and advancing northwards along the east coast. The Allied forces were then to lure the enemy into a trap in the north east corner and, by cutting him off, prevent any attempt to cross the Messina Strait to the mainland.

The emphasis is on the last sentence. In the contrast between this plan of campaign and what actually occurred lies the vindication of our conduct of the operations. In place of the Allied plan there was a slow frontal push northwards by Montgomery's army with its right shoulder along the coast. Following upon this the western part of the island was "combed out" by Patton's army, and this led indirectly to a coherent German front at Etna. The Italo-German forces were only very slowly squeezed out of the north-east tip of the island, and could be transferred to the mainland with the main body.

As usual the figures of losses are controversial and full of contradictions. General Marshal reported to the Secretary of State for War that "through strong concentrations of heavy flak (A.A. batteries) the Germans succeeded in transfering thousands of their best armoured and air-landing troops to the mainland".

---

* Extract from the *U.S. Infantry Journal*, Feb. 1945.

CHANGE OF GOVERNMENT

After handing over my command I spent a day with the Italian 6th Army commander. We were at a height of 1,000 metres at the crest of a pass, about halfway between the northern slope of Etna and Cape Milazzo on the north coast. With my friend Rohr I was accommodated in a tent in the wood. This position had the disadvantage that the road, like all roads leading to Messina, was under continuous attack from low-flying fighter-bombers, and we were frequently in the slit trenches. In the car on the open roads of the pass we could move only by rushes. The wood where our first camp was situated was set alight by a shot-down aircraft. The second camp too was close to the road, as the precipitous countryside precluded any diversion from it. As far as service matters were concerned life here became quieter. I was often visited by General Baade, who on the far side of the Messina Strait was in charge of the arrangements for transferring the army. Both of us had the feeling of having left the stage, in order—as Baade expressed it—to watch this cosmic event from the box. I sometimes bathed on the north coast with Rohr, when I took along the little tea-boiler that had been my faithful companion throughout the war; and over a cup of tea we had time once more to admire the beauty of the landscape. In the spring the island is said to have a wonderful wealth of flowers, but in high summer it is somewhat lacking in colour. At the water's edge the deep blue sea contrasted with the chalky face of the cliffs, which glowed pink in the setting sun. Then there was a welcome change in the temperature. On the drives along the coast and over the black lava of Etna the African heat was oppressive, but at night in our tented camp on the pass I needed three blankets to keep me from freezing.

I had my meals with Guzzoni in his comfortable dining caravan where we enjoyed the plentiful Italian fare, usually without other company.

The change of government that occurred at this time did not seem to affect the conduct of the war. Already as liaison officer in Turin I had repeatedly reported that for Italians the loss of Libya meant the loss of the war, and now the loss of Sicily portended that the motherland could not be adequately defended. The Italians frankly admitted their own weakness, yet they hoped that the strong forces now fighting in the east would be sent back to defend their country. Their confidence was weakened, mainly due to the absence of the Luftwaffe.

Guzzoni accommodated himself to the declaration by Badoglio's new government that the war was to go on. But at our table talks he admitted that the King evidently had no intention of continuing along a path that only led to a blind alley. This attitude might affect both politics and the conduct of the war. It was known that

Mussolini had not objected to Hitler's idea of defending Italy at the Apennines. In this matter the Fascist Grand Council, in other words his own party, had let him down. Those officers who had not been let into the conspiracy could believe that Badoglio wanted to pursue the war more vigorously, especially to defend the entire mainland, and that for this purpose he would make demands on the Germans.

But naturally it was Badoglio's aim to end a war that in his view was already lost, even if it meant going behind Hitler's back. This aim was shared by the majority of his generals, though these were not necessarily in the plot with him. It was these generals in particular who were disgruntled at the ever-increasing German tutelage. The loss of Sicily was the latest of a series of reverses which they laid at the door of the Fascist government. Badoglio himself had withdrawn from the scene at the start of the campaign in Greece because of his differences with the party, and he was vindicated by the subsequent course of the war.

There was moreover an internal political development due to the realisation—not only by the Allies but also by the Fascists—that Mussolini's mental and physical powers were rapidly waning. Consequently when it came to discussing a successor, there was no need to be a traitor in order to envisage a change of government. Badoglio, regarded as Italy's most outstanding military man, was expected to lead a strong government which would also introduce military reforms.

Even allowing for the well-known weaknesses of the Fascist régime it is amazing how inglorious, how frictionless and colourless was its overnight disappearance. Neither Guzzoni nor I was aware of the extent of the tension between the new Italian and German governments. We knew each other as unenthusiastic adherents of our respective political régimes, and this favoured our friendly relations.

It was soon noticeable that the new government no longer insisted on the Italian 6th Army commander retaining the overall military command in Sicily, but complied with the German claim to assume it. Naturally the mood in the dining caravan was gloomy. After the change of government the Prefect and the Commissioner for Sicily continued to join us occasionally for meals, when Guzzoni would expound his reservations against Fascism, blaming Mussolini especially for neglecting the country's armaments. To add weight to his argument, he pointed to the state of the Italian forces in Sicily.

This last comment sheds a light on the outlook of the Italian upper strata, who were always predominantly in favour of the monarchy and to some extent pro-Fascist, though usually far more anti-German than the party officials. The anti-German feeling was now uppermost. The loyal old Guzzoni was carried along by the tide of events. He saw the world with shrewd, wide open eyes. On the wall above him hung the portrait of the King and beside it an empty frame, symbol of the current vacuum in the constitution. I suggested filling the frame with a portrait of the Queen, as is the custom with monarchies.

Before finally relinquishing my post, I paid a last visit to General Hube, commander of XIV Panzer Corps. The road leading through Taormina was hewn out of the rocks and barely negotiable because of the damage caused by bombardment from the ships. I wondered why the enemy had not brought all movement along this road to a standstill. Early on the morning of August 8th I drove along the north coast towards the Messina Strait, which looked like some wide river. From past experience at the front I knew that the safest time for a crossing was at first light of dawn, when the night fighters have left and before the day fighters have appeared. Baade arrived on time to fetch his old commander back. He stood like an Admiral on the bridge of the motor torpedo boat. We made the crossing in half an hour without incident and breakfasted in his mainland battle H.Q., situated at some height above sea level. It was an unforgettable moment when I looked across to Sicily. I had the idiotic sensation of having been rescued, and the relief was all the greater for the fact that I was now free of all responsibility.

Next I drove northwards up the coast. At noon we had a bathe in the sea. As we were sitting peacefully on the beach a flight of enemy bombers came roaring up at a height of a hundred metres. We rushed into the water and took cover behind some rocks, for we were used to being attacked by every sort of aircraft. But the bombers ignored us. We spent the night near Castrovillari. Naples made a bad impression with its ragged people, hungry and sick. Spending the second night in the town of Cassino, we visited the Abbot, who invited us to lunch. The monastery had been in close contact with General Hube, who had spent a considerable time at Cassino. The Chief Abbot, Baron Stotzingen, was due to arrive that day, but I could not stay. I had no inkling of the significance that this place and the road I then took to Rome were to hold for me in the months and years that lay ahead.

On August 11th I reported to Kesselring in Rome. He was pleasant and I felt that nothing was left of the tensions that had existed between us during the fighting in Sicily. He handed me a picture of himself with a flattering inscription; it may be that he decided to do so on the strength of my prediction of the turn of events in Sicily, which had proved accurate. To send further reinforcements to the island would have changed nothing, but could only have delayed the completion of the evacuation.

I remained with Kesselring while he had a discussion with the newly appointed Italian Minister of Marine, who had formerly been military attaché in Berlin, but I was unable to deduce the minister's personal attitude. The two participants in the conversation were agreed that the Italian Fleet could play no active part while it remained in the harbours of La Spezia and Taranto. Many people failed to understand that operations by naval forces demand even stronger air cover than land forces. Air power had provoked even more revolutionary changes in naval tactics than in military operations. Consequently to send the Italian warships out on operations could only be described as a gesture of desperation. Every professional man realised that a battleship putting to sea would immediately have been identified and destroyed by an opponent who possessed air and naval supremacy.

Kesselring placed at my disposal a DO-217, which I boarded on August 12th with Major von Rohr and my batman, Feuerstak. We sat very cramped under the glass dome of the bomber, while the baggage was stowed in the bomb-racks. But this time we only had to wear on our backs the parachute bag, and not the additional life-saving jacket for flights across the water. Within a hundred minutes we reached Munich, where I caught the familiar train to Göttingen.

SARDINIA AND CORSICA—INITIAL SITUATION

Remembering Sicily with mixed emotions, I cannot claim to have evinced much enthusiasm for the new task I was given at the beginning of September—as commander of the Wehrmacht forces to take charge of the evacuation of Sardinia and the defence of Corsica. The prospects were even worse, while the political situation had become more acute. The O.K.W. treated the Badoglio government with a discouraging abruptness, whereas people with a sense of diplomacy, such as our military attaché in Rome, advocated a *modus vivendi* even though they knew the attitude of this government. I had to reckon with the probability that our ally would leave us to our own devices in these islands, and the prospect was hardly attractive. In that eventuality the C.-in-C. South had ordered that the Italians were to be immediately disarmed. But the German forces in the islands were numerically too inferior to achieve this, and there was a possibility of interference by native French insurgents. Lastly, there was the threat of landings by the Allies. By jumping across from Sicily to these islands they would acquire a base for landings deep in the rear of the German forces on the mainland. Geographically the islands are more isolated than Sicily, being almost as far from the mainland as Sicily is from Africa. Then there was the Allied superiority at sea and in the air. In my view the directive to defend isolated islands of this type was another example of the failure to appreciate the vital contribution of the sea and the air to modern operations.

Nor did there seem any compensating merit in the instructions I was given that in the event of Italian defection the German garrison on Sardinia was to be transferred to Corsica, which then alone was to be defended. The Allies could hardly be expected to watch idly while the two garrisons were being united; sooner or later Corsica too must fall to them.

On September 7th the DO-217 flew me to Ajaccio, my staff having already been sent over from Leghorn. I proceeded to call on the Italian VII Army Corps at Corte. Its commander, General Magli, was considered pro-German, as he had worked with Cavallero, and on this account he was appreciated by Kesselring. Yet I noticed a very frigid atmosphere among the officers. The fact that Kesselring was counting on "loyal co-operation" with Magli particularly complicated the political part of my mission. Neither Kesselring nor Hitler's O.K.W. realised than an Italian officer might find himself in a position where he would have to carry out the orders of his legitimate government, orders that could end in the laying down of arms. For such a decision would ultimately have to end this war, as it had ended all other lost wars. As things stood, the order could only be issued behind the backs of the Germans. But the unpleasant taste of "treachery" by statesmen must not be allowed to obstruct the path leading to the salvation of the people. In this case the officers had to obey. Consequently I was not surprised when Magli refused my request, as he had previously refused Kesselring's, to send German detachments to serve with his own coastal batteries. He felt that the request was humiliating and would damage the high morale of his troops.

Magli had four divisions, while at that time I had at my disposal the "SS-Assault Brigade Reichsführer SS", which had only two battalions of infantry, but was relatively strong in artillery and possessed one anti-tank battalion. This brigade was assembled in the south, near Sartena, for the purpose of preventing enemy landings, or if necessary to form a bridgehead at Bonifacio to enable the withdrawal of German troops from Sardinia. The anti-tank battalion was situated at Porto Vecchio.

The Italian VII Army Corps commander with his four divisions was in charge of all other defences. I was allocated to him as liaison officer, which corresponded to the position I had held in Sicily.

I agreed with the corps commander that the entire east coast of Corsica was endangered. The Italian divisions were so grouped that they could only repel a landing on the west coast. Yet a sudden enemy descent on the east coast was not only possible, but promised rewarding results. It could have cut off the German forces that were tied down in the south from the important harbour of Bastia on the north-east coast.

I therefore intended, in the event of Italian defection, to spread sections of 90 Pz. Gren. Div. (which would then arrive from Sardinia) along the east coast, thus establishing a link between the southern tip of the island and Bastia. Magli approved this plan. If a landing occurred on that coast he wanted to be associated with its defence by launching counter-attacks from the interior of the island!

Conditions in the port of Bastia were particularly unfavourable. Here were three A.A. batteries and one or two German administrative centres: the local administrative officer, the important sea transport office, the Wermacht supply officer and some small administrative units. A German battalion that had arrived by way of reinforcement immediately had to allocate half its strength to guard duties for the depots. This released the crews of coastal batteries, whom I hoped (if all went well) to employ at Bastia and Bonifacio in place of the Italian ones.

THE DEFECTION OF ITALY

Within twenty-four hours of my arrival the situation was radically changed through Badoglio's conclusion of an armistice with the Allied High Command. All Italian forces on the island were neutralised, while the French insurgents went into action. General Magli was now ostensibly without a command. He offered as far as was possible to back the German control of operations, to facilitate the transfer of German forces from Sardinia, to suppress the uprisings of the French guerillas, to order his coastal batteries to reply if fired on from seaward, and to continue to put his communications service at my disposal!

Under these circumstances there was of course no question of taking action to disarm the Italian forces, as Kesselring had ordered in this very situation. The only available German force—the S.S. brigade—on receipt of the code-word "Axis" moved into the bridgehead at Bonifacio to safeguard the removal of German troops from Sardinia and their junction with those in Corsica. Thus the brigade was tied to its southern function.

The agreement that had been reached through diplomatic channels and without which I could not have carried on any independent activity was now considerably upset. On the evening of September 8th the weak German naval garrison in Bastia, acting on a code-word passed to it on a naval communications link without my knowledge, undertook a sudden raid on the harbour and on the Italian ships lying in it. The attack failed due to the resistance of the Italians who were in superior numbers, but both sides suffered casualties and lost some prisoners. This enterprise was senseless and harmful to our position. I had to be careful to placate the C.-in-C. of the

The Author

Maas River. Crossing at Maestricht: the author in the foreground

Martinvast

Candebec: after a bomber attack

Rouen in flames

"Phoney War": in Rouen special "props" are rigged for a German propaganda film

My batman, Feverstak
(right)

Cavalry monuments in a Brittany churchyard

Russia: German tanks attack. A German war artist's impression

Russia: a billet behind the lines. A German war artist depicts one of the very rare rest periods

Lynbizkije, 14th May, 1943

Russia. Tank advance

(Above and below) Russian prisoners, January, 1943

Russia. A last taste of hot food before the attack

Russian front. Bizarre transport

The front line in Russia

In Russia, a hot meal was a rare but welcome treat

The author reporting the situation to Field Marshal Kesselring,
20th May 1944

Views of the Monastery of Monte Cassino before the bombardment

The Monastery after the bombardment—a nightmarish shambles

Difficult climb. Mules bring provisions and ammunition over extensive fields of snow to the forward positions in Italy

Only by using mules could supplies be brought up across the cleft terrain

Fighter bombers—the terror of the highways—have set fire to a truck

Bishop Diamare of the Abbey testifies on behalf of the Germans
after the bombardment

The Archbishop of the
Cassino Monastery brought
to safety by General von
Senger und Etterlin

Italian forces until such time as sufficient units of 90 Pz. Gren. Div. had arrived for me to be able to confront him with demands in the form of an ultimatum. For this reason the negotiations that took place on September 9th resulted in the re-establishment of the *status quo*. I did not attend the negotiations in person, because while driving to Bastia we ran into an ambush laid by the French insurgents, to which my leading escort car fell victim.

On September 12th the advance units of 90 Pz. Gren. Div. reached Bonifacio. That evening the position became more strained when on the mainland the Wehrmacht began to disarm its former ally. General Magli was conscious of the danger that threatened him and of the impossibility of any further co-operation with the Germans —even as "neutrals". We had a highly dramatic discussion, during which he surprised me by consenting to let the German personnel join up with his coastal batteries. He agreed to concentrate his troops in the centre of the island and to refrain from any hostile act.

Yet he refused to evacuate Bastia on the grounds that he had to maintain communications with the mainland. I reserved the right to take any measures—troop movements in particular—that might be necessary for the defence of the island.

It had become evident that the position in Bastia could only be cleared up by resort to arms. In my bivouac close by Corte I had no protection and could easily have been captured by the Italians. I therefore moved off after dark and made for a battle H.Q. at Ghisonaccia, a suitably central site for directing any fighting on the eastern side of the island. Meanwhile the Fliegerführer 2 had reached this place from Sardinia.

The situation compelled us to seize Bastia. The Italian divisions would not allow themselves to be disarmed by a single German one. And we were even less in a position to disarm the French insurgents. Although we did not know their numbers, there was unmistakable evidence of their fanaticism. Even if we established covering forces along the 160 kilometre-long eastern road and seized Bastia, the situation would remain extremely critical. If there were a landing, the German forces, widely dispersed along the east coast, would present the invaders with a long unprotected flank, exposed on both sides. The transfer of 90 Pz. Gren. Div. was delayed because the conditions prevailing on the island of Maddalena could not be ascertained. An attempt to capture the island had failed. The sea route from Sardinia to Corsica lay within range of its guns. But the commander of the division, General Lungershausen, thanks to his past relations with the Italian C.-in-C., managed to persuade the Italian troops in Sardinia to allow the Germans to retain their arms when evacuating the island. (General Basso later found himself under a cloud on this account, but was acquitted.) But in Sardinia—unlike Corsica—the

Italians were on their own soil. They were not disarmed as on the mainland, and therefore suffered no degradation. Nor had they to guard against insurrectionists as the Italians in Corsica had to do. The latter would also soon be subject to the Allied Control commissioners and would no longer be able to implement their own decisions.

It would not be possible before September 13th to provide adequate German forces for the seizure of Bastia and at the same time have a covering force for the exit road to the west. Until then we would have to prevaricate with the Italians and make them believe that we were merely thinking of evacuating the island in the same way as we had left Sardinia.

This mixture of artifice, delaying negotiations and preparatory movements was complicated by the heterogeneous German garrison on the island. I had no doubt of the complete loyalty of the army division that was just arriving in the island, but I was not so sure of the troops already there. The twenty-four hours that I had spent in Corsica before the Italian capitulation had been too short for me to see to the discipline of the troops under my command. This was evidenced by the Navy's unsuccessful attempt at Bastia. The Luftwaffe units too showed their habitual reluctance to subordinate themselves to the unified command that was now so essential. The Fliegerführer, a colonel twenty years younger than myself, fought his own battles with quite inadequate resources, and charged me with "irresolute prosecution of the war". Fortunately he was soon recalled to the mainland, leaving the difficult task of organising the impending air evacuation to a very loyal and co-operative senior supply officer. The attitude of the S.S. brigade was different again. This unit, which stood outside the regular Wehrmacht and was really only allied to it—like those S.S. formations that I had got to know in Russia—behaved in an extremely correct manner towards all superior Army commands The senior officers of the regular army were of course aware of the direct official link that existed between these S.S. units and their superiors in the party, and of their consequent independence in all questions of personnel and organisation. Yet in fairness I must admit that the officers of the Waffen S.S. with whom I had any dealings were always correct and modest. On the other hand it is probable that they were continuously reporting back on the senior officers of the Army, and on their reliability in matters of political policy.

The Fight for Bastia

On September 11th the local German command posts again tried to negotiate the Italian evacuation of Bastia, but as this was unsuccessful, the weak German forces were withdrawn from the town so as not to obstruct the attack by the S.S. brigade, which was arriving there in stages.

On the 12th I sent over an officer with a flag of truce to General Magli with a telegram from Kesselring. Reminding the Italian of the years of mutual collaberation and expressing his personal admira‑ tion for him, Kesselring now requested his further co-operation. I thought it best to seize the opportunity to ask Magli to evacuate Bastia and other places which I needed for the defence of the island, otherwise I would have to resort to arms. His reply was not only evasive, but contained accusations. I thereupon received orders to disarm all Italians encountered in the districts occupied by our troops. The only Italians involved were those who had disobeyed the order to withdraw to the interior, probably because they preferred German to French captivity.

On this day those elements of the S.S. brigade that had been sent ahead to Bastia broke the Italian resistance at Casamozza and reached their assembly area south of the port. Here the Italians succeeded in blowing up a large road-bridge behind the German troops who had crossed it. This complicated and retarded the advance on the port. A railway bridge to the east of it could be quickly adapted for road traffic, and the attack on Bastia was ordered to take place on the 13th.

The attack made only slow progress, as the Italians kept the low-lying approach road under heavy fire from numerous batteries that had been skilfully sited in the hills south-west of the town. I myself investigated the difficulties caused by the terrain. Particularly con‑ fusing was the duel between the German and Italian flak batteries, often at very close range.

Seeing that success could only be achieved by a night attack, I arranged the details for starting it, and at 8 p.m. the spearheads of the S.S. brigade penetrated into the town. Only those sections of the Italian division that had ceased to fight were taken prisoner. The others withdrew southwards into the mountains.

On September 14th I went to Bastia to organise the formation of a bridgehead. Our infantry strength was inadequate and I had to re‑ nounce capturing the peninsula extending northwards, as this opera‑ tion would have thinned out the forces even more. Returning to my battle H.Q. that evening and feeling pleased at the capture of Bastia and the withdrawal of the Italians to the interior, I found my G.S.O. in a despairing mood over the orders that had come in. On Hitler's instructions all Italian officers were to be shot and the names of the victims reported that same evening. The order had been issued on the strength of a general directive by the O.K.W. to the effect that all Italian officers captured after September 10th who had fought after that date were to be treated as guerrillas and shot.

The Italian officers had obeyed the orders of their legitimate government. Most of the two hundred-odd captured officers had preferred becoming prisoners of the Germans to being held, if only temporarily, by the Free French Forces, which seemed the only alternative. They hoped thereby to be sent back sooner to Italy. And they had friends among their former allies, who gave them a hearty welcome as prisoners.

It was thus obvious that for me the time had come to refuse to obey orders. I at once spoke by radio-telephone with Kesselring, informing him of my decision. He accepted it without comment and agreed to pass it on to the O.K.W. I arranged for the officer prisoners to be returned immediately to the mainland, where the execution order could not be known. I am grateful to Kesselring because he more or less accepted my decision and left it at that.

Through fresh instructions the situation on the island underwent a change. On September 13th Kesselring's Chief of Staff brought over a directive that the island was not to be defended and that all German forces were to be transferred to the mainland. While this did not render the capture of Bastia superfluous, I no longer had to think in terms of subjugating the whole island. The only way to remove the 30,000 German troops (of whom two thirds were Army and the remainder Air Force) was by air from the two airports at Ghisonaccia and Borgo-Bastia. It became necessary gradually to withdraw down the long eastern road, with continuous flank protection towards the west.

The rate of evacuation was 3,000 men per day. While the arrangements were being prepared, the Bastia bridgehead had to be extended and further covering forces provided for the eastern road. This involved thinning down the infantry strength to such an extent that it was out of the question to launch any offensive operations into the central mountain massif. Even the assault forces were unsuccessful when launched against the supply depots in the interior at Ghisoni and Quenze, which had fallen into Italian hands. It was proved here even more than in Sicily that on mountain roads tanks can be quite easily resisted and ambushed.

Although the situation demanded the concentration of all resources on the evacuation and rescue of all men and equipment, the Chief of Staff of the Army Group, General Westphal, brought over an order from Kesselring as late as September 16th, to the effect that the mountainous road running north and south through the middle of the island, on which the Italians were assembling, was to be mopped up, in order to re-conquer the island before our withdrawal. Westphal himself was far too experienced in the General Staff to overlook the absurdity of this order. He agreed with my emphatic objection. On return, he informed Kesselring of my views, and that evening I received his concurrence. On September 19th Kesselring, who never shirked danger, visited the island and issued his own directives for the further evacuation.

CLOSER CONTAINMENT

In the first few days the evacuation proceeded according to plan, the troops being flown out from the two aerodromes while the equipment was sent by sea from Bastia. On September 20th the enemy became more active on land, at sea and in the air. The evacuation was continued, but communications with the mainland were increasingly threatened and interrupted.

On land, regular French troops of General Giraud—which we regarded at that time as belonging to General de Gaulle—began to launch attacks from Ajaccio, where they had landed. These were mainly Moroccan and Senegalese troops, and according to prisoners they amounted to twenty-three battalions. Supporting their operations were American tanks, while their equipment and the mules for mountain warfare were supplied by Badoglio's troops.

Thus the enemy was in a position to evade the German patrols on the mountain tracks, to cut some of them off before they could be relieved, and finally, towards the end of the campaign to advance right up to the life-line of the German troops. On the night of October 2nd they threatened my battle H.Q. near Bastia, but from the bridgehead I could still launch counter attacks, since the reduction of my forces had compelled me to shorten the perimeter of the defensive front. Consequently the enemy lost several hundred further potential prisoners. We had blown up all the roads leading to the area under our occupation, with the result that he could not bring up any artillery or fighting vehicles.

On September 21st the Allies attacked the harbour and town of Bastia with twenty-one Liberators, sinking the steamers *Tiberiade, Nikolaus* and two smaller vessels, all of which had been detailed for evacuation of special equipment. That night the harbour was raided by twelve Wellingtons, resulting in the loss of two Siebel ferries. On the 29th the aerodrome at Borgo was bombed by thirty-six Liberators and rendered unusable. But the powerful 88 mm. flak batteries that were now closely concentrated there prevented the raid from being fully effective, and by evening the aerodrome was again seviceable.

The air transports suffered serious losses. On September 25th alone, eleven Junkers transport planes were shot into the sea. On the previous day enemy submarines torpedoed the steamer *Champagne* in the harbour of Bastia. The ship could be repaired but after leaving harbour on the 27th she was again hit by two torpedoes and ran aground.

On the 24th I moved my battle H.Q. from Ghisonaccia to the

southern outskirts of Bastia. Here I had a slight attack of malaria. From my tent I saw the air transports being shot down over the sea and watched the raids on my remaining extempore airstrips. I was pleasantly surprised at the unexpected arrival of my faithful friend Rohr. He had not received the order to await me on the mainland, or had ignored it, which would be in keeping with his nature. So he shared with me the last fortnight on the islands.

On the night of September 20th the Bonifacio bridgehead was evacuated after the last units of 90 Pz. Gren. Div. had been air-lifted. Porto Vecchio was evacuated at night on the 22nd, the aerodromes at Ghisonaccia on the 25th and at Borgo on October 2nd. The sixty bridges on the eastern road were demolished, as were the harbour installations at Bonifacio and Porto Vecchio. The aerodrome at Ghisonaccia was made unserviceable. Borgo was not very useful as an aerodrome, so Poretta was also used. In the last days the air evacuation was done only at night, which reduced losses. When these last aerodromes had been abandoned, the remainder of the Bastia bridgehead garrison and I myself had to rely on sea transport. But the lurking submarines now prevented the ships from sailing, so our only means of escape was by the shallow-draught lighters and the Siebel ferries, and even these were very doubtful starters since the autumn storms had now set in. Being rather unseaworthy, they frequently had to turn back. As each day passed we wondered whether we would ever see our transport fleet again.

When the last airstrips had been given up on October 2nd I reported that the bridgehead could be held only until the following night. This meant abandoning several hundred lorries. The last Siebel ferries had to embark a number of flak batteries that were essential for holding the bridgehead. They were loaded outside the harbour, for the enemy had meanwhile so narrowed our bridgehead with its diminishing infantry that he could cover the harbour with his guns.

RETURN FROM CORSICA

The battle was moving towards its dramatic end. In reality we were surrounded—on land by the rapidly approaching Free French troops and insurgents, at sea by the submarines, in the air by the un-challenged supremacy of the Allied air forces.

On the final night I shifted my battle H.Q. from the southern border of Bastia towards the north, as the enemy threatened to descend from the surrounding hills. The transport fleet had arrived and both inside and outside the harbour was loading up with the last tanks and guns. Somebody had the idea of setting fire to the lorries that were to be left behind. The fire spread to the port threatening the quays, and had to be extinguished from the ships. The tension mounted; we had to watch idly while the ammunition exploded. To ease the feeling of strain I bathed in the sea, while Rohr had a talk with an attractive Frenchwoman, a nurse from the hospital. At 4 p.m. I boarded a small ship as it reached the quay, and from the water I supervised the final embarkation points and directed the last loadings. The overladen vessel was barely afloat, and all around us were the high splashes of falling shells. When a little way out, I transferred to a motor torpedo boat, but it had no lifesaving jackets. So we returned to the seething harbour, where we took some jackets from a torpedoed ship. Our flak batteries, fortunately free from anti-aircraft commitments, directed an uninterrupted barrage fire against the hills. They had a surplus of ammunition since it could not be embarked, and this proved our salvation. Then the batteries themselves were put on board, and the only guns still firing were those of the ships and lighters, aiming at the heights already fading in the evening twilight.

In this war I never saw anything more picturesque than this scene of battle. In the harbour and between the ships the fountains of water shot high in the air. The tracer ammunition from our ships' guns drew a pattern of lines over the town and the adjoining countryside. While the rearguards were embarking, the air was rent by the pre-arranged demolition explosions within the town limits. Then it was dark, the din suddenly ceased and was followed by an almost embarrassing stillness in which not even the noise of the departing ships could be distinguished. The loading of the ships could no longer be supervised. I still doubted whether it could be completed.

Once more I arranged to be taken close in to the land to ascertain what had happened to the last ships and the rearguard troops The officers around me became restless. At last I got a message from a naval officer that the commander of the rearguard had embarked everything and was already heading for the mainland. I kept my vessel at the landing stage a little longer in order to pick up any stragglers that might still arrive, and at 11 p.m. I finally gave the order: "Cast off, full speed ahead!" which came as a great relief to us all. We stood well to the north to avoid any submarines. On deck I wrapped my overcoat around me, glanced up at the stars, then fell into a deep slumber. Not until first light of dawn was I woken by some noise, the ship was already tied up in the harbour of Leghorn.

The naval officers in charge of the crossing who had attended to us all night, insisted—even before we could get to our new quarters—that we should celebrate our safe arrival with them. Near these quarters was the military unit occupying the coast of Leghorn, in which my son was serving. From his vantage point he had watched the Junkers planes flying back from Corsica, just as in the spring of that same year he had waited for me at Stalino after those weeks of fighting in the Kalmuk steppes. On the evening of October 4th we were again under the same roof at Prince Buoncompagni's Villa Pozzo.

October 5th was one of the days of my life that I shall long remember. After breakfasting with my friend Rohr and my son, with the broad valley of the Arno below us, we spent a delightful day in Florence. The Wehrmacht bulletin would have reassured those of my family who were back home, for it gave prominence to the evacuation of Corsica, which meant, incidentally, that I was not regarded with disfavour. Indeed I received a telegram from Hitler expressing his appreciation of my handling of "a movement whose fulfilment in such completeness could not have been expected". Later I heard that in the O.K.W. I had been the subject of a controversy in which my supporters had won the day. Nevertheless my refusal to obey an order caused my name to remain on a black list.

For the next five days I recuperated in the Villa Pozzo, paying daily visits to my son at Lucca who was expecting an appointment to the Russian theatre of war. On October 11th I drove over to Kesselring's H.Q. at Monte Soracte, where I picked up only some of the details of what had meanwhile occurred on the mainland. On his last visit to me Kesselring had expressed the hope that the enemy would not land on Corsica, but on the mainland, where adequate troops were available to throw him back into the sea. His hopes had proved illusory, the enemy having made a successful landing at Salerno; yet we could claim a great success in holding Rome. The Allies had planned to land at Salerno simultaneously with the capture of Rome by Italian troops, thus destroying all German forces on the peninsula. Yet Rome was again in German hands thanks to a combination of threats and force and diplomatic negotiations. Its Italian commander, General Count Carlo Calvi, was the King's son-in-law. The Germans had gradually infiltrated the town until they could disarm the beleaguered Italian divisions.

The German Embassy seemed to have suffered considerably through being occupied by German troops. My friend Rohr had been an eyewitness to their precipitate departure. Ambassador von Mackensen and General von Rintelen had already been recalled because their readiness to enter into negotiations with Badoglio had brought them into disfavour, and the remainder of the embassy personnel had hurriedly caught the last diplomatic train. The embassy papers had neither been destroyed as prescribed, nor handed over to a German military command.

I was surprised to find Frau von Mackensen at Monte Soracte. She had returned from Germany on her own initiative in order to rescue her personal possessions from the embassy with the help of Kesselring, and she seemed very disillusioned. Her husband had always advocated close co-operation with Italy. I remember my discussion with him after I had expressed differing views in my report on the dependability of the alliance. He would never admit that all alliances are based on considerations of power politics, and that any foreign power will always display a measure of mistrust, even towards an ally. Moreover, he had over-rated the strength of the Fascist régime —a mistake that can easily occur in times of autocratic government where all opposition is suppressed. General von Rintelen, who never over-estimated the influence of Fascism, had favoured respecting the Italians' vanity and their desire for independence in both political and military questions. If he had not foreseen Badoglio's "treachery", this could not be held against him. So long as the Italian Marshal had not broken with Germany, we had to deal with his government in order to prosecute the war in Italy. A break with him would have worsened our position and justified his government's antagonism to us.

The Hotel Flora in Rome, where I spent the night after dining with Kesselring, had become a kind of soldiers' recreation centre. On October 12th I started the journey home, accompanied by Rohr and my batman. We felt rather like travellers on a holiday, wandering through old Viterbo buying grapes, eating in Siena in the half-round square with its picturesque town hall and slender campanile. Then we made a diversion to re-visit our old quarters in the Villa Pozzo at Pontedera, passing through the little town of Gimignano, dotted with towers and set in the midst of the rich Tuscan landscape. That evening our small car climbed towards Volterra, squarely and majestically perched on its hill. Etruscan walls, huge in height and length, formed a screen round the precincts. We approached the town from the east as the sun was setting and left it after moonrise, when its outline stood out boldly against the silvery night sky. On the 13th we reached Verona via Bologna and Modena. At Innsbruck I met my colleagues from the Turin days, Count Hans Trapp and Prince Hubert Hohenlohe. Two days later my staff reached Munich, where I reported to the deputy corps commander. As no appointment was awaiting me, I took the night train to Göttingen.

Now I bade farewell to Rohr. In 1940 he had accompanied me in the western campaign, had shared my sorrows and anxieties in Sicily and Corsica and the small joys of our journey through Italy. We kept in touch, but he died all too soon. I shall not forget him.

THE ISLANDS IN RETROSPECT—HISTORICAL BACKGROUND

Within the brief span of three months it had fallen to me to be in charge of the withdrawal from the three large islands off the Italian mainland. The task brought the dubious distinction of being the first

German commander of this war to have to abandon any of the home-land of our Italian ally or of France.

In order to understand the nature of any self-contained country one must know its history. Island peoples develop their own attributes: they are stationary, possess no neighbours and, to that extent, no frontiers. A notable example of this is to be found in the British people. Yet the Italian islands have suffered many invasions. The predominance of the Mediterranean was even more significant in ancient history and during the Middle Ages than in modern times. In those days the limits of the political world could be said to extend only to the shores of the Mediterranean. The nations struggling for domination strove above all to gain a foothold on the islands, which could easily be conquered. The great sea powers of the Middle Ages —Pisa, Venice and Padua— lay in a protected position in the northern indentations of the Mediterranean, not on the exposed islands and not on those parts of the mainland that protrude into the sea.

The most exposed and most coveted of the islands was Sicily. Being centrally situated, it was already a bone of contention in the Middle Ages between all the seafaring nations of the Mediterranean. The Phoenicians appropriated the western part, the Greeks the eastern part. Prolonged struggles ensued between Greeks and Carthaginians. Then Rome came to the fore, while Sicily became the no-man's land, perpetually contended for by Rome and Carthage, until it finally became a Roman Province, the granary of Rome and a corner-stone of her economy. Later, when her power was waning, Rome could no longer maintain control over the island, which had become so much the target of maritime expeditions that it could not have been held by any purely military means. The comparison of these historical variations with the events of 1943 is inescapable.

During the first millenium the tide of maritime enterprises flowed from east to west, and Sicily was bound to be affected by this. Like Sardinia and Corsica it had become a part of the Eastern Roman Empire. As early as the seventh century A.D. the Arabs raided the island, and it was subjected to both eastern influences, the Byzantine and the Arabian.

The start of the second millenium heralded a change in the current of Mediterranean affairs. For almost nine centuries the island of Sicily was lured away from the Italian mainland towards the West. The Norman conquest had begun in the north, passing around and through France and sweeping eastwards from the Atlantic into the Mediterranean up to the Near East. Sicily, far from being submerged, improved her status when through marriage the Hohenstaufen inherited this legacy of the Norman Kings. The brief century of the Norman domination had left its imprint on the island, as can be seen to-day in its capital, Palermo. Here is a fusion of the cultures of the Saracen, the older Byzantine and the Norman. Here one may see mosques with flat cupolas and Romanesque interiors like the churches in England or Germany. It is not without reason that the English describe the Romanesque style of architecture as "Norman". The walls of these churches scintillate with the gold of Byzantine mosaics.

Sicily sought neither annexation to the Italian mainland nor incorporation in the western Roman Church. The German Imperial Power for a time made the island the centre of the western world. The Saracens and later the Normans had extended the might of the southern kingdom northwards beyond Naples to the Garigliano, the river which thereafter for centuries formed its northern boundary under the Hohenstaufen Kings and their successors from other dynasties.

After the Sicilian Vespers and the expulsion of the French claimant to the throne, Sicily became virtually if not constitutionally a Spanish dominion, and in consequence was ruled by Spanish dynasties. The northern boundary on the Garigliano was extended westwards across the sea, terminating at the old Franco-Spanish frontier, the Pyrenees. As Sardinia lay south of this line it came within the same group of states as Sicily and the Kingdom of Naples.

It was in Sicily that dependence on Spain was most marked. For at least 150 years after the Sicilian Vespers, Naples experienced the interregnum of the House of Anjou until the middle of the fifteenth century, when the two countries were united with Aragon under the Castilian Line.

This dependence on Spain endured until 1860, which for Sicily meant 600 years. The claims of the French Crown for hegemony were finally disposed of in 1504 at the Battle of Cassino, on the northern frontier of the southern kingdom, when Spain remained dominant.

The Napoleonic Wars need not be considered here. They brought Sicily to Savoy for six years, and to Austria for fourteen. After 1820, as part of the Kingdom of the two Sicilies under a Spanish branch of the Bourbons, the island was independent, but separated from the mainland states and orientated towards the West. Nor was this spiritual attachment to the West upset by the dynasty's reactionary mismanagement or the social backwardness of the island. In 1848 British intervention fostered development on constitutional lines. The island's contribution to the unification of Italy was of a different nature to that of dynastic Piedmont. Starting in the south, Garibaldi, the liberal, anti-reactionary, anti-clerical hero of the liberation, began his victory march. It was he, more than the liberally inclined House of Savoy, who added the concept of freedom to the movement for unification—in contrast to Germany, where unification evolved within the shackles of an authoritarian dynasty.

The fortunes of Sicily as outlined here bear a resemblance to those of Sardinia, which, being more remote, was not as directly involved in the alternating current of events between East and West Carthage ruled here before Rome had become a sea power. With the Roman conquest of the western Mediterranean, Sardinia together with Corsica became Provinces of the Roman Empire. Like Sicily, Sardinia in the first millenium remained either east or west Roman. Islam barely touched the island and the Normans by-passed it, believing it not worth conquering.

At the beginning of the fourteenth century Sardinia was wrested from the Republic of Pisa to become part of the southern kingdom under the Crown of Aragon. This separation of the two islands under different sovereignties has a sound political basis. In regard to its latitude, Sardinia belongs to the south, where it remained for 400 years, sharing the fate of Sicily.

Events now took a turn that proved decisive for the present political structure. Following the War of the Spanish Succession, Sardinia was taken out of the southern kingdom, and after a brief interlude under Austrian suzerainty, was given to the House of Savoy, which thereby assumed a royal status. Having no territorial contact with Piedmont or even a Piedmontese Residency, Sardinia became the first non-Piedmontese part of Savoy and the precursor of all the other individual states that in the nineteenth century united under the Crown of Savoy to form the Kingdom of Italy. So ended Sardinia's lengthy adherence to the southern kingdom. The island assumed the character of a Piedmontese military state. With the unification of Italy this special position was lost, but the historical heritage was proudly cherished.

Corsica's history was very different. In the Punic Wars its fate was similar to that of the sister islands. But at the time of the Carolingian partitions Corsica was already regarded as part of the Italian mainland and allocated to the northern kingdom, to which it remained tied. At the end of the thirteenth century it went to Genoa, under whose sovereignty it stayed until the end of the eighteenth century. When Genoa lost its influence the island had to be sold to the protecting power, France. But that country had to assert its authority by force of arms, and in the French Revolution the island once more rebelled against its new master.

In the Second World War, Corsica with Tunis and Djibuti became one of the Italian war aims. Nice, claimed only at the time of France's greatest humiliation, was soon written off again.

POPULATION AND LANDSCAPE

The character of the islands' populations derives not only from their history, but also from the nature of the landscape. The three island have much in common. Their ethnological features are to be found inland, rather than on the coasts. The coastal population, the fishermen and seafarers, are influenced by their environment, and live in the ports where foreigners land. Foreign industries support a proportion of these people and tend to obliterate their individuality.

But the bigger towns are also located on the coast. Here live the educated people. They are more conscious of history than the peasants or the simple inland dwellers, and take an active part in current politics. This is where Napoleon grew into a man.

Sicily has a bigger population than the other islands. Although of similar size to Sardinia, it contains four times as many inhabitants, or 4,000,000 people. It does not live merely on its great past. Palermo is more modern and cleaner, for instance, than Naples, its victorious rival for the seat of the Dual Kingdom. Yet despite the modern culture in places like Palermo, Catania and Messina—the latter so often the victim of earthquakes and in the end practically destroyed by the invasion—the interior of Sicily has remained almost untouched by European civilisation. The country has lost its significance as a granary, nor does the production of sulphur play the same rôle in the island's economy as in former times. Consequently the inhabitants of the interior are extremely poor. The language too is a bastard one, or rather an Italian dialect influenced by Arabic, Greek and Spanish. The attitude of the natives towards foreigners is one of passive indifference, probably due to their long-suffering experience of invasions.

As in all these islands, Sicily has never had a fully developed constitutional status. Even to-day the population is susceptible to blood feuds, while the brigand chiefs who place themselves outside the law enjoy admiration and protection.

All the land is in the hands of feudal Latifundian owners, who lease it out on the "share cropping" system; very few of them live in the island. The Spanish influence has left the people with a strong attachment to the Catholic Church, which rejects all interference with private property—even by the State. The processions during Holy Week—even in Palermo and Trapani—are run by Brotherhoods, as in Seville. They are without spirituality, and include masquerades dating from the period of pestilence, with huge figures of the Redeemer and the Madonna, all very reminiscent of Spain.

The mountainous contours of the island add to the isolation of the inland dwellers. In the north-east, the main scene of activity during the invasion, Etna rises to a height of 3,000 metres. But this cone does not harmonise with the surrounding landscape; only when in eruption does it disturb the life of the people. A more important feature is the mountain range that runs along the entire north coast, some of whose peaks rise to 2,000 metres. The mountains sweep down into the numerous bays, forming a series of natural harbours such as Milazzo, Patti, Cefalu, Termini, Palermo and Castellamare. These offer many possibilities for military landings. Towards the south the mountains gradually disappear, leaving only a few steep precipices. It is impossible to move quickly, which explains why Patton's army took so long to advance. Only in the south is the island level enough for tanks to operate, but as the beaches are very shallow, landings can only be made at certain points along the coast. All the harbours used by the Allies for the invasion were of artificial construction, such as Sciacca, Porto Empedocle, Licata. The numerous small airstrips, mostly military, are situated along the south coast.

The south-east coast has a number of natural harbours which were used in ancient times by the shallow-draft ships of the period. Farther north there are several harbours fit for modern shipping; their economic growth was due to the development of the towns of Messina and Catania.

Lacking experience of landing operations, the Axis powers made faulty estimates of the importance of the terrain. They assumed that the enemy would choose to land mainly in the shallow bays, where he could quickly operate his light tanks. They failed to realise that to put tanks ashore it is best to choose relatively steep beaches with roads running close to them. In Sicily there are numerous places that fulfil this requirement at the eastern end of the south coast, except in the bays, and also along the north coast.

In Sardinia too the coastal dwellers differ from those who live inland. Although they are poor and their country never enjoyed the political importance of Sicily, the Sardinian sailors and fishermen have a less restricted outlook than the peasants who live in the hills of the interior.

In Sardinia the inhabitants of the interior are mainly peasants and shepherds. At the start of the Fascist period, forty per cent of those over six years of age were illiterate. Blood feuds are rooted in the families and continue from generation to generation. Though rough and unacccommodating, the islanders are hard-working and steadfast, and as with all simple people, hospitality is natural to them. As part of the old southern Spanish Kingdom, Sardinia is pledged to the Roman Church. Hunted bandits make use of certain lonely chapels where priests appear at predetermined times for confessions. Anyone who earns the confidence of a Sardinian has gained a faithful friend.

Their long attachment to Piedmont has made the Sardinians loyal monarchists. They are less susceptible than the Corsicans to liberation movements, but under certain conditions they would make useful resistance fighters. The men are cast in a small, thickset mould and are undemanding and persevering, all of which makes them particularly good soldiers; the military tradition runs in their veins.

The relatively slight cultural impact of Sardinia is illustrated by the fact that the capital, Cagliari, and the universities there and at Sassari are almost unknown to most people who have not visited the island.

Cagliari, in the bay of the same name, is the chief harbour in the south, from which traffic flows to the central Mediterranean, Sicily and North Africa. In the north the minor harbour at Porto Torres in the Gulf of Assinara serves shipping to the European mainland, mainly to Savona and Genoa.

General Basso, Italian C.-in-C. in Sardinia, considered that the island could be easily attacked, particularly in the west and the south. Yet the east coast with its deeper water and steeper beaches is possibly better suited to landings, although I do not know it well enough to form an opinion. In the south there were fifteen airstrips which between them could have provided a major air base.

Corsica is separated by a narrow strait from Sardinia, with which it has geological and ethnological affinities. The native population is no more definable racially than that of Sardinia. Yet Corsica is even more backward culturally.

The island is ruled by a moderately prosperous French upper stratum, consisting mainly of officials and people of independent means. This makes the advancement of the native inhabitants even more difficult than it already is through the isolation of the coasts. To-day it is difficult to find any native gentry like the one from which Napoleon stemmed. Despite the gloss imposed by the French, the natives have remained very wild; here too, blood feuds are common. On my very first night in the island a landowner was murdered without any political motive.

I believe that the inhabitants have become entirely apolitical due to their foreign rulers. This accounts for the fact that the numerous partisans, who were supplied with arms through air-drops, were not as active as might have been expected from their numerical strength and the contacts they had with the Allies along the open west coast. The ambush that I ran into after the Italian capitulation was laid by French gendarmes. The French were far more anti-German than the native Italians.

The social structure is affected by the small area available for agriculture. Not more than 5.5 per cent of the total land area has been made fit for cultivating corn, fruit, wine, olives and chestnuts. The rest is fields, woods and barren mountains, which certainly enhances the beauty of the countryside. Quite near the coast the mountains rise to 3,000 metres.

The harbours of Ajaccio and Bastia, though inconsiderable, fulfil their purpose as supply ports for the 350,000 inhabitants. The few airports are situated on the east coast.

In contrast to Sardinia, the west coast of Corsica is steeper than the east coast where the Germans were concentrated before the evacuation. The narrow strip of coastal land in the west was at that time so threatened with malaria that all who could afford it withdrew to to the interior for the summer.

THE OPERATIONAL SIGNIFICANCE OF THE ISLANDS

As already mentioned, we had to reckon with the strong possibility that the Allies would land in Sardinia, either directly from North Africa or after their landing in Sicily. Field-Marshal von Richthofen, C.-in-C. of the German air forces in Italy, had moved the main concentration of his A.A. defences to Sardinia because he thought this a more likely Allied objective than Sicily. This air expert therefore considered Sardinia to be not too remote from the existing base of the indispensable Allied fighters. And we know that Badoglio, greatest authority on Italian military geography, described the Allied choice of Sicily in preference to Sardinia as "a serious strategic blunder".

What made the Allies nevertheless choose Salerno for their landing? In his report to the U.S. Secretary for War (Biennial Report, July 1943 to June 1945) General Marshall maintained that the fighters operating from Sicily could only remain for fifteen minutes over the Salerno bridgehead. But this does not constitute an argument either for or against the choice of Sicily. The southern part of Sardinia lay within the radius of action of fighters coming from either North Africa or Sicily.

The attraction of Sardinia would have been enhanced for the Allies by the prospect that after the Italian capitulation they could have occupied the island without any fighting. The one-and-a-half German divisions stationed in Sardinia and Corsica could have effectively resorted to arms against the Italians, but could not have simultaneously repelled an Allied landing. From Sardinia the Allied fighter squadrons could have ranged over the whole of central Italy and from Corsica they could have covered all Tuscany and a good part of the plains of Lombardy and the Po valley.

Nevertheless the enemy had many good reasons for landing on the Italian mainland. His political and military preparations had been designed with an eye to the major propaganda effect of a successful landing on the Continent, thus precipitating the defection of Italy, which could not have been acheived by the occupation of further islands. He probably even hoped for a general collapse of the Axis, and this might well have happened if in Germany political conditions had been different.

It must also be taken into account that although Sardinia and Corsica had ample aerodromes, their harbours were hardly adequate for major landings and simultaneous preparations for an invasion of the mainland.

Probably the Allies were also afraid that a leap across from the two islands into the Leghorn district would bring them too close to the main German air bases in the plain of the Po, whose importance they were inclined to exaggerate. Had they landed here, they would have had to eliminate the naval base at La Spezia, which was still strongly protected by A.A. batteries. On the other hand the Italian Fleet could only have put to sea as a desperate last gesture, since it lacked air cover.

Yet there were further points in favour of an invasion of the mainland, and these are no less worth examining because they conformed to a strategic concept which to-day is obsolete. According to that concept the tactical air force has an important rôle in land fighting, as exemplified in General Marshall's report: "Operating from Foggia, our heavy bombers could easily strike against the passes of the Alps, and against air force installations in Austria and factories in southern Germany; they could also attack centres of industry and communications in the Balkans, thereby relieving the pressure on the Red Army". The same report describes how supplies to the heavily engaged Allied land forces had to be throttled down in the weeks following the landing in order that a major air base could be developed in the Foggia area. The area was more suited to this purpose than any other part of southern or central Italy. The Allied air forces alone were allocated 300,000 tons of shipping, 35,000 flying personnel were sent to the mainland and ten aerodromes with steel-covered runways were put into service—all within three weeks. Added to this were fuel tank storages, oil pipes to the aircraft sheds, workshops and so on. Marshall does not deny that it was a grave decision to build up this organisation at the expense of the land front, the neglect of which allowed the Germans to strengthen their defences. We know how much this strengthening was to cost the Allies.

It was not until the end of the war that I realised the extent to which the Allied leaders had counted on their air forces to produce a swift decision. I then had the opportunity to discuss the matter with the C.-in-C. of the Allied air forces. He wondered why the repeated interruption by the Allies of the German supply line over the Brenner had not forced the Germans to break off the fighting. He seemed to have been too optimistic as to the possibilities of tactical air warfare. General Sir Harold Alexander (now Earl Alexander) reported to the Combined Chiefs of Staff that as late as December, 1944, when the Allied bases had been moved considerably farther north, air reconnaissance on twenty-seven days of the month had established that the bomb damage was repeatedly made good by the German organisation.

The American General Mark Clark is another who in his book *Calculated Risk* designates as "wishful thinking" the Allied calculation that the Germans could be disposed of from the air through the permanent severance of their supply lines in the Alps and on the narrow back of the Italian mainland. What would the Allies do to-day if they found themselves in a similar position? That is the big question. Would they again land on the mainland by way of a political demonstration and in order to build up a major air base, when they could not even cut off the southern German forces located in Calabria? Would they again be willing to face a year of costly fighting with occasional fierce battles like Cassino, or again involve themselves in a laborious campaign, advancing northwards along the boot of Italy merely to be brought up at the Gothic Line? Or would they take experience in the Pacific into account and realise that against an enemy already beaten in the air and at sea, the most effective method is the combined application of air, sea and land forces?

The classic teachings of war stipulate that an enemy should be attacked at his weakest point, not his strongest. Our softest spots were Sardinia and Corsica. These were unsinkable aircraft carriers, which the Allies could have used as bases from which to provide fighter cover for an operation between Pisa and Elba. Probably it would not even have been necessary for the Allies to assemble their convoys here, since they could have started from more remote ports, and while on passage would have enjoyed far better protection than was available for any other landing operation. To realise the importance of the islands one has only to recall how the Allies used unconquered Malta throughout the war for dominating the west-east Mediterranean route. If in the autumn they had formed a bridgehead so far north on the mainland, it would have attracted, or even cut off, such considerable German forces as to greatly curtail the Italian campaign. But instead the Allies merely attempted a deception by moving the U.S. 7th Army Command (Patton) to Corsica, but without any troops. I do not know whether this deception succeeded; at all events the German Army Group did not react to it.

And so I hold the view that the Allies greatly over-emphasied the land aspect of the campaign in Italy and also over-rated the usefulness of their tactical air force.

These views are naturally speculative, since there is no evidence as to the result if other decisions had been taken. It is also questionable whether an investigation on these lines could benefit the future. It seems unlikely that Italy will ever again be fought over from north to south or vice versa.

5

THE CASSINO BATTLES

PENETRATION OF THE BERNHARD LINE

To me it came as a relief when on October 8th, 1943, I took over command of XIV Panzer Corps. After the ambiguous posts as liaison officer to the Italian C.s-in-C. in Sicily and Sardinia I now at last found myself back in a normal appointment in command of troops. In the islands I had stood alone, with no German superior officers, no proper command organisation and no definition of my authority. Yet the responsibility for the conduct of operations on the German side had been vested in me, and I bore the imposing title of a Wehrmacht Commander, implying that all branches of the armed forces came under my authority, as they should do in an island war of this kind. But even under normal Army conditions the units of the Luftwaffe and the S.S. would acknowledge the authority of the local commander only in regard to tactics, while retaining their own independent channels for all other service matters. All the less were they prepared to accept the executive authority of an Army general with an *ad hoc* appointment and with no communications link of his own.

It was reasonable to suppose that I had been given the new command because my conduct of the operations on the islands had reflected no discredit on me, and this was an encouraging thought. In my own mind I was confident of having done my best under adverse conditions, yet the character of the Supreme Command at that time was such that recognition of my services was by no means certain.

I was appreciative of the fact that my new position involved taking over by far the most important part of the Italian land-front—the western sector, extending more than half way across the peninsula. Because of its extent and the size of the forces it was the equivalent of an Army. The sector of the front covered by my corps faced the U.S. 5th Army under General Mark Clark.

The corps H.Q. staff that I found established in the main headquarters at Roccasecca was already known to me from Sicily. The Chief of Staff, Colonel von Bonin, had been Rommel's G.S.O.1

in North Africa, where he had a reputation for thoroughness. Yet I soon discovered that this corps H.Q. was still very much bound to "the party line". The C.O.S., moreover, had become strongly influenced by Rommel's personality and consequently displayed a marked antipathy towards the C.-in-C. South, Field-Marshal Kesselring. Indeed, the latter was more or less disliked by most of those fighting in Africa, and specially by Rommel's immediate entourage, which was understandable. The Wehrmacht's structure was such as to make large sections of the troops dependent on the party leaders. There was always a danger that Luftwaffe and S.S. commanders would want to further their own ambitions by making out that the situation was more favourable than the more experienced Army commanders judged it to be. In this way they acquired the reputation of loyal and enthusiastic stayers, which was easy as long as they bore no responsibilities. As I was not in North Africa I cannot judge whether Kesselring deserved this kind of reproach, but having worked with him in connection with Sicily I knew that his optimism and belief in the Führer were not motivated by ambition, but sprang from his innermost conviction.

The North African campaigners' prejudice against the Field-Marshal was strengthened by the fact that after the North African defeat Rommel ceased to believe in a German victory. Ever since the campaign in the West I regarded him as the prototype of an energetic and confident divisional commander, but I had not been able to follow his later career at all closely. Hence I cannot say whether his apostasy had an "intellectual" basis, in short, whether he had decided that the war was lost or could now only be fought as a delaying campaign. It was not surprising that he had little enthusiasm for his new task. As leader in the North African campaign he had been so much accustomed to making quick decisions on his own initiative that he was unlikely to find pleasure in the kind of static warfare in which he was now involved.

The appreciation of the situation in the Italian theatre of war was influenced by the controversy between Kesselring and Rommel. The latter thought it right to defend Italy in the Apennines on the so-called Gothic Line, whereas the former wanted to offer resistance wherever an opportunity might present itself. Although there was no definite indication of Hitler's attitude, it had somehow filtered through that he subscribed to Kesselring's concept, which came much nearer to his own outlook. If that should prove true, it would accentuate the contrast between Rommel and Hitler. But nothing was known for certain.

It was just possible that all the directives for a delaying defence were only designed to avoid a precipitate withdrawal to the Apennine mountains, which would perhaps have been undesirable; or maybe the aim was merely to gain time for building up the Apennines position. My C.O.S., being an adherent of Rommel, seemed to reckon only with this last possibility. He was already regarding all orders for a delaying defence as a dishonest betrayal of the troops, and blamed it all on Kesselring, whom he reproached for indulging in extravagant tactics designed solely to prevent his being replaced by Rommel in this theatre of war.

Army sources were equally unhelpful for gaining an insight into the intentions of the High Command. Colonel-General von Vietinghoff-Scheel, C.-in-C. of the 10th Army, was a knowledgeable commander with a General Staff background. As an old Prussian infantryman of the Guards, competent, sure of himself and adaptable, he was an excellent intermediary between the fighting troops and the High Command, not that he had any special standing with the soldiery. His C.O.S., General Wetzel, was a professional of long standing at a time when other Army Commanders already had Chiefs of Staff too young to have undergone a thorough peace-time training. The 10th Army staff was the best that I ever encountered in this war.

As for Kesselring, he possessed in General Westphal "one of the best horses in the stable". Highly intelligent, very energetic and a quick worker, Westphal never strayed from the point; his attitude towards incompetent officers could sometimes be very cool, and this did not add to his popularity. Up to this period my relations with him had been unclouded. He had always accepted me as one of the few high-ranking commanders, had personally recommended me for Sicily, and had always approved my conduct of operations.

When I took over command of the corps, the High Command's appreciation of the situation was important to me inasmuch as the intention to put up a resolute defence south of Rome called for one method of fighting, whereas a delaying resistance with a view to withdrawing to the Apennines required a different method. For the time being the German divisions fell back to the "Bernhard Line". which the Allies called the "Winter Line". Our task was to put up so tough a resistance on the Volturno that there would be time to prepare the Bernhard Line. Some sections of the troops fighting in the immediate front were already being withdrawn into this line to link up with advanced detachments that were falling back more quickly than planned, and to help in preparing the new positions. If the intention was to make a stand south of Rome, then it was certainly right to hold the Bernhard Line as long as possible, thereby gaining time for building up the Gustav Line.

It was my predecessor, General Hube, who had chosen the Bernhard Line. He evidently considered it much better than the Gustav Line, which rested on the Garigliano, the Gari and the Rapido, ran across the plain without including the great blocks of Monte Camino and Monte Samucro, that stand like watch-towers commanding the approaches to Cassino.

Yet the Bernhard Line had its weaknesses. Its southern half could be overlooked on the flank from the dominating Monte Croce, west of Roccamonfina. Here the line ran almost in an east-west direction until in the north it joined the massif of Monte Camino, which was included in the line.

Facing the centre of the Bernhard Line was the dominating Monte Cesima, situated to the east of the low-lying hill-pass between Mignano and S. Pietro. In our opinion this was where a breakthrough threatened, and we gave the place all our attention. We assumed that the enemy would attempt to capture the pass, send his tanks over it and over-run the broad valley of the Liri at Cassino and southwards, thus preparing the way for a bold operation to capture Rome. That he would attack the mountainous part of the front seemed unlikely to me as well as to the commanders of the Army Group and the 10th Army, although we had not excluded this possibility at our conferences.

Neither I nor my staff knew very much about most of the German divisions composing the corps. On the right wing was 94 Inf. Div. under General Pfeiffer, a soldierly personality who inspired confidence. This division was spread a considerable distance along the sea shore, as it also had to defend the coast as far as Terracina. This was one of the weak points of the entire defence organisation in Italy. There was always a danger of tactical landings in the rear of our positions, and to meet the danger it was decided, for want of other reserves, to fold back the right wing where it met the sea, extending it rearwards. This made the fronts too long. The wing divisions had to keep one eye on the sea, and they were right in maintaining that in the event of a major attack they would not be equal to both tasks—defence on the land front as well as against an invasion from seaward.

The 94 Inf. Div. was already in position on the Bernhard Line and had the advantage that this sector was identical with the Gustav Line, so that the division could work on its ultimate defensive position or main battle line without enemy interference. The Army Commander saw confirmation of his view that the enemy would attack at Mignano in the fact that this division remained unmolested.

On the left of 94 Inf. Div., and touching it, was 15 Pz. Gren. Div., which I had known in Sicily, and whose commander, General Rodt, was known to me from the time we served together in the Cavalry in South Germany. I appreciated his quiet and confident if somewhat dispassionate manner, and felt that I could rely on this division. The regimental commanders whom I visited on Monte Faito and on the western slope of Monte Camino confirmed this impression of reliability.

Things were rather different with 3 Pz. Gren. Div., which was stationed in the centre. Its commander, General Gräser, was a typical Prussian officer. Having been seriously wounded on several occasions, he walked with the aid of sticks, which however did not prevent him from appearing in the forward line, after getting as near it as possible in his car. This restriction on his personal mobility had not affected his bravery or his spirit. And yet he affords an example of the fact that although the personality of the leader can contribute vitally to the spirit animating a division, it cannot eliminate every deficiency. During the fighting withdrawal at Salerno this division had reported troops "missing" in numbers that bore no relation to the intensity of the fighting. It contained a considerable number of so-called *Volksdeutschen* who came from the occupied zone of Poland and were serving in the Wehrmacht on probation. Although these men could earn decorations for bravery, they could receive no advancement until their period of probation had expired. This discriminatory treatment according to "racial principles" was not calculated to enhance the morale of the troops. Moreover, these soldiers were receiving complaints from their relatives at home that they were being badly treated by the local party officials. The division had been exposed to the severest trials, and I got the impression that even the German elements among the troops had been shaken by the many reverses and uninterrupted withdrawals. There was nothing surprising in this, for even the more credulous soldiers and those loyal to Hitler must have realised that repeated failures could never result in victory.

The 305 Inf. Div., which linked up at the northern end with 3 Pz. Gren. Div., consisted of Würtemberg-Baden men, who according to First World War experience must be rated effective fighting men; indeed, they were soon to show their mettle in the critical battles that lay ahead. Their commander, General Haug, was a very conscientious and zealous officer, who took any reverses most seriously to heart. He had taken the trouble to select the right men to command his regiments and battalions—an essential condition for a good division. His division suffered, of course, from the organisational weakness of all infantry divisions—the reserves were not sufficiently mobile, the anti-tank defence was too weak, and there was a lack of experience in co-operating with armour.

The fighting that led to the penetration of the Winter Line and heralded the Cassino battles was characterised by the fact that the enemy held the initiative. When heavily attacked, the German divisions were nowhere capable of holding their so-called positions. Nor could their morale be enhanced by any successes. Initially the corps conducted a frontal defensive in the centre and on its left wing.

The attack on the left took us by surprise because we still thought the enemy's most likely tactics would be to attempt a breakthrough in the centre with his armour. Yet his attack against the left wing of 3 Pz. Gren. Div. offered him prospects because here a "balcony" protruded from the main battle line.

We knew very little about the enemy. My Intelligence Officer received continuous guidance from the 10th Army G.H.Q., who usually knew which enemy divisions stood opposite us. We had practically no reconnaissance of our own; occasionally a prisoner would be taken by chance and interrogated at Corps H.Q. before being sent on to Army H.Q.

It was essential for me to get an impression of my own troops and of the enemy during his attack on the "balcony". I therefore moved up to the front line at Pozzili. What struck me most was the futility of our own positions, which consisted of single strongpoints, all weak and unco-ordinated. Too often such positions are traps rather than useful defensive works. But at short notice it was no more possible here than in Russia to create continuous defensive positions. In Russia, the Todt Organisation and other organised bodies ruthlessly enlisted the civil population for building the defensive installations. But here in Italy the troops had to rely on their own efforts, and their numbers were of course quite insufficient to dig out positions similar to those of the First World War. Even that would have had a limited value, since the entire length of the positions could never have been manned. This inspection persuaded me that it would be a mistake to worry very much about the loss of this or that "position". The serious aspect of any such loss was the question of accommodation. I had experienced this problem in Russia, and now it cropped up again in the foothills of the Abruzzi. If in this raw climate of a rugged mountain district the troops could find no kind of accommodation, then their capacity for resistance would diminish. They would feel that conditions were much better behind the lines, and that would be disastrous.

I found difficulty in assessing the fighting value of the battalion that was engaged in this part of the line, because it was actually during my visit that its battle H.Q. was driven out of its strongpoint during some close fighting. But I noticed that the enemy was swift in attack and did not shun close-in fighting. Evidently the Americans were no longer affected by the novelty of battle. In Sicily they had hardly learned how to adapt themselves to the conditions, and their attacks still lacked spirit. Here they showed no such shortcomings. This also held good for their attacks on the centre of the front, which we still regarded as the most threatened. To begin with, a German company engaged in a forward position on Monte Cesima was thrown back. The German parachute rifle battalion that was sent into action failed to recapture the hill, which dominated the important defile north-west of Mignano. Shortly afterwards we lost Monte Rotondo, which was on the defile itself. A few days later the enemy made a successful attack astride the road between Venafro and S. Pietro, quickly reaching a point from which the whole valley could be overlooked as far as Cassino. It now seemed that we had lost our key position in the Bernhard Line. At the same time the enemy's attacks in the sector of 305 Div. were being extended north-wards, forcing the division back astride the sole mountain road from Filignano westwards to Aquafondata. Thus the division was every-where driven out of its positions in the Bernhard Line into the open mountain country.

The enemy had broken into the Bernhard Line in the centre and in the contiguous northern sector of 305 Div. Although the divisions exposed to the attack succeeded in keeping together, they could not have stood up to the enemy's pressure if the Corps Commander had not thrown in sufficient reserves. Astride the road that ran east-wards from S. Elia into the mountains I arranged for a division to be sandwiched in between 305 Div. and 3 Pz. Gren. Div. This was the famous and above-average 26 Pz. Div. (formerly the 23 Potsdamer Infantry Division), but naturally it was no more equipped for mountain warfare than the other divisions. It formed a buffer at Viticuso. I myself made certain that the somewhat shaken infantry of 3 Pz. Gren. Div. and its neighbouring division to the north were given support, particularly with artillery. The 26 Pz. Div., like all armoured divisions, was weak in infantry and could not be expected to occupy anything more than a narrow sector. Being tied to the road, there were special difficulties in its use of artillery and in getting supplies. The 26 Pz. Div. stayed for three weeks in this sector, where under its calm and confident commander, General Count v. Lüttwitz, it contributed much to the progressive consolidation of the front.

Even more important for the stabilisation was the replacement of 3 Pz. Gren. Div. by 29 Pz. Gren. Div. under General Fries. This division, which I had got to know in Sicily, had the well-merited reputation of being one of the best in the Italian theatre of war. The general always gave a sound professional appreciation of the situation; he was a stickler for truth, steady and unostentatious in the exercise of his command. Being warm-hearted towards his troops, he could demand much of them and inspired confidence everywhere.

At the end of November, after a month of fighting, the Bernhard Line had been dented in the centre and to the north of Venafro. To replace 26 Pz. Gren. Div., a new and still unknown unit was moved in. This was the "Reichsgrenadier-Division Hoch-und Deut-schmeister", the Vienna Division. The 29 Pz. Gren. Div. had held fast on the reverse slope of the Mignano defile. Opposite 15 Pz. Gren.

Div. all attacks and advances against the Monte Camino massif had failed. In the south 94 Inf. Div. had been able to continue building up its positions.

The weather now caused a reduction of fighting activity. For the second half of November, despite the loss of some important sectors, I could claim a measure of defensive success:

1. Although we had lost some commanding hill positions and the Magnano defile, the enemy's breakthrough had come to a standstill only a few kilometres behind the main battle line.
2. The two mighty pillars of Monte Samucro and Monte Camino, north and south of the Via Casilina,* which commanded the valley, had remained firmly in our hands.
3. The arrival of the two experienced divisions had strengthened the front occupied by the corps. For a time these divisions and 15 Pz. Gren. Div., which adjoined them in the south, had stood at the focal point of the attack, where they had raised the morale of the whole corps. The troops had regained confidence.

FIGHTING ON THE GUSTAV POSITION

Although the enemy had achieved penetration on the fronts of H. & D. Div. and 305 Inf. Div., we did not take this too seriously. We believed that his progress in the mountain was bound to be slow and that this front would probably have to be pulled back if the enemy were to make a vigorous attack on its centre. True the H. & D. Division was an unknown factor, and its commanding officers did not inspire confidence. It could not be compared with 29 or 15 Pz. Gren. Divs., for it had not been tested in battle and as an infantry division it possessed no armour or quick-moving reserves. There could also have been political reasons for its weakness; I was inclined to accept the latter explanation, knowing what these political handicaps were. There was all the difference between armed forces originating in a country whose people had brought Hitler to power and those coming from Austria, which had been annexed.

We wondered whether the enemy would attempt a narrow breakthrough from the positions he had won at the high passes or whether he would decide first to seize the two dominating positions on Monte Camino and Monte Samucro. On December 2nd I proceeded on a long walk to inspect the battalion stationed on Monte Samucro. While descending from the hill I found the answer to this question. What I had experienced here astounded and dismayed me. The northern slopes of the Camino massif on the opposite side of the valley were under bombardment of an intensity such as I had not witnessed since the big battles of the First World War. This bombard-

* Known as "Highway 6" in Allied reports.

ment, lasting for days and marked by repeated fierce infantry battles, led to the enemy's capture of Monte Camino. He gained ground most rapidly in the direction of Vallevona and Padre Eterno. The single battalions of the Hermann Göring Division—the only available reserves—were unable to overthrow the enemy; the most they could do was to bring his advanced spearhead to a halt in the region of Monte Maggiore. The penetration was deep enough seriously to threaten the neighbouring forces. For Monte Camino itself a weak battalion of 15 Pz. Gren. Div. was putting up a heroic fight, enduring the heaviest fire, until on December 6th it lost the summit. After some hours a report arrived from the positions on the rear slope that the defenders were still holding the summit; a runner who was sent to investigate confirmed that no living troops but only corpses were still there.

Tactically these losses were not so serious as the enemy's advance to the south of Monte Camino. If he should succeed in advancing boldly from there to the Garigliano, the southern regiment of 15 Pz. Gren. Div. would be in danger of encirclement. It could not fall back across the river, whose bridges had been destroyed by gunfire and flood water. It seemed as if the catastrophe suffered by the French troops in 1504 would be repeated. After bitter arguments with the O.K.W., permission to disengage was obtained at the last minute, but in the process the regiment lost nearly all its heavy weapons. I had the painful duty of ordering an official enquiry, as was the rule in all cases of withdrawal involving heavy loss of equipment.

During the last ten days of December we also lost Monte Samucro, which in any case was now no longer tenable, and the front was withdrawn to the so-called Poccia position. This ran in the south along the Garigliano in the Gustav Line up to the confluence of the Poccia, then along the narrow sector of this stream, thence eastwards to the massif of the low Monte Lungo, which nevertheless dominated the valley, then to S. Pietro where it joined up with the mountain positions of 29 Pz. Gren. Div., H. & D. Div. and 305 Inf. Div. Astride the Via Casilina there was further heavy fighting for Monte Lungo and S. Pietro. Prolonged resistance became more pointless in proportion as the enemy gained more ground through single attacks against the H. & D. Division in the Abruzzi mountains, which are nearly 2,000 metres high. In the middle of the month a general withdrawal to the Gustav Line was approved. In the centre 29 Pz. Gren. Div. was still fighting for every inch of ground, and this governed the rate of withdrawal of the whole corps. On Christmas Day, returning from a visit to the front, I attended Mass in the crypt of the Abbey of Monte Cassino. I was the only soldier who had entered the abbey since the start of the major battles in this region. Soldiers were not allowed to visit the place, and a sentry placed at its entrance ensured that the rule was strictly observed. I, too, had avoided being seen from the abbey itself, so as not to infringe the agreement. I made this visit only in order to ascertain from the monks themselves whether the neutrality was being strictly maintained. While driving towards the abbey on the double bends of the ascending road I noticed how the entire width of the Cassino valley was filled with uninterrupted harassing fire. This continued day and night with very heavy expenditure of ammunition. In contrast to the wide-ranging mobile battles in Russia, the conflict here resembled the static fighting of the First World War.

During the first half of January 1944 I re-grouped the corps in the course of the disengaging movements, while it was being heavily attacked. I arranged for the H. & D. Division to fall back more quickly to the Gustav Line so that it would have more time to settle down. The 29 Pz. Gren. Div., which was fighting on the same sector, would be pulled back from the front later and by stages. From it I wanted to create the essential reserves for the main battle on the Gustav Line itself and hence for the Liri valley that led to Rome.

Thus for a limited period the defence in this region was conducted with two successive lines. But after its protracted fighting, 29 Pz. Gren. Div. was now really overdue for relief and rest. True that there was a risk in handing the sector over to H. & D. Division. At a discussion in the battle H.Q. of 29 Pz. Gren. Div. at Piedimonte between Kesselring, myself and General Fries, it was left to the latter to decide how much longer he would continue to fight in the immediate front of H. & D. Division.

But now a crisis developed on the left wing of the corps. It was here that in the last ten days of December 305 Inf. Div. had been gradually—but as it proved, too quickly—relieved by 5 Mountain Division. We were all agreed that this terrain was more suited to mountain troops than any other parts of this theatre of war. But the exchange of mountain for infantry divisions that suggested itself was out of the question because transportation between Italy and Russia was too costly, too lengthy and exposed to air attacks. There were only two railway lines to Germany across the Alps; these were so dominated by the enemy from the air that our own aircraft could do little to protect them, and only the A.A. defences could provide a measure of defence. By hearsay the transfer of 5 Mountain Div. to Italy could be ascribed to the personal relationship between its commander and Hitler. The division had certainly imagined this theatre of war to be different from the reality. To begin with there were none of the joys of the "sunny south". Germans were apt to visualise this part of the world in terms of the tourist attractions;

these did not include the high mountain regions of the Abruzzi where the winter is severe and where the snowstorms could be so dangerous that the troops had sometimes to descend from a crest *towards* the enemy in order to survive. The 5 Mountain Div. also suffered serious setbacks due to its battalions being sent into action immediately after detraining, and frequently without their essential pack-animal units. Here and also later on we found that divisions arriving from other theatres of war were not immediately equal to the double burden of icy mountain terrain and massed bombardment of a kind that is usually associated with major battles. Although the temperature did not fall as low as in Russia, there was the discomfort of alternating rain, snow, frost and storm.

The senior commanders were busy almost every day discussing what tactics would be most effective. If we pulled back the front, we would lose valuable time for building up the Gustav position. If we held on too long, there was a danger of the troops being thrown back to that position and even beyond it; in the process they would suffer such casualties on the immediate front that on reaching the main battle line they would be too weak to defend it effectively.

In the centre of the corps front there were two successive battle lines; not so on the left wing, where the divisions were new and largely untried. Here I wanted to break off the fighting on the immediate front in sufficient time to enable them to occupy the Gustav Line in good order. I accepted the disadvantage that the Gustav positions had not yet been fully built up; it was better to run that risk than to fall back precipitately under heavy enemy pressure. The enemy was here attacking in the direction of the low-lying Atina basin. This basin, completely surrounded by hills, had no direct operational outlet towards Rome; because of this, no rearward fixed positions had been constructed. If the enemy should effect a breakthrough in this place, he would be able to unhinge the Gustav position that had taken so much effort to build up, and even the "Führer-Barrier" position that had been erected behind it in the southern sector. I was therefore particularly anxious about this sector, not only on account of the tactical implications and the inexperience of 5 Mountain Div., but also because of the nature of their opponents—Moroccan and Algerian troops under General Juin. These were native mountain people, led by superbly trained French staff officers, equipped with modern American weapons and accoutrements. This formidable opponent naturally aggravated the already critical situation of 5 Mountain Division.

Nevertheless we managed to hold down the enemy in front of the main battle line sufficiently long to enable the division to build up the Gustav Line to some extent, a task that it was well equipped to do. The position could be occupied in good order, and here the enemy's attack was brought to a standstill. But I must confess that there were moments when the whole thing seemed to hang by a thread.

This was hardly encouraging. The decisive battle for the Gustav Line was still to come, and except for the 15 Pz. Gren. Div. which was in need of rest, I had no divisions available with battle experience in this theatre of war. The 94 Inf. Div. had its hands full with coastal defence. In the event of a battle its centre would have to fight with its back to the wall. Although this gave the division an incentive, the lack of depth would make it impossible to keep it supplied during the battle, and it ran the risk of being split in two. In the centre and on the left were the H. & D. Div. and the 5 Mountain Div., neither of which had yet shown themselves to be outstanding in battle.

Added to this, the operational effectiveness of the Gustav position was altogether conjectural. Moreover, in the given organisation of the divisions it was questionable how much importance should be attached to defensive positions that were too often assessed by senior officers on the basis of recollections of the First World War.

The First Battle of Cassino

The big attack on the Gustav line (map 10) started on January 18th, According to the Allied plan this was to mark the end of the slow and laborious advance since crossing the Volturno. Once they had reached the Liri valley they could use their armour, and the gateway to Rome would be wide open.

The large-scale attack, employing material resources of unknown extent, resolved itself into three phases of separate thrusts against XIV Panzer Corps along its whole front, and an outflanking operation from seaward. It now transpires from American sources, especially from Mark Clark's *Calculated Risk*, that the attack already mentioned on 5 Mountain Div. was actually the first part of an overall Allied plan to outflank Cassino in the north. But we still counted this attack as one of the battles on the immediate front, because it had come to a halt before reaching the main battle line.

Yet the attacks were all parts of one plan. The thrust by the British X Corps against 94 Inf. Div. had special significance, for if it had led to a breakthrough, the entire German front would have been rolled up from the south. Compared with this, the subsequent attacks in the centre by the U.S. 36 Div. against 15 Pz Gren. Div., and north of this, the attack by the U.S. 34 Div. and the French Corps against the H. & D. Div. would have been of secondary importance. As so often happened, the attack on 94 Inf. Div. came as a surprise. The enemy over-ran the battle outposts through a tactical landing in the rear. Thereupon his first onslaught captured the division's lengthy fortified position on the slope and over-ran it, as had been done before in the

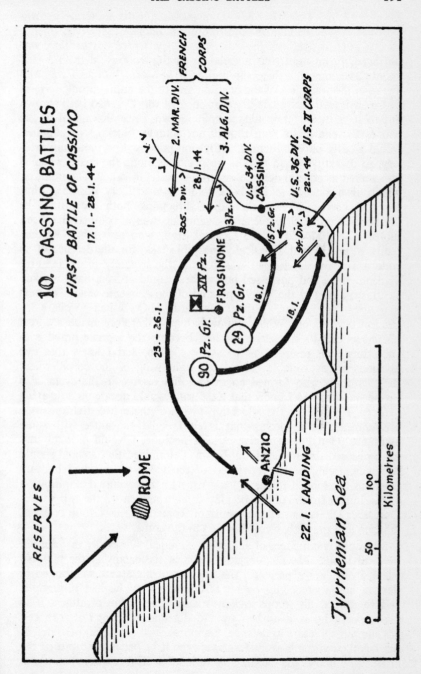

10. CASSINO BATTLES
FIRST BATTLE OF CASSINO
17.1. - 28.1.44

Bernhard Line. Thereafter he took possession of the moderately elevated terrain lying behind this position in the floor of the valley, whence
he was able to overlook the Aussente valley, where our artillery was
stationed. From numerous inspections of the troops and from a visit
as late as January 17th to the region of S. Maria Infante I was well
aware of the weakness of the position and of the unfavourable terrain.
I also envisaged the possibility that once 94 Inf. Div. had been thrown
out of its position, it would be split in two, since the massif of the
Monte Patrella in its rear, though not actually blocking its supplies,
would greatly impede them. The division possessed no mountain artillery, so its artillery had to take up positions along the coast, where it
also served as coastal defence, or in the Aussente valley. The infantry,
which always tends to fall back to its own artillery positions, thus
had the choice of two alternative directions, both eccentric. The
divisional commander, General Steinmetz, was a competent officer,
thoroughly grounded in the General Staff, who saw things as they
really were. He had a basically insoluble task, for the defence of so
wide a sea and land front was beyond the capacity of an infantry
division. If he had possessed tanks, these could at least have blocked
the narrow part of the Via Appia and of the Aussente valley. Visiting
him again on January 18th at his battle H.Q., I had to share his
pessimistic outlook. While still with him I therefore made a direct
telephone call to Kesselring. It had become the regular practice to
subordinate all reserves to the Army Group, and I knew that two
divisions were available behind the right wing of the corps, where
they naturally also formed an operational reserve in the event of a
further landing. As I knew that Kesselring would decide on a delaying
defence, I asked for the allocation to me of these two divisions as a
pre-requisite for a success that I felt I could guarantee with some
assurance. Had I been in Kesselring's position, I would probably not
have released the divisions, but he was determined that a stand should
be made. Being firmly convinced of the value of so-called built-up
positions, he looked to the Gustav Line for the eventual stabilisation
of the Italian front. And so he played his trump card: the two Panzer
Grenadier Divisions stationed south of Rome as Army Group reserves,
the 29th and the 90th, were allocated to the corps.

I was pretty confident of achieving a tactical success by throwing in
these divisions. The counter-attack struck the enemy at the moment
when, from long experience, the impetus of his attack was bound to
slacken and there could be no resumption until he had re-grouped
and reinforced his troops and drawn up a new plan of attack. If in
this process he is disturbed by the defender's counter-attacks and
has himself to resort to defence, his morale will suffer, and the defender has then virtually won the game, even if he has not recaptured the
main battle line as the German operational doctrine expects him to do.

The 29 Pz. Gren. Div. was sent into action through Ausonia and Correno Ausonia in the direction of Castelforte, since I was particularly apprehensive of any further advance here by the British 46 Division. As I discovered for myself on the spot, the enemy threatened to outflank the left wing of 94 Inf. Div., thereby separating it from the adjoining 15 Pz. Gren. Div. and blocking the Aussente defile at Ausonia.

The 90 Pz. Gren. Div., arriving later, was sent astride the Via Appia to lend support to 94 Inf. Div. For a time this produced a confused situation as to who was in charge, but this difficulty was overcome. The division arrived by battalions and could not be used in the counter-attack. Meanwhile the situation had changed.

When the fighting temporarily ceased, 94 Inf. Div. had lost the greater part of the positions which it had taken months to construct. It had been forced into the open terrain behind the former main battle line. The mountains here, especially on the left wing, were so chalky that the infantry could not dig itself in as it had been taught to do. Indeed, the positions had to be fortified for mountain warfare, as in the Abruzzi. But constructions in the manner of the old main battle line were out of the question.

The attack against the front of 15 Pz. Gren. Div. between January 20th and 22nd proceeded in a completely different manner to that on 94 Inf. Div. The 15 Pz. Gren. Div. lay on the plain behind the Gari river, in a terrain that was more familiar to the German soldier, and it put up a completely successful defence. The enemy crossed the river during the night and under cover of the morning mist. The main battle line did not follow the river-line, but was laid out behind it in zig-zag fashion, with the result that those enemy units that had crossed the river came under ambushing fire and immediately suffered heavy losses. Despite this setback the enemy repeated the hopeless attempt on the following day. According to reports from the division, he lost 400 dead and 500 prisoners.

At that time neither 15 Pz. Div. nor the corps fully realised the extent of the enemy's failure; it was not until the U.S. Congressional Enquiry into the costly attack by the U.S. 36 Div. that the facts came to light. The German Command paid little attention to this offensive for the simple reason that it caused no particular anxiety. The repulse of the attack did not even call for reserves of 15 Pz. Gren. Div., still less the reserves from other parts of the front, and it proved unnecessary to postpone the relief of 19 Pz. Gren. Div., which duly took place after the battle. I am unable to say whether the higher Allied commanders had ordered the plan of attack in such detail as to leave their local commanders no scope for initiative.

On January 22nd the enemy landed at Nettuno (the Anzio bridgehead). The 29 Pz. Gren. Div. had to be rapidly taken out of line in order to take part in the Nettuno fighting. The 90 Pz. Gren. Div. became the new Army Group reserve behind the Cassino front, but was still under my orders. In view of the Nettuno landings, Kesselring may later have considered it a mistake to allow the two divisions to reinforce the front of 94 Inf. Div. Yet one may also regard this assignment of the reserves as a fortunate example of dual employment. Their absence from the scene of the landing had no adverse consequences, for while the actual landing could not be prevented, the enemy was robbed of success since he was unable to issue from the bridgehead into the interior. The 29 Pz. Gren. Div. thus joined the 14th Army, assembled at Nettuno, in sufficient time to prevent a breakthrough, but not soon enough to throw the enemy back into the sea. This division's task with XIV Panzer Corps had been accomplished to the extent that the offensive by the British X Corps failed. It is true that the division's withdrawal from the front caused some friction, for the Army Group, for whom things could not go quickly enough, was most insistent. Yet the division was able to claim several successes in rapid succession when used as an operational reserve.

After the Nettuno landing I could no longer rely on being supplied with Army Group reserves to the same extent as before. In all responsible quarters this situation naturally provoked the question whether the Cassino front could really be held in the event of a major attack, or whether it would be better to withdraw the front so far that it would run behind the Anzio bridgehead, thus allowing the two German armies to unite and economise their forces. Kesselring, who now visited my battle H.Q. as he had frequently done in the past, emphasised that he was against withdrawing the front, "because the present line is shorter and therefore more economical, than a line running directly in front of the gates of Rome straight across Italy". Yet the Field-Marshal's appreciation of the situation pre-supposed that a big attack on the Nettuno bridgehead would clear it of the enemy—an assumption in keeping with his known optimism. An offensive plan of this nature against the bridgehead meant that we would have to give up the idea of operational reserves for use in northern Italy in the event of further landings, and XIV Panzer Corps would have to rely mainly on its own resources for the defence of its own front. I had to create reserves without denuding those sectors of the front that were under attack.

On January 25th, shortly after the second attack on the front of the corps, there was a third attack. This time the enemy attacked to the north of Cassino, and as the town was directly threatened, the troops designated the operation "the first battle of Cassino". In tough fighting that lasted nearly a month the U.S. 34 Div. achieved a deep penetration to the north of Cassino, and in association with this the French Corps attacked from the region of the Secco and Rapido rivers up the mountains towards Terelle. Their colonial troops lived up to their reputation by fighting most stubbornly without regard to losses. The H. & D. Div. was in a difficult position. As with most of the German divisions at this time, its battalion commanders were young men who led their forces, amounting to no more than 100 men, in the forward front line as if they were mixed assault companies. The garrison of Cassino itself and the battalions to the north of the town would have been overrun if I had not been able to throw in a completely fresh regiment of the newly arrived 71 Inf. Div., which was due to relieve 15 Pz. Gren. Div. Fortunately the regiment held its position.

In the Belmonte valley, which was the first under attack, I likewise attempted to launch a counter-attack with parts of 71 Inf. Div., but this resulted only in sealing off the area without gaining any ground. When in the course of its attack I visited the regiment in the Belmonte valley, I was struck by the inadequacy of our infantry in comparison with the French colonial troops. The regimental battle H.Q. was located in a rock-cave. In the intense bombardment, whose rumbling was greatly magnified by the narrow mountain valley, it was almost impossible to make oneself understood. These lowland troops, unaccustomed to the hills and unsuitably clad in overcoats, were expected to attack up the steep mountain slopes, passing through a barrage fire that was intensified by the rock splinters.

During the first week the front to the north of Cassino became deeply indented through the continuous attacks, and finally the enemy captured the hills to the north-west of the place. This enabled him to overlook the Via Casilina, the only road communication with Cassino. He threatened the village of Terelle, from which place he could pass north of Monte Cairo and within one hour's marching time reach Roccasecca, where my corps H.Q. was located.

The H. & D. Division was no longer able to defend the position. I therefore threw in 90 Pz. Gren. Div. which I had again taken out of the southern front, and gave command of the division to General Baade, who was well known to me. It was risky to withdraw the division from the southern front, where the enemy's continued attacks were gaining him ground to an alarming extent. But his activities to the north of Cassino had gone on long enough to indicate that this was now his point of main effort. I did precisely the same, accepting the risk of committing my main reserves, the 90 Pz. Gren. Div.

From the still intact forward line of 5 Mountain Div. on Monte Cifalco, I could look from the northern slope towards the Belmonte valley, get a view of the arc of the enemy's penetration and watch his infantry from their rear as they attacked in the direction of my H.Q. at Roccasecca. I also saw the enemy's movements in the area of S. Elia, in places only two kilometres away and below me. As this was the front and an excellent vantage point for observation, I concentrated all the artillery there that was covering the arc of penetration as far as Cassino. The eventual defensive success can be ascribed among other factors to this operational use of the artillery.

Meanwhile the divisions engaged in the main battle area were losing fighting strength at a daily rate of one or two battalions, and it would be only a matter of time before they were annihilated. As the individual battalions were weak, the divisions' figures of losses remained small in relation to its total victualling strength. Thus, a single division which within one week has lost the infantry strength of six weak battalions can be considered as used up, although its victualling strength has only dropped from 12,000 to 11,000 men. The attempts that were made by some command centres to maintain the infantry strength of a division by filling up from other parts of the division invariably failed. A modern division is too complicated to undergo organisational changes on the battlefield. The so-called "emergency units" that were formed at short notice from the artillery, from other battle groups or from supply and communications units were unaccustomed to infantry fighting and were usually "eaten up" much sooner than the regular infantry.

Consequently at the moment when the enemy's penetration had given him an unimpeded view of the Via Casilina, I mustered all the weight of my authority to request that the battle at Cassino should be broken off, and that we should occupy a quite new line—the so-called C Line, situated much farther back and behind the Nettuno bridgehead—instead of exposing the mass of the German forces in Italy to inevitable defeat south of the bridgehead. My request was not approved. However, the fortune of war now turned in our favour to the extent that the enemy too was declining in strength. He, too, seemed to have no further reserves.

When I look at the Allied plan for a breakthrough from the point of view of the defender who was not overthrown, I cannot refrain from criticism. According to the original plan, which was tactically well thought out, there was to be an attack against the right wing of my corps, followed by a number of blows against the Cassino front. But after the first attack had failed, the original plan was followed too rigidly. This gave me the chance to draw reserves from the sectors where the attacks had failed, to constantly change the operational boundaries of the divisions, and to parry the blows one by one.

Nor did I understand why the enemy attempted to break through at so many points of the front. It seemed to me that in so doing he was dissipating his forces. The British X Corps attacked the German right wing with three divisions side by side, and had no reserves with which to feed the attack. Linking up with this operation both in time and in area came the attack by the U.S. II Corps. First the U.S. 36 Div. attacked alone to the south of Cassino, then the U.S. 34 Div. to the north of the town, and here there was a simultaneous and continuous attack by the French Expeditionary Corps under General Juin.

After the war I had the opportunity of meeting the erstwhile commander of the British X Corps, General McCreery, in England, as well as General Keyes, former commander of the U.S. II Corps, in Washington. Through my discussions with them I obtained a more precise picture of the planning of those days, but I still have cause to be critical of it.

After the British X Corps' attack had been brought to a standstill, there was no point in the Allies continuing with their original concept of rolling up the German front from the south by means of a thrust into the Liri valley. The subsequent attacks by the other Allied corps in the centre and in the north had now lost their original purpose and achieved only tactical results.

One must in truth concede to the commander of the U.S. 5th Army that it was the attack by the British X Corps that made it possible to land at Anzio. The British Corps had drawn our reserves from their dispositions in depth towards itself, so that when the landing occurred we lacked the forces that should have attacked in the first phase and might even have annihilated the landing force. In later Allied operations this bridgehead provided a springboard for a second attack at the time of the breakthrough in May 1944 when the bridgehead was still in the rear of our main front.

Yet even on the Allied side the first battle of Cassino was marked by excessive casualties. But the Allies drew the right conclusions from their setbacks. In May they formed a centre of pressure *south* of Cassino by launching a simultaneous offensive by three Army Corps, leaving the northern front unmolested and under the threat of being outflanked.

In the first Cassino battle the centre of pressure had lain *north* of the town. After the New Zealand Corps had been brought up, this area contained six of the nine Divisions that the U.S. 5th Army launched into the attack. According to the German operational doctrine at least three of these six divisions should have stood behind the Allied right wing, ready to force a breakthrough into the mountains. Even in the fighting at the Gustav position I feared a possible thrust by the French Corps into the Atina basin. This anxiety recurred during the first Cassino battle. But even if the Allied commander did not wish to run the risks of mountain warfare to achieve so ambitious an objective, the six divisions could have been sent into action at the centre of pressure, which was also the weakest German position on the front, and could have forced their way downwards either from Terelle to

Roccasecca or from south of Terelle towards Piedimonte. For the attacker differs from the defender in that he is able to thin out or even entirely denude those parts of the line that lie outside the zone of the offensive operations.

CHANGE OF SURROUNDINGS

After the first battle of Cassino I reflected on the part I had played in this event. In modern war a commander in the field, with his complete system of communications, is so much the executive agent for directives already received that he cannot claim the mantle of fame. For my corps the battlefield ranged from the Tyrrhenian Sea to the hills of the Abruzzi. The entire mainland front was shared by two Army Corps, of which mine was the right hand one. I knew this whole field of battle better than anyone else, for even the divisional commanders could overlook only a limited sector of the front, and then only while the division was in its front line positions. I, on the other hand, had ranged over the entire sector of my corps, seeing all the focal points on the 80 kilometre-long front, as far forward as the battalion battle H.Q.s. I had climbed every single hill that offered a long view, and this gave me a complete picture of the fissured mountain terrain. I could thus appreciate fluctuations in the situation from changes in artillery fire and air activity.

For three months I was accommodated in a decrepit old *Palazzo* at Roccasecca. As usual I had made my room as homely as possible with some fine old pictures and cretonne-covered furniture. An adjoining house contained a library that was not very extensive but included books in every language,which is unusual in Italy. I found the reason when on one of my occasional walks I encountered an old lady. Her dessicated face, her solid shoes and walking-stick proclaimed her to be of Anglo-Saxon stock. American by birth, she had been educated in Germany and France·and had married an Italian. When visiting the front I enjoyed climbing the hills; this gave me the necessary exercise and benefited me physically. I loved spending whole days in the open with the wind whistling in my ears, when I could see something of the fighting and look my men in the face. In the evening I would relax for an hour over a good book or radio concert. Having to stay up late into the night during the big battle, we often sat with a bottle of wine by the fireplace in the large cosy hall, which at other times served as a reception-room or cinema or dining hall for big functions.

The town of Gaeta was nothing but a·heap of rubble. But the drives to the coastal fortifications were a pleasant relief, for here was no fighting and the roads, relatively unmolested by enemy fighters, led to the sea, to the oranges and lemons.

Minturno was a frequent centre of attacks. It was always oppressive to pass the Ausonia defile, for operationally it was a source of anxiety. Farther back lay Esperia, which during the winter still accommodated a divisional staff, but by May had become the centre of bitter fighting. Towards the north the scenery changed as one approached the famous Liri valley. The precincts of Pontecorvo were under almost continuous fire. I cannot recall a single drive to this place when I was not aware of smouldering shell craters all around me. Aquino, the birthplace of St. Thomas Aquinas, was soon in ruins. The castle where he was born lay outside the town and close above my corps battle H.Q.

During the winter until January Cassino could be negotiated without difficulty. I had to drive through the town on my visits of inspection to the concentration of divisions at Mignano, and to all the intermediate country of the Bernhard Line.

One of the most unpleasant passes was on the road from Elia to Aqua Fondata. It may be a coincidence that I never drove along it without running into heavy artillery fire at the latter place. On returning from these journeys my Chief of Staff used to make a reproachful inspection of the little Volkswagen, usually spattered with shell-splinters.

By passing through the Atina basin I reached the more northerly battle area. I liked to come to this place. The basin lies like a circular plate in the middle of the Abruzzi, and in the spring these high hills still sparkled in the snow.

The front occupied by my corps was a truly historic line. It corresponded to the northern boundary of the Saracen and the Norman kingdoms. It was precisely on this line that in 1504 the Spaniards defending southern Italy had stood facing the French, whose strategic objective was the same as now, but in reverse: breakthrough at Cassino in the direction from Rome to Naples. The battle had likewise started north of Cassino. In those days the French had vainly besieged Roccasecca, where my staff quarters were now situated. They then failed to break through on the lower Garigliano. The pages turn. . . . The Spaniards crossed the Garigliano at Suio, at exactly the same place where the Allies broke through in May 1944. The Spaniards, who until then had been on the defensive, now completely defeated the French, driving them into Gaeta. The floods prevented the French from bringing back their heavy gun. They tried to save it by sending it down the Garigliano on rafts, but it was lost in the open sea. After the French defeat the Spaniards remained undisputed masters of southern Italy.

During the first battle of Cassino I found it necessary to move my battle H.Q. from Roccasecca. At Castell Massimo we were in a more secluded and quiet position, but the drives became longer, and instead of reaching a regiment or a battalion in an afternoon, it now took the whole day to visit it. Castel Massimo too was rich in history. In earlier wars it had been the headquarters of Murat and of Garibaldi. I deliberately chose to move to this place immediately after one successful battle, thus obviating the risk, in the event of a setback at the front, of having to be the first to withdraw—a situation that can be harmful to the morale of the troops. For me the position was materially improved by a change of Chief of Staff. My new C.O.S., Colonel Schmidt von Altenstadt, also saw eye to eye with me on political questions. After the move the two of us formed a smaller household away from the big officers' mess, and this we shared with the G.S.O.1., the adjutant and one of my assistant adjutants. Being thus among ourselves, we could talk openly, which had never been possible in the past. My C.O.S. was a friend of Count Stauffenberg, having got to know him while they were working together in Berlin. He told me of their combined efforts to persuade the individual C.-in-C.'s of Army Groups to opt for the overthrow of Hitler. My G.S.O.1 was a son of General Oster, whom we knew to be at the head of the resistance movement and who had many irons in the fire. These young officers were not afraid to criticise Hitler and National Socialism, and consequently a more trustful relationship developed between us than with the previous staff. In the operational control of the corps there was also less friction. We always managed to agree quickly on the current situation and on the decisions that had to be made. Those generals and officers of the General Staff who were followers of Hitler took the setbacks in a very personal way. In their blind optimism they readily ascribed failures to this or that third party, who in their opinion was prejudicing the leadership of Hitler, the man of genius. We, on the other hand, saw clearly that from every point of view the war was lost, that wars cannot be decided with uncompleted secret weapons, that it was immaterial whether the fight was continued on this or that battle line, and that it was now only a question of ending hostilities and getting rid of the régime. True that at this period opinion varied among us as to how this was to be achieved—not that we became heated in our discussions. My younger friends were more confident of results than I, who was very doubtful of the chances of forcibly overthrowing Hitler and ending the war. Opposition to the prevailing instruments of state authority was too weak, and there were too few opportunities for co-ordinating the individual currents of resistance. The overthrow could not be prepared in detail if so few people were in the know, but if the number were increased, the essential secrecy of the plot would be compromised. Moreover, it had to be admitted that the mass of the people, and even the generals, property owners, industrialists and the universities were in favour of Hitler. My young friends failed to realise something of which I myself was convinced, namely that the Russians, having at this stage made immeasurably greater contributions to the defeat of Hitler, would claim the lion's share of the spoils by occupying the country and establishing spheres of influence.

I felt it as a personal tragedy that the defensive success of my own Army Corps at Cassino would reduce the Allies' chances of asserting themselves at least as much as the Russians. I felt that the Allies must at all costs establish a second front by a landing in Europe. That alone would prove that the collapse of Germany and the Russian invasion were imminent.

Sometimes my friends would discuss the oppression of the Jews. Although we had no precise information, it was common talk that evil things were afoot. We felt ashamed at these developments, at this discrimination against a small but intellectually gifted minority of the population. This in itself was sufficient to brand the responsible authorities as sadists and perverts.

To me the anti-Semitism displayed by a high proportion of the population, which had degenerated into murder, seemed particularly outrageous. I recalled the saying of an old Jewish friend, that it was "a higher form of patriotism to feel ashamed of one's people if there were cause to do so". Here there was every cause for shame, what with the incitement against a so-called racial minority, the false and unsubstantiated accusations, the defilement of a moral code to which all were entitled to look for protection. There was a lack of compassion for women and children, and this perverse streak was even eulogised as "strength" by those whose moral values had become completely distorted. How could those who laid violent hands on defenceless people claim to be advocates of a fighting or soldierly ethos?

After the situation conferences the C.-in-C. of the 10th Army, Colonel-General von Vietinghoff, was a frequent guest at my battle H.Q. I found him and his C.O.S., General Wenzel, to be in harmony not only with my views, but also with those of my operational staff. All of us had a similar attitude towards the political leaders and consequently towards the problems of high command.

Destruction of the Abbey of Monte Cassino

On February 15th, 1944, at the end of what we called the first battle of Cassino, the abbey was destroyed from the air. We could not see any military reason for choosing this moment for its destruction, for although a few single attacks were to follow, the main battle had already petered out.

Before I took over the command, XIV Panzer Corps under my predecessor had already developed friendly relations with the monastery in the summer of 1943, as it was then stationed at Cassino before being moved to Sicily. On my return journey from Sicily I had paid a visit in the monastery to the abbott and Bishop of the Cassino Diocese. I had again been up there for Christmas Mass in 1943, in order to confirm that no German soldiers were visiting the place once the fighting had broken out in the general area. Kesselring had always tried to find ways and means of protecting valuable works of art and places of worship from the ravages of war, and had accordingly issued the order to "neutralise' the monastery. Now he also looked to me to ensure that if I were forced to retreat, no harm should befall the ancient bishoprics at Veroli, Alatri and Anagni.

I was only too pleased to agree that the principal abbey should be spared from military operations. Nobody would want to sponsor the destruction of a cultural monument of this kind merely to gain a tactical advantage. But even under normal conditions Monte Cassino would never have been occupied by artillery spotters. True, it commanded a view of the entire district, the town and the Via Casilina. But on our side it was the considered tactical opinion that so conspicuous a landmark would be quite unsuitable as an observation post, since we could expect it to be put out of action by heavy fire very soon after the big battle had started. It was the German practice to place the artillery observers half way up the hills in a concealed position with a camouflaged background.

I did not know whether any proper agreement had been drawn up with the enemy over the neutralisation of the abbey, but I doubted it. I assume that it was a unilateral German decision. But in my opinion the Allies must have known, especially through the Vatican, that for months the Germans had been sparing and neutralising Monte Cassino. Evidently the abbey assumed that such an agreement existed between the Germans and the Allies, and relying on this, had given shelter to many homeless persons including some from the town of Cassino. Thus there were several hundred refugees who had come from the neighbourhood to join the monks in the abbey.

Some months earlier the treasures of the monastery had been removed to a place of safety. On assuming command of the corps I discovered that this operation had been assigned to the Hermann Göring Division, and that the precious convoy was on its way north from Rome. Making enquiries, I was informed that the convoy had been halted near Spoleto and ordered to proceed to the Vatican. After all the details that have since been made public, it can at least be said that Colonel Schlegel, who was in charge of the salvage operation, acted in good faith.

The bombing had the opposite effect to what was intended. Now we would occupy the abbey without scruple, especially as ruins are better for defence than intact buildings. In time of war one must be prepared to demolish buildings which are required for defence.

Now the Germans had a mighty, commanding strongpoint, which paid for itself in all the subsequent fighting.

When the abbey was destroyed, the eighty-two-year-old abbot formed a procession with his monks and with those refugees who could manage it, and carrying a crucifix, led it through the zone of barrage fire. The direct descent to the Via Casilina was too much under fire to be used, and so the procession marched over the hill until it reached the vicinity of Piedimonte, whence it descended into the valley. Down there I arranged for the abbot and his companion to be picked up by a car and brought to my H.Q. at Castel Massimo, where he spent the night. I received a directive from the O.K.W. that I was to arrange for him to be interviewed by a radio reporter about the behaviour of the German troops. I was reluctant to do this, as it seemed an abuse of hospitality. Yet I realised that the German political leaders could not afford to miss this ready-made opportunity for a piece of propaganda, since the destruction of the abbey was bound to arouse world-wide discussion. I therefore asked the abbot if he would receive the reporter, and he agreed to do so. Unfortunately my intention to shield the old dignitary from further importunities came to nothing. I wanted to move him from my H.Q. to the central Benedictine monastery at S. Anselmo on the Aventine. I knew this monastery, and the abbot himself wished to be there. The Chief Benedictine Abbot, Baron Stotzingen, came from the same Baden district of Lake Constance as myself. His family still owned property there, whereas mine had been landowners a hundred years ago. I had got to know other members of his family before I met this well-known member of a religious order, and we had many acquaintances in common.

In S. Anselmo, Abbot Diamare would have been safe. But the attempt failed when the small car, which on my orders was escorted by a competent orderly officer, was intercepted outside the gates of Rome. The weary old man was immediately dragged off to a big transmitting station, where he was not even given a meal. Here he had to give an account of the difference in the behaviour of the Germans and the Allies, an account that although specially written was essentially true. Disillusioned at being made the unwitting tool of others, he was not even allowed to go to his monastery late that evening. Foreign Minister von Ribbentrop could not allow Dr. Goebbels, who had arranged the interrogation of the abbot, to rest on his laurels. Tired, hungry and dejected, the abbot was dragged to the German Embassy at the Vatican, where he was asked to sign a memorandum that bristled with propaganda against the Allies. But once again Ribbentrop had miscalculated and had merely shown how little he knew of another Power—in this case the Catholic Church. Naturally the abbot refused to put his name to such a document. He collapsed and asked to be released from his captivity. All those who knew the circumstances realised that the abbot would always honour the truth and would exonerate the Wehrmacht from all blame for the destruction of Monte Cassino, but also that his testimony did not imply his becoming a protagonist of the Axis. Even if he had been friendly to the Axis, he would never have taken the side of Germany in the face of the wrongs that Hitler's government had inflicted on the Catholic Church, bearing in mind that the great majority of the Benedictine Conventions were either neutral or favoured the other side. The abbot disassociated himself from the blunders of this propaganda; that which could have been achieved with a little tact thus came to nothing.

Late that evening my orderly officer returned, disappointed and shaken by his failure and by his experiences. When I sent a protest to the C.-in-C. of the Army Group on the treatment of my honoured guest, Kesselring assured me that he had nothing to do with this *gaucherie.*

Ever since the abbey was bombed there had been argument over who was to blame. In this matter it is perhaps best to quote the other side. In 1951 General Mark Clark, the responsible C.-in-C., wrote:

"I say that the bombing of the Abbey . . . was a mistake, and I say it with full knowledge of the controversy that has raged around this episode. . . . Not only was the bombing . . . an unnecessary psychological mistake in the propaganda field, but it was a tactical military mistake of the first magnitude. It only made our job more difficult, more costly in terms of men, machines, and time."

This passage from Clark's *Calculated Risk* was quoted by Fred Majdalany in his own book *The Battle of Cassino,* and he added: "So the bombing . . . expended its fury in a vacuum, tragically and wastefully. It achieved nothing, it helped nobody."

Much as I respect Majdalany's objective account, I cannot approve his condemnation of Mark Clark. He bases his judgment on the fact that while Clark himself gave the order for the bombing, he later denied responsibility for it. Majdalany details the motives for the bombing, and these agree with the official war history of the New Zealand Government. (Wellington, New Zealand, 1957.)

With the decision to move the New Zealand Division and the 4th Indian Division from the eastern side of the peninsula into the major battle in the west, a political factor entered into the military considerations.

The New Zealand Division belonged to the Commonwealth. During the first world war its commander, General Freyberg, had commanded New Zealand contingents with distinction. Like all leaders of small contingents in a coalition war, he was responsible to his government for the fate of his division. The Allied High

Command graded up his divisional staff to the status of a corps command over two divisions, the New Zealand and the 4th Indian Divisions, which were to force a decision at Cassino. Where the Americans, the British and the French had failed, the New Zealanders were to do the job. The objective, which was to be captured in an outflanking operation, was the dominating hill on which the monastery stood, as they saw it, intact, hostile and threatening. In extenuation it can certainly be said that the ordinary soldier refused to believe that the place did not contain Germans, or that German observers would not be sent there very soon.

In the course of the attack the New Zealanders suffered heavy losses. Were they to run the risk of still heavier losses in order to avoid destroying the abbey? Were the people of New Zealand to be asked to pay for the preservation of the monastery with the lives of their own sons? These questions show the dilemma confronting not only the British commander, General Sir Harold Alexander, and the British government itself, but also the "accused", General Mark Clark. Germans and Italians alike were convinced that the bombing of the abbey could not have been ordered without the prior approval of the British government, and that once the decision had been made, even the commander of the U.S. 5th Army could not disregard it. This kind of inter-dependence is an inevitable feature of any coalition war. Strangely enough the New Zealand Corps waited for two days after the bombing before making serious and costly efforts to force a breakthrough by means of a pincer movement from Hill 593, north-west of the abbey, and from the railway station at Cassino, south-west of the abbey. Despite three further days of intense effort and sacrifice there was no result. The exact time of the bombing had not been decided, but the situation in the Anzio bridgehead made it necessary to ante-date it by twenty-four hours, a fact that was unknown to the troops! But even without this error the result could not have been different. On all the hills to the north-west of the abbey that came under attack the grenadiers of 90 Pz. Gren. Div. had built powerful strongpoints in the cliffs, against which all attacks by the brave 4th Indian Division failed. In Cassino itself the Allies captured the station, but it was re-captured by German tanks on February 18th. The tanks had taken advantage of the smoke from the enemy's artillery to force their way into the station in a surprise attack. The impressions left by these events were not the same on both sides. In our war histories we do not regard the bombing as a special "second battle for Cassino". In general we still had the same troops in the battle. The newly-arrived battalions of the 1 Parachute Rifle Division were allocated to the local commander, General Baade. The ordinary soldier on those parts of the front that were not under attack witnessed the destruction and looked upon it more as a devastating gesture of disillusionment over previous failures than as a serious military operation.

It is idle to criticise the enemy's tactical failure in the fighting between February 15th and 18th. It goes without saying that there were military failures on the side of the Allies. It has already been said that the 4th Indian Division was unaware of the decision to advance the time for bombing the abbey. But there was no need for the infantry attack and the bombing to be so close together. In any case the first objectives were the hills to the west of the abbey. The opposite argument is also valid, namely that tactically it would have been wiser if the Allies had not launched their infantry attack at the moment of increased watchfulness after the bombing. But as one who was brought up in the German school of tactics I cannot refrain from making another criticism. What we described as the "slackening of the battle" after the bombing was in reality a quite serious Allied effort to break the monastery hill out of the German front by means of a smaller pincer attack. The plan was so similar to the first one (which was a combined attack by the U.S. 36 Div. across the Rapido at S. Angelo, followed immediately by an attack by the U.S. 34 Div. north of Cassino) that it could not hold any surprise. There was nothing new in it. I knew the terrain round Albaneta Farm, Hill 593 and Hill 444 from the day that I proceeded on foot to visit a battalion of 90 Pz. Gren. Div., when the trail of blood from the wounded that had been brought back marked for me the way up the track. These were all defensive positions in excellent condition, and they were being improved every day. According to German ideas, anyone wishing to continue the attack in the same direction from the terrain won in the earlier assault would have had to assemble a much more powerful mass as an attacking force. To achieve this, the attacker could have ruthlessly denuded his secondary fronts, a measure that I too was constantly compelled to adopt for my defensive operations. I feared an attack from the hills down to the Via Casilina, which would have severed my supply line to Cassino. But what I feared even more was an attack by Juin's corps with its superb Moroccan and Algerian divisions. I anticipated a wide-sweeping operational thrust into the Atina basin against our thin lines, behind which we had no collecting positions. I have already described the implications of that danger. The enemy could indeed have avoided the costly battles for Cassino.

GENERAL BAADE

It was natural that I should be on intimate terms with General Baade, commander of 90 Pz. Gren. Div., for it was he, with his two divisions, who had been instrumental in averting defeat in the first battle of Cassino. At the outbreak of war, when I was C.O. of Cavalry Regiment 3, he had one of the squadrons. I remember a day shortly after I had taken over the regiment when he opened a personal conversation about his immediate future with the remark: "I assume that in my service records I must have been given the worst confidential report of any Army officer." He was evidently considering giving up his career. He was the son of a Brandenburg landowner and had married into a wealthy family, so that he was financially independent. Both he and his wife were in the international class in show jumping. I made no immediate comment. Not until I had seen his squadron "from the inside" did I advise him to stay on. The squadron was stamped with his own personality, the troopers worked together exceptionally well and displayed a natural, relaxed discipline. And that was now a characteristic of 90 Pz. Gren. Div. When I inspected this division, I was overcome by a feeling of regret that I was no longer at the head of my old 17 Panzer Division. When one assumes a higher command than a division it is of course impossible directly to influence a larger number of subordinates with one's own personality. Many a superior officer would have found that relations with Baade were not easy and might even end in a clash. Baade was an original character, and I gave him plenty of rein because I knew that his influence on the troops was partly due to his originality. He was the subject of countless anecdotes. In North Africa, for instance, he and his regiment had broken into the British lines. For his return passage he took a captured British officer along to pilot him through the minefield. Having safely passed through it, he rewarded the prisoner by sending him back to his own troops.

Before I reached Sicily, Baade had been attached for special duties to the German General in Rome. For the impending evacuation of the island he had organised the way back to the mainland by the air and sea routes. He had arranged for the establishment of small concealed depots, at which provisions and bottles of brandy were available as if for some polar expedition. He always organised things thoroughly and with an eye for the future.

At the end of 1943, I was rung up by an excited officer in the O.K.W. who wanted to know whether it was true that on Christmas Eve Baade had accepted an invitation to dine with the enemy. Of course this was nonsense, but on New Year's Day he had exchanged greetings by radio with his former opponents in the North African campaign. In Africa, having driven well up to the front, he would sometimes send a message to the enemy before returning: "Stop firing. On my way back. Baade"—and sometimes this was effective!

Over his riding breeches Baade used to wear a Scottish khaki kilt.

In the place of the large leather sporran worn by Scotsmen he had a large pistol, suspended in a holster from his neck. He spent most of the time at his forward command post, where he was hard to get at. On one occasion I passed through some intense barrage fire in order to meet him in the front line. But there I was told that he was up among the advanced outposts, so naturally I had to go on!

During the first battle of Cassino, Baade's command post was situated on the Via Casilina, between Piedimonte and Cassino, where I often visited him. He had found accommodation in a cylindrical concrete dug-out containing two bunks, which had just been completed as part of the defensive works. At these forward command posts he was in the habit of leaving behind for the benefit of future generations a "bottle-mail", containing the names of himself, his adjutant, his dog and the date of the battle.

It was from his command post that we witnessed the bombing of the abbey. Both of us were at a loss to know what this appalling spectacle signified. I should have been in the battle H.Q. of the corps, not in Baade's forward position. We still had a communications link with his divisional staff in the caves near Piedimonte, so that I hoped before my return to get a picture of the enemy's intentions and to bring back the first authentic reports on the attack against 90 Pz. Gren. Div. But the lull in the battle seemd to drag on. As a tactical prelude the destruction of the abbey appeared to have no significance. We felt sad at the failure of our efforts to preserve the abbey in the midst of the battlefield. The prototype of all western religious Orders, the venerable mother of monasteries, lay in ruins. All further attempts by the New Zealand Corps to attack from its positions north-west of the abbey were invalidated by the brave and costly resistance of 90 Pz. Gren. Div.

To the journal of Cavalry Regiment 3, which for the sake of continuity was still being published, I contributed the following memorial on Baade: —

"The lonѕger the war lasts, the more does the personality of the fighting commander come to the fore. For the true fighting man only begins to reveal himself in a protracted struggle where setbacks are not lacking. In this fifth year of war we may wonder what are the qualities of leaders such as this one, who has just been awarded the Oak Leaves.

"Through his personality alone he manages in a few days of fighting to restore half-defeated divisions, breathing new life into them, putting them into better shape, enhancing their powers of resistance by the very fact that he commands them. The magic stream of confidence begins to flow.

"In these severe battles we saw him in his hole in the ground with shells exploding all about him, sitting there with a clear view of the fighting around the monastery hill. Logs are burning in a crater, giving off a steady heat. The water boils in the battered little tea-kettle—indispensable in many a campaign and battle.

"Others may argue as to whether a senior commander so far forward and away from the routine work of his staff is capable of controlling larger troop formations. Yet it is in his nature to be here in the midst of his fighting men, sending the battalion staffs into the front line in times of crisis. Above all, it is here that he sees everything, and like an artist at the piano, masters the keyboard of the battle.

"Being a true commander he husbands his resources. Behind him lies the experience of command in every theatre of war. This was his method in Poland, France and Russia, in North Africa or when in charge of the Messina Strait. He dismisses irrelevancies in order to concentrate with a sure instinct on what is really needed. He will give directions for supplies of ammunition, for the co-ordination of weapons, for fire plans. He seems to be playing a game of chess with single pieces, with an assault-gun, a raiding party, the construction of a single concrete dugout. Yet in the end it is the purposeful aggregate that achieves results.

"Trained in the old Cavalry, he understands the meaning of mobility. No one phase of the battle resembles the next. With the assurance of the historian he frames the sentences with which he judges the day-to-day situation. From the fluctuating picture of the fighting he is ever reaching new and confident decisions, but avoids dogmatic orders. The practice of concise directives dates from the era of 'orders from the saddle', when the commander himself was always on the move.

"Those who have trained many horses will appreciate the significance of economy of forces, which is as important for the men as it is for the animals. Where the average commander will throw exhausted reserves into the breech, Baade will incur the greatest risk in withdrawing them so that they can be freshened up in the shortest time and be used as new assault forces.

"He was victor in the first battle of Cassino. The principle of restoration of energy is one that he also applies to his own person. Like any good boxer, he knows how important it is to relax between the rounds. He may have spent weeks on end in some hole in the ground, but we might meet him again in a big hotel or comfortable quarters. When neither of these ways of relaxing was available, we might see him in a small hut, sitting by the stove reading Aristotle or Seneca. Between battles he arranges to have a little volume of well-chosen verses printed for his friends. He likes fine things, sports clothes, good weapons, shiny mahogany-coloured leather in a smart saddle-room, strong well-schooled hunters. Is there anyone in the regiment who does not remember those lovely horses?

"There are other inborn sources of quiet strength from which such leaders draw their inspiration. In war he will not countenance anything mean, will never sully the warrior's ethos by the least violence towards defenceless people; this steadfast attitude springs from faith in the eternal values."

On the very last day of the war, as he was nearing his home on the estate in Holstein, Baade was so severely injured in an air attack that he died shortly afterwards.

The Second Battle of Cassino

The second battle of Cassino, which started on March 15th, 1944, will go down in history as one of the most perplexing operations of war. To understand this battle (Map 11) it is essential to study the sources on both sides, and even then one is left with a puzzle, for the commanding generals on each side had widely differing impressions of it.

When the battle started I was on my way to the front in the region of Piedimonte and ran into the fringes of the monstrous carpet-bombing. All that happened to me was that occasionally the blast from the falling bombs would hurl me a few yards forwards or backwards before I could reach some hole in the ground. I knew the effect of these aerial bombs from my time in Sicily.

Two days after the Allies had laid this great carpet of bombs in such a minute area, I was already convinced that their effort had failed. But their leaders, or at any rate the commander of the New Zealand Corps on this small sector, thought otherwise. From the Tyrrhenian coast to the 2,000 metres high watershed of the Abruzzi the battles were part of a general plan, as already explained. The second battle of Cassino developed out of the first battle in accordance with operational laws. It was the natural consequence of the failure implicit in the destruction of the abbey without any compensating tactical advantage. The responsible Allied leaders therefore decided on a much more extensive bombing than that of February 15th, but this time it was to be directed against the German troops in the plain, and the result immediately exploited. And so it came to the bombing of the town of Cassino on March 15th.

Once again political considerations were involved. General Freyberg was directly responsible to his government. He had authority to veto a continuation of the battle if losses in a single action should exceed a thousand men. This had already occurred; the losses in the first battle of Cassino were higher than this. Even after the abbey had been bombed the 4th Indian Division, which was part of the New Zealand Corps, kept up its attacks without success, and the New Zealand Division also suffered losses. Yet Freyberg was reluctant to apply the veto, as this would reflect on the honour of the New Zealand contingent. He enquired from Sir Harold Alexander whether, if the veto were used, another division would be detailed for the task. When this was confirmed, he decided to accept the risk of a further operation by his division as part of the corps, hoping that success would compensate for the losses already incurred. The plan of battle was decided on immediately after the failure of the last attacks in the first battle of Cassino. At that time it had the additional purpose of tying down German forces at Cassino in order to relieve the pressure on the Allied bridgehead at Nettuno through the counter-attacks by the

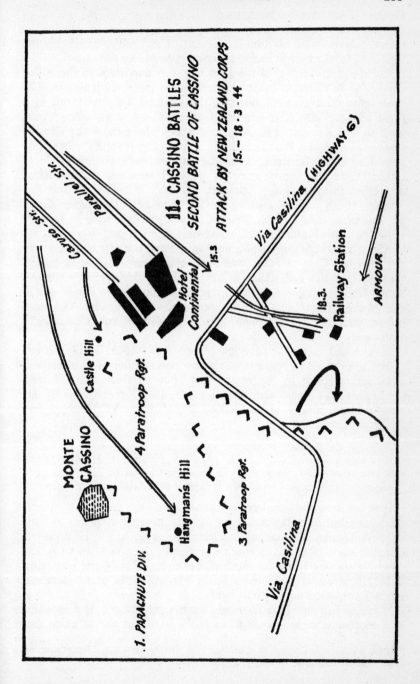

11. CASSINO BATTLES
SECOND BATTLE OF CASSINO
ATTACK BY NEW ZEALAND CORPS
15 - 18 · 3 · 44

German 14th Army (Mackensen). But the start of the attack at Cassino was repeatedly postponed by bad weather, so that this additional purpose was no longer relevant. The counter-attack by the German 14th Army was finally abandoned on March 4th.

But the continuation of the fight was also important to the Allied Command in order to invalidate reproaches from the Russians. The Red Army had crossed the Bug, the Dniester and the Pruth in a rapid advance into Rumania and Galicia. The western Allies would have to attack somewhere. A general attack along the entire Cassino front would require time-consuming re-grouping of forces; meanwhile something must be done. Thus the extraordinary second battle of Cassino was the consequence of political tensions, considerations of prestige and past disappointments.

After Juin's attacks against the left wing of XIV Panzer Corps in November 1943 and McCreery's against the right wing in January 1944 the Allied attacks had concentrated more and more on the centre of the corps' long front, until in the end the sole objective was the town of Cassino. This was not an arbitrary choice. A breakthrough into the Liri valley would allow the deployment of major armed forces. Cassino was the key point on the road to Rome, and it offered the quickest link with Valmontone, where General Alexander hoped, after the breakthrough, to seal the fate of von Vietinghoff's 10th Army.

This Allied tactical evaluation of geography could hardly be expected to produce an operational surprise. Instead the Allies attempted a tactical surprise to the extent that after all their setbacks they again went for Cassino without re-grouping their forces. In the official New Zealand history of the Second World War, A.C. Philipps has this to say about it: —

"From the military standpoint no competent soldier would in March 1944 have selected Cassino as the objective of an attack. He would have rejected the idea of assaulting the strongest fortress in Europe in mid-winter, using a single corps without the aid of diversionary operations."*

It is hardly to be wondered at that not only the decision to launch the attack but also its further prosecution brought surprises to both sides. A layman without any local knowledge could not be expected to make sense of even the initial direction of the attack. In an Allied offensive starting from the southern extremity of Italy one inevitably thinks in terms of a south to north movement. In actual fact the attack was made from north to south.

It is necessary to bear in mind that the peninsula runs diagonally in a south-east direction. At Cassino the front ran almost north and

* *Italy, Volume I, Sangro to Cassino,* War History Branch, Department of International Affairs, Wellington, New Zealand, 1957.

south, and the enemy had on many previous occasions attacked due westwards. But now he adopted a special plan, whereby instead of penetrating into the town along the plain from east to west, he would start from the places into which he had broken during the first battle of Cassino, which lay north of the town, and thence push southwards into the town. By this means Freyberg wanted to seize the slope of the monastery hill in order from there to cover his forces against the flanking strongpoint of the ruined abbey. Together with the main central thrust, a pincer movement would be made by means of attacks from the hill position west of the monastery towards the south, and from the southern edge of the town westwards towards the Via Casilina.

For this purpose a very careful plan was elaborated, which in the German opinion went into far too much detail. The crux of the plan was to destroy the town and its garrison by using all available bombers, including the strategic bomber force. Consequently on the morning of March 15th something over 1,000 tons of bombs were dropped on Cassino from 300 heavy and 200 medium bombers. Perhaps this no longer impresses people living in the atomic age, but its effect then was staggering.

The strategic bombers had not been trained to the method whereby a target is bombed until it is ready to be assaulted by ground forces. While they were still approaching the target, things went wrong. Some released their bombs prematurely, killing several hundred civilians at Venafro, which they mistook for Cassino. This also caused some casualties among the French Corps. Bombs released too late fell on Piedimonte and Castrocielo. The Allied commanders had assembled at the New Zealand Corps H.Q. at Cervaro, whence they could overlook the battlefield. The New Zealand historian Philipps, already quoted, has this to say: "In the relative security of the hills round Cervaro the picnic atmosphere was both inappropriate and unavoidable". Yet from the Allied viewpoint it was perhaps not so "inappropriate". Their assault infantry had been moved well away from the danger zone. In view of the destructive capacity of these huge bomb-loads there seemed no urgency for the ground attack. Consequently the assault battalions had a co-ordinated timetable that reduced the rate of attack to a minimum, allowing for various alternative situations. A German plan would have been wary of this kind of co-ordination, which was bound to put too much of a brake on the development of the first attack, thereby missing the opportunity of sending up reserves. Nor did the Allies conform to the orthodox doctrine of street-fighting, whereby enemy strongpoints are isolated and by-passed, their destruction being assigned to subsequent waves.

The bombing was an erroneous concept inasmuch as it failed to destroy all life in Cassino. The bombing of the abbey had already shown that the many arched cellars provided secure shelters because aircraft bombs are not designed to penetrate deep into the ground.

At Cassino the bombing was not directed against frightened refugees but against the Wehrmacht's toughest fighting men. The 1 Parachute Rifle Division had slowly relieved 90 Pz. Gren. Div., thus allowing the new troops gradually to familiarise themselves with the terrain. Their commander, General Heidrich, had taken over on February 26th.

This step-by-step handing-over was a minor tactical expedient. But what exceeded all expectations was the fighting spirit of the troops. The soldiers crawled out of the shattered cellars and bunkers to confront the enemy with the toughest resistance. Words can hardly do them justice. We had all reckoned that those who survived the hours of bombing and the casualties would be physically and morrally shaken, but this was not so.

In all armies the paratroops are an élite of fighting men. To begin with, the parachute jump calls for self-control, and the more numerous the jumps, the greater the demand on self-control. Contact with the ground still resembles a free jump from a height of several metres. the parachutes are smaller than the normal life-saving ones. Their size is limited by the need to keep the units close together while still air-borne. However, the units usually land without any co-ordination, which they have then to establish on the battlefield, despite the lack of any communications with the rear. This tradition proved its value at Cassino. It was no longer a question of permanently occupying the town. The fighting was done from fortuitous new strongpoints which usually had no contact on the flanks or towards the rear, and were ignorant of what was happening elsewhere on the narrow front.

The individual nests of resistance had not become isolated through the bombing alone. Such isolation is typical for all fighting in towns. At first the fighting in Cassino fluctuated, then the New Zealand Division slowly forced its way south deeper into the town, and was able to hold parts of it. But between these parts were strongpoints that the Germans had not given up or had recaptured in counter-attacks. The fighting was at such close quarters that one floor of a building might be held by the defender while the next was occupied by the attackers. If the latter wished to use their artillery to soften up the building before storming it, they would first have to evacuate this floor!

The town area of Cassino came under Paratroop Regiment 3, Colonel Heilmann. When the bombing started, the divisional commander, General Heidrich, happened to be at Heilmann's command post, two-and-a-half kilometres south of Monte Cassino. Heilmann stayed there during the entire battle, and this was right, for it was the centre of resistance. In order to meet both these commanders at that place I had to cover much ground on foot from Aquino through a seemingly unoccupied terrain. I crossed a large field full of craters which had been ploughed up more and more by heavy calibre shells although it seemed to be unoccupied. No tree escaped damage, no piece of ground remained green. On my lonely walk the only accompaniment was the jarring explosion of shells, the whistling of splinters, the smell of freshly thrown-up earth and the well-known mixture of smells from glowing iron and burnt powder. Yet distributed round this terrain were hidden batteries, whose men rushed from cover to man their guns for sudden bombardments, then disappeared again with equal speed. What I saw and felt took me back across twenty-eight years, when I experienced the same loneliness crossing the battle-field of the Somme. Hitler was right when he later told me that here was the only battlefield of this war that resembled those of the first.

It was never possible to obtain a clear picture of the course of the battle from the command post of Regiment 3. The paratroops were in the habit of not reporting the smaller losses of ground, because they hoped soon to recover it. Often reports from the corps artillery, which I had allocated in good measure to this division, were more accurate.

I gave the division plenty of freedom to fight the battle in its own way. Exhortations of the kind that one addresses to other troops to shake them up would have been out of place here. I also said nothing when we lost the railway station due to a tank attack from the east, when our counter-attack failed to recapture it. It was more important to preserve our irreplaceable forces than to hold on to this or that part of the town.

To the west of the New Zealand Division, the 4th Indian Division also attacked in a general southerly direction on the monastery hill. Anyone who has climbed this hill with its gradient of 500 metres up for every 1,000 metres horizontally will know the difficulties of attacking across a slope of this kind. And the strongpoint in the ruins of the monastery was still on the flank of the enemy's thrust. The slope of the hill was, however, so cut up that this gave the outstanding Indian troops the possibility of pressing on, with the result that Castle Hill (Hill 193) north of the Continental Hotel was soon lost. In the end the Gurkhas thrust forward as far as the well-known Hangman's Hill (Hill 434) which is 350 metres south of the Abbey, and here they formed an isolated strongpoint. This was the western arm of the pincer which was intended to unite with the other pincer movement that had developed from the Cassino railway station. In this way the Via Casilina would have been cut off and the town of Cassino surrounded.

But this did not happen. The fighting on the hill continued for a week without any decisive result, until a balance of forces was achieved, and so we maintained our position in Cassino. Here as elsewhere the the onslaught had failed due to the steadfastness and desperate courage of the paratroops. It will not detract from their fame if I fill in the picture with one or two lucky incidents of the kind that in war always seem to assist the brave.

Although the bombs falling on the town had extinguished many lives and destroyed many defensive works, they also eased the burden of the defenders. The Allied infantry attacks showed clearly that they had been wrong in thinking that their tanks could operate in the town. The bombs had produced an area of craters so extensive that the tanks could only force their way along narrow lanes after the pioneers had laboriously cleared the obstructions. The craters were filled with the rubble of the houses, so that they could not even be negotiated by climbing over them. We were also aided on the very first night by the rain showers which turned the rubble into sticky sludge. Consequently in the first assault the infantry lacked support from any forward rushing tanks. The German infantry in Cassino and the few tanks knew their job because they had long been on the defensive. The tanks, operating singly, were held back under cover until at very close range they engaged the enemy's tanks, then immediately disappeared into fresh cover. That the Continental Hotel was held is attributable to one tank, which had been built into the entrance hall.

The enemy's artillery had difficulty in laying a creeping barrage in front of the infantry, which was advancing too slowly. The mass of this artillery was located in the valley east of Cassino, not north of the town, whence the infantry had started out. More than one critic of our opponent at that time maintains that he did not suffer too much from the German artillery fire. But this is a characteristic of all street and town fighting. We, however, were in no doubt that our artillery, consisting of many batteries concentrated in the corps unit and centrally directed, made a substantial contribution to the success of the defence.

In my opinion the smoke-making battery under Lt.-Colonel Andrae was a highly effective weapon. Thanks to its well-directed searching fire, its demoralising effect, stifled the enemy's initial effort to assemble his tanks and infantry, and helped our own infantry in many an apparently hopeless situation.

From sources provided by our opponent we now know that his own tactical mistakes made our task less difficult. These were mistakes which in another context we had learned to avoid as a result of experiences at Stalingrad. The slow tempo of the first infantry attack was in line with the reluctance to throw in reserves at the very places where the attack needed backing. During the first two days the enemy had no battalion staff in the town. This went against our principles. With us, if the situation demanded it, the battalion commander would normally be seen in the front line, sometimes even rushing out of his bunker armed with a hand grenade, like any patrol leader. Thus he could be expected to send back tactically relevant situation reports and to make his own decisions. In the end the strength of our battalions at the climax of the battle was never more than about a hundred men, of whom a proportion were tied to anti-tank guns and mortars.

As was always the case in this type of close-in fighting, the physical proximity of the opponents induced a comradeship between the front line soldiers which showed itself particularly in the imperative need to remove the wounded. Frequently a local armistice was arranged to allow both sides to rescue their wounded. I myself had often seen this in mountain warfare. Sometimes the paratroops on the hills would allow wounded to pass unmolested without any prior agreement. In places where there was no alternative the wounded were rescued in broad daylight under the shield of the Red Cross. The negotiators usually imposed a limit on the time allowed for rescue. When at the end of the battle the enemy had to evacuate the salient formed by Hangman's Hill, he left his wounded behind, as the last of his occupying forces would not otherwise have been able to fight their way back through the German lines. But the lightly wounded got moving and, giving each other mutual support, passed through the lines. The local German commander had intimated his approval for this procedure. To quote Fred Majdalany:

"The medical orderlies of both sides fell into the habit of wandering, almost at will, in a mute kinship that in its spontaneous charity was perhaps the most ironic witness of all to the folly that made it necessary*".

I associate myself with these sentiments of my young friend, and I bow to those New Zealanders, Indians and Germans who in the midst of a hellish, death-dealing battle saved others at the risk of their own lives.

On March 19th, only four days after the bombing and the start of the attack, General Freyberg had to consider sending into action at Cassino the reserves that had been intended for the pursuit following a breakthrough.

The next day Churchill asked General Alexander to explain why he was attacking on the Cassino front on a width of only two or three miles, which had already used up five or six divisions against the German pincer defence, and why he had attempted no flanking movement. Alexander was at pains to explain the peculiarities of the battlefield to the Prime Minister.

---

* *The Battle of Cassino*, Houghton Mifflin Co., Boston, 1957.

But on the same day Alexander summoned the Army Commanders and General Freyberg to discover whether a continuation of the attack would be likely to lead within the next few days to the capture of the abbey, or whether the offensive should be broken off while holding on to important points with a view to later operations. The council of war decided in favour of breaking off the attack. In Cassino, Castle Hill and the north-west sector of the town were held on to, as were the botanical garden in the centre and the railway station with the adjoining hill. The salient strongpoint on Hangman's Hill, immediately south-east of the abbey (Hill 435), was evacuated under great difficulties.

THE CASSINO BATTLES IN RETROSPECT

The world's attention was attracted to the Italian theatre of war through the tough German resistance on the Cassino front, which cost the Allies three whole months for an advance of fifteen kilometres; then there was the equally stubborn German resistance in Cassino itself, where for three months the Allies vainly tried to break through. Moreover, at that time this was the only European land activity of the Western Allies. The Germans fully exploited the propaganda value of their success in order to bolster the unwarranted optimism of their people. The difficulties encountered by the Allies led them to false conclusions. To me the great weakness of the Axis leadership was only too apparent despite all our defensive successes.

Our real weakness lay in the lack of facilities for reconnaissance. In reality all the enemy's major attacks came as a complete surprise. Although we still possessed a good intelligence service which functioned through the General Staff organisation, we could no longer use the normal means of reconnaissance. The Luftwaffe had been so decimated that it could barely venture into the air for routine reconnaissance. Prisoners were seldom brought in. Agents could pass behind the lines by the sea route, but they probably worked for and got paid by both sides, and of course they knew nothing of any preparations for attacks. To obtain warnings of such preparations from agents would have needed a very close-knit mesh, which we did not possess.

The Allies' air supremacy had far-reaching consequences. They had a continuous and uninterrupted air spotting service for their artillery fire over the German lines, which operated unmolested by German fighters. Through the observers in the Allied planes the fire could be directed against any desired part of the front. This advantage proved ineffective only because the Allied attacks moved forward too slowly, so that we always found time at night to move up the necessary reserves for the counter-blows.

Yet all this did not blind me to the fact that our successes were of a temporary nature. If the enemy should succeed in going over to a war of movement, then the nightly movement of reserves would no longer suffice. It would have to occur by daylight on the battlefield itself, because the enemy would also be moving in daytime. Only if there were parity in the air could restrictions be imposed on the day movements of the enemy, and this would also re-establish parity in the conduct of operations.

During the six months' fighting in the Cassino area I achieved a successful defence by paying constant attention to the morale of the troops, by establishing a system of stop-gaps, by having under my single control all the operations in the entire sector of the fighting, by my precise knowledge of the terrain and by continually adapting the grouping of forces and their centres of resistance to the changing circumstances of the battle. It is no vain boast to say that the sum of these activities constitutes what is generally termed the art of leadership.

All ranks in the German Army were well trained in leadership, for with us this was a tradition. In regard to the quick and accurate appreciation of a situation, the making of clear decisions and the framing of concise orders our General Staff was probably superior to those of all other countries. In manoeuvres, discussions on the terrain and General Staff exercises all our officers had been constantly schooled to acquire a mastery of the subject. The tasks were always set in such a way that the local leader was compelled to make more or less independent decisions. In peace-time, moreover, certain mandatory conditions were imposed on the situation. For example, if a "new enemy" came into the picture, it was stipulated that all communications had broken down or that some other snag had cropped up, as indeed had often occurred up to the time of the Battle of the Marne in 1914. By this means the pupils were to acquire great skill and a readiness to make decisions and accept responsibility—important assets for any leader. Sometimes this independence was carried too far. In 1935 I attended the manoeuvres in East Prussia in the company of the future British C.I.G.S., Field-Marshal Sir John Dill. Afterwards we visited the battlefield of Tannenberg, where Sir John wanted to know how the Germans had achieved such success despite the notorious disobediance of the junior commanders.

One might wonder how much of all this had survived into 1940. The answer is: nothing, or very little. We, the higher German commanders suffered excessively from a narrow tutelage. This subservience found its nadir in sheltering behind the directives of Hitler, who was regarded as the real cause of degeneration in the so-called "promulgation of executive orders for a task"*. This promulgation should have

* AUFTRAGBEFEHLSGEBUNG.

been confined to essential directives for carrying out any particular task, so that the relevant commander could remain as free as possible in his choice of means and tactics.

Yet it would be a grave mistake to attribute this degeneration to Hitler alone. The true reasons lay deeper.

Firstly we must consider the effect of developments in communications, as a result of which it would be almost impossible to have a recurrence of the chaotic conditions during the Battle of the Marne in 1914. In the Second World War every commander could in a matter of minutes be put in touch with his superior headquarters or with the O.K.W. itself, so that he could converse with his superior officer or with the General Staff as though these were in the adjoining room. From Corsica I used to have clear conversations with Kesselring over a decimetre radio-telephone link. This technical perfection in communications naturally diminishes the independence of a local commander, and of course every commander will whenever possible report his decisions to a higher quarter, knowing that his superiors' decisions will depend on his own. In consequence the superior authority will give his opinion on the decisions of his subordinate, if only because, being in the know, he must inevitably share in the responsibility for those decisions. Under certain circumstances important decisions can be passed up the chain of command until they reach the highest quarter, and at each stage responsibility for those decisions is accepted by the forwarding authority. All this militates against the local commander, who becomes more and more reluctant to take decisions on his own initiative, knowing that he must bear the whole responsibility. Yet if the local commander fails to make use of his communications to keep his superior in the picture, but decides to make his own decision, then he is guilty of another kind of transgression.

This is the second innovation as compared with the days when a higher commander was in sole command. The new tactics make it essential for all neighbours to be kept informed of decisions made, and this is effected through the commander-in-chief. In the new tactics nothing is left of the tradition that survived from the nineteenth century, namely of "separate marching and united fighting". Modern armies fill continents from sea to sea, and in all decisive campaigns this leads to "line tactics". Lines must be held because neither of the contestants dares to dissolve his stabilised front and withdraw sufficiently to regain full operational mobility. Already in the First World War the risk was too great, although the movements were still only at the pace of marching infantry. How much less could they now risk such a method, when every disengaging movement was immediately pursued by fast motorised units which were not in the least prepared to forfeit the initiative they had thus acquired.

However much and however rightly all the commanders and General Staff officers may have complained about Hitler's "halt" tactics, the fact remains that no army commander was able to show a successful example of any other. But if it were only a case of withdrawing from untenable sectors of the front, then the unattacked neighbouring sectors nearly always became involved. It was these sectors that had consolidated their positions all the more effectively the longer they remained unmolested, and consequently they were reluctant to withdraw their positions to unprepared terrain. Yet if they were not pulled back, the result was the notorious indentation of the front, which consumed more forces than any straight-running front line.

It was considerations of this nature that made it necessary to hold a sort of council of war with all concerned whenever a disengaging movement was contemplated. It is not necessary for the corps commander to make a personal appearance at the council, since extensive communications allow him to keep in touch before any important decision is made. Neither the corps commander nor even the army commander play any more significant part in such a council than the local expert who puts his proposals to the vote and must act according to the council's decision.

When an attack develops from the front line, the conditions become more favourable. The attacking groups at the centre of pressure move their front towards the enemy, thus assisting their neighbours, whereas in a withdrawal they would embarrass them. But the commanders do not retain much independence as in the days of the battles of the pockets, where the area of operations was limited geographically.

The one exception was the North African theatre of war, where in desert warfare mobility was limited on one side by the sea, on the other by the desert. The front being narrow, this led to those total breakthroughs with wide-sweeping attack and withdrawal movements, the local commanders enjoying a large measure of independence and consequently earning fame more easily. The North African campaign did not, however, change the historically established pattern of the modern battle with its characteristic frontal pressure, its yielding or holding fast.

In addition to the perfection of means of communication and the inescapable line tactics there was a third reason for the reduced independence of commanders in the field—the dwindling forces. This was due to line tactics; the interminably long lines had to be occupied notwithstanding the basic zonal defence and deployment in depth. Yet the proportion of a modern army that can be engaged in the front line has grown ever smaller. There were never enough infantrymen to occupy the defensive lines. I have tried to show this in the numerous examples of the Cassino battles.

The lack of forces made it increasingly difficult to earmark troops as reserves. As long as the commander has sufficient forces at his disposal, it is normal and understandable that he will possess reserves bearing some relation to his overall stregth. Thus the army group will have reserves amounting to a corps, the army will have a corps or several divisions, and the corps will have one or more divisions, depending on its own size. Despite all the restrictions imposed by communications and by line tactics, these reserves enable the commander to preserve a measure of independence. He may feel obliged to report his decisions, but as long as his superior authority has his own reserves with which to influence the general situation, that authority will only be too ready to leave the subordinate commander to use his as he thinks best.

If the forces shrink so much that these normal reserves are not available at each level of command, then the forces so detailed are put at the disposal of the highest commander in the area, while the local commanders, having none for themselves, can no longer expect to exert any decisive influence on the operations. It often happened that the only available reserve division was allocated to the corps, but not subordinated to it. This division was moved into the corps zone, and even its order of battle was prescribed, but its operational employment was, quite rightly, decided by the "council of war".

Where there is a lack of forces it is right to keep the operational reserves under the authority of the army group, which will then hand them over to an army under attack, without stipulating the time and place of their employment, That is what happened on January 18th with the 29 and 90 Pz. Gren. Divisions.

At Cassino the only occasions when XIV Corps had entire divisions in reserve was when these had been moved forward into the corps zone waiting to relieve other divisions, but had not yet been released for operations. In an emergency I could have made use of these reserves, but otherwise I had to create my reserves by an *ad hoc* procedure. Thus I used those parts of divisions that had been relieved, or the parts that the divisions had themselves sent back, and formed them into the corps reserve. It is true that this unsatisfactory procedure was thus passed on down the chain of command. But it was only in cases of dire necessity that the corps operated such reserves in the sectors of divisions that were unfamiliar to them. Then one was faced with the tricky business of tidying up the formations. Either the battalions that had been operating temporarily in unfamiliar sectors of the front were relieved as soon as possible and sent back to their own divisions, or the division itself was moved to the threatenend place, while the detailing of troops and consequently the boundaries of the divisions were adjusted while forming a new centre of pressure. This was a frequent occurrence. In my opinion the daily detailed work by the General Staff with a view to re-assembling broken-up divisions was a substantial contributory factor in our success. One cannot fight with broken-up divisions. A battalion should be under its divisional commander, who knows it and with whom it feels a home.

The better the point of main effort could be organised by this daily adjustment of divisional boundaries and of the chain of command, the easier it was to compensate for the lack of reserves. During the entire war it was shown that every commander believed he had created a point of main effort when he had assembled reserves behind one sector and had moved several batteries to that place. The true art of leadership is displayed only when the commander deliberately risks denuding his unmolested fronts so extensively that a major attack here could never be repulsed. I found that divisional commanders who were tuned to my methods showed an understanding for this type of operational control. They could see the result and realised that if they themselves should be attacked, help would come to them in the same way as it had come from them to their neighbours.

In order to cope with the ever more noticeable shortage of fighting troops, the German High Command had adopted the emergency measure of forming so-called Emergency Units, and this was a failure Experience showed that this type of unit never had any great fighting value when single battalions or even companies were sent to reinforce divisions to whom they were strangers. It was always found that when relieved at the front the "totally battle-weary" divisions had a victualling strength of 10,000 instead of the full 12,000 men. The decrease of 2,000 was due to losses in the front line, which made the infantry unfit for battle. The idea was to comb out the supply and rearward services. But it was an unpromising start to replace the lost infantry by artillerymen drawn from the batteries or by the valuable technical personnel of the pioneers, the communications troops, the truck drivers or the supply units. Apart from the opposition that this provoked among the commanders of these specialised troops, there was no ultimate advantage to operations in creating these units that virtually existed on paper only. In a major battle they melted away like butter in the sun. Not only were they physically isolated on the battlefield, but they lacked the essential experience of the front that can only be acquired by living there.

Here I must again mention the enemy's air superiority, which presented one of the biggest problems to the German command. During the preparations for a major attack the air force of the attacker tries to inactivate that of the defender through air battles and through attacks on his aerodromes. The Allies never had to go through that process, for at the start of the Cassino battles the German air force had already been so weakened and so completely forced on the defensive that it had no chance of gaining parity, let alone air superiority.

Yet the Allied air force was confronted with a special problem, due to the peculiarities of this mountainous theatre of war. As is usual before launching an offensive, the attacker here tried to destroy the bridges in the hinterland. Normally the attack follows close up on this action, allowing the defender no time to restore the bridges. In the flat country of the Liri valley there was usually no difficulty in building up fords to serve as submerged bridges in place of those that had been destroyed. But in the high mountains the bridges span ravines that can be over a hundred metres deep, so that one cannot improvise a ford or other alternative crossing, such as a pontoon bridge or a ferry. Moreover, the narrow approach routes come under intense fire as soon as the bridge is destroyed. The destruction of these bridges emphasised the vital importance of having means of supply that do not depend on roads. Operationally it was right not to count on these bridges for supply purposes, and to treat them as though they did not exist. Indeed if they were at all accessible the defender himself preferred to prepare them for destruction. Then the enemy, having broken through, would be confronted with obstacles that his photographic reconnaissance had not revealed to him.

During the actual major attack our front-line troops were usually free from air attacks. Carpet bombing could only be used by the attacker if his own troops had first been withdrawn from the area. But this would lose him the element of surprise, for it would then take hours before his infantry and armour could begin their attack.

The enemy's mastery of the air space immediately behind the front under attack was a major source of worry to the defender, for it prevented all daylight movements, especially the bringing up of reserves. We were accustomed to making all necessary movements by night, but in the event of a real breakthrough this was not good enough. That was what actually occurred in the May breakthrough. In a battle of movement a commander who can only make the tactically essential moves by night resembles a chess-player who for three of his opponent's moves has the right to only one.

In the discussions on operations there was frequent debate over the relative value of the excessively diversified types of divisions in the German Army. I preferred the Panzer grenadier divisions, apart from the special types of parachute rifle divisions and mountain divisions, of which there was a real shortage in this theatre of war. As for the old type of infantry divisions, I was compelled to look on them as second-rate as regards their weapons, since the tank was indispensable in any attack against an enemy who used even a small number of tanks. In the wartime order of battle the infantry divisions possessed no tanks, and consequently they were inadequately organised. At this stage of the war the armoured divisions seldom had more than a quarter of their full intended strength in tanks. But as their infantry strength did not exceed four battalions, an increased allocation of tanks would not have produced the correct relationship for this kind of fighting. Thus the Panzer divisions were too small, and their fighting capacity did not bear a satisfactory relation to their large supply organization and their other auxiliary weapons and services. The Panzer grenadier divisions had the correct balance as compared with these two extremes. They possessed six battalions and as much armour as the Danzer Divisions. Hence they were more suitably organised for all kinds of use in attack and defence than other types of divisions.

Perhaps I should say a word on the activities of the higher commanders themselves. At the start of this section of the book I tried to establish the reasons for the decline in the art of leadership as an *independent* and responsible form of action. Commanders who were incapable of accommodating themselves to this situation were deemed unsuitable. Modern leadership demands the effacement of one's own person. At a council of war the commander carries the most weight because he will neither be affected by the urge to make himself felt, nor be dependent on his subordinates. If his professional judgment of a given situation should cause him firmly to reject some line of action, this is what makes him a real commander, and justifies the confidence of his subordinates. During these long battles I invariably found that I gained the confidence of superior officers and subordinates alike.

In recent times the higher commanders had less independence, and their tactical and strategic abilities were thus of less account when it came to selecting them for appointments. The more the dispassionate observer realised that defeat was inevitable, the more did the German higher commanders display other characteristics. A calm evaluation of the situation was always a sign of true leadership. The intellectual type came more and more into disrepute. People were expected to have "Faith". The military leader was supposed to have unshakeable faith in "his Führer" and to animate his troops with this faith and with belief in ultimate victory. Consequently there was less and less scope in the Führer hierarchy for the best type of independently critical officer that the Prussian General Staff had always produced. This disastrous development was precipitated by the well-known political weakness of the Germans. Even in Ludendorff's day generals had forgotten that all strategy contains a political element.

Consequently many generals could be found who fulfilled the requirement of faith in victory. But even among the most competent generals a new kind of leadership had evolved, which conformed to the wishes of the régime, and was typified by the so-called "thorough commander", who was expected to be present in the front line, especially while advancing. The reputation of this type was enhanced if he went over the heads of his subordinates to intervene in the battle—thereby infringing one of the elementary principles of command. It is obvious that a senior commander who remains far up at the front thereby forfeits his influence over the operations of his corps or of his army. He leaves the conduct of operations to his Chief of Staff, and thus ceases to be the real commander. Frequently this practice of being absent was deliberately chosen as an easy way of avoiding the unpleasant telephone conversations of the council of war, and it was also a form of self-advertisement. In the impressive advances during the first phase of the war it often happened that the responsible commander was unattainable, somewhere in the front line, though he could hardly be reproached on that score. The effect on the front-line troops was all the greater in proportion as their morale suffered with the repeated reverses in the later phases of the war.

I do not, however, wish to contest the value of frequent visits to the front by the senior commander. At the time of the protracted and heavy static fighting at Cassino I myself visited the front several times every week and always in day-time, as this was the only way to obtain a complete picture of the situation on the lengthy front. I used to drive up to within five or ten kilometres of the front, then stalked my way nearer, usually accompanied only by a young orderly officer, and I was glad of my strong constitution when climbing the high hills. In this way I acquired a very precise knowledge of the whole terrain, saw the troops in action, could here and there effect changes, and could provide the higher command with important information, particularly in regard to the boundaries between the divisions, where the danger was always greatest. It was especially to my advantage that I knew some of the terrain from the attacker's point of view. At the beginning, when looking back from the Bernhard Line I was able to get a vivid impression of the terrain and of the Gustav Line.

For a divisional commander it is an easy matter, and also essential, to visit his battalion commanders during a big action, but it is not quite so easy for a corps commander, especially if he has more than six divisions under him. But the front line begins with the battalion commander, for he is both the battle commander of a very mixed unit and the leader of the assault force.

The corps commander's contacts are made more difficult by the fact that his divisions are constantly being changed round, so that the troops cannot exactly regard him as a "father". His solicitude for them is intangible, unless he occasionally shows himself to the troops.

One secret of personal leadership is to discover the man whose bravery and whose influence on others deserves immediate recognition, to make him feel that he is appreciated and that others rely on him. The obverse is less pleasant, when a visit to the front shows that some commander ought to be replaced as quickly as possible because he is not up to his job. In this respect any leniency towards subordinate commanders does more harm than good.

In Hitler's army there was no satisfaction in being a commander. To me it seemed doubtful whether it was a sign of strength to regard every situation as an occasion for optimistically proclaiming one's faith in the ultimate victory. I could not help recalling the words of Montherlant: "Optimism is the elixir of life for the weak". Only those who are strong will face the facts without flinching. From my experience of colleagues I could not maintain that the optimists were particularly strong characters, and indeed they could hardly be so, since they shrank from any sober appreciation of the situation or from using their own judgment. Yet they were the best agents for a system that was determined to fight to the death and to eliminate all who thought otherwise.

What will be the judgment of history on those of us who had the perspicacity and the integrity to recognise that defeat was inescapable, yet continued to fight and shed blood?

My battle H.Q. at Roccasecca lay in a sheltered cut in the valley and was shielded from Cassino by the steep protuberance of a mountain on which stood the ruins of a castle. It was here that St. Thomas Aquinas was born in 1225. To-day his teachings are still basically relevant to Western morality. They stipulate that no man can be held answerable for the misdeeds of those over whom he has no power.

INFANTRY—QUEEN OF THE BATTLEFIELD

The forces available at Cassino were so numerous that one could think in terms of the defence of a continuous line of positions. Yet it was no more possible here than elsewhere in the war to occupy the entire length of these positions. The line consisted rather of a number of strong-points, some very powerful. In the daylight fighting it was not possible to move from one strongpoint to another except via the ridge positions on the high mountains.

But even a system of trenches could not have been manned like those of the First World War, for the infantry strength in the front line had become too weak. The vast arena of war between the armament centres in the homeland and the fronts required so many men that even the populous military powers were unable to afford anything more than an attenuated occupation of their front lines. In any case the increased effectiveness of weapons makes it necessary to save lives by thinning out the troops in the front line.

A few figures may serve to illustrate the conditions on a major battle front. In the centre of the line occupied by the corps—that is, in front of Cassino, and later, in and around the place—each division held a sector six to eight kilometres long with an infantry strength of about 1,200 men. In the first world war this would have been regarded as inadequate for a continuous defence. Naturally these 1,200 men were not arrayed shoulder to shoulder in one line, but occupied a depth of at least 500 metres. True that during the attempts to break through there were in this sector always two divisions, one behind the other. One of them fought ahead of the line while the other was busy building up and at the same time manning the main position in order to act as a rallying force in case of a breakthrough. I have already described the weakness of available reserves, but this was reduced to some extent by the fact that they were motorised, so that they could be thrown forward as quickly as they could be withdrawn.

The numbers of infantry had steadily declined relatively to the numbers of other fighting troops, yet paradoxically the infantry remained more firmly established as queen of the battlefield. In battle the clash is between the war potential of the opposing powers. The thrust that develops from great depth and is constantly nourished finally ramifies into the fighting of handfuls of soldiers for a few blocks of houses or for the jagged part of some hill.

At the start of a battle about a quarter of all the fighting troops might under the most favourable conditions be in the front line. It was these men who were quickly reduced in a major battle, while the other three quarters, the supporters of the infantry, remained intact. Strenuous efforts were made to even out this gross disproportion. But it did not pay to use the specialists of the auxiliary units in fighting for which they were not equipped. Thus the disproportion became every day more acute.

We did not care to have large masses of infantry at the focal points. Even if the units were still at full strength we kept the companies small. After 1943 the maximum number permitted was ninety, and we reduced it to seventy. Very experienced divisional commanders limited it to forty. The most important task of the command was to prevent the complete atrition of numbers, always to assemble new units and to hold fresh battalions in readiness, even though they were smaller.

At Cassino the terrain was difficult. In the mountains the infantry was unable to dig itself in on the front line. The demoralising effect of the intense bombardment was increased tenfold by the echoes from the valleys. There was no possibility of deviating from the tracks used for supplies. Often the strongpoints were a kilometre apart and separated by a deep ravine, so that it took two hours to go from one to the next. Especially at night it was easy for the enemy to filter in between these strongpoints and to cut them off from the rear. Consequently the troops were anxious to occupy the forward line in sufficient strength to act as a screen and so prevent undetected attacks from developing. Against this there was the need to deploy in depth and to segregate reserves. The two requirements were incompatible.

The enemy, knowing that we could not attack, was in a position to completely denude some parts of the front, while strengthening other parts and deploying his forces in depth in the sector where he intended to attack. He could relieve his battalions and bring them up to strength behind the lines, so that they were always rested when it came to the first attack.

The severe fighting around Monte Cassino, Monte Samucro, Monte Lungo, Monte Trocchio, Monte Abate and among the pile of ruins in Cassino itself was the business of twenty-five-year-old battalion commanders at the head of assault parties, each consisting of a handful of first class fighting men. It was the business of men like Struckmann, Zapf, Baron Heyking, Maitzel, Schneider, Count v.d. Borch, and others of the same calibre.

After the Cassino battles it fell to me to pay tribute to these men in a talk on the radio:

"I take this opportunity of speaking to listeners about the Cassino battles, and all the more willingly since it enables me to bear witness to the heroism of the troops under my command.

"The German public has been kept informed about these battles, but I would here like to emphasise once more that our successes were the outcome of heavy fighting throughout the entire winter. In this characteristic mountain terrain many a high peak was defended during the winter with the same stubbornness as was later displayed among the ruins of Cassino. The enemy's assault on the front of the corps had virtually never ceased since last autumn. All the divisions which at one time or another fought here, divisions that had to give up battalions to other main fighting fronts, weak divisions that sometimes had to stand up to a much stronger enemy— all these had their share in the successes at Cassino. For it is only through the orderly re-disposition of forces and through anticipatory measures to forestall the enemy's blows that defensive successes of this kind can be obtained. This method of fighting and this co-ordination of all the divisions alone made it possible to continue the struggle at Cassino without interruption even after the enemy had landed behind our back at Nettuno.

"It is difficult for those at home to appreciate the achievements of the individual soldier in this struggle, for the many reports of the winter in Russia have influenced the public and inevitably given them a false impression of the "Sunny South" in the Italian theatre of war. Indeed, it is difficult to explain that in the zone of the corps on the Tyrrhenian Sea the oranges ripen throughout the winter, while in the fighting area, sometimes at a height of 2,000 metres, the raging snowstorms seem to exterminate all life.

"In this theatre of war, moreover, the situation is characterised by very heavy expenditure of material in battles at the focal points, and on a scale hitherto unknown except in the First World War. It is clear that our Anglo-American opponents have been able to prepare and apply a terrific concentration of artillery fire not only at points like Cassino, where the prospects seemed good, but also during the preceding winter months at many other focal points. Standing up to this kind of artillery fire and carpet bombing from the air, under the appalling weather conditions already described and among the coverless rocks of the high mountains where there can be no digging-in, the troops have proved in this fifth year of hostilities that they have fully maintained their fighting efficiency.

"Our success at Cassino reflects the numerous examples in the history of war where results depend on the personality of the commander in the field. It is widely known that the main credit for the outcome of the first battle of Cassino goes to Major-General Baade, also that in the second battle the laurels for holding on to the town go to Lieut.-General Heidrich. These two divisional commanders were at the same time paragons for their troops. But here I must put in a word for the young company commanders, the battalion commanders and the commanders of regiments, most of whom must remain anonymous. For it is they who bear the brunt of the close-in fighting, whose merit and courage and devotion determine the value of the troops. Many of them carry the Knight's Cross of the Iron Cross, many others rest in eternal peace among the adamantine rocks. Your steadfast bearing in the hour of greatest crisis and your loyalty to your commanding general will not be forgotten. If I mention one of the best by name, let him represent all of you. For I would like to take this oppprtunity to lower my sword before the grave of Major Knuth, the defender of Cassino in the first battle, who while leading his regiment into action found a hero's death on the day after I had decorated him with the Knight's Cross. As this leader fought, so did the soldiers fight, especially the infantry, but also the pioneers, the gunners, the smoke-mortar men, and not least, the medical orderlies, the mine-detectors, the truck-drivers and the mule-drivers on supply roads that were constantly under fire.

"In the coming engagements the opponent will once more come face to face with these hard fighters."

MOUNTAIN WARFARE

The Cassino battles were essentially mountain warfare. Usually this fact was not fully appreciated by German soldiers coming from the north or even by the Anglo-Saxon troops until they were actually in the area. That at any rate was my experience with nearly all the German troops and with my occasional visitors. Even those who had got to know the south of Italy through their travels nearly always pictured it as a land of sunshine, sea and oranges, and this was because they usually passed through that kind of country. But only a very small portion of the war was fought in these typically southern regions. The range of hills lying between the sea and central Abruzzi may not be very high, but they have enough of the character of high mountains to be taken seriously even by experienced alpine troops.

In regard to the difficulty of accustoming the troops to these surroundings I was often reminded of a parallel case. The Western soldier is at a disadvantage, compared with his Russian counterpart, because he is far less accustomed to darkness. When we have to do a job at night, we produce our own light. On the other hand the Russians still perform a large part of their nocturnal tasks in the dark—milking, feeding, carting and long marches during the long winter months. For them the night is a cloak of invisibility and an ally, but to Western man it is an enemy and adds to the terror of battle. It is the same with the mountains. For the soldier accustomed to flat country the mountains intensify all fears and demoralise him. But people living in the mountains regard them as a protection and also as a weapon which becomes all the more effective when the opponent does not know how to make use of it.

At first I had no mountain division at my disposal. It was difficult to convince the O.K.W. of the mountainous character of the theatre of war, and there was also the problem of moving such divisions from the Eastern front. The only mountain division that came from Russia could attribute the move to the personal relations between its commander and Hitler. It was significant that this division, consisting of Austrian mountain dwellers, suffered from a severe moral strain. Although the men were familiar with mountains and had been trained in the hills, they knew nothing of hard mountain warfare. At first their "field postcards" contained remarks indicating that they "would rather return to Russia on all fours". But once the division had got over the first shock, it proved itself a good match for the Algerian and Moroccan attackers who were well acquainted with mountains.

The acoustically magnified noise of bombarding guns is the first unpleasantness. In the plains it was still possible to hold a conversation in the intervals between the single detonations, but in the mountains it became almost impossible because of the lingering peals and echoes. The broken stones greatly increased the splinter effect. Unlike the lowlands, the rocks absorbed nothing of the detonation, but provided a means of ricochet firing, whose effect resembles that of firing with time fuses. Anyone suddenly overtaken by artillery fire while on a mountain track had no possibility of evading it by moving away into open country.

In the mountains the soldiers felt lonely, and the proximity of death was more real under heavy fire. In the Liri valley and in the town of Cassino the fighting men could always reach some neighbouring strongpoint after dark and verify that "the front" still held. But those on Monte Camino or Monte Samucro often spent days without any other contact. A track that was 500 metres long as the crow flies might take as much as three hours to negotiate.

In the positions on the mountain ridges the communications were better. Those familiar with mountains always favoured such positions. But the great majority of German commanders and subordinate commanders came from the plains and found that ridges were too conspicuous and attracted the enemy's fire. It is true that lowland strongpoints had become more and more inconspicuous. But the infantryman did not take long to realise the advantage of ridge positions: all the enemy's shots that fell short or beyond the ridge were ineffective.

The troops also learned to use crowbars, hammers and explosive charges to dig themselves in at the ridge positions. The spade supplied as standard equipment was useless, and we had to purchase the additional equipment in the open market. Training usually occurred on the actual position. Once the technique was acquired, the troops settled into the rocks relatively quickly, finding excellent cover on the ridge in excavated dugouts resembling swallows' nests.

The adaptation of supplies to the conditions of mountain warfare proved difficult for troops and commanders alike. At first the columns of pack-animals did not function too well. The soldiers were unfamiliar with mules, but in the end the animals and actual experience provided the best training. Mules will only work if they are correctly handled and not, as with many horses even to-day, by some inexpert driver. Yet the mule-trains of the ordinary infantry remained an improvised method, whereas they should have been an organised section of each company, as they are with regular alpine troops.

The mountain soldier needs a special diet. A German research establishment started investigations and would in time have produced results. However, we had to do our best with what we had. The only usable nourishment was in the form of concentrated or powdered foods, which the soldiers could prepare while in their positions. These foods had to be tasty and also contain chemically nutritious materials. Hot food that had been prepared behind the lines and brought up the mountains in special containers usually did not arrive until after dark, by which time it was cold. But in the snow and when a battle was in progress this was not acceptable. I ordered the cooking canteens to be moved as far forward as possible, and arranged for the insulation of food containers with straw, but even this was an inadequate expedient.

The transport of the wounded caused us worry because the stretcher-bearers had to be provided by the fighting personnel. Often the fighting for dominating summits was done by battalions with a strength of only 200 men, and companies with only sixty men. In these circumstances every single man counted. If the organisations were bad, four men were detailed for every wounded one. I tried to improve this situation by arranging for the provision of seat barrows and tractor barrows that could be worked by one man, as used in ski-ing.

RESERVES AND COUNTER-ATTACK

The decision to throw in reserves is nearly always decisive for the outcome of a defensive battle. Since the lines are only thinly held, a surprise attack will always result in penetrations. It is only too well known that Hitler with his amateur concepts wanted to counter this state of affairs by simply ordering certain lines to be held under threat of disciplinary action. It was nearly always impossible to comply with a demand of this nature. We adopted a method of keeping at least the local reserves so close to the front line that they could immediately be launched on a counter-thrust. If, as usually happened, a regiment had no complete battalion as reserves for its sector, the forward line would be thinned still further in order to occupy the zone in depth and form reserves. But this naturally made the forward line even more assailable.

The "halt order" and the resulting discrepancy between wishing and doing cannot be attributed to Hitler's ideas about the First World War. For these very ideas could also be found in the inter-war German regulations, which required that on the conclusion of a battle in the deep zone, the forward edge of the battlefield must again be in the defender's hands—which means that the line must be held. The defence of Cassino over a period of months proved that this requirement was impracticable when one side is completely driven on to the defensive because of its inferiority in numbers and equipment. In these battles the forward line was never regained once there had been any serious penetration. On the other hand linear resistance was often put up in the zone of depth where nobody would have expected it.

The lack of local reserves could not always be avoided. But the reserves of the higher command were indispensable. If none are available, the responsible commander is robbed of the possibility of a successful defence. In the art of operational control it is still a most important rule to keep one's reserves intact and to replace those that are used up. A commander cannot hope to arrest an attack unless he has adequate reserves at his disposal. To commit them to action is one of the most difficult decisions of war. Here the famous dictum no longer applies, that "mistakes in the choice of means are a lesser affliction than inactivity". In the case of enemy penetrations, the higher commander must wait until he is sure that this is not merely a diversionary attack, and he must also wait until the right moment has come for the counter-attack. That may see like inactivity. But if the only available reserves are prematurely committed, he will have no other resources to fall back on, and that is usually disastrous. The O.K.W. was more and more insistent that weak reserves be held available well forward in the back area, that is, within 1,000 metres of the front line, where they were expected to fulfil the old requirement of "mopping up" the penetrations by means of immediate counter-thrusts. But this dispersion of forces could accomplish nothing except deprive the commander and his subordinate command posts of the possibility of controlling the operations.

I will give two brief examples showing the right and the wrong use of reserves in the Cassino battles. One of these has already been described in detail and is mentioned here only as a reminder. It was the attack on January 18th against the right flank of XIV Panzer Corps where it rested on the Tyrrhenian Sea, which resulted in a dangerous penetration. The army group threw in its two reserve divisions, the 29 and 90 Pz. Gren. Divs., on the threatened flank. This was taking a risk which subsequently became obvious with the Anzio landing on January 22nd. Yet here 29 Pz. Gren. Div., was quickly pulled back again and was able to help in delaying the Allied exploitation of their successful landing.

This was a truly classic example of the right use of reserves: keeping them far back, exploiting their mobility for dealing with the threatened main front and also with the invasion threat on the coast; then the definite step in committing two divisions, accepting a great risk, and withdrawing one of them after the enemy had been halted, although this withdrawal occurred before the counter-thrust had regained the old line.

The other and opposite example occurred four months later on the same sector of the front. On this occasion the Army Commander, acting on pressure from the O.K.W., had in my absence moved the available 15 Pz. Gren. Div. into the southern sector, deploying the individual battalions far forward. The concept of powerful reserves was abandoned in favour of counter-thrusts to be launched immediately after the enemy had broken through. Thus the battalions were nothing more than reinforcements for the regiments in their forward positions. At this period events would probably have taken the same course even if the operational control had been unimpeachable. The time was ripe for the collapse of this front. Had it been successfully defended, it would still have fallen when the enemy broke out of his Anzio bridgehead.

CO-OPERATION OF WEAPONS

The principles underlying the co-operation of all arms, which governed the training of the inter-war German Army, proved themselves in the defensive battles of Cassino. The exceptional circumstance that the big front of six to eight divisions came under a single corps commander contributed greatly to co-operation between infantry and artillery. It avoided the usual narrower corps boundaries that are so often a hindrance to the formation of points of main effort. Thus it was easy for me by means of repeated and usually slight adjustments of divisional boundaries to create a depth of frontal disposition at the points of main effort which I could not otherwise have achieved.

But above all it was possible to conduct the artillery battle irrespective of divisional boundaries and with a far-reaching concentration of fire-power. Units that did not belong to the divisions' order of battle were ruthlessly withdrawn from other sectors of the front and moved to the point of main effort.

It was precisely the collective fire from numerous batteries in the sectors threatened with a breakthrough that made it impossible for the enemy's tanks to operate, or wrecked the assembly of his armour. A defence such as that at Cassino could only be effective if the massed artillery worked in conjunction with grenade-throwers and smoke-batteries to prevent the enemy using his armour. Resumption of armoured warfare spells the end of any persistent defence.

As always when there is a shortage of ammunition, the special concentration of stocks at certain pre-selected places proved very useful. In a big battle there were three classes of batteries. Those whose fire covered the point of main effort could help themselves without restriction to the ammunition that had been brought up, and this was the maximum that the supply situation permitted. The divisions situated on either side of the point of main effort could, if the attack shifted to their sector, make use of the prescribed daily allowance. Under certain conditions they had to report the consumption of ammunition, indicating the nature of their targets. The third category, the artillery of divisions not participating in the battle, were usually ordered not to fire at all, so that all supply resources could be applied to the centre of pressure. On the basis of the number of batteries engaged, the German artillery was not really inferior to that of the opponent, but it was handicapped through inferiority in the air. Being able to maintain the requisite number of airborne artillery observers, the enemy greatly increased the effectiveness of his guns. His helicopters circled over the German positions every day, almost unmolested. We had no such possibilities. After the breakthrough and in the 1944 withdrawal this enemy air superiority proved disastrous to us because we were compelled to perform all movements under cover of darkness.

The co-operation with armour at Cassino illustrates the character of this phase of the war and of this theatre of war. Purely armoured warfare never occurred again in Italy, not even in the later stages of the retreat.

The central and western European terrain, being dotted with buildings, woods, narrow passes, canals and agricultural land, is by nature less suited to armoured warfare than the Russian or African steppes. Yet it was not for this reason, but because of new methods of anti-tank warfare, that purely armoured operations suffered an eclipse. Both sides now always committed their tanks at the same time. The terrain hindered the tanks and favoured the anti-tank defences, so that the armoured formations could not regain the initiative for themselves, least of all during the bitter defensive battles on a front as narrow as that at Cassino.

True that the Allies made repeated attempts to use their armour for a breakthrough with a view to accelerating the slow tempo of their offensive, but they never succeeded. The floor of the valley between Minturno through Cassino into the Liri valley and on to Rome was intersected by the courses of the rivers Rapido, Gari and Garigliano —all difficult obstructions for tanks.

For an attack on the town of Cassino there were suitable areas for the approach and subsequent breakthrough of tanks, but they had no success here either, for the width of the front involved was too narrow. The German front, tested in defence and organised for it, was able to apply concentrated fire to destroy the enemy's tanks while they were still in the assembly area.

On the German side the anti-tank defence naturally included a considerable number of tanks, which were still available in the Panzer and Panzer grenadier divisions. Of course they had to be operated in accordance with the pecularities of the terrain and of the battle, and not in the form of an armoured wedge as prescribed in the classic rules of armoured warfare; instead they were attached to groups of other units with assorted weapons. And they no longer fought only in their own element—the plain—but also in houses, fields of maize, and on the passes and slopes of the mountains.

HIATUS AND LEAVE

The second battle of Cassino was followed by a relatively quiet period at the front. The reputation of the corps had been established. Sometimes we would sit together in the evenings and exchange ideas. The H.Q. house was owned by the Marchese Campanari, with whom we had developed a friendship. He lived in near-by Alatri and occasionally came over for a meal, accompanied by his wife and daughter. When Alatri was bombed he moved into a neighbouring farmhouse. Like myself, Campanari was a cavalry officer. He had fled from Bologna as he considered it beneath his dignity to allow himself to be disarmed by the Germans; disguised as a cattle-drover he had journeyed to his home. I understood him well and took him under my protection. The Republican-Fascist myrmidons tried to arrest him because of "desertion", and he was also under suspicion because he had been *aide-de-camp* to the Duke of Aosta. Yet he was in no way hostile to Germany.

We were also on friendly terms with the Benedictine nuns and with Bishop Baroncelli in nearby Veroli. The nuns invited me to a meal on several occasions. The convent was situated in a quiet piazetta; a woman opened the door, as nuns are not allowed to leave their seclusion, and we ourselves had to remain in a room outside their quarters. A coal fire glowed in a grid at floor level. The only ornament in this room was a crucifix, but in the centre was a table invitingly laid with food. Then our hostess, the abbess, accompanied by a German nun, appeared behind a doubly-barred small window. In the half-light behind the thick iron bars it was difficult to distinguish their faces, but they displayed the winning kindness, amiability and equanimity that are frequently in evidence with nuns. While we seated ourselves they remained silent behind the grid. Through a revolving door the dishes were passed from the cell to the guest-room and served to us by a woman.

After the battles had subsided I occasionally managed to visit Rome for the afternoon. Driving back from the front, I came within earshot of the thunder of guns as I reached the vicinity of Anzio. After all the hard battles, my senses were more receptive than ever to the beauty of the land. Between the house-high hedges of the Villa Medici in Rome I moved up to the Pavilion, where one gets a view of the entire city. And I looked up other old haunts—Santa Cecilia with its porch and campanile, redolent of the early Christian era despite the eighteenth-century gloss of its interior. Here is the reclining statue of the saint whose undefiled body was discovered at the place of burial some 700 years after her death. In Trastevere the narrow little streets with their simple inns lead to Maria Capella, a little known church that is approached through peaceful cloisters and has the warm atmosphere of the tenth century. Walking back across the Tiber I passed Maria Cosmedin, a church that since its thorough restoration is probably the most representative of the turn of the millenium. Up on the Aventine I came upon the street that runs past S. Allessio, the Villa Maltese and S. Anselmo, all as peaceful and remote as in the long period when nothing of importance happened in that district. At last I could satisfy an old whim to visit Santa Saba, where the German Jesuits have their seat. It was the Saturday of Holy Week, and the archaic building was flooded with the light of hundreds of candles in celebration of Resurrection Day, while the pure voices of the choirboys filled the air. This was a large-scale festival of a kind that unfortunately is rarely seen at St. Peter's or the Sistine Chapel.

Rome still had its concerts and operas. My Italian and German friends had told people that I was very fond of these voices that rose so naturally in song. So the artists from the opera came out to my place at Castell Massimo to sing. But these full voices needed a large space, which was not available there. Several times I visited the Chief Abbott, Baron Stotzingen. The old man had preserved his keen mind and generous kindliness. From his hand at High Mass on Maundy Thursday I received Communion immediately after the Grand Master of the Order of Malta, Prince Chigi, and afterwards both of us lunched with him.

The success at Cassino had the effect of somewhat stabilising political relations in the German-occupied part of Italy. Belief in German invincibility had not entirely vanished. True, the Fascist régime that had been re-introduced after the liberation of Mussolini was nothing more than a façade. Even if better men had been available they could not have wielded any influence since they had no executive powers. The Prefects had little success in their attempts to help the population of the fighting zone with evacuation and supplies. Rome became more and more crowded with people; the masses went hungry while the thunder of the Nettuno guns could be heard. In all this uncertainty there was no let-up in the entertainments of a certain set. Because of the curfew in Rome, Italians invited to parties had to stay on until morning.

On each side there was now an Italian government friendly to those fighting the war. Italians naturally wanted the Allies to occupy their country completely, as this was the only way to end it. Italians in that part of Italy occupied by the Allies had at least escaped bombing from the air, and for them the war, if not the occupation, was already to some extent over. The Germans would never re-conquer that part. Reports reaching us indicated that life for Italians in the Allied zone was not easy; the nourishment was only moderate and treatment by the Allied troops naturally not very satisfactory. Old squabbles were re-animated and prices were rising. An American soldier's pay was equivalent to that of a German staff officer. He had little opportunity of sending it home and therefore spent it. At Castel Massimo I was once visited by a Princess P. who had managed to pass through the lines at Castelforte. She maintained that a large part of the population of Naples was living by prostitution, and that Fascism there was experiencing a certain revival due to dissatisfied elements. I could well imagine it. The Princess had come over in order to obtain funds from the Duce for recruiting Fascists on the other side. She actually carried out her plan and some weeks later slipped back through the lines. Incidentally, she spoke German fluently.

Yet even in Mussolini's new-fangled Republic there were people who never lost their faith in the Germans. These were the incorrigible Fascists who had adopted the outlook of National Socialism; to us German commanders they could become a great nuisance, since their activities involved a horizontal link between the two peoples. These Fascists saw their enemies, not among those who were on the other side of the war front, but among the Monarchists, the Church, the nobility and the General Staff. They regarded the defection of Italy as due to the treachery of those circles that were "hostile to the people"; they joined forces with similarly minded persons on the German side and had close relations with the S.S. and the S.D.; to the latter organisation they served as informers against Wehrmacht commanders under suspicion—a category which naturally included myself. Yet these Fascists constituted only a small minority

I was particularly sorry for the women in the fighting zone. On cold winter nights they had to evacuate hearth and home with small children in their arms, fear and grief in their eyes. But the migration northwards of the population was not much bigger than the other way, for in the north there was nothing to eat. Many could only be removed by force, saying that they preferred death by shelling to death by starvation. For this reason I put up a passive resistance to all evacuation. It was worst in the spring, when last year's harvest had been consumed and no transport was to be had from the Fascist government or the German military administration for carrying flour from the more plentiful areas. It was not surprising that these people prefered to be killed by a shot to other forms of extermination. The noble families of the old Papal State were more honestly friendly to the Germans than the nobility of Piedimonte. They have numerous blood ties with the German nobility and are proud of it. They also feel a need to lean on the big German neighbour, which may be due to historical reasons. Prior to the unification of the Kingdom the Papal State was closely associated with the Habsburg dynasties in North Italy and was also the natural opponent of the House of Savoy, which had allied itself with Liberalism against the Conservatives. But now the House of Savoy was beaten. It had lifted Fascism out of the cradle, and according to the old particularist families had paid for its megalomania by losing its independence. Nor did the strict Catholicism of these families estrange them from Germany. They knew that many of their German relations and friends had remained loyal to the Church.

With these people I led a kind of second or double life in my house, enjoying the advent of spring, finding pleasure in the setting, with the lambs under the blossoming trees. I had a long view across the gentle slopes of the hills towards the chain of white crests of the

Abruzzi standing out sharply against the blue sky. And, in the midst of war, all was peace here in the soft morning light when the dove cooed and the cock crowed.

On April 17th I handed over the command of XIV Panzer Corps to a deputy before proceeding to Führer Headquarters to receive a decoration. I was reluctant to part with the officers of my staff who had become my good friends, and to leave the little house where I had spent so many pleasant hours. I sensed that all this would soon be changed.

The drive in the car took me over the Apennines to the Adriatic. When we reached the sea I felt that I must cast off the clothes that I had worn too long. I got out of the car and surrendered myself to the peacefulness of the ubiquitous spring. It was a blissful hour.

The deserted coastal road led to a goal that had long attracted me. Ravenna, I knew, was not situated on a height or the summit of a hill like so many Italian towns, but lay in the broad, almost featureless plain. People speak of the spell of Bruges, a lifeless city that reflects the Middle Ages only in its walls and the run of its streets. Yet the great days in Ravenna vanished not six but twelve centuries ago. Monuments from that period are completely intact; it is fascinating to realise that here one is face to face with the seventh century. Since that time nothing further seems to have occurred. It is not just any town of the period, but Ravenna, seat of the Goths, a part of Byzantium, the bridge between East and West.

Because of the danger of destruction the mosaics of St. Vitale and of the tomb of Galla Placidia had been protected and hidden, but in St. Apollinare everything was on view: the strange procession of the identical virgins offering the Crown to the Creator. Across a thousand years the mosaics have kept their sparkle; the striding women seem to be moving along a path that leads from the earthly burden to the heavenly peace, and their even steps are like a hymn of rest and prayer. These effigies exude a spirit of solemnity and purity.

Ravenna is the point of contact between East and West. Not far from the picture of the walking virgins stands the massive tomb of Theodore. Salvation comes from the East, and is eagerly taken up by the Romans and the Teutons. What in Byzantium seems courtly, liturgical and formal here forms the corner-stone of the great world of the Middle Ages. From these basilicas comes the development of the sacral style of architecture known as the romanesque. And so the Middle Ages have their beginning—that era of kingdoms imbued with godliness and of men turned towards God. Now the French and German Cathedrals arise, and the sculptures of Naumburg. The last flowering of this period can be seen in the Siena school of painting, whose ultimate paragon is Simone Martini. Then it dissolves into the naturalism of the Renaissance. Hellenism and Latinism break through, the heavenly world becomes earthbound, the gods become human. The pathos is gone, the balance is upset. Calm is succeeded by movement. The melody in stone of the virgins of St. Apollinare Nuovo has faded into history.

REPORTING TO HITLER ON THE OBERSALZBERG

The ceremony of bestowing the decoration proceeded according to a practice dating from the beginning of the war. At that time the award of the Oak Leaves of the Knight's Cross was still confined to a few dozen soldiers of all ranks. The ceremony had lost any personal significance now that hundreds of people wore the decoration, which was being awarded to commanders of successful corps or even divisions, and was thus intended to honour the troops under command.

It was impressive in rather a negative sense when the selected candidates were received on the Obersalzberg. The impression made by Hitler was utterly depressing, and involuntarily I wondered how the young officers and N.C.O.s attending the ceremony would react. This man, to whose fiendish tenacity and nihilistic will the German people were committed, was still regarded by many of these young officers as a demi-god, a man deserving of complete confidence, whose handshake inspired new strength. He wore a yellow military blouse with a yellow tie, white collar and black trousers—hardly a becoming outfit! His unprepossessing frame and short neck made him appear even less dignified than usual. His complexion was flabby, colourless and sickly. His large blue eyes, which evidently fascinated many people, were watery, possibly due to his constant use of stimulating drugs. His handshake was soft, his left arm hung limp and trembling by his side. Yet a striking feature, contrasting with his notorious screaming during speeches or fits of rage, was the quiet and modulated voice that almost inspired compassion since it barely concealed his despondency and weakness.

More noteworthy than this outward impression of Hitler were the words he spoke to this small circle of fortuitously assembled front-line soldiers when he sat down with them at a round table. As regards objectivity his review of the general situation left nothing to be desired. He described the disastrous situation on the Eastern front, where one defeat succeeded another. He informed us that the Battle of the Atlantic had entered a critical phase for the Germans because of the enemy's use of radar. He barely mentioned our successes on the Italian front, which Goebbels' propaganda was exploiting to the full. On the other hand he made no secret of his anxiety over the impending invasion in the West and the prospect of a second front that would use up his forces. The only consolation that he gave to these fighting men was a muttered sentence to the effect that all difficulties must be surmounted through "faith". There was not even a comforting allusion to the hopes centred on the famous secret weapons, hopes on which the ordinary German citizen was being constantly nourished.

It may be that I, who had eagerly absorbed his objective analysis of the situation, was even more strongly impressed by it than those a-political listeners who for the past eleven years had been trained not to see or hear anything that might weaken their "faith"—not even a depressing description of the situation by Hitler himself. But other friends of mine such as General Baade, who had also been summoned to Hitler's presence to receive a high decoration, had the same impression as myself: "The government and the Army are finished—defeated over and over again in the field, damned by history, heading for downfall—and they know it."

This impression was confirmed during the course on *Weltanschauung* which we had to attend at the castle of Sonthofen after receiving our awards. At the end of the course, which was attended by several hundred senior officers, it was intended that Hitler should give a reception. But in the end the shrewd directors of the course preferred not to suggest this to him, much to the disappointment of the many participants! During these sessions the atmosphere remained oppressive, despite Field-Marshal Keitel's optimistic speeches and the artificial joviality of the "Reichsführer S.S." Himmler. I was aware that certain officers of the O.K.W., like General Stieff, who attended the conference, were anything but enthusiastic at having to listen to such propaganda nonsense at a time when the general situation was nothing short of disastrous. But these officers thought it best to conceal their feelings. Fear of a revolution had made the die-hard followers of Hitler keep an eye on the "unreliable generals". The senior National Socialist political officer, who had organised the "spiritual education" of the Army and the "informer" service on its commanders, showed noticeable reserve towards me, as did General Burgdorff, of the Army Personnel Office, whom I had known well in former days. Only the head of that office, General Schmundt, known in the Officers Corps as "John the Disciple", was completely forthcoming and apparently without guile; for hours he held forth to us about his good fortune in being allowed to work with so great a man in these great times!

What was to be done? Perhaps Hitler could be got rid of, but that would not dispose of the whole gang who held the reins of power and were determined to assert themselves like criminals. Many of my younger friends imagined that the Western powers would negotiate with a new German government consisting of generals in revolt. They little knew that even foreigners well acquainted with Germany—

and in this war there fewer of these than formerly—regarded "militarism" as responsible for setting up Hitler, despite the fact that no single group had produced more opponents to him than the German Army. They fancied that they would be known abroad as opponents of Hitler because they were known as such in Germany, and this made them believe in the possibility of negotiations. But our opponents were only interested in unconditional surrender, not least because of the state of public opinion abroad. That the German Man in the Street was politically immature was evidenced by the fact that in contrast to the First World War he was not even disposed to act on his own initiative.

After the course at Sonthofen I went on leave, but was soon recalled. The offensive of May 12th had started.

BREAKTHROUGH AT CASSINO

It was not until the 17th that I returned to the front. I found my quarters at Castel Massimo occupied by the C.-in-C. of the 10th Army and his staff. They had been bombed out of their own headquarters.

In order to explain the situation as I found it, I must refer briefly to events in the German 14th Army facing the Nettuno bridgehead. During the first battle of Cassino an unsuccessful attempt had been made, after thorough artillery preparation, to penetrate the bridgehead. I cannot assess the cause of this failure. In a private conversation Kesselring told me that the newly constituted divisions had shown a lack of offensive spirit, and he seemed very concerned at this. But even if the fighting quality of the men was understandably lower than in the first year of hostilities, there could be little hope of a successful attack against an opponent who was fighting under the artillery protection of a Fleet that remained almost unmolested. The subordinate divisional commanders ascribed the failure to the excessively detailed plan of attack that was ordered by the higher command. While I can offer no opinion on that, it is certain that the results expected from the massing of the German armour were not achieved. Once more it was demonstrated that the Italian terrain, whether in the hills or the plains, is unsuited to operations by tanks in close order. Some of the attacking divisions suffered considerable losses.

After this failure the question had to be considered whether to go on maintaining both the army fronts. The C.-in-C. of the army group decided to do so, despite the fact that after the second Cassino battle had petered out the situation was no better.

A month earlier, on April 13th, I had submitted a memorandum in which I predicted the attack fairly accurately. I was pretty certain that in view of the costly defeats the enemy had suffered since January he would not again choose the Cassino area for his next attack. He would have better prospects of success if he tried to crumple up the German front by operating from the coast. At the very first attempt his attack against the right flank of the corps together with his simultaneous deep outflanking movement coming from the sea, had nearly caused the collapse of the Cassino front. Although there would be no originality or surprise in repeating this direction of attack, it would be a logical exploitation of the Anzio success, where the mere holding of the bridgehead was in itself a victory for the Allies.

In reviewing the situation I was again concerned about 94 Inf. Div., whose task was beyond its strength. I was not so worried about the adjoining and more northerly 71 Inf. Div. Although this division had no experience of mountains and had not yet been able to prove itself as a unit under its commander, General Rapke, some of its regiments had nevertheless already shown merit at Cassino. What distinguished this division from 94 Inf. Div., was that it was already located in the mountains and would have to fight there. In the event of a setback it could not be pushed with its back to the mountains as in the case of 94th Inf. Div., but would be able to evade into the Liri valley where it would be more at home than in the hills. Furthermore, in April I could still assume that in the event of such a setback in the Liri valley I would be able to gather in this division with my fast mobile reserves.

The tactics adopted by the enemy were thus fairly correctly estimated. Yet when his attack was launched on May 12th it came as a complete surprise (Map 12). This can be seen from the fact that many important German commanders were away when it started. The Chief of Staff of the army group was sick. The C.-in-C. of the 10th Army and I had been superfluously ordered to meet Hitler to receive our decorations, after which we had gone on leave. My deputy, an excellent but not so young general, had been rash enough to send my C.O.S. on leave as well, and without his experience to fall back on, the general was not up to his task in this major battle.

This lack of concern was not merely due to inadequate knowledge about the enemy's immediate intentions. To us the Italian front seemed to have generally declined in importance. We expected that the Allies would create the now inevitable second front in France; they would still want to capture Rome, but at a much later date. After the war it became known that the Allies had actually contemplated something of this kind: The Italian offensive was to be halted in order to build up the necessary forces for the offensive in France.

The enemy had made a penetration to the north of Itri. On resuming command of XIV Panzer Corps I at once proceeded to that place. Detached sections of the H. & D. Division had been ordered to seal off the area. Kesselring had achieved one of his favourite ideas

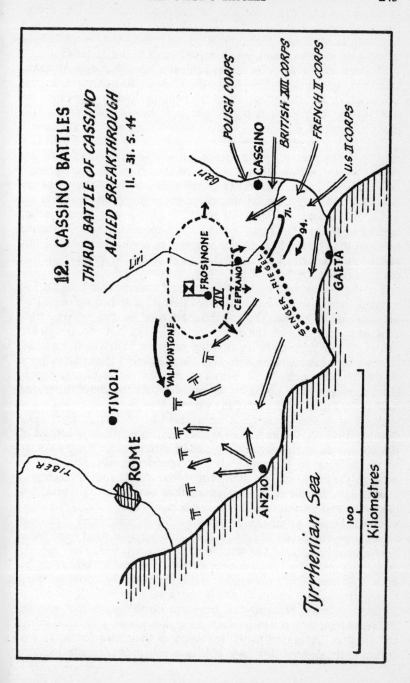

12. CASSINO BATTLES

THIRD BATTLE OF CASSINO

ALLIED BREAKTHROUGH

11. – 31. 5. 44

by sending a specially constituted machine-gun battalion into action, but it fell back. The current explanation was that this unit had first been surrounded and then fought its way out. But in reality the enemy was in hot pursuit, and I myself came under his M.G. fire.

The next day a conference was held at a place between Avezzano and Sora, attended by Kesselring, the C.-in-C. 10th Army and their Chiefs of Staff. I had to report to the field-marshal that this time the front of my corps had not just been penetrated as so often in the past, but that it had been broken through, and that it was now a question of preventing a considerable part of my forces from being cut off if the enemy should attack out of the bridgehead. For this reason an orderly withdrawal should be started, which must proceed while offering continuous resistance from line to line. But even at this late stage the only question that came under discussion was how far south of Nettuno and south of the "C" Line a new defensive line could be built up. The basis of this faulty appreciation of the situation was that the Cassino front (which was not under attack or only slightly under attack), remained intact and was likely to provide further effective resistance.

Yet the enemy had no need to attack Cassino. This time he had avoided the mistakes of his January offensive and had staked all on his outflanking groups. One of them attacked on the extreme right wing of the corps front, the other, operating from Nettuno, threatened to cut off our retreat. There is really no point in trying to establish whether or what mistakes were made in the period immediately prior to the breakthrough. Yet I must criticise two measures and expose them as errors to be noted by the historian. At the above-mentioned conference I made no secret of my views.

The first mistake was the altered chain of command. Ever since October 1943, XIV Panzer Corps had been in continuous control of the operations in the fiercely contested Cassino sector. In the course of the fighting an intimate feeling of confidence had developed as between the corps and the 10th Army, whose staff always functioned with admirable efficiency. This association was based on mutual appreciation and proved itself in the results achieved. Similarly the corps was well known to all the divisions on the fighting front. This had not only psychological advantages, but also purely tactical ones. Once the Nettuno bridgehead had been formed, the corps had to rely entirely on its own resources for forming reserves. These had to come from the front, and could only materialise if the front of the corps included broad stretches of inactivity and if there were no limitations due to corps boundaries. Naturally an army can do the same, but with the difference that it will always have to contend with individual corps commanders' resistance to the reduction of their own forces. It was crucial to the defence that I was able to attenuate the divisional sectors in favour of the main front under attack, and moreover this enabled me to form artillery concentrations. For many months now the artillery was accustomed to being assembled under the corps artillery commander, regardless of any divisional attachment. This alone accounts for our earlier defensive achievements. But now the corps sector had been split up. I doubt whether this would have occurred if I had been able to state my objections to Colonel-General v. Vietinghoff. The result was that we no longer had unified control of operations in this sector of the front. A further handicap was that when the main attack was launched, neither of the two corps commanders knew the front or had ever been in command during such an attack. They lacked my long experience with the troops and my knowledge of the terrain.

Due to the fact that north of the Liri LI Mountain Corps remained in its position while XIV Panzer Corps fell back after the break-through, it was now no longer possible to swivel the entire former sector of XIV Corps round the pivot of Cassino as I had originally intended to do. Hence the "Senger barrier" that I had caused to be built for this very purpose could not be utilised. All through the winter this barrier had been very strongly built up with the help of the Todt organisation and of Slovak contingents. It ran from Terracina through Fondi to Pontecorvo, thence in the general direction of Aquino, and terminated at Piedimonte to the west of Cassino.

Thus the line was particularly suitable as a rallying position for resisting precisely this direction of the enemy's thrust, for which purpose it had been designed. The forces needed to man the barrier were lacking. The divisions were not pulled back into this line, but had to fight in front of it in order to preserve the junction with LI Mountain Corps, which was fighting north of the Liri and was not much exposed to attack. Thus in the enemy's attack on the completely unoccupied Senger barrier the divisions were thrown back and never made a stand at that position.

It was not only the lack of cohesion of the whole front that proved fatal to the issue of the battle. Equally damaging was the second German error, perpetrated before the start of the battle. I have already mentioned that 15 Pz. Gren. Div. which had been correctly set up as a reserve behind the right wing of the corps, was mistakenly split up into battalions in anticipation of the attack, and allocated as local reserves or actually as occupying force for a second line far forward in the battle zone of the threatened area. The mistake is a textbook example of the degeneration of military leadership under the influence of Hitler. A higher commander who in anticipation of being attacked hands out his reserves to his regiments must in consequence confine himself to supervising his subordinates, for he has surrendered the one decisive means of influencing the course of the battle.

The 15 Pz. Gren. Div. had been quite wrongly deployed. Clearly the solution that presented itself was to assemble this division in the area of Fondi and Pico. Here it should have remained intact under its commander and none of its units should have been allocated to other divisions until the start of the attack. It could then have been operated either against the enemy landing on the coast, or in the Liri valley. Above all, the division was in the correct position to cope with the anticipated attack on the right flank of the corps. Not until May 19th did the enemy move westwards across the road between Itri and Campodimele. From the start of the attack there was thus a whole week in which to send forward this battle-worthy reserve division into the gap between the defeated 71 and 94 Infantry Divisions, thereby perhaps halting the onslaught, as had so often occurred before. This counter-attack should not have been launched too soon and its wings would have been dependent on support from the Senger barrier. Then the entire XIV Corps and consequently the LI Mountain Corps would have been able to occupy the Senger barrier in an orderly manner and without being routed. That is how we had operated in the winter months round Cassino.

But now XIV Corps was compelled to fight in front of the Senger barrier in order to maintain a link with LI Mountain Corps which was deployed far forward. As might be expected, my corps was thrown back beyond the barrier without making any stand.

It was left to me to prevent the annihilation of the corps. I saw to it that the units rushing back were sent in a general northerly direction while offering occasional resistance here and there, and I formed an assembly point at Frosinone. Meanwhile, I had to maintain communication with LI Corps on the left until such time as all the troops fighting in the Liri valley had again been put under my unified control. Since the British corps attacking there was not exerting any great pressure the task was relatively easy. It was far more difficult to repel the French corps, which to the south of the Liri was now thrusting swiftly and vigorously towards the north-west. Here for a time no contact could be established to the west with the defeated 14th Army. The 29 Pz. Gren. Div. was ordered to engage the French and came temporarily under my orders. On a broad front the division had varying success in repelling the French advance from the mountains towards the Via Casilina. Under this cover I more or less allowed the enemy to push on westwards past XIV Corps, while I myself withdrew northwards with the main body.

In view of the enemy's rapid progress north-westwards towards Rome it became increasingly doubtful whether the corps could be withdrawn from the region of Frosinone. On May 26th, when the enemy had established a junction with his forces in the Nettuno bridgehead, I felt I should advise the 10th Army commander to take the mobile divisions out of the corps as quickly as possible and to employ them to screen its deep right flank at Valmontone. This was the point of greatest threat to all German divisions standing south of the line Valmontone-Sora. If the enemy should succeed in firmly securing the key position at Valmontone, the withdrawal of these forces would be jeopardised. The remaining available mountain roads east of the Via Casilina were now of doubtful and limited value in view of the enemy's overwhelming air superiority Moreover I anticipated that the enemy could use fast troops to block even these mountain roads, particularly the road from Tivoli via Subiaco to Alitiri—the only one left for the corps' withdrawal. Prior to the attack in May, the Allies too had their differences of opinion as to the best direction to attack once they had established contact with their bridgehead. General Alexander held that a thrust on Valmontone offered the best prospect of embarrassing the German withdrawal.

Afer May 26th I believed that I could throw in a division every day at this threatened key point. I still had a slight hope of thereby establishing a junction between the two defeated German armies, and perhaps of preventing a breakthrough to Rome by means of an attack towards the Alban Hills. If only we could halt the enemy's advance on Rome, then at least the retreating 10th Army could pivot round this key point, and if the situation took a particularly favourable turn, it might even be possible to occupy and defend the "C-position" from the Alban Hills in the direction of Subiaco.

Quite possibly it was already too late to adopt this operational proposal of mine. I had no precise knowledge of the situation with the 14th Army, which had suffered defeat at the bridgehead. Here the enemy quickly achieved big successes in a direction that was of greater operational importance, for it resulted in his capture of Rome by June 4th. This breakthrough caused the already broken front of the 10th Army in the eastern part of the peninsula to waver all along the line. There was now acute danger of the enemy thrusting northeastwards from Rome and driving a wedge between the two retreating German armies, which would probably seal the fate of both.

Although whole sections of the armies might well be destroyed, it was not until June 3rd—the day before Rome fell—that XIV Panzer Corps was given freedom of movement.

HISTORICAL PERSPECTIVE

As the commander of troops on one side I could not rid myself of a feeling of destiny when I reflected that the same battle had already been fought here in an almost identical manner in 1504. History affords a number of examples of this strange duplication. It shows that many a passage of arms derives almost compulsively from the special features of the terrain. The issue of battles like these at such places nearly always decides the fate of the district that is being fought over.

It will be remembered that in 1504 the attacker came from the north. The French, wishing to contest Spain's possession of southern Italy, were initially on the offensive. Their left wing however did not extend so far into the Abruzzi as the wing of my corps; it reached only as far as the region of my first H.Q. at Roccasecca. But in both cases the fight was for possession of the Mignano-Cassino defile—in those days in order to advance from there to Naples, this time in order to capture Rome. On both occasions the breakthrough failed and the opponent occupied the position that we called the Gustav Line.

Then the Spaniards changed over from defence to attack. At first they had as little success as the Allies in 1944. They tried to get operational results by means of a breakthrough at Cassino, just as the Allies did. But then they hit upon the same idea as the Allies did 440 years later. They crossed the Garigliano farther south because of the mountains, and approximately at the same place as their successors —the British 56 Division, which thereby created the basis for the successful May offensive.

The fate of the French was sealed when the Spaniards crossed the Gustav Line. They had the same experience as we did, except that in those days the movements took less time to perform. The French were thrown back on Gaeta, their army was destroyed and southern Italy remained Spanish.

Our war, however, dragged on. It is the distinguishing feature of modern warfare that single battles no longer decide the issue of a war. The battles were mere items on a much bigger account.

Yet our fate seemed to me to be more clearly settled than that of the French in 1504, even if we should be able to continue fighting. In the earlier case the French embarked on an unsuccessful plundering expedition, of which the citizens of the Auvergne or of Brittany were probably not even aware. But in our case the outcome would decide the destiny of Europe. In the broadest sense our passage of arms was the last in Europe's thousand-year-old story. The new world powers, the U.S.S.R. and the U.S.A., had started their encroachment on Central Europe. Gone are the days of independent policy by a Richelieu or a Bismarck. The nations of Europe are compelled to close their ranks, to surrender their thousand-year-old regional sovereignties, to live with one another for better or worse.

THE PURSUIT

The pursuit of a beaten opponent has always formed a special subject of military studies. I feel therefore that it is worth while to examine the pursuit of the German 10th Army, defeated at Cassino, and of the German 14th Army, likewise defeated at Anzio, from the viewpoint of these pursued and numerically inferior armies. Such a study may allow us to formulate ideas on the general aspects of an operational pursuit in modern war.

On January 22nd, 1944, the enemy had established a beach-head at Anzio and had maintained it ever since. Although it was possible to frustrate his simultaneous attacks on the Cassino front, the fact remained that this beach-head, established deep in the rear of the German 10th Army, provided a basis for an operational pursuit of the German forces in the event of a breakthrough on the Cassino front.

We now know that the Allies were in two minds as to the best direction in which to launch the attack from their beach-head in order to be sure of destroying the German 10th Army. That was bound to be the main object of the pursuit. Lord Alexander was particularly anxious to swing the forces in towards the locality of Valmontone, while his subordinate, General Mark Clark, commander of the U.S. 5th Army, considered Rome to be the most important goal. While this latter viewpoint, like all strategic decisions, had a political basis, it also fitted in with the tactical concept of the parallel pursuit, which leads far into the rear of the evading opponent, thus forcing him to capitulate without any major battle.

Let us consider the effect on the German 10th Army of the opponent's dual offensive action—the frontal atack at Cassino and the attack in the rear at Anzio. On May 11th and subsequent days XIV Panzer Corps, whose right wing had rested on the sea, suffered a total breakthrough. On May 17th I had once more assumed command of the corps. Up to May 31st the situation developed as follows:

The corps had been thrown out of the long-defended Gustav Line and had evaded into the Liri valley. The U.S. II Corps had thrust forward along the coast and had joined up with the forces of the U.S. VI Corps breaking out from Anzio. To the north of the U.S. II Corps, the French corps with its Algerian and Moroccan divisions under General Juin was engaged in a rapid advance on Valmontone and had reached the important supply and withdrawal road between Cassino and Rome. Holding back a little was the British XIII Corps which was thrusting from Cassino towards Frosinone.

My suggestion that we should rapidly push towards Valmontone had been turned down, so that the only remaining possibility was to disengage as soon as approval had been obtained from the army group, and putting up a defence on three sides, fall back towards Subiaco along a road in the foothills that was still open.

While one division was deployed rearwards on the right, the others remained committed to the battle. The object was to maintain

a link, even if only tenuous, with the 10th Army which was taking
evasive action northwards, and to prevent the French corps from
throwing us back into the mountains. In addition we had to prevent
any further advance by the British corps towards Frosinone. Hence
we had to maintain our freedom of movement for further moves in a
general north-west direction. I remained at Frosinone at my advanced
battle H.Q. until just before it was over-run. So the operations were
controlled from a forward position towards the rear, which, though
hardly a normal state of affairs, may be desirable for psychological
reasons in order to prevent dissolution.

My friends the Campanaris had gone into the mountains to find
their daughter, but failing to do so, returned to their small farm. Not
until gun batteries were placed near the house did they pack up again
to find accommodation in some remote monastery in the hills.

Castel Massimo became more and more deserted and inhospitable
until finally my own staff moved off, leaving me there alone with my
orderly officer. On the last day Baade thought he would move in,
but he too could not stay, since the light artillery guns were
already barking behind us and the front line would be running right
through the place within a few hours. In the company of Baade and a
British airman who had just been shot down I had a last cup of tea in
that beautiful garden.

The break-away movement of the corps succeeded well enough.
Along the only mountain road, which had no cover, seven divisions
were pulled back in five days and nights. This was achieved despite
the fact that the road was practically unusable in daylight because
of the enemy's air superiority, while one of the vital bridges had been
destroyed by bombs and had first to be rebuilt.

The enemy's attempt to utilise his break-out from the Anzio bridgehead to cut off the retreat of XIV Corps had failed. Yet from this it
must not be concluded that Alexander's plan to use strong forces
from the bridgehead for an attack towards Valmontone would have
met with success. XIV Panzer Corps could only have been annihilated
if the enemy had then also succeeded in pinning it down at Frosinone
or alternatively if he had pushed forward beyond Valmontone towards Subiaco, which would have involved him in major difficulties
of terrain.

Assuming that it is more correct to follow close upon the heels
of defeated troops, then the German 14th Army, which had been
defeated at the bridgehead by the U.S. VI Corps, should have been
pursued beyond Rome along the Tyrrhenian coast, which is what
actually happened. But in the initial planning of the May offensive
Alexander had probably already applied his thoughts to the question
as to whether and when it would pay to wheel inwards in order to
separate the German 10th Army, which was still far back, from the

14th Army, thereby partially or completely blocking the 10th Army's withdrawal.

The German higher command anxiously considered the possibility or even the probability of such a decision by the enemy. That the latter was still thinking of cutting off the German 10th Army became apparent through the new direction of his thrust from Rome north-eastwards towards Tivoli. It was here above all that the 10th Army's right flank would have to be screened.

A far more dangerous situation would have arisen, however, if the line of pursuit had been directed deep into the rear of the German 10th Army. This would have been feasible if the 14th Army had been forced back northwards at such speed that the crossings of the Tiber in the region of Orte had fallen into Allied hands. True that this direction of thrust led into hilly terrain, but the region was better supplied with roads than that to the south of Rome. Had the enemy succeeded in advancing from Orte in the direction of Spoleto, he would have reached the important road running north through Rieti. He would then have been in a position to cut off the retreat of the 10th Army on the line Terni-Spoleto-Foligno, and to separate it from the 14th Army—a result that would have been tantamount to a total defeat of the German army group.

In order to counter this menace XIV Panzer Corps, which with its main body was still fighting to the north of Frosinone, was at last ordered on June 1st to disengage from the enemy and to take over at Tivoli the protection of the right flank of the army. When the corps reached Tivoli it was given the further task of seizing the Tiber crossings northwards as far as Orvieto so as to prevent the enemy breaking across the river. This task therefore involved moving over a stretch of 200 kilometres from Frosinone to Orvieto, for the route included mountain roads with many bends. The whole length of it was incessantly threatened from the air, and the individual divisions could only reach their respective destinations after first warding off enemy attacks at Tivoli, then leap-frogging forward and mutually screening each other. It must also be borne in mind that the U.S. 5th Army in pursuing the German 14th Army northwards was repeatedly delayed by the rearguards of that army.

The war diary registered the race between the pursuing Americans and the screening XIV Panzer Corps in the following terms:

2.6: Enemy breaks through the lines of our right-hand neighbour between Alban Lake and Palestrina.

3.6: 1 Para. Rifle Div., 94 Inf. Div., 15 Pz. Gren. Div. on the march in Tivoli area as flank protection for 10th Army. 90 Pz. Gren. Div., 305 Inf. Div., 26 Pz. Div. cover the move towards the general line Cave (3 km. north-east of Valmontone)—Acuto (20 km. east of V.).

4.6: Enemy in Rome.

5.6: 1 Para. Rifle Div. has occupied a position round Tivoli resembling a bridgehead. Heavy attacks there. (These attacks seem to indicate the enemy's intention of wheeling at least some of his forces inwards in order to cut off XIV Pz. Corps.).

Enemy breakthrough north of Bagni Albula (3 km. west of Tivoli). 29 Pz. Gren. Div. sent into action to the west of 1 Para. Rifle Div.

6.6: Breakaway movement to the general line Tivoli-Subiaco has succeeded. The impetus of the enemy's attack in the mountains has been broken. (This refers to frontal pressure by the pursuing British XIII Corps). Further attacks on 1 Para. Rifle Div.

7.6: Enemy penetration north and north-west of Rome.

8.6: 26 Pz. Div. occupies Tiber crossings at Orte and to the south and holds them against attacks by weaker forces. 334 Inf. Div. is arriving from 10th Army. 90 Pz. Gren. Div. on the march to Orvieto.

9.6: Attacks on the Tiber bridgehead repulsed. Advanced units of 90 Pz. Gren. Div. reach Orvieto.

Here I must turn briefly from consideration of the situation to my personal experiences during these fighting days. My corps H.Q. was again caught up in the bustle of a war of movement. On May 29th we moved into a battle H.Q. at Abbadia della Gloria, near Anagni. It was a romanesque ruin standing amidst tall elder bushes, and not exactly comfortable. From here we wanted to move to Bellegra, near Subiaco. When on May 31st I drove there alone, the road already lay under the fire of the enemy's forces pushing north between the 10th and 14th Armies. Laboriously we repelled our pursuer, but we could not reach the intended quarters, which were situated close to the pass road and were subjected for hours to the fire of low-circling fighter-bombers. We had to drive on at random and find lodgings somewhere for the night. Awaking the next morning in the camp at Ciciliano, we found ourselves in a wonderful wood of chestnut trees in a beautiful setting. I had not had so refreshing a night's rest for many a month.

I spent the following night in a castle at Orvinio, which lies at a good elevation. Here in the deserted but well-furnished bedroom of a young *Marchesa* I slept in a wonderfully wide bed, with clean linen and a bath provided.

Our next stop was a wooded camp at Cantonella near the Tiber, where in the meantime we had succeeded in establishing contact between the two German armies. But we remained very uninformed about the fighting on the far side of the river. My most northerly division had reached Orvieto and on June 10th we moved into a new wooded camp at Fratta Todina, north of Todi. On our way there we passed through the towns of Narni and Todi, both still completely of the Middle Ages. At Narni I was impressed by a basilica that was unusual in not being overlayed with seventeenth-century ornamentation; it still conveyed the potent charm of the turn of the millenium.

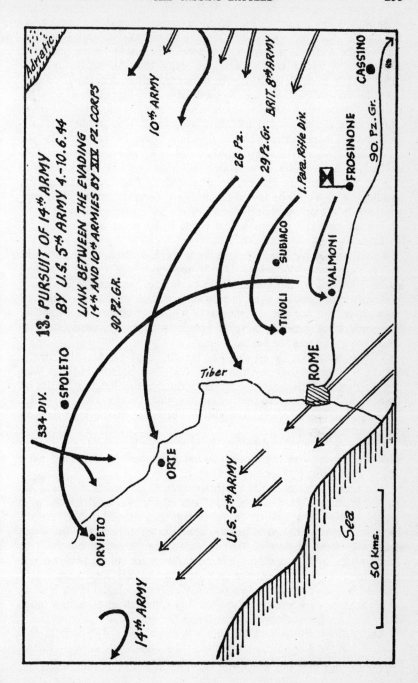

13. PURSUIT OF 14th ARMY BY U.S. 5th ARMY 4.–10.6.44

LINK BETWEEN THE EVADING 14th AND 10th ARMIES BY XIV PZ. CORPS

As at Cassino, so now I again had seven divisions under command. To control the operations of so many divisions was only possible because the staffs of Panzer corps usually had a far more generous allowance of radio communications units than those of infantry corps. With such far-ranging movements, often requiring several days to complete, the only method of exercising control was by radio.

The orders were issued as "saddle orders". This implies that on receipt of general directives the divisions must be prepared to act independently and to improvise. My battle H.Q. was often as primitive as that of a battalion commander, but that is to be expected in a war of movement. In the corps commander's tent by the light of a candle, orders would be issued to divisional commanders on their way through. While on the march the divisions had to report their position at regular intervals to enable the corps to keep the march table up to date.

This march table could not be very rigid, since air attacks could in any case cause alterations. Due to the scarcity of roads, these had to be allocated to individual divisions for set periods. Within these periods the divisions moved in marching groups which supplied their own cover, but for the division as a whole no cover was provided. The orders for supplies were of special importance, particularly in regard to the figures for fuel supplies.

The co-ordination of all this was facilitated by the fact that nearly all the divisions under my command had long become familiar with the methods of the corps command during the lengthy battles at Cassino and also because the commanders of the motorised divisions, being former cavalrymen, had got to know me in the long days of peace-time training.

Having been prevented from driving a wedge between the retreating German armies, the enemy also found it impossible to cut off parts of the 10th Army by blocking their way.

The commander of the U.S. 5th Army had declared on the occasion of the breakthrough to Rome that "one of the two Kesselring armies would never fight again"—a prophecy that proved too optimistic since no overtaking pursuit had been accomplished. On the other hand the short history of the war that was published by the War Department in Washington while hostilities were still in progress was right in the following assessment: "Field-Marshal Kesselring's 10th and 14th Armies, whose destruction was the goal of the struggle in Italy, were not completely destroyed, but found themselves in a headlong retreat after suffering severe losses".

The 10th Army Command, with whom we had only sporadic contact, evidently judged the situation in the same light as XIV Panzer Corps, as can be seen from this teleprinter message:

"XIV Panzer Corps has been able to relieve the Panzer and Panzer grenadier divisions engaged on its front and to apply them to their new task of protecting the right flank with such speed that at the very last moment the enemy's northward break-through and the concomitant disruption of the German front were frustrated. Exceptional difficulties were involved in the execution of this movement. That they were overcome constitutes a masterpiece in the art of military leadership and is in line with the corps' previous high achievements."

(Signed) v. Vietinghoff.

The purusit by the Allies in the Italian theatre of war cannot be regarded as entirely typical for pursuit in modern war. The operational hypothesis deriving from the Nettuno bridgehead was applicable only to the particular geographical form of the peninsula in this theatre of war. The attacker, operating from the coast, had already come to grips with the defender in his rear before ever he needed to initiate any new attack. As we have seen, the pursuit by the forces issuing from the bridgehead always held more promise of results than the frontal pursuit by the British 8th Army or even by the U.S. II Corps and the French Corps. When the decisive pursuit was invalidated, the Allied attackers were robbed of the initial operational advantages of their situation.

When the enemy had to switch from an overtaking to a frontal pursuit, he reverted basically to a form of pursuit that had prevailed throughout the war. Thanks to the motorised mobility of the mass of the defender's fighting troops, these are able over and over again to form loosely associated lines across whole Continents, and this precludes the old classic form of the overtaking pursuit. Even if these lines were penetrated and indeed frequently broken through, they repeatedly formed themselves anew. In this sense the history of the war in the east after Stalingrad was simply that of an uninterrupted slow pursuit by superior Russian forces exerting frontal pressure. It is noteworthy that even the massing of armour could not alter this state of affairs. Even after a decision had been achieved in such conclusive battles as Stalingrad, Alamein, Tunisia and Normandy, it was still possible for the tenacious loser to continue his fighting withdrawal for years on end. In our case we suffered from the general strategic illusion that we had not been decisively beaten by any out-flanking manoeuvre in the manner of the nineteenth century. In a modern war this concept is no longer tenable.

In Italy the breakthroughs of May 1944 did not lead to any over-taking or decisive pursuit, and so it may be worth examining the possibilities that the Allies missed.

In retrospect I must come to the conclusion that the Allies were not at the time fully conscious of their great opportunities in the Italian land operations. They could have landed anywhere on the lengthy coast to operate in the rear of the defender, who was inferior at sea and in the air. True the fighter protection that the Allies considered essential was still dependent on land-bound bases, and the choice of landing sites was therefore limited by the short radius of action of the fighters. That will not be so in the future, when ship-borne fighters will allow a choice of landings that is limited only by the radius of action of the Fleet itself.

Yet there remains an unmistakable connection between the unsatisfactory course of the Allied land campaign and the missed opportunities of operating from seaward.

I must again refer to my earlier surmise that a landing in Sardinia and Corsica instead of at Salerno would have given the campaign an entirely different complexion, for these two islands off the main-land were equivalent to aircraft carriers. From them the Allies could have landed at Leghorn at any time, thereby possibly saving them-selves a whole year of laborious and costly fighting.

6

THE DEFEAT

WITHDRAWAL THROUGH TUSCANY

In order to prevent an enemy breakthrough between the two German armies, XIV Panzer Corps had been deployed far in the rear of the 10th Army and consequently the corps now found itself in the zone of the 14th Army. On June 12th, while driving up to the front at the Tiber, I was ordered by radio to report to 14th Army H.Q. For me this was an unwelcome change. We had got used to working in with the 10th Army Command, felt that we belonged to it and knew that we could count on its sympathy and understanding. Col.-General v. Vietinghoff and his C.O.S., General Wenzel, were capable leaders with clear ideas, whose decisions were always unambiguous. Between them and myself there had never been any differences of opinion. On those occasions when they had to carry out decisions that they could not approve, it meant that like all of us they were victims of developments that I have attempted to describe in the preceding chapter.

In Italy I had always had the best German divisions under my command, but now I found that they were mostly third-rate. It was poor consolation that I and my corps H.Q. staff had been deliberately chosen for the task because of the precarious situation on this sector of the front. My old divisions were subordinated to I Parachute Rifle Corps on the left wing of the 14th Army, while I was pushed in between that corps and LIV Corps which was stationed along the coast. During the fighting the allocation of forces as between the latter corps and my own underwent a number of changes.

Since there was as yet no corps H.Q. staff in the zone that I had taken over, the divisions had been subordinate to a so-called corps command, which was nothing more than a divisional command entrusted with controlling the operations of the other associated divisions, and therefore lacked the requisite facilities for communications.

Two of these divisions were so-called Luftwaffe Field Divisions, which had been constituted from redundant air force personnel and

had retained this appellation although they had been incorporated
into the Army. Lacking fightng experience, they were not battle-
worthy. One of them, the 19th L.F. Div., was disbanded during the
fighting withdrawal. The other, whose officers consisted mainly of
former cavalry officers, did better but it too was later disbanded.

Another unit here was the Turkmens Division, consisting of
Turkmens with a 25 per cent. leaven of German key personnel. The
Turkmens have many good qualities, such as modesty and loyalty
to any leader whom they know and trust. Their bearing was better
than I expected, yet like many primitive peoples they were sensitive
to artillery and aircraft fire, against which they could not defend
themselves. In close combat they showed fighting qualities. However,
they lacked the spiritual motivation that makes people want to fight.
Like all those who had agreed to enlist in the so-called Eastern
Battalions, the Turkmens had chosen military service because it
enabled them to escape the inadequate food in the prisoner-of-war
camps and because it offered them greater freedom. Under fire they
frequently ran away, but could be easily re-assembled and led forward
again.

When I reported to the C.-in-C. of the 14th Army, General Lemelsen, the successor of Colonel-General von Mackensen, I found Field-
Marshal Kesselring there. Mackensen had been relieved owing to
disagreements with Kesselring. In the spring of 1943 as a divisional
commander I had fought under him when he commanded the 1st
Panzer Army, and I had learned to appreciate him.

The conference lasted several hours. I noticed that unimportant
details, such as operations by individual pairs of tanks took up too
much time. In all the fighting that lay behind us this kind of detail
had never formed the subject of discussion between the 10th Army
commander and myself, for von Vietinghoff always adhered to the
principle of giving general directives, and avoided interfering in the
detailed control of operations, as indeed was the normal practice in
the German armies. But this conference between the C.-in-C. of the
army group and the 14th Army commander was more in the nature
of an enquiry.

For my part I informed Kesselring that the forces at my disposal
were quite inadequate for the task which had been assigned to me.
I could not understand why it had been decided to choose this particular part of the front for operating all the weakest divisions.
Clearly the main axis of the enemy's offensive thrust was along the
Tyrrhenian coast, for he had recognised this as being the region of
least resistance. Moreover, apart from the movements already described, which might have led to the separation of the two German
armies, this was operationally the enemy's most favourable direction.
On several occasions during the fighting that ensued in this sector

I suggested that this very part of the front should be reinforced with higher quality divisions. True, such proposals are always being put forward by commanders; yet in this case I was quite sure of the priority of my claim over that of the other corps commanders. If a stand were to be made at all, then this must occur on the army group's western wing. The corps on the right wing must form the pivot round which all the other corps would gradually wheel back. Only in this way could the front be slowly shortened while assuming a line running across the boot of Italy from north-east to south-west.

I fear that the 10th Army was not pulled back more rapidly simply because it was not attacked with sufficient vigour, and in consequence it could boast of some local defensive successes. I wanted to fall back to the Gothic Line. The reason later advanced for adopting the other and to my mind mistaken plan was that the important port of Ancona must still be held—an argument that seemed to me devoid of logic.

So long as I lacked efficient divisions the front of the corps was more than once in danger of disintegration. It was not until such divisions were brought up that there could be any ordered control of operations in my sector. The divisions that eventually arrived were: first the severely battle-strained 3 Pz. Gren. Div., then the outstanding 26 Pz. and 90 Pz. Gren. Divs.

Before these units arrived my more or less scattered divisions had been thrown back into the mountain terrain south-west of Siena by the enemy's northward thrust from Grosseto. During the twelve days following the capture of Rome on June 4th, the Allied 5th Army had moved forward 140 kilometres—a rate of advance that amounted to the pursuit of a defeated opponent. When XIV Panzer Corps took charge, the rate of advance was slowed down to thirty kilometres in the week from June 16th to 23rd and to another thirty kilometres during the subsequent three weeks.

On June 12th, my corps H.Q. staff occupied a wooded camp in St. Fiora and four days later moved to Montalcino, where I experienced some of the blackest moments. What a change had set in since the days of Cassino and Castell Massimo! We had moved into Tuscany, and I was staying with a landed family of the lesser nobility. The household struck me as peculiarly German in character; the very hospitable occupants led a happy family life and never complained. They made no pretence of any particular culture but were evidently wealthy. The adolescent daughter of the house with her blonde plaited hair could have been equally at home in northern Germany.

In one of our moves by night the car belonging to Colonel von Altenstadt had crashed over a declivity—the sort of thing that was liable to occur during nocturnal marches. Miraculously the Colonel escaped with his life, but suffered severe lacerations of muscles. For a time he continued his duties as my Chief of Staff, but eventually had to go home for treatment. He seemed to be making a slow recovery, but on the day before he was due for discharge from the hospital he died of thrombosis. How often in moments of acute crisis had he encouraged all of us with his unfailing cheerfulness! Now he had died within a few seconds with a song on his lips. My staff of Cassino days was no more.

In my new quarters I also had to give up the hope I had always cherished of being able to see my children unscathed in limb when the war was over. After a great deal of close combat my son was wounded in the forearm—it was his eighth wound—and the plaster bandage caused gangrene, necessitating amputation of the arm.

In addition to the difficulties at the front there was now a new one of which we had so far been unaware. The rear areas of the fighting line were no longer free, but were dominated by guerrillas whose raids became a regular feature. In particular the roads in the wooded district north of Massa Marittima were being repeatedly blocked. We had no choice but to divert the supplies or fight laboriously to clear the roads again. Nor could the battle H.Q. be situated behind the centre of the corps sector, since the telephone connections had to lie outside the area threatened by the partisans. Hence in the days before we crossed northwards over the line of the Cecina we usually sited the corps H.Q. staff somewhat to the left of centre. The divisions could only be reached in a roundabout way through Volterra and Siena.

Consequent upon the strengthening of the front through the arrival of the Panzer and Panzer Grenadier divisions the enemy's advance had been slowed down. I therefore hoped to be able to put up a delaying defence in the Cecina sector for some time at least. Meanwhile the Normandy invasion had started. It was a considerable relief to us in the Italian theatre of war when strong elements of the enemy's air force were withdrawn. At the time we in the corps had no idea of the extent of the reduction of Allied forces to meet the needs of the new front in France. From June to the beginning of August one Allied division every week was taken away. Italy had become a subsidiary theatre of war.

Although the terrain in the Cecina sector had no particular significance for defensive purposes, yet the hills in the north of the region afforded an extensive view of the enemy-occupied country as well as providing cover for our own hinterland. This was once more under our effective control, since it contained few wooded areas and was therefore free from guerrillas. Some of the low-lying parts were sufficiently open for armoured operations.

Yet any prospect of prolonged resistance on this line was illusory. Despite the favourable terrain and the reduction in enemy air activity, even our best divisions found themselves driven farther north in a series of heavy engagements. Halting on the heights just north of Cecina, I saw for myself how at a distance of two kilometres ahead of and below me dozens of enemy tanks were preparing to attack. Inevitable they would break through our tenuous lines. The Etruscan walls of Volterra, though several feet thick, had no tactical significance in this type of fighting. Moreover I no longer possessed the comprehensive communications network that at Cassino had enabled me to suddenly concentrate the corps artillery on targets of this nature.

In this summer battle of Tuscany I was torn between the grim prospect of defeat and the sheer beauty of my surroundings. My duties frequently took me through Siena. The collection of Sienese *Trecentisti*, especially the paintings of Simone Martini, Duccio and Lorenzetti, had been hidden away and were inaccessible, so that I had to be content with the wonderful freshness of the set of Pinturicchios in the Cathedral Library. Yet I was too much under the spell of the *Trecentisti* for the library pictures to arouse in me anything more than the admiration of an ordinary museum visitor.

As usual, Baade had his battle H.Q. just behind the front line. From his room I could look out on San Gimignano with its numerous steeples. The pure, fresh cathedral contains the chapel of Santa Fina, ornamented by Ghirlandaio. It is a strikingly simple chamber with the reclining Holy Virgin, the two chairs, the table and the homely repast. It was in this town and at this time that Savoranola began his thorny path—the zealot vainly endeavouring to arouse humanity, contrasting with the ingenuousness of the dying Virgin. Which of these two concepts had the deeper appeal—the profound calm of this simplicity or the strident cry of the preacher of repentance?

In the more open country to the north of the Cecina we could at least oppose the enemy's tanks in a battle of armour and thereby prevent a breakthrough. While we were still fighting in the wooded country south of Volterra, our tanks, which unfortunately included numerous Tigers, could only operate on the roads. They were indispensable as support for the defeated and the demoralised infantry, yet dozens of these monsters had fallen out of the fighting because even when only slightly damaged we had no means of dragging them away. Guerrillas blew up the bridges ahead of and behind the tanks or quickly made barriers with felled trees. One reason for the heavy losses was that tanks newly arrived from Germany were sent into action piecemeal, usually not more than two at a time. Having had much experience in operating tanks in the East, I protested against this squandering of irreplaceable material, but it was useless, for the orders came from a higher quarter—from persons with no personal experience of armoured warfare. Nor did the infantry have any close co-operation with tanks, with the result that the latter acted independently. Experience had taught me that the tanks often wanted to give up the fight for inadequate reasons, such as minor technical faults. If a Tiger became temporarily immobile, it could only be towed away by another Tiger. Such targets were very conspicuous to the enemy with his good air and artillery observation and were soon under fire, which inevitably caused further damage to their propelling mechanism. To the south of the Cecina the losses among our ranks were painfully high.

But even in the open country north of the Cecina we could not get the better of the enemy's armour. We had to content ourselves with the knowledge that as long as we opposed his attacks, this would upset his plans to launch major concentrations of tanks in close order deep into our positions for the purpose of achieving a breakthrough. It was always the same story—major formations of tanks never succeeded in breaking through, be it in the mountains, the woods, or the so-called open terrain which at first sight seemed suitable for armoured operations. In the western theatre of war the only employment that remained for tanks was to attach them to the infantry as its mobile, armoured, heavy weapon.

Especially in its last phases our withdrawal under frontal pressure to the Arno conformed to the concept of delaying resistance as laid down in the German instructions for the 100,000-man (pre-war) Army. True that these regulations had been designed for the fighting technique of the infantry divisions of those days, which had since been re-organised. Here in Italy the divisions were all motorised, and whenever an infantry division was engaged, we at least tried to improvise motorisation of its rearguards. In practice this resulted in many departures from the last German peace-time regulations.

It was not only the motorisation that led to different tactics, but also our tenuous occupation of the front lines, whose density was no greater than the old regulations would have prescribed for rearguards. Now the forces detached as rearguards were much weaker still; to give them any big fighting assignment would have impaired their confidence. Under prevailing conditions they were little more than battle-worthy patrols. These will always suffice where the main forces, prior to a rush withdrawal, have secured a major defensive success against the enemy. Rearguards as weak as this must on no account lose contact with the main forces.

But if the main forces exploit their mobility to retreat at once to a greater distance—say thirty kilometres—then responsible commanders must be detailed for the rearguards in order to co-ordinate their disengaging movements, as prescribed in the regulations. In order to harmonise these duties as between the various divisions the corps issued timetables on which the break-away rushes were precisely prescribed in regard to time and space. Naturally these tables presupposed that the enemy would exert normal pressure. The control and co-ordination of such weak and scattered rearguards was a particularly difficult problem that called for experienced commanders amply equipped with radio facilities. In addition they needed to have mobile main bodies at their disposal in order if necessary to fight for longer periods at vital points, and so provide a backing for the weak advanced units and also safeguard the essential contact with neighbouring units.

When the rearguards had been withdrawn to within some ten kilometres of the new main positions, the control of operations was again centred on the main forces. The moment for the final gathering in of the rearguards was then governed by the requirements of the main forces themselves. Only in exceptional cases did the corps commander intervene with direct orders for harmonising the operations of the divisions.

The nearer XIV Panzer Corps came to the Arno, the fiercer was the fighting, for here the divisions would have to make their stand. If the corps had declined to do battle, the enemy could perhaps have exploited the open terrain to break through the actual Arno position. He could have thrown our weak rearguards back on to the main body and have over-run the main forces before these had been able to organise their more permanent defences.

In any case we had to fight decisively before reaching the Arno. Before occupying a new main battle line that is to be held for some time, it is essential to involve the enemy in considerable exertions, thereby weakening him and preventing him from at once launching a spirited attack across the new obstruction. If the defender breaks off a successful defensive battle, he will gain time and can the more easily settle into the new defensive line.

That method had already brought us success at Cassino. Of course the new main battle line had to be occupied while strong elements of the divisions were still fighting in the forward positions, unless whole divisions happened to be available for manning the line. The elements in the forward positions had to be ready to fall back at any moment into the main battle line. If they succeeded in this, the defender would acquire the initiative, at least for a certain time.

The burden of the increasingly bitter fighting fell on the 26 and 90 Pz. Gren. Divs. On my way up to the front I usually proceeded via the old Imperial Palace of San Miniato. The only way to reach General Baade's battle H.Q. was by passing through the barrage fire at Palaia. Laboriously we crept up-and-downhill through the thicket trying to find a way through gaps in the shell-fire. In memory of this experience I wrote the following for the excellent little daily newspaper of Baade's division:

For me it was always a pleasure to visit your division when it was in my corps, for with you I saw and shared the real fighting. The battle headquarters were always observation posts. Here one could see the enemy assembling and attacking, could observe his fire and the co-operation of our own weapons. Seeing all this was of great value to me as your higher commander, as it gave me a true picture of the situation.

But what attracted me even more to the main battle line of your division was to see you in action. Here "every man pulled his weight"—to use the expression of your divisional commander. The activity of all the forces seemed to be controlled by an invisible thread. Every man made the impression of a veteran fighter, not waiting for instructions but seeming to know from past experience what was required of him in every situation. Above all, each man seemed to realise that in any critical situation there was no better solution than to fight, and fight hard.

However great the exertions, however strong the enemy, however serious our own losses, I was always greeted by cheerful faces. This gave me renewed strength for my own task. I thank the division and all the soldiers whom I got to know during these days of battle.

On the ride back from this scene of bitter fighting it was not long before my senses were again steeped in the beauty of the Tuscan landscape. Behind long rows of cypress trees some large villas reflected the light from their ochre-washed façades. Nature luxuriated in the full bloom of summer. A short way from the big road and near Castell Fiorentino, where all was peace, I came upon the little church of the Sighing Madonna with its frescoes by Benozzo Gozzoli. For 500 years it has been an object of interest mainly to historians, and for me, too, this was an historical visit, recalling the same artist's frescoes in the famous Camposanto in Pisa. These great Florentine painters had not forsaken naturalism in their work. Fra Angelico is by no means representative of them.

When my corps occupied the Arno positions the enemy confined himself to destroying the river-bridges in the rear of the divisions, but this did not cause a crisis. Owing to the low state of the water it was possible within a few days to build up ford-bridges which had the advantage of remaining hidden from air reconnaissance. Behind the Arno a period of relative quiet now ensued in the sector of the corps. Again it was proved that a river line can be a great advantage when used as a defensive front. Here the river bank covering the length of our line gave the German forces the feeling of security that they so badly needed. Immediately in front of them the field of fire was open, and at many points the river was an obstacle to tanks.

WAR OF POSITION ON THE ARNO

On July 16th my corps H.Q. staff moved its battle headquarters to the vicinity of Pistoia, where it remained for one month. The valley of the Arno lay sweltering in the sun. The walls of the exposed villa standing on the southern slope absorbed the heat to such an extent that it continued to radiate from them all through the night. We had a swimming-pool and many other amenities, but in my view these were not pleasant quarters, for they lacked any homely appeal.

My journeys to the front now took the form of tours of inspection. It was now full summer. At this time of year the green becomes darker, purple peaches and golden-yellow pears grow above the ripening vines and corn. The maize stands high as a jungle while the earth gets more parched.

The sector of the corps included Pisa, Lucca and Pistoia. Like Florence, Pisa was in the front line, but here there was no fighting. I paid another visit to this town, so distinct from all other Italian places, and lingered again over the Camposanto frescoes which display the work of so many masters.

Lucca lay behind the front. It is shut in by a circular wall and suffers from no architectural blemishes. In these war days it probably appeared even more dead and deserted than in peacetime. I was able to steep myself completely in the spirit of the twelfth century, in which the majority of its splendid churches had their origin—examples of romanesque art such as the purity of San Frediano, the magnificent façade of San Michele; San Pier Somaldi, San Alessandro and Santa Maria fuori portam. The Cathedral of San Martino together with the neighbouring San Giovanni and the gardens form an *ensemble* in which architecture turns into landscape.

Pistoia also lay behind the front, but it suffered far more. S. Giovanni Forcivitas and S. Dominico were destroyed by bombing. Other romanesque jewels such as the lovely, tall S. Andrea and the well-preserved S. Bartolomeo were still standing. The favourite church of the inhabitants, who lived behind locked doors, seemed to be S. Francesco, which is rated Gothic, though locally described as Franciscan because it originated with the dissemination of that Order. It is simply a large hall, which for a long time was out of use until in recent years it was furnished with new decorative windows and re-consecrated. Its sacristy contains frescoes by Capana.

On one visit to the front I got out of the car as was my custom and continued on foot in order to dodge the enemy's fire. In the burning sun with bare torsos we strode across the meadows and vineyards. Towering high against the sun was the church of a village that we wanted to avoid. But as the enemy's artillery remained silent and did not disturb the noonday peace of summer, we climbed up to the place and obtained a long view of the Arno valley. The background of the landscape turned more deeply blue, as in the paintings of Leonardo da Vinci. After we had left the place I consulted the map to establish our whereabouts. We had been looking down from Vinci into the valley of the Arno!

While we were still moving into the Arno positions the High Command was already wondering how long they should be held. It was entirely against the practice of the O.K.W. to give up a position that had not been broken through by the enemy. The Gothic Line was not yet ready; indeed, a new position never is. I myself did not fancy this line, for again it was fully exposed to the enemy's view, being situated on a forward-facing slope. For long stretches it ran through wooded terrain. In order to create a field of fire it was necessary to fell trees in the extensive areas of the woods immediately in front of the positions, and this made them all the more conspicuous. Experience had taught me how easily such wooded positions, possessing a limited range of vision, can be lost through enemy infiltration. While we were still fighting in the centre of Italy I remembered hearing some severe criticism of this Gothic position by experts in mountain warfare.

Nevertheless there were weighty reasons for giving up the Arno positions, the most important being Florence. The German High Command was unwilling to bear responsibility for the possible destruction of the city. Field-Marshal Kesselring had always advocated sparing the Italian towns. Moreover it was barely possible to feed the population. Florence was not in my own sector, but I had similar problems. It was ridiculous to think that the destruction, for instance, of the unique Pisa square with its Cathedral, Campanile and Baptistery could be justified merely because the German military commander wanted to hold a defensive line along the Arno rather than one running slightly farther back, through the woods and hills. Although Lucca was farther back from the front, both it and Pistoia, on the left wing of the corps, contained irreplaceable works of art. In addition there were countless frescoes that could not really be protected. They were in the smaller villages, like those by Filippo Lippi which I "discovered" in the otherwise unremarkable Prato. These frescoes had taken the artist sixteen years to complete, and were unique in illustrating the change between the first and second half of the *Quattrocento*.

Less obvious was the fact that a defence of the Arno position might endanger a collection of works from the Uffizi Galleries that was supposed to be in safe hiding. Because of the risk of Allied bombing these pictures had earlier been removed from Florence to the countryside, but this did not render them immune from artillery fire. Indeed, they were located right in the middle of the fighting. It was a strange experience when in some villa being used as a battalion command post we happened to find a locked room in which priceless treasures were stored without any security measures. Specially detailed collecting parties as well as the staff of my corps and divisions did their utmost to salve these works of art, sometimes incurring personal danger. It is a tragic thought that all such efforts came under suspicion because of the concurrent "salvage" activities of Göring's special commandos.

Florence was abandoned on the night of August 2nd, and gradually the entire Arno front was evacuated. On August 18th I moved my corps H.Q. from Pistoia a long way west, to a position north of Bagni di Lucca, since I had meanwhile been charged additionally with the entire coastal sector up to Genoa. Without any notable fighting the corps was slowly pulled back from here to the Green Line.

Yet in areas away from the front on the roads over the mountains life became increasingly insecure. Large sections of the Italian people had rebelled against their former ally. The routes we used for the withdrawal ran for 100 kilometres across bleak and coverless pass roads into the plain of the Po, which we were unable to dominate. Raids were a daily occurrence, and it was difficult to capture the guerrillas, who roamed about the high mountains. Some were under Communist leadership, others under the British. At first one could distinguish the so-called patriots from the Communists. Thus it might happen that our trucks would be intercepted by bourgeois partisans who respected their Red Cross markings; they would be allowed to proceed after being warned of a Red partisan ambush farther along the same road.

The justifiable anger that was generated by these raids, especially when the situation was critical, and the fact that the perpetrators were not caught, led to reprisals by the German troops. But the guerrillas evaded these counter-measures, which unfortunately fell too often on innocent people, thus producing the opposite effect to that intended. Consequently the Germans were hated by more and more people. Most Italians wanted only to see the end of the war and live in peace. When the guerrillas terrorised certain villages, the Germans regarded their inhabitants as implicated in the plot. Yet it was wrong always to hold them responsible for the acts of the terrorists. Certainly a few individuals were ready to help the bands, but the majority had acted under duress. Nearly every house was expected to provide accommodation for men and equipment, nearly every woman and child was told or forced to be an agent or an informer. I took great trouble to oppose these aberrations and also gave instructions for German transgressors to be dealt with. This was not easy, particularly in the case of divisions that had been under my command for tactical purposes only, but were not under my jurisdiction as regards discipline.

The development of the situation had robbed the Fascist-Republican Government of its last support from the Italian people. The government-sponsored Blackshirt Brigades were probably more loathed by the population than were the German occupying troops or the Allied liberators, or the guerrillas of whatever political colour. The compulsory co-operation with the Blackshirts, far from easing the task of the German armed forces, made it more difficult, for it meant that the Germans were put in the same category with the most hated section of the population. It is true that we were in no position to dispense with the services of spies for keeping an eye on the activities of guerrillas.

Reconniassance into the enemy's hinterland showed that the situation was not much better for the population, except for the fact that they were free from terrorist activities and from the consequent justified or unjustified reprisals. Meanwhile, those Italians who were engaged in prosecuting the war more or less left the population to its fate. It was, after all, the population of a country that had fought long enough on the side of Hitler against the Allies. Being weak economically, the Italians experienced a situation in regard to supplies that was as catastrophic as the German one. On the side of the Allies the Italian political parties—now again permitted—denounced each other. The enemy began to enlist Italian partisans in the fighting, which brought them pay and food.

The war had moved from a purely military setting into a politico-military one—a sure sign of its impending termination.

The increasingly acute situation caused by the guerrillas compelled me to move my quarters into the village. The German General Crisolli had been shot by them shortly after he had entertained me to lunch on the occasion of his departure from the corps.

While the neighbouring corps on my left had been steadily driven back towards Bologna by incessant enemy pressure from Florence, XIV Panzer Corps had remained in a position far up in front without being attacked. My battle H.Q. at Villa Collemandina was at the southern end of the Apennines, whereas the other corps was already at the northern end or in the Po valley. Consequently on September 29th we also moved back to the northern edge at Albinea. The route thence to the two divisions still in my corps was long and infested with guerrillas. The front itself remained free from attack.

Autumn was spreading across the country. We lived in a large house that seemed empty and inhospitable. But I had the time and inclination to install myself comfortably in one of the top rooms, from whose windows I had an unrestricted view over the extensive vineyards of the plain of the Po. It was harvest-time, as depicted in the paintings of Benozzo Gozzoli in the Camposanto of Pisa. At midday I usually wandered through the vast maze of vine plantations. Very gradually the vine-leaves changed their colour under the steel blue sky, at first to a faint yellow tint, then to ever-deepening shades of red. In the foliage hung the ripe clusters of blue velvety grapes. Among the harvesters there was usually much merriment. Youths and girls with bare legs stood on the ladders singing and cackling. When they placed the loaded baskets on the ground there was much shouting and snatching, and in the grass were laughing couples. A young peasant woman showed her pretty face and sparkling teeth under her large Florentine hat. With her ample shoulders and hips she was the embodiment of healthy fertility. Grazing in the dark grass were spotless lambs with a shining pinky hue on their coats. An ox-drawn cart drew up to load the full baskets. The white oxen had hides the dull colour of parchment, and over the yoke towered their huge horns with a span of two metres. The sweet fruit was carted home and the trampling with bare feet started, all the men, women and children of the farm joining in. The sweet scent of the fresh grape-juice filled the air, adding spice to the odour of the sun-baked earth.

THE TWENTIETH OF JULY, 1944

I was at my headquarters in Pistoia on July 20th when the anti-Hitler coup was attempted. I had long been aware of the plan for the conspiracy. Now we very soon learnt that it had failed. In the interest of the German people the conspirators had attempted to precipitate events. Among my intimate friends I had repeatedly expressed doubts over the prospects of success, and these were now confirmed. I had always realised the dangers; the secret could only be maintained if the circle of conspirators remained small, but in that case there would not be enough people in key positions with a knowledge of the plot. Yet it was here that the conspirators should be. Even after the attempt had failed there were people ready to give their services and turn it into a success; others hesitated for fear of their own safety. Still others —the fanatical followers of Hitler and those who had lived through the last phase of German history in ignorance of events—took sides against the conspirators and frustrated the coup that the persistent Stauffenberg was still trying to bring to a head in Berlin on the evening of his attempt.

My first reaction was of acute anxiety for the fate of the participants. I was personally acquainted with Stauffenberg, who as a south-west German was a fellow-countryman and had started his career as an officer of Cavalry Regiment 7 in the same cavalry brigade as myself. I was concerned too over the fate of his family and his brothers, who had done their training in my squadron. I also anticipated that many of my acquaintances would have to pay with their lives, although not directly involved in the plot.

I felt there was a special tragedy in the fate of Col.-General Beck, the highly respected former Chief of the General Staff, who had sacrificed his position at the dictates of his conscience and had retired in protest against Hitler's policy of war. He had realised the malfunctioning of political strategy. The rôles had been reversed: the politician had figured as a pseudo-strategist, while the general had opposed him because, in the situation in which Germany found herself, a warlike policy was even more irresponsible than it had been at the start of the First World War.

It was these two men of different generations, Beck and Stauffenberg, who stood at the centre of the resistance movement. But its spiritual core had for years been General Oster, whose son had become a friend of mine while serving on the staff of the corps. I reflected how worried he would be about his father.

It was hardly surprising that many officers of the General Staff were involved in the conspiracy. Beck had modelled this organisation with a view to maintaining its independence of judgment and its right to express opinions freely in the presence of superiors. This privilege had indeed been the corner-stone of the General Staff, but under Hitler it was bound to disappear. Yet even he never succeeded in creating a compliant General Staff, deferential to the régime. The habit of clear and sober deliberation was too ingrained in its traditions for this intellectual training to be displaced by an uncritical faith in the mystical sagacities of Hitler, which too often reflected the inadequacy of his education. Moreover, the numerically small General Staff still re-cruited its personnel from the higher and more educated stratum of society, and for them there was never any question of compromise with the criminal edicts of the Führer. Consequently the conflict of conscience had led the officers of the General Staff to link up with intellectuals and fighters from other walks of life. A large proportion of the leaders of the conspiracy came from the General Staff, which proved that it preferred to go under rather than defile itself morally.

Those who had sacrificed their lives had risen far above the duties normally expected of the leaders of any community, and had become heroes of the nation's liberation. To me the future of the nation now seemed to hinge on whether this liberation movement would succeed in acquiring the place in history that it merited. It was the only libera-tion movement in German history that—on the basis of conscience—aimed at eliminating a criminal despot. The heroes of July 20th gave the lie to those who regarded the German people as little more than servile vassals. In this context I must utterly reject the implication in Sir John Wheeler-Bennett's book *The Nemesis of Power**, where he scoffs at the military leaders of July 20th in the very hour when they. were sentenced to death by the People's Court of Justice.

But what was now to be the pattern of events? Was the war to continue now that Hitler and his sycophants had revenged themselves on defenceless persons? Surely the conspirators had given the signal

* Macmillan & Co., London, 1954, pp 679–688.

for capitulation. Should we not offer to capitulate even though the opponent would reject anything short of "unconditional surrender"? Did a totally defeated country have any right whatever to make conditions? Each further day would make the war more meaningless than it already was, claiming the blood of thousands of people, of fathers and of adolescent sons. It would present the advancing Russians with more and more territory and would accelerate our internal dissolution, for by now the misleading picture of "a firmly led nation unanimously set on victory" had lost all conviction. If fate should spare those of us who were not involved in the conspiracy, if our names did not figure on certain lists of opponents to the régime— what road were we to take?

In the impending collapse of the Reich, would it be possible to save some part of the German substance, to find enough followers of the heroes of the resistance to enable us to lead the nation back resolutely into the community of peoples?

Another thought that oppressed me was that further thousands would probably now be made to start their journey to the gas chambers. We had the ghastly pictures before our eyes: those railway trains into which the victims were crammed, never leaving them until they reached their destinations, unless they died of hunger on the way. What should a mother do when a last crust of bread was thrown to her— divide it among her starving children, or eat it to gain strength to help the children? It was a vain hope. Next would come the march to the gas chambers. To be forced to take half-grown children with them was the most brutal violence that the fathers and mothers had to suffer. Such children realised what was in store for them, and their parents were racked with compassion. Families were brutally separated according to sex. If their nerves held out, they walked the final steps; if not, they were dragged or carried in. It was against this disgrace, which had fallen on all of us in the name of the German people, that the heroes of liberation had staked their lives, evidently in vain.

In my corps headquarters the daily routine continued as in other staffs. Outwardly I took no notice of the attempted assassination. Some time later my attitude was responsible for an anecdote that when the news of it arrived I was sitting at a bridge-table and gave the answer "I pass!" But I have never played bridge. A young staff officer, who naturally knew my attitude, held forth very disparagingly about Hitler in the officers' mess. My N.S.F.O. (the National Socialist leadership officer) used the occasion of a drive to the front to inform me that his subordinate N.S.F.O.'s in the divisions had criticised me for not raising my arm in the correct manner when giving the so-called "German greeting".

Never had we been in a situation like this. Every prospect was

forbidding, particularly in regard to the more distant future. To-
morrow we might no longer be free soldiers. We might find ourselves
prisoners of the Allies or meet each other in some German concentration camp. The very continuity of human existence had been
placed in jeopardy. But now the question was: how to make this event
understandable to the troops? To maintain their morale, those in
authority had to give them daily doses of propaganda on the need
to hold out. Basically it was tragic enough that this propaganda was so
effective. Nowhere had there been any sign of the disintegration that
occurred in the First World War. The moral front was holding out
while the military front was crumbling more and more. I avoided
taking up any attitude in front of the troops, and I never referred to
the attempt on Hitler's life. The more alert of them could draw their
own conclusions. It would have been suicidal to champion the conspirators. As the plot was immediately recognised as having failed, it
led to no complications in this theatre of war.

It remained a sad fact that resistance to the Hitler régime found
no real response among the German people. The Nazi propaganda
over a period of eleven years had progressively undermined the
capacity of the people for political discrimination. And this had not
even changed with the deterioration of the situation, which was apparent to any layman. The legend of "the stab in the back", invented
by Ludendorff, had done much to mislead a people already dazzled
by Hitler into thinking that this time the war could be won, since there
was no *Dolchstoss*. The general lack of political and military perspicacity was a measure of how the situation was judged by ordinary
people, loyal as they were to the flag and accustomed to an optimistic
outlook. It could hardly be imagined what would have happened at
the front if a partially successful *putsch* had resulted in a state of
instability akin to civil war. Certain divisions that contained figure-
heads associated with the party were more reliable to the régime than
those of the Army proper, which was more strongly imbued with the
traditions of Prussia and of the General Staff. Yet the core of the
resistance was to be found in the General Staff, as was proved by the
events of July 20th.

I myself was in no doubt as to the moral justification for opposing
a corrupt régime, for the burden on my conscience had been too
heavy over the past eleven years. The tortured and misled German
people would find salvation after the collapse, when it could demonstrate its undivided support for the martyrs.

For those implicated in the plot it must have been terrible to involve
their families in such great danger. If we consider these difficulties as
well as the unpromising prospects for the attempt, it is easy to understand those senior commanders who refused to become involved. All
of us were left only with admiration for the martyrs of freedom.

And yet the July 20th plot had caused some kind of a break among the people as well as the officers and the ordinary soldiers who accepted the party line. It had become patently obvious that not all the officers stood behind Hitler, while many of them also realised that mere ambition could not have been the motive of the brave conspirators. Many had long doubted whether Hitler's "exemplary fanaticism" could be relied on.

After July 20th I seemed to encounter among my troops more questioning faces, more men looking for guidance in regard to Hitler, men to whom my bad reputation as a non-party general now stood in a better light.

The worry about our friends in the conspiracy was capped by our anxiety over the fortunes of the state. How was Germany to raise herself once more to the status of even a medium power after she had lost the essential political basis? Would she be in any position to impugn the criminals of the régime and thus establish the elements of a new moral order? The tribunals of the victorious powers later took this burden off our shoulders. Even if their judgments did not convince the mass of the people, it was the only course to adopt, since the authority of the German state was non-existent under the occupation. The leaders of Nazism had ended their lives by suicide. Consequently justice by the will of the people, as applied by the Italians to their Duce, was denied to the Germans. Perhaps this was fortunate for us, for Germany contained so many men who were indictable on penal charges that neither mob-law nor the new "People's Courts" would have been adequate to deal with them. We had to trust to the courts of the victors. But they included the Soviet Union, whose legal code could never stand as an example to the tottering judiciary of Germany.

A word is needed about these differences. Russia had no machinery for implementing a change of government or for registering the will of the people. There, any such change involved criminal conduct. Crimes were committed in order to bring a group into power or maintain it in power, usually by simply eliminating the opponent. Among the more established section of the Russian social order thousands had to forfeit their freedom because they regarded those in power as dangerous, and this state of affairs had continued for many years. Such symptoms of disease in the body politic have also occurred in other nations in times of upheaval.

The Germans had fallen even lower. Racial and religious minorities were brutally liquidated by a "chosen" and ostensibly "legal" government in the crass delusion that these massacres would add to the happiness of others. Man had taken it upon himself to improve upon the Creation. The mass killings involved innocent people who had lived loyally within their families and within the state. These were the children of God, as all men desire to be who do not take the wrong path.

DEFENCE OF THE GOTHIC LINE

For me the period between mid-September and mid-October was depressing. My corps H.Q. staff was tucked away on the right wing of the 14th Army on a dead sector of the front. From intelligence reports we knew that here the enemy had no battle-worthy divisions. Moreover the pattern of his further operations was now quite clear. By the end of August the British 8th Army had already begun to launch attacks along the Adriatic coast with a view to rolling up the left wing of the German army group. Doubtless this plan took into consideration that the flat terrain in that region offered better prospects for the offensive use of armour. Here the Allies could hope to achieve a breakthrough with their massed armoured forces and at least provide their infantry with sufficient armoured support to enable it to penetrate the German left wing. That these operations failed to achieve an armoured breakthrough confirmed my appreciation of the changing conditions for tank warfare, which I have already outlined.

By the middle of September the U.S. 5th Army had also resumed its offensive with the object of breaking through from Florence towards Bologna. After our experiences of the enemy's superiority in the mountains, this attack was bound to cause us even more concern than that of the 8th Army on the coast.

Although I was not directly involved in this fighting, I could see enough of the situation to realise that we would not have to reckon with any further surprises. It could be assumed that the enemy would maintain the direction of his attack against the left wing of the 14th Army. Movements across the mountains were difficult and too time-consuming because of the fresh deployment of artillery that they demanded. And so we were the sorrowful witnesses of the enemy's almost daily successes against our neighbours, 1 Parachute Corps. The incessant prodding against our front across the Futa pass was like jabbing a thick cloth with a sharp spear. The cloth would give way like elastic, but under excessive strain it would be penetrated by the spear.

The war diary of XIV Panzer Corps shows that at this time the staff were almost more concerned with events on the neighbouring corps' front than on my own. While this reflected my own appreciation of the general situation, it also derived from a personal factor. I will not deny that I had been spoilt in the leadership of the corps, which for so long had stood at the focal point at Cassino. Despite my inherent scepticism, which was a product of the intellect, I felt the urge to apply the lessons of my earlier experiences to the new situation;

self-consciously I believed myself better fitted to cope with it than the senior commanders whom the turn of fortune had brought into the limelight. There was also a physical side to this. Anyone who is conscious of his fitness for higher command will always become fascinated by the problems involved in decisive battles. If he has to stand aside, he is like a hunter chafing at the stable door when the other horses are led out and he has to remain behind. I do not think this fever has anything to do with the aptitude for military matters. It is quite possible to condemn a war for its futility or its hopeless strategic concepts and yet be impelled towards the decisive battle-ground through the inescapable force of destiny.

I stated earlier that it was only on September 29th that I moved my corps H.Q. to the northern edge of the Apennines, where the other corps H.Q. had already been installed for some time. Every time I drove to the front I now had to pass through a guerrilla-infested district. Normally I drove in the little Volkswagen and displayed no general's insignia of rank—no peaked cap, no gold or red flags. This may have saved me from the fate of one divisional commander who after conferring with me in this area was ambushed and shot.

From this H.Q. at Albinea there was nothing I could do beyond watching and even hastening the further depletion of my sector of the front. Indeed I felt that this process did not go far enough. At Cassino I had repeatedly expected of the divisions free from attack that they should not complain if they were thinned out; and now I myself had to follow that example.

On October 15th an unexpected opportunity at last presented itself for me to join in the fray. The C.-in-C. of the 14th Army was suffering from acute catarrh and for five days I assumed his responsibility. Looking back on those days, I have a definite feeling that I managed to bring the advance of the U.S. 5th Army on Bologna to a halt. For the measures that I took also left their mark on the days that followed. By the end of October all enemy attacks had ceased. The Allied radio messages stated that Kesselring had massed so much artillery in the region of Bologna that there was no point in continuing the offensive in that locality. Kesselring sent me his flattering acknowledgments.

THE OPERATIONAL PROBLEM IN THE BOLOGNA SECTOR

At the end of October I exchanged my battle H.Q. at Albinea with that of LI Mountain Corps at Vedrana, and for reasons of suitability I at once moved on to Baricella, a bigger place. I breathed more freely, for I believed that my corps H.Q. was once more at the centre of events. But further developments belied this hope.

When I took over the sector previously occupied by LI Mountain

Corps, it was extended westwards at the expense of 1 Parachute Corps, and consequently the city of Bologna and the important Futa pass-road came into the zone of XIV Panzer Corps. This zone now covered a line running from the range of hills between the Setta and the Savena valleys as far as the river Santerno, where LXXVI Panzer Corps linked up.

In accordance with previously made plans 90 Pz. Gren. Div. and 362 Inf. Div. were taken out of the line at the beginning of November. The front of my corps now included the following in the order given, starting with the right wing: 65 Inf. Div., 29 Pz. Gren. Div., 42 Inf. Div., 1 Para. Div., and 334 Inf. Div.

When the British 8th Army opened its offensive on November 20th, this started a process of weakening the front of my corps in favour of the neighbouring corps on my left. The 90 Pz. Gren. Div., which until then had been held ready behind the corps as army group reserve, was sent before the end of the month to join up with LXXIII Corps. At the end of November my corps boundaries were altered when 334 Inf. Div. on the left wing was incorporated in the neighbouring corps. Early in December 98 Inf. Div., which had then formed the left wing, was taken out of the line. This division was originally earmarked as reserve behind my corps, but because of developments elsewhere it had to be handed over to LXXIII Corps without a substitute, so that its sector had to be taken over by 1 Para. Div., which now became the wing division. We thought that as the front of the corps had to be weakened, this was the place where we could best risk doing so.

On December 6th, 362 Inf. Div, until then in reserve and being freshened up, took the place of 29 Pz. Gren. Div., the latter being allocated to LXXVI Pz. Corps. Thus from December 15th the following Divisions were in the sector of XIV Pz. Corps in the Bologna area: 65 Inf., 362 Inf., 42 Rifle Div. and 1 Para. Div.

In his report to the Combined Chiefs of Staff for the period 12.12.1943 to 2.5.1945, Field-Marshal Alexander gives the following picture of the German Order of Battle:

"XIV Corps was occupying a quiet sector of the front directly to the east of Road 65 (Florence to Bologna) with two divisions, the 715 and 314 Inf. Divs. The immediate approaches to Bologna on each side of Road 65 were held by the permanent corps of the 10th Army, I Parachute Corps with the following six divisions at the front: 1 Para. Div., 42 Rifle Div., 362 Inf. Div., 4 Para. Div. and 84 Inf. Div."

This picture is inaccurate. From the end of October the whole Bologna sector came under XIV Pz. Corps with the divisions that Alexander has ascribed to 1 Para Corps excepting 94 (not 84) Inf. Div. and 4 Para. Div., both of which came under 1 Para. Corps, adjoining my corps on the west. On the quiet sector east of the

Florence-Bologna road it was not the 715 and 314 Inf. Divs., but the 42 Rifle Div. and 1 Para. Div., that came within XIV Pz. Corps.

At the beginning of January 1945 a new crisis developed in LXXIII Corps. The enemy had "pushed through" to Lake Comacchio, and in consequence 42 Rifle Div. was relieved by 305 Inf. Div. and attached to LXXIII Corps. At about the same time 362 Inf. Div. was also pulled out of the line and handed over to that corps. Its sector was taken care of by extending the divisional boundaries of 65 Inf. Div. and the new 305 Inf. Div.

Between January 6th and 8th, XIV Pz. Corps, which already occupied the Bologna sector, took over the entire sector previously held by 1 Para. Corps, including that corps' 94 Inf. Div. and 4 Para. Div. At the same time 1 Para. Corps was pushed into the line between XIV Pz. Corps and LXXVI Pz. Corps, thus taking over the sector of 1 Para. Div. from XIV Pz. Corps. These changes were effected less for tactical reasons than out of consideration for Göring, who despite the dwindling Luftwaffe still had great influence. Evidently Army circles still bowed to his authority, although it was rumoured that he had fallen into disfavour with Hitler. The re-disposition of the divisions was made in order to subordinate both parachute divisions, which belonged to the Luftwaffe, to 1 Para. Corps. This kind of collective employment of individual corps had already been discarded in the First World War.

The course of the fighting already described shows the extent to which the higher command was forced to meet the operational developments by changes in the centre of pressure and concomitant changes in the distribution of divisions among the various corps. In exempting the two parachute divisions of the Para. Corps from these changes and leaving them united within that corps for reasons of prestige, the higher command was liable to involve itself in considerable operational difficulties.

The 4 Para. Div. was relieved by the virtually untried 157 Mountain Div. and allotted to 1 Para. Corps. Thus from the end of January the following divisions, from right to left, stood in the zone of XIV Pz. Corps: 94 Inf. Div., 157 (later designated 8) Mountain Div., 65 and 305 Inf. Divs. This was the order of battle of the corps when it was later faced with the breakthrough.

The foregoing description of re-groupings has been given to show that the Bologna region was not really a fighting sector of the front. There were no further attacks by the enemy until he broke through in April. It is true that all the German operational commands anticipated a renewal of the attack in this direction—a direction which the enemy had maintained up to the time of our defensive success in October, 1944. This was his shortest way into the plain of the Po, for in this sector he had carried his old offensive farthest northwards.

It seemed likely that he would exploit this advantage even if it meant having to forfeit the element of surprise.

My corps became progressively weaker as the weeks passed. This was understandable, since it was being depleted in favour of the two neighbouring corps which were under attack astride the Via Emilia and at Lake Comacchio. Nevertheless my sector remained relatively strong, since the German side had all the advantages of interior lines.

A glance at the map will show how centrally all the reserves that had been assembled in the Bologna area were placed for operating either on the Adriatic front or at Bologna itself or with the army in Liguria. This situation was useful to me inasmuch as I could always feel that behind the comparatively weakly held Bologna sector were reserves that could immediately be launched in a counter-attack. Moreover I had always maintained a focal point here for artillery, of which there was a powerful concentration. All I had to do now was to arrange for an adequate disposition in depth of the front line divisions and for corresponding protection with armour.

The defence of the valleys of the rivers Savena, Zena and Idice, all running due north, was assured with the forces available. The ridges of the hills between these rivers, also running north and south, could be easily dominated from positions that had been arranged in chess-board fashion. From these positions the infantry also dominated the three valley roads with flanking fire. On the actual roads were anti-tank guns in concealed positions, while tanks and assault-guns were held in readiness so that after slight changes of position they could become mobile and engage any enemy tanks that had managed to break through. If there was any weakness in these positions, it was due to the rather too ingenious organisation that they acquired in the course of months. This is always a handicap, since subordinate commanders tend to evolve a formula for every contingency. If there is then a sudden setback, the art of improvisation lags behind. That is what occurred with the Atlantic Wall, which also had other weakness.

I tried to remedy this disadvantage by arranging that the current courses for officers should include a series of small exercises at the southern edge of Bologna. I was particularly anxious that the experience gained at Cassino in the co-ordination of infantry and armour should be understood. Eventually all battalion commanders belonging to the more permanent divisions of my corps passed through this course, and I could therefore hope that they would avoid the mistakes that had been all too common while we were still south of the Gothic Line.

I found that the sector we had taken over from 1 Para. Corps at the beginning of January was much less secure. Here two divisions covered a width of twenty-six kilometres in difficult terrain. The 94 Inf Div., which I knew from the days of Cassino, had a particularly efficient and conscientious commander, but it had taken part in only one battle, when it was supported by army group reserves. In the May offensive this division had been routed, which was not unexpected in view of its insoluble task. The adjoining 157 Mountain Div. was untested, and I was concerned as to how it would stand up to major fighting.

The shape of the defensive line that we had assumed after the easing up of the fighting in 1944 caused me added anxiety. Hardly any part of this line conformed to the rules of mountain warfare. Positions on forward slopes deep into the valley alternated with normal bridgehead positions which would have been immediately over-run if subjected to a major attack. I tried to change this as quickly as possible, but although the improvement would merely have involved the abandonment of worthless territory, the mentality of certain higher commanders who depended on Hitler's tactics was such that they regarded this proposal as an intention to withdraw. Consequently I could achieve only part of the adjustments that I considered essential, and those had to be either approved by the O.K.W., or kept secret from it whenever the situation was desperate.

The peculiarities of the terrain added to the difficulties. Behind the front line divisions lay the confluence of the rivers Reno and Setta. Their valleys were broader than those running directly from the south towards Bologna. Monte Adone, formerly marking the western boundary of the corps, had a number of summits which ran through the front line, but they had no connecting ridges, like those at Monte Sole and Monte Rumici. If the enemy should succeed in over-running these summits, he would secure an unimpaired view of the entire valley of the Setta, and if he then advanced astride this valley, he would imperil all the positions of the westerly and adjoining 94 Inf. Div.

The position occupied by this division was even less capable of resisting a frontal attack than that of 157 Mountain Div., for here the defender had no mountains that could be utilised for defence. The hills, being flat and without cover, favoured armoured operations. Nor did my visits to the troops allay my anxiety Despite the integrity of its commander, the division showed certain deficiencies in its personnel. But at this stage of the war I could not afford to take it out of the line, as I would normally have done.

There were no insoluble problems on the sector of the adjoining, easterly 1 Para. Div., which I had handed over at the beginning of January. Being near the Via Emilia, it was a dead sector, and no special attack was to be expected here. Between October and January this division again proved its worth and initiative in the weekly raiding parties that always brought in a haul of prisoners.

Naturally the front-line troops were constantly occupied with building up their positions. The higher command ordered so many of these constructions that their individual quality suffered. There were three categories of them. The first were the so-called "tendon and cut-off" positions* situated in or directly behind the front line, which were selected and set up in such a way that if penetrated, the troops could link up with other parts of the front that were still intact. In the course of time it was possible to calculate how long it would take the enemy, at the rate of attack that he maintained during 1944, to unhinge the defensive line of XIV Pz. Corps through his advance along the Via Emilia. In order then to occupy a correctly developing line, we had to choose one that ran along the chain of hills between the valleys of the Savena and the Idice, and this was now built up. This second line ran due north and south, with the front facing east. If the Via Emilia were crossed in the Po valley, the line would follow the river Idice in a general north-easterly direction and be continued towards Lake Comacchio. These tactics of conducting the operations on the basis of pre-determined lines originated in the O.K.W. Actually the line was not much longer than the erstwhile Gothic Line. But if the enemy should penetrate into the plain of the Po, that would necessarily lead to the destruction of all the army group elements situated south of the point of penetration, for they would have no alternative to continuing to fight to the end.

A third category of line ran through the actual plain of the Po. My occasional brief visits of inspection convinced me that it was barely usable. In most places the slightest digging immediately exposed the sub-soil water. To the north of Bologna there were no rivers that ran in the tactically desirable south-west to north-east direction. In the Po valley the river Reno forms a wide north-westerly loop.

Each new day in 1945 lessened the chances of a persistent defence in the sector of XIV Pz. Corps. The story from the Allied point of view has since been made available, and it can be taken into account here. The German higher command and I myself anticipated a break-through at Bologna, but it occurred elsewhere. The Allied war diary shows that our estimate was not so wrong, however.

In his report to the Combined Chiefs of Staff, Field-Marshal Alexander stated that "In December 1944 sufficient forces were still available in the Italian theatre of war to undertake an offensive, although several divisions had departed for France." The plan that Alexander produced on December 12th shows that he was still think-ing in terms of an attack on Bologna. In accordance with the British

---

* Sehnen–und Riegelstellungen.

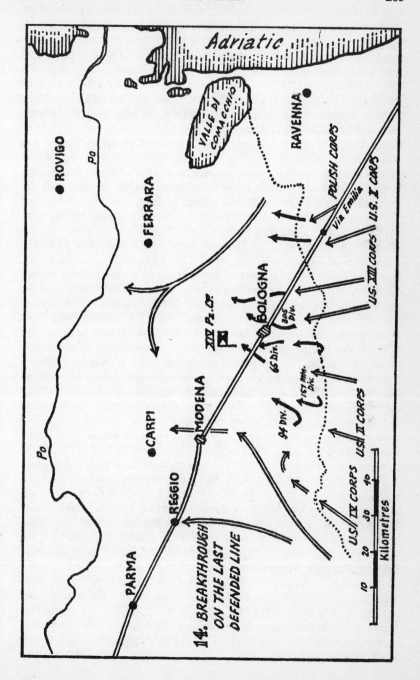

14. BREAKTHROUGH ON THE LAST DEFENDED LINE

operational technique he proposed first to launch an offensive with limited objectives against certain sectors, and later to follow this up with the real spring offensive. As soon as the first objective had been attained, there would be a re-grouping of the forces, and especially a period of rest for the troops prior to the spring offensive. Alexander's report proceeds: —"In my opinion we would not have been able to throw the enemy back as far as the Adige before it would be necessary to have a pause. I therefore decided to limit the objectives to the capture of Bologna and Ravenna."

For this purpose the Allied C.-in-C. planned an attack by the 8th Army in the plain of the Po. When the Germans were tied down by this fighting, the U.S. 5th Army was to withdraw two of its divisions from the front and launch them by surprise in "an all-out attack on Bologna". This attack was first timed to take place on November 15th, then postponed to the 30th. The time-table could not be kept because of the disappointingly slow progress of the 8th Army's offensive. Consequently the U.S. 5th Army was to be ready to attack on receipt of orders any time after December 22nd. But even this date was cancelled on receipt of intelligence of an imminent German offensive in the Serchio valley, which was anxiously compared to the recently launched German offensive in the Ardennes. This impending German attack appeared all the more threatening since "the mass of the U.S. 5th Army forces had been concentrated in the centre of the front, whence they were soon to be launched on a breakthrough thrust at Bologna". Consequently on January 8th, Alexander reported that he had decided to go over to the defensive since "the enemy has built up his field fortifications around Bologna into a fortified zone sufficiently strong to make it impossible with the forces available to drive him out of them during this winter".

A further contributory factor was that a frontal attack on Bologna was no longer considered feasible. The defensive installations immediately around the town were "strong and getting stronger every day". In the new plan the U.S. 5th Army was to attack west of the Reno towards the north, reaching the road Modena-Ostiglia-Verona and so avoiding the defensive fortifications of Bologna. The British 8th Army for its part was to cross the lower reaches of the Reno, thereby avoiding the numerous smaller tributaries that ran into the Reno from the south. This plan succeeded and led to the destruction of Army Group C in the spring.

Alexander's report confirms my opinion that the Allies regarded an attack on Bologna as too costly in view of the German success against their October offensive. There is no doubt that a contributory factor was the relatively high morale of the German troops engaged in this sector. As the war diary of XIV Pz. Corps shows, these troops were not just passively employed on construction work, but were kept

on their toes with repeated raiding operations which not only scared
off the enemy, but gave us a clear picture of his situation. They also
gave the troops a feeling of superiority which, though hardly justified,
helped to maintain their fighting spirit.

Bologna presented a problem not only operationally, but also in
regard to administration and policy. It was not merely a question
of controlling and pacifying the town, but of feeding it and neutralising it on the eve of a major battle.

Before I took over the command, certain unwise administrative
measures had irritated the population. I discovered that especially in
the southern precincts of the town, where the partisans were most
numerous, there had been serious excesses by the German troops.
The corps commander previously in control of this area had instituted
raids on the streets to round up able-bodied men capable of doing
work. The result was a temporary stoppage of essential services such
as electricity and waterworks, and strong representations had to be
made by the responsible Italian authorities before this practice was
discontinued in the German interest. These incidents once again
showed that despite all its resources an occupying power is incapable
of governing an economically difficult district. In a situation of this
kind the fighting troops are prone to act too severely and inconsider-
ately, little realising that in the end they are piling up trouble for
themselves. Moreover the specialist officials engaged in administering
the rear areas rarely had first-rate personnel at their disposal. The
best of them, if soldiers, were at the front, and if administrative
experts, were employed in the homeland.

The most pressing problem was to cope with the partisans. They
were the underworld and the gangsters who ruled the town. Before
I took over the sector, they had made an armed raid on the leading
hotel, firing indiscriminately on the guests in the hall, most of whom
were German officers or Italian Republican Party adherents. Our own
security service came to the conclusion that it would not be possible
to arrest any large number of partisans in the town, since they could
always go underground again. In this respect they had the advantage
over partisans working in the open country. Murders even among
the civil population were a daily occurrence. The partisans not only
struck at their political opponents, but were often actuated by purely
personal motives of hate or revenge. They sought to cover their traces
by pinning to their dead victims a label with the inscription *SPIA
TEDESCA* (German spy). Although this accusation might deceive
a few credulous Italians, it was not so with us, who had means of
checking up on the perpetrators.

In Bologna by far the greater part of the partisans belonged to the
Communist wing. They could hardly have been led by Allied agents,
and they were incapable of any military tasks such as severing

lines of communication or fighting the German troops. On the other hand they were definitely in touch with the other movement, the so-called *Comitato di Liberazione*. They were getting reinforcements all the time from the plain, for we were powerless to stop the incessant stream of deserters. In the Bologna area the partisans became especially dangerous through their close contact with the increasing number of German deserters from the colours. These gave the partisans first-hand information on conditions in the Wehrmacht, which was useful to them since they were working as spies for the Allies. We knew about this through occasionally catching some of these spies. Nor could we trust our own spies, who seemed to be moving about much too freely on the enemy's side, and were probably taking money from both sides.

To pacify and at the same time to rule Bologna was of course a political problem of the first order. I considered it too tricky to leave to some inadequate military commandant or town major. Instead I made myself the *de facto* if not the official commandant by setting up an office in the town and appointing an officer from my corps H.Q. staff as head of it, with orders to report to me once or twice a week. In his office I received the Italian administrative officials.

Fortunately the heads of the Italian administration were excellent men of integrity. The Prefect, Signor Fantozzi, still a young man, was a fighter against Fascism, an idealist, and an administrator by profession. I could never discover whether his "faith" outweighed his common sense to such an extent that he, like many Germans, still believed in a German victory. In contrast to him the Mayor, an engineer called Agnoli, was not committed to any party, and as his only concern was for the welfare of the town, he remained at his post although convinced that the end was near. I greatly admired and respected him, and we frequently discussed our mutual troubles. The Commissioner for Emilia, who had been appointed by Mussolini, was an unsuitable and not very educated man, but even he eventually proved himself to be an unselfish and upright patriot. He was an old soldier who had been wounded many times and possessed a number of decorations for bravery. Mussolini, who had sent him here from the seat of government on Lake Garda, was kept directly informed by him about the situation at the front.

These more or less responsible Italians were not as difficult a problem as were our relations with the new Republican-Fascist organisations of a military or para-military character. The loyalty of the *Guardia Republicana Nazionale* was beyond doubt. They had been founded as the successors of the famous Royal Carabinieri, and were animated by a genuine fighting spirit. Their battalion in Bologna was so insistent on having a share in the fighting that I sent it to a threatened sector of the front where it fought bravely. Our common

enemies were the Blackshirts, the *Camicie Nere*. They were the real
scourge of the people, equally detested by the peace-loving citizens,
the officials I have mentioned, and indeed by myself. They recruited
all the extremist party men. These reckless, brave and uncritical
devotees of the Duce would not stop at murder or other atrocities
to achieve their purpose of eliminating all internal political opposition.
Their attitude towards people in my position was hostile, if only
because they regarded the S.D. and S.S. as their real German associates. From these organisations they received information about the
German commanders, which governed their attitude towards them.
Yet the Blackshirts and their leaders represented only that small
proportion of the Italian people who were set on sacrificing themselves
for Hitler's idea of the German cause, and they opposed everyone,
German or Italian, who saw things in a different light. These people
really amounted to a new *Internationale* whose outlook on the world
had little to do with the purely national interest. As long as Italy
was ruled by a monarchy the Fascists had pilloried the Church, the
nobility and the General Staff for being international, but they were
quite wrong, for these circles thought in terms of the nation and
consequently treated the German brand of National Socialism with
reserve.

The evil spirit of Bologna's Blackshirts was a university professor
of the medical faculty. As soon as I arrived in the town he was pointed
out to me as a plotter. In general the disruptive elements among both
the Nazis and the Fascists made themselves more prevalent in proportion as the situation became more desperate. The professor opposed
the Prefect and the Mayor, which meant that he was also against me.
But he kept himself in the background, refused to enter into any
discussion and shielded himself behind the so-called *Federale*, the
head of the Blackshirt Brigade, who was himself inaccessible.

At the end of November four respected citizens of Bologna were
treacherously assassinated. Being avowed opponents of Fascism, they
had compromised themselves when in 1943 they tried to revive the
old political parties after the fall of Mussolini. The population attributed these murders to the professor, but naturally there was no proof.
It was also difficult to proceed against him owing to the fact that in
their fight against the partisans the Blackshirts were acting in
support of the German cause, and had incurred considerable loss of
life in the process. The professor had a supporter in Pavolini, the
secretary of the party, whereas the Minister of the Interior, Buffarini,
and the Prefect were in favour of the Professor's elimination.

Meanwhile Rahn, German Ambassador to the Fascist-Republican
Government, also had objections to removing the professor, for this
would have constituted a political act against extreme Fascism, which
certainly was held in higher esteem by the German government than

by Mussolini himself. Yet Rahn showed understanding for the way in which I chose to deal with the Italian population. But when he reported in this sense to his chief at the German Foreign Office, Ribbentrop let it be known that he preferred the uncompromising methods of my predecessors. The usual rôles of soldier and diplomat had been reversed. Normally a military commander at the front had to be prepared to take severe measures in the interest of his troops, while the Foreign Ministry had to maintain good relations with the ally; but now the opposite was true. Ambassador Rahn had appointed a young attaché named Sachs to act as liaison officer with my corps, for he quite rightly attached the greatest significance to conditions in Bologna.

Despite the objections I decided to proceed against the professor. He and the *Federale* were banished from Bologna. In a conference I explained to them that since the district was in the forward area of the front, it was essential for the maintenance of administrative authority that the Italian factions should form a united front. But as they were not doing so, I had to remove them from their sphere of activity despite the sacrifices that his own units had made. The modest and loyal district leader of Cremona, named Cerchiari, was appointed as his successor.

The banishment of the professor brought peace to the political factions in Bologna. The authority of the garrison troops and of the state and urban officials who worked in with them was consolidated. The fight against the Blackshirts was popular; their encroachments had been aimed at civilians, not at German soldiers.

It was clear that I could survive the hostility of the Blackshirts; more dangerous was the deterioration of my relations with the S.D. (the German political security service) which had resulted from my action. The S.D. regarded the removal of the professor as a slight on its own position. In Bologna the normal animosity between the Wehrmacht and the S.S. had become particularly acute. Everywhere the S.D. had over-riding police powers Yet Bologna was an operational zone which according to all precedents should have been under Wehrmacht authority. But this was not attainable under the prevailing circumstances. Although the S.D. chief in Bologna was only of captain's rank, he was in no way subordinate to me, but on the contrary regarded himself as my equal. We knew very well that in order to safeguard the "security of the Reich" one of his duties was to report continuously on the senior military commanders, whom the party rightly mistrusted. When the collapse occurred a few weeks later I was told by General Wolff, senior S.S. and police commander in Italy, that Himmler had several times demanded my dismissal, which had only been avoided through his and Kesselring's intervention.

I tried to relieve the S.D. of any responsibility for the security of the troops in the Bologna area and to limit their functions to guarding and removing the civilian prisoners. For the rest, I gradually transferred the proceedings against the Italian delinquents to the Italian authorities. In cases where the offence had been committed against the German occupying forces I arranged for them to be tried in the ordinary civil courts.

Because of Bologna's proximity to the front it was difficult to give it the status of an open city. On his own initiative Kesselring had written several times to the Mayor assuring him that he wished to spare the town the horrors of war and to treat it as an open city. When on taking over the command I prohibited access by all German troops to the centre of the town, my action was regarded as a consequence of Kesselring's decision. The mayor publicised this measure by every means, thus, as it were, anticipating the fact of neutralisation, which he believed to be in the best interest of the town and its inhabitants. My chief reason for keeping the German troops out of the centre of the town was that the guerrillas could then be dealt with; moreover, it would be easier to protect the troops, and there were advantages from the disciplinary angle. But when the enemy's air attacks on the town ceased completely, its inhabitants believed that a mutual understanding had been reached between the belligerents. I naturally assumed that the Allies had got to know about Kesselring's efforts for neutralisation and about my own measures to pacify the town. There is no doubt that both the Vatican and the Badoglio government intervened to safeguard the town; however, with Bologna it never came to a binding international agreement any more than in the case of Monte Cassino or Florence.

Yet developments might well result in my having to put up a defence of Bologna in a series of rearward lines, a contingency that had been provided for. In that event the propaganda for neutralisation could easily involve me in the risk of infringing some international agreement. Consequently it was in my interest to secure a statement showing that in the event of a breakthrough at this key position I had reveived no orders other than to defend the town to the utmost. Such a defence was possible in this as in all towns; moreover the terrain on the southern outskirts of Bologna lent itself to defence, and there were numerous natural caves.

In the end I had no alternative but to request Kesselring either to cancel the order to defend the rearward built-up positions where they ran near the edge of the town, or to inform the Mayor of the true position. Kesselring opted for defence, and had to write to the Mayor to tell him so. (In the event it was fortunate that Bologna did not have to be defended, as the enemy's offensive spared the town; without any fighting or disturbances it was isolated and abandoned.) The letter received by the Mayor did not alter the population's belief that the town was "open". There was a continuous inflow of refugees, and insofar as these came from the battle zone we could do nothing to hinder them.

It was evident that we would not surmount the difficulties unless the population were kept nourished. This was feasible because of ample supplies in the surrounding provinces, agriculturally the richest in the land. Bologna had meat supplies sufficient for several months. The farmers had driven their livestock into the town, where cattle were to be seen in the entrances of houses, in courtyards and even churches, until such time as they were slaughtered. There was a shortage of fats and especially of salt, which could be made good from the big military depot. During the winter the shortage of fuel became acute. Since their country possesses neither wood nor coal, the Italians are more indifferent to the cold than the Germans. But we needed coal for the gas, electricity and water-works, and it had to be hauled laboriously across the bridgeless Po. The normally scant stocks of wood in the neighbourhood became smaller than ever, but had to be kept up in the interest of the German troops. Consequently we began to dismantle railway sleepers from unused tracks. The sanitary conditions were still bearable despite the increased population due to tens of thousands of refugees from other parts. We were worried only about the summer months.

Because of earlier experiences I forebade the installation of brothels for the troops. They encourage breaches of discipline, nor do they by any means lessen the amount of venereal disease. Experience showed that in the brothel-free zone of Bologna there was less venereal disease than in the zone of the neighbouring corps, where brothels were allowed. The worst feature of brothels in time of war is that they are generally established as a supply area amenity for the rearward services, but not for the front-line soldiers.

During the winter I had my headquarters first at Baricella, then farther west at Padulle. Near Baricella, in the castle of S. Martino, lived a former professor of Bologna University, Count Filippo Cavazza, who was a good friend. His wife had died and his only son had been killed in action. He was somewhat of a misanthrope, and now the prospect of the possible destruction of his house made him particularly bitter. He was a violent anti-Fascist. When visiting him I frequently met a very intelligent man who kept me informed about every detail of the situation in Bologna. He acted as spokesman for the wishes of the inhabitants and showed me lists of the victims of the Blackshirts, which enabled me to take action and generally to do everything I could to ease the burden for the people. This was Father Casati, Prior of the Dominican convent and a friend of Cavazza.

An official directive from the army commander stated that we should co-operate with the Church, which throughout the war and in the absence of proper state machinery had represented the starving people. Shortly after taking over command in Bologna I therefore paid a formal visit to the Archbishop, Cardinal Count Naselli Rocca. But in him I found a Prince of the Church who either did not wish to become compromised or else had an understandable antipathy towards all Germans. At any rate we never got beyond the customary exchange of courtesies, and even my complete mastery of the Italian language and my Catholic faith failed to smooth the way as they had so often done before in a situation of this kind. Yet I knew that the Cardinal was trying to spare Bologna from destruction, using his contact with the Vatican and the Papal Nuncio in Berne. On the other hand, he did little to settle the internal political difficulties.

In such matters it was Father Casati who sprang into the breach. When I asked him if in his capacity as Prior of the Dominican Convention he also represented the Church—which in this case was the Cardinal—he gave an affirmative reply. For the rest, he was an impressive personality, a man of intellect and learning, like the founder of the Order. Hence it was a pleasure to negotiate with him, but also a strain because of the sharpness of his logic. Clearly a particularly good brain had been chosen for the Convention in Bologna. In the late Middle Ages the town's university enjoyed the highest esteem, equal to that of Paris. St. Dominic had sent his sons here first in order that they should propagate the creed in the learned circles of discussion among the spiritual élite. In this he was followed by St. Ignatius, who had the same idea after the Reformation. Their spiritual programme distinguished the Domincans for all time from the mendicant Order of Franciscans, which was founded at the same period. The monastery at Bologna contains the relics of the founder of the Order.

We had frustrated all the enemy's attempts to break through and had thus seemingly created a stable front. Yet the German position was deteriorating, and everybody realised that Germany was nearing the end. Consequently the relative quiet in this theatre of war was something of a paradox. I did what is usual among senior commanders in such a situation: I wore an air of confidence that belied my better judgment. I wandered unaccompanied through the bookshops of Bologna and through architecturally interesting buildings, and despite the protests of my staff I rode out alone into the partisan-ridden countryside. Even my Italian friends, who were well aware of the danger, began by warning me. But then the disgruntled partisans let it be known that they would do me no harm!

I kept up the outward pretence of confidence by arranging for the Bologna Opera to re-open, which involved considerable difficulties. As a substitute for the non-existent brothels I arranged for hundreds of German soldiers to be sent every evening from their rest billets to the performances. Italian variety troupes were formed and sent to the rest billets. Although this was against the regulations, I considered that such diversions were a necessity for the troops during their periods of rest. I did not take the danger of espionage very seriously; as each of the thousands of partisans was already a spy, what did half a dozen artists matter? In the spring we also had classical concerts, and I arranged for an officer's club to be opened on the outskirts of the town. Here day-time courses were held on co-operation between armour and infantry, and in the evenings there were films, variety acts and concerts. The club got extra rations and wine from local suppliers.

At Baricella our quarters were indifferent. The officers were on good terms with the population, and especially with the energetic and kindly priest, in whose house the junior officers established their mess.

On January 8th we had to move unexpectedly to Padulle. It was a poor place compared with Baricella, and the change was unpopular. But then I found a secluded medium-sized house for myself. It belonged to a rich man who had moved into Bologna, where he had been murdered by the partisans. The furnishings that remained in this house were in bad taste, but with the available resources I had a room furnished for myself, in which I was very happy. As usual the walls and ceilings were painted white. The floor consisted of red tiles. For the lamps we made our own large white shades. There was a large round table of high quality wood and chairs covered in red and white cretonne. In another house near Bologna I came across seven large prints in mahogany frames, representing the Seven Sacraments. I borrowed them, taking care to inform the town authorities of my action. These pictures in their broad frames were hung low and exactly covered the white surface of the wall. The room had good proportions, being square with a very low ceiling. The area between the two wide windows on the south side was completely filled by a huge fireplace.

For that latitude the winter was very severe, with four weeks of snow and hard frost. Usually I returned from the front thoroughly frozen. After the hard walking at the front I was usually sweating when I got into the draughty little Volkswagen, my feet and shoes sodden with snow or water from the streams I had waded through, and it was in this condition that I returned to the comfort of my room. The sunlight, reflected from the broad expanse of snow, streamed through the large windows, settling on the snow-white walls, where the effect was intensified by the flickering firelight. Each time it was the same—a feast of light and warmth and inner contentment. Here I could lead my own life away from the world's affairs, burying myself in the books that I had brought from Bologna. Occasionally I had guests. On the ground floor was a dining-room and a small drawing-room with pictures that I had borrowed (with consent) from the museums of Bologna. Apart from the accommodation for the household there was only one spare room.

The property included a large orchard and a few farm buildings, the whole being enclosed by a tall hedge and trees that towered above the house. Beyond them lay the broad open fields of the plain of the Po.

The thaw ushered in the spring. Now we could drink our coffee in the orchard, where I whiled away many an hour. The hedges broke into pale green, the trees sprouted their red buds; and the first delicate pale shroud of leaves glistened in the east wind—a picture that never lost its spell. The colours grew deeper, the prolific white blossom of the fruit trees gradually gaining over the green. Then came the bloom and perfume of lilac.

From my corner of the garden there was a view through a wide, open gateway towards an alley of poplars which terminated at a small red house. No noise of the town, or of war or machines, disturbed the festive morning song of the birds.

I sent for my horses. Round the hedges on the border of the property a jumping course was laid out. Once again I experienced the joy of applying the well-tried methods to schooling a horse to jump lithely and with confidence.

The problems of operations and administration had been so well settled that I could enjoy this god-given relaxation just as at Lubitzkije in the spring of 1943. I surrendered myself to this peace in full awareness of what sooner or later must be my fate.

I now wrote frequently to my beloved children and I could also reach them by telephone. While Germany was already being invaded from both sides, they remained in the narrow strip of land that had not yet been occupied—in Bolzano and in Berlin.

INDOCTRINATION OF THE TROOPS

Naturally it became more and more difficult at this stage to cater for the mental and spiritual well-being of the troops. It gradually dawned on all who had retained a measure of common sense that the war could no longer be won, irrespective of whether and for how long there could be any effective resistance south of the Alps.

While we were still at Cassino I had selected as N.S.F.O. (Nazi leadership officer) a Reserve officer, a friend of mine from the days of my old cavalry regiment, who was occupying a minor post on the corps H.Q. staff. He was qualified for the job inasmuch as he had once belonged to the *Stahlhelm*. When that organisation was dissolved, he was compulsorily transferred to the S.A. Here he had held an intermediate rank, but not for long, as he resigned. With him I could openly discuss all our difficulties. There was no need for him to dissociate himself from National Socialism, since he had never adopted it. This was a great relief to me, for otherwise I would probably have been saddled with a wild party man acting as informer in the midst of my staff.

Up to July 20th everything had in fact gone well, but thereafter the party headquarters kept a very suspicious watch on the composition of the corps staff and also on myself because of my attitude, which was well known to the S.D. My N.S.F.O's appointment had never been confirmed by the party as prescribed by the regulations, and I repeatedly refused to have him replaced. At this stage an inspector was sent from the homeland to investigate the circumstances.

The outcome was that I was allowed to retain my N.S.F.O., and at regular intervals I even held my own N.S.F.O. sessions for the corps. I thus achieved a two-fold purpose: I fooled the N.S.F.O.s of the army and the army group, as well as the party informers; but above all I kept the indoctrination of the troops in my own hands, so that these political officers could not assert themselves outside the jurisdiction of the senior military commander, as was occurring in higher staffs. I ordered the N.S.F.O.s of the subordinated divisions to attend these sessions, and on the occasions when I myself spoke, the divisional commanders were also present.

One of the subterfuges by which I restricted the activities of the subordinate N.S.F.O.s was to confine the indoctrination to the battalions that were resting, away from the front. Indeed this was the only way of getting the instructions over to the men. But the practice for battalions undergoing rest periods was that the first three rest days were spent really resting, bathing, getting fresh clothing, and enjoying sports and other recreations. Not until this period was over could they be available for indoctrination. However, the rest period could never last more than three days, for if the battalion was not sent back to the front it would then be detailed for building up the rearward positions. Since no N.S.F.O. was capable of penning a usable article, the divisional newspapers, which came under the direction of the divisional commanders, were a practical means of restraining Nazi dominance.

There were two categories of N.S.F.O.s—the fanatics and informers who were feared, and the credulous, the so-called "decent fellows". I urged the divisional commanders to choose the N.S.F.O.s from their own divisions and naturally from the credulous category. This was all the more easy since the fanatical ones usually failed to qualify as regards the stipulation that they should have proved themselves in action at the front and wear the decorations awarded for such service. If any fanatics with such qualifications were still to be found at the front, they usually had little enthusiasm for taking on the job. They had begun to smell a rat and were disinclined to have themselves branded in this way. Consequently most of the N.S.F.O.s were of the easily led and limited type, who, even without decorations, were glad to accept the post in order to avoid a worse evil.

Despite these restrictions on the effectiveness of the N.S.F.O.s, the indoctrination of the troops became increasingly difficult. In the summer of 1944 German maps could still substantiate the claim that the areas under German occupation were bigger than all the territory reconquered by the Allies. Yet this kind of map strategy had become dangerous, and soon defeated its purpose, for it spoke all too clearly against us. Until 1942 the Axis powers were always advancing, but thereafter the occupied territories began to shrink perceptibly. Until 1941 the success of German offensive operations had caused certain people, whom we would have credited with a better judgment, to believe that even after severe reverses Germany would always be able to resume the offensive. Such people, being more optimistic than understanding, eagerly seized upon any news like that of the Runstedt offensive in the Ardennes. They ignored the fact that as early as 1942 the German attacks in Russia were producing only an impression of success. The balance of military power was even then swinging in favour of the Allies, nor could this development be stopped by the genius of all the commanders in the field, whose plans in any case could no longer affect the issue of the war. The optimists were greatly disappointed when the Rundstedt offensive revealed itself as the last convulsion of an already defeated nation which possessed no political system capable of ending the war. To do this meant abolishing the régime, and the atempt to do that had failed on July 20th.

In the German army in Italy the spirit of the troops, which had so long remained at a high level, was now undermined by a further and not unjustified fear. It was anticipated that Hitler would seek his last refuge in the southern Alps, in which case these soldiers would be called upon to fight to the bitter end, as Hitler had always expected them to do. He had once uttered these words: "God forgive me the last hours before the achievement of final victory", and there were actually people who believed in this oracular reference to wonder weapons—instruments of war that by means of "electricity" or "death-rays" would destroy all Germany's enemies so completely that only the German people would be left. . . .

In the face of these hallucinations and fears it was important to keep calm. We had to avoid senseless sacrifices and spare the greatest number of people so that they could return to the homeland. If that were impossible we would prefer captivity, for, in contrast to the eastern front, this would bring us safely home.

I could not even disclose to my divisional commanders the knowledge I possessed of the army group's measures for winding up the local theatre of war. Even so, it was not certain that peace would result. The better one knew the troops, the more obvious it became that peace efforts would be opposed not only by the die-hard Nazis, but also by numerous officers of the old school who, especially in time of war, repudiated any suggestion of breaking the oath. I confess that I was always amazed how little even anti-Fascist officers knew of the criminal nature of our political leadership. They considered it their duty to close their ears in time of war to all unfavourable news. For them Hitler still remained the "rightful authority" to whom they had pledged obedience and loyalty. Such people, who were numerically preponderant in all the German armies, would not be easily talked into a separate capitulation in this theatre of war.

In proportion as the reasons for continuing to fight became less cogent, so it was more difficult to suggest the right attitude to the troops. In the end all one could do was to urge them to stick together in the hour of danger, to trust the "Führer" and to maintain discipline.

It was a difficult position, since this type of exhortation is a characteristic of military defeat. Naturally nothing raises the morale of troops so much as victory; how long we had been without one! Every day we were suffering a defeat on one front or another, and we were reduced to claiming a "victory" if we even successfully defended some position. But our opponents were now in sight of a real victory, involving the annihilation of their enemy. Meanwhile we, the defeated, sought consolation in a utopian optimism—"the elixir of the weak"—which in the end deceived nobody.

Those who stray from the truth must forfeit the trust of their fellow-men. Yet anyone describing the situation as it really was would have been spreading despondency. Nor did Nazism find any escape from these alternatives. Consequently in this last phase the troops that had seen the light were more dependable than the misguided followers of Hitler. He who looks his destiny in the face will understand the adage: *Nec metus nec spes*—Neither fear nor hope.

DESTRUCTION OF ARMY GROUP C IN THE PLAIN OF THE PO

It had always been clear to the senior German commanders in Italy that the Apennine front would not be tenable against a major enemy offensive. Col.-General von Vietinghoff, who had succeeded Field-Marshal Kesselring as C.-in-C. of Army Group C, warned the O.K.W. of this on several occasions.

Naturally I pondered the situation that would confront XIV Panzer Corps. I still thought the corps would have to meet one of the enemy's main thrusts. The routine of begging for more troops necessitated my producing evidence of the enemy's anticipated centres of pressure, and this I was constantly doing. Yet even the army group and army commanders considered that the enemy would thrust downwards from the Apennines to the plain of the Po from whatever position was nearest to the plain, which implied that he would move in the direction of Bologna. However, in the course of the winter offensive I began to doubt whether the enemy would do so. During his offensive on the Adriatic side and subsequently, the enemy had never seriously renewed his autumn attacks against the Bologna positions. He could dispense with his costly and time-consuming attack in the mountains, and instead roll up the entire Apennine front from the plain of the Po. The conditions for such an operation were presented to him after his successes against LXXVI Pz. Corps and LXXIII Corps. If he could exploit these successes to the extent of achieving a deep breakthrough at only one point, this would seal the fate not only of the 10th Army, but also of the westerly 14th Army and the Ligurian Army. A further advance from the area south-west of Lake Commachio would take him via Ferrara directly towards Verona. This town was the sole gateway to the north for all German troops still fighting in Italy. If the Allies concentrated all their air power on the Brenner road, they could effectively block it. This was one of those situations when concentrated paratroop units could still be used for that purpose. It would not even have been a desperate venture, since partisans would have assisted the paratroops everywhere in the plain of the Po. Under such circumstances the rôle of XIV Pz. Corps would have been possible but very difficult. I anticipated that the corps would be kept in its position as long as possible to act as a pivotal point for the retreating 10th Army and also as flank protection and later as rearguard for the 14th Army; and that it would only be allowed to start a disengaging movement under the severest fighting conditions. I did not anticipate that the Ligurian Army under Graziani would be pulled back. If there were a precipitate retreat, the Italian troops in this army would disintegrate, while the still numerous admixture of German forces on the western Alpine front would probably be gathered in north of the Po.

These prognoses could hardly inspire me with confidence. True, the fighting spirit of the troops remained reasonably good, but it could not be put to the test until the big offensive. Raiding activities were limited to a few small operations, while the mass of troops vegetated in their fixed positions. The better these were constructed, the more difficult would be a new war of movement, and this worried me. Although I possessed good divisions, I lacked any élite, such as the motorised divisions that were truly mobile and capable of putting up a defence against armour.

When the attack developed on April 14th, it came as a surprise against the right wing of my corps and the left wing of my right-hand neighbour, LI Mountain Corps. Indeed the surprise attack was so complete that after it had started we still regarded it as a diversionary operation. It was launched against the left-hand regiment of the left-wing division of the mountain corps, and at once gained considerable ground. Then the enemy wheeled against the right wing of 94 Inf. Div. on the front of my corps, and quickly unhinged its entire position on the right-hand sector. In anticipation of the imminent threat I had placed the division's reserve battalion in a state of readiness behind the boundary of the two corps, but its forces proved insufficient. For any crisis that might develop between Bologna and the Tyrrhenian Sea the only available operational reserve was the 90 Pz. Gren. Div. The further reserves of the army group—26 Pz. Div. and 29 Pz. Gren. Div., which could be considered élite troops—were regarded by the C.-in-C. as indispensable at Commachio. Since an attack from that direction could cut off the entire army group, there was nothing he feared more.

In retrospect it is impossible to decide whether a correct use of 90 Pz. Gren. Div. would have prevented the breakthrough between LI Mountain Corps and XIV Pz. Corps. Presumably the end result would have been unchanged. Yet the manner in which the battle was here conducted provides another instance of the incorrect employment of reserves. One regiment had been sent prematurely against guerrillas on the roads leading south from Parma and Reggio, and this splitting of the reserves prevented their concentrated use against the gap in the front, which should have been vigorously defended. Moreover the remainder of the division was prematurely thrown into the battle, actually against the penetration at the left wing regiment of LI Mountain Corps. Although the division stood up for a time to the frontal attack, it could not prevent the enemy from turning against 94th Inf. Div. on the now exposed flank of XIV Pz. Corps. When the army realised that this was the critical point, it had no reserves left. The units of 90 Pz. Gren. Div. that had been engaged were now moved eastward to their base line. Because of the direction of this movement, any counter-attack would have been useless, and in any case a movement of this kind always requires considerable time. Nor could I with my only corps reserve—a battalion from the Bologna area— arrest the breakthrough, for by the time it had arrived, the right wing had already crumpled up after the shedding of 90 Pz. Gren. Div. The enemy now had freedom of movement.

The Allies had chosen their direction of attack wisely and with a view to further developments. After their forces had passed through the village of Tole they entered a terrain that had always caused me anxiety—the country that I have already described, with its gentle and uncultivated slopes descending towards the Po, where armour could at once be operated. The mobile anti-tank defences in depth that I had kept in readiness did not get into action, and now the communications links began to break down.

The defeat took its inevitable course. I did manage once more to establish a kind of operational front on the northern slopes of the Apennines, but it no longer had any sort of a backbone.

Having discovered the weakest part of the German defensive system, the enemy assembled his troops to exploit it. The U.S. 1 Armoured Div. overpowered the German mobile anti-tank defences on the northern slopes of the Apennines. The excellent U.S. 10 Alpine Div. and 88 Inf. Div. pushed ahead correctly towards the Via Emilia between Modena and Bologna. After the German 94 Inf. Div. had been defeated the Bologna complex collapsed of its own accord. In conjunction with 94 Inf. Div., the untried 8 Mountain Div. was compelled to fall back. On the other hand the disengaging movements went according to plan with 65 Inf. Div. at Bologna and the adjoining 305 Inf. Div., the latter again under my command. Bologna was evacuated without fighting. This conformed to the wishes of its population and also of Kesselring and myself. The partisans in Bologna remained quiet, which was probably a reward for our peaceful evacuation of the town. Our policy of pacification during those months had borne fruit. But I also insisted that all the troops falling back should by-pass the town.

As we had to assume that the enemy knew the location of my advanced H.Q., we moved on April 13th to a prepared H.Q. at Riolo, east of Castelfranco and close to the Via Emilia. Meanwhile the enemy's air superiority had become so preponderant that nobody dared show himself on the roads in daylight. My faithful batman Feuerstak was persistently attacked by fighter-bombers when with his dogcart he was trying to fetch provisions for the staff. He was badly wounded and had to have a leg amputated. I quickly visited him in the field hospital and sat a long time at his bedside, holding his hand. We both had the same thoughts: after seven years of soldiering together we would now be parted. Neither he nor I knew where he would fetch up. As I feared, we were never to see each other again. He felt himself deprived of my help, and I of his. Such moments in a soldier's life are among the saddest of memories. Now he leads the life of a peasant somewhere in the Eastern zone, but how long will he be able to endure it?

By April 20th the enemy already had knowledge of my new headquarters. I was alone in the house when it was attacked from the air. Several bombs exploded very near it, the neighbouring house burst into flames, the cattle stampeded, and my washing on the line was carried by the blast into the trees.

It was no longer possible to pull the corps back in an orderly retreat across the Po. The threat from the air forced us to restrict all movement to the dark hours, yet so rapid was the enemy's advance that movement in daylight could not be avoided. The corps H.Q. staff was continually chased by enemy armour from one H.Q. to the next.

The zone immediately south of the Po is completely coverless to a depth of ten to fifteen kilometres. There were no natural obstacles behind which the now disordered mass of troops might have made some kind of a last stand while streaming back. Allied reports indicate that it was part of their plan to reach this coverless zone in good time.

In the area of the left-hand neighbouring 1 Para. Corps the enemy had already reached Modena. While shifting the battle H.Q. we came under artillery fire from the exposed left flank. On the right of XIV Pz. Corps the gap between it and LI Corps grew wider. The latter had either already been cut off or, as we presumed, was falling back northwards to Mantua. To our west the enemy had reached S. Benedetto on the Po and was attacking Poggio Rucco. Elements of 65 and 305 Inf. Divs. that were still capable of fighting had assembled at Camposanto. The remnants of 8 Mountain Div. were falling back towards this group, but were unable to cover the completely exposed western flank. As far as the corps was concerned, 94 Inf. Div. had completely vanished—presumably forced westwards or already rounded up by the enemy. The 90 Pz. Gren. Div. had pulled back towards the west with LI Mountain Corps. The commander of 65 Inf. Div., Lieut.-General Pfeiffer, was killed at the bridge at Finale. I had no hope of re-assembling a battle-worthy force to the south of the Po.

On the night of April 22nd I had to decide whether to be taken prisoner with my corps H.Q. staff while still south of the Po, or whether to cross the river. I decided to attempt the crossing. My H.Q. staff was dissolved into separate groups. At dawn on the 23rd we found a ferry at Bergantino. Of the thirty-six Po ferries in the zone of 14th Army, four only were still serviceable. Because of the incessant fighter-bomber attacks it was useless to cross in daylight. As the level of water in the Po was low, many officers and men were able to swim across. The access road at Revere was blocked by many columns of burning vehicles. I had to leave my cars behind. In the morning twilight we crossed the river, and together with my operations staff I marched the twenty-five kilometres to Legnano. We were unable to establish any communications. Major-General von Schellwitz, who after General Pfeiffer's death had assumed command of the remnants of 65 and 305 Inf. Divs., was captured south of the river.

We spent the night of April 23rd in Legnano, then tried to cross the Adige in order to reach the corps' base at S. Stefano. All the bridges had been destroyed from the air, and again we had to find a ferry. Meanwhile, even at night the roads were under continuous fire from fighter-bombers. At S. Stefano I assembled the corps staff insofar as the separate groups had managed to escape across the Po. On the 24th I was again at the disposal of the army commander at his H.Q. which was between Verona and Lake Garda. During the night we tried to proceed via the Adige valley road and the eastern road of Lake Garda to the village of Ala, but were held up by traffic blocks and obstructions. On the following night we succeeded in crossing the Pasubio pass and reached the remote mountain village of Ronchi. There we installed a battle H.Q., and recuperated in the mountain air after the many sleepless nights.

At this juncture two of the former divisional staffs—from 94 Inf. Div. and 8 Mountain Div.—turned up again. They organised a front from Lake Garda to the Pasubio pass with an odd assortment of troops, mostly from other units. From the rear some fresh troops in small numbers had been brought up, consisting of a Parachute Officers' School and an S.S. Mountain School. Consequently it was to some extent possible again to provide infantry forces for occupying the Adige valley and the mountains between it and Lake Garda, but there was no longer any artillery, and its tasks were taken over by the A.A. batteries of the army and the Luftwaffe. Now the enemy had everywhere ceased attacking. We wondered whether this was due to exhaustion, but thought it more likely that he now saw no point in risking the lives of any more soldiers.

The roads leading north were filled with an unending stream of stragglers. We would have regarded this as a sign of dissolution if we had not long been accustomed to such scenes. The defeated infantry had been streaming back ever since the Cassino breakthrough, some with their commanders, others without them. Movements of this type were far more feasible with the all too weak forces on this front than they had been at the time of the serried

companies of the First World War. Because of this, too, there was no
occasion for the troops to mutiny. Every soldier to whom one spoke
told the same tale as in similar situations in the past: he had been
"over-run" or "outflanked", had fought his way through, and now
wanted to carry out the order to proceed to the assembly-point in
the supply area. It was never possible to discover who had given
such an order. Nor was it possible to assemble these stragglers
directly behind a new defensive line among unfamiliar troop units.
Every soldier abhorred the idea of being cut off from his mail and, in
general, from his military home circle.

Nevertheless these infantrymen gave no impression of demoral-
isation. In contrast to 1918, their conduct was honourable. Without
exception they were innocent of cowardice or disobedience of orders.
In cases where an organised order of battle no longer existed
at the front they were accustomed to going back to their supply
areas, which in their view was the only way to freshen them up for
further action. In the same way my corps H.Q. staff had gone far
back to its rear base, where it hoped to find new vehicles and other
equipment.

While still south of the Po, I had repeatedly tried to get these
stragglers to rejoin their units which were still fighting. But these
piecemeal orders could have no real effect, for the commanders themselves were physically too exhausted to appreciate the value of such a
procedure. After a catastrophe of this kind, which involves the break-
ing-up of whole formations, long marches, swimming across rivers
and many sleepless nights, there is only one way to deal with the
exhausted infantry, and that is to follow the instinct of the ordinary
soldier and to re-form the troops far back in the supply area.

We had occupied the so-called Blue Line, where for the first time
in the long years of war we found really powerful and deep fortifications. They dated from the First World War! But the enemy was
content to circumvent the blocked eastern road of Lake Garda by
using amphibious vehicles and landing on the north shore, thereby
rendering the Blue Line untenable.

I spent April 29th and 30th in quarters in the house of Count
Frederigotti at Pamorolo near Roverto. The situation was tense. The
Count was aware of my attitude towards the Nazi régime. His family
belonged to the aristocracy of South Tyrol, and had long since
become Austrians although their home was in the Trentino. He had
married a Countess von der Straaten, whose father had been head of
the Spanish riding school in Vienna. So I found myself the guest of
Germans as well.

Frederigotti was giving shelter to a senior member of the Todt
organisation, a man with the equivalent rank of general, who
apparently wanted to go over to the enemy. I urged him to drive

northwards, but in Rovereto he carried out his intention.

I knew that Frederigotti sided with the Italian Committee of Liberation. Each day he drove down to the town to discuss measures to be taken against the Germans, and indeed this was his right and duty as an Italian citizen whose legal government was now at war with Germany. He would return from his council of war for dinner in his elegant house, and we would ponder the problem of how to save the district from further hostilities, which had now become pointless.

CAPITULATION OF ARMY GROUP C

May 1st, 1945. In the forenoon I gave up my quarters with the Count and moved to Matterello, seven kilometres south of Trent, where I found a pretty villa with a baroque garden and a distant view into the valley of the Adige. It would have been a pleasant place to spend a fortnight, but I stayed there for only two days and spent the nights elsewhere, for in the meantime fateful events were taking their course.

On the previous evening my own C.-in-C., General Lemelsen, had called me on the telephone to say that Kesselring had transferred von Vietinghoff, C.-in-C. of the army group, and General Röttiger, his Chief of Staff, to the reserve of generals. The army group had been taken over by a General Schulz, a man unknown to us, but fortunately his Chief of Staff was to be General Wenzel, whom we knew well as the former C.O.S. to von Vietinghoff.

On the afternoon of May 1st General Lemelsen called me again to say that Röttiger had ordered the arrest of the newly-appointed Generals Schulz and Wenzel, and had asked Lemelsen as the senior commander of an army to come at once to army group headquarters to take over the command. Lemelsen had refused, since he could not take orders from Röttiger. Von Vietinghoff and Röttiger had evidently exceeded their authority in negotiating with the enemy. Lemelsen also informed me that he had received a written instruction from Kesselring prohibiting negotiations without a special order.

At 4.30 p.m. I was urgently summoned by Lemelsen to take over at army headquarters at Fay, as his presence at army group headquarters had become a necessity.

At Fay I was given the following picture by Colonel Runkel, the C.O.S.: Generals Schulz and Wenzel were free again, and exercising command. Col-General v. Vietinghoff, who had left Bolzano as instructed, together with SS *Obergruppenführer* Wolff, had through the medium of Lt.-Colonel von Schweinitz entered into an armistice agreement with the Allied C.-in-C. of the Mediterranean theatre of war, Field-Marshal Alexander, which would come into force at

2 p.m. on May 2nd and could not now be rescinded. The commanders of the German 10th and 14th Armies, the commander of the Luftwaffe in Italy (General von Pohl) and especially SS *Obergruppenführer* Wolff accepted the conclusion of an armistice, since the utterly defeated army group had been cut off from the homeland through the enemy's advance from Garmisch in the direction of Innsbruck, and also because the lack of weapons, fuel and ammunition, and the impending shortage of provisions had made all further resistance impossible.

As there had been no clarification of the position, I rang up my friend Wenzel to obtain information. He told me that both he and his C.-in-C. were now keeping to the agreement and that everything had been settled in a very "honourable" manner. I was not entirely satisfied with this information, and asked to speak to Lemelsen, but instead Schulz came to the telephone. He said he was faced by a *fait accompli* which he could do nothing to alter. As the time allowed for compliance was running out. he had of his own accord suggested to Kesselring that his approval should be forthcoming within half an hour.

Later, Lemelsen rang me again with the order that by 2 p.m. on May 2nd the army was to cease fire and stop all movements other than those needed for supplies. Kesselring was unattainable, but his C.O.S., General Westphal, had been kept informed. General Schulz, new C.-in-C. of the army group, realised the necessity for complying with the agreement already concluded. Generals von Pohl and Herr had already issued the relevant orders to the units under their command. Hitler had died in Berlin.

It was clear to me that the death of Hitler would soon result in the liquidation of all the fronts, and the troops of my army group would have to conform. Nor was there any further disagreement among the higher commanders, as there had evidently been between Kesselring and Vietinghoff. Towards midnight I gave the appropriate orders to General Haug for LI Corps, to Colonel Kras for my XIV Pz. Corps and to General Heiderich for 1 Para. Corps. None of them questioned the orders.

May 2nd, 1945. In the morning I returned to my H.Q. After the conclusion of the armistice I was free to explain the situation to the troops. First I assembled the officers of my corps staff, telling them that the more realistically minded senior commanders had long foreseen this situation, since our fighting potential had been deteriorating almost hourly. I had to reckon with the possibility that some fresh units recently thrown into the battle, such as the Parachute Officers' School or the S.S. Mountain School, would decide to fight on, as that accorded with the mystical attitude of their commanders. Consequently I drew attention to the hopeless operational situation, the enemy's advance towards the Brenner, the complete annihilation of the German 10th Army to the east, and the likelihood that the enemy would reach the Brenner from both east and west, and block it. I described the difficulties that had faced the higher command ever since the Cassino battles. I reminded my listeners that for a long time already our material and numerical inferiority had led to the routing of our troops in major battles, that many of them had streamed back completely disorganised and could only be re-assembled with difficulty, that the battle on the Po had resulted in complete dissolution, from which the corps H.Q. itself had not been spared. I also reminded them that we had fought for years against the senseless orders to halt at certain defensive positions, orders which had resulted in the unnecessary sacrifice of troops when we should have tried to break contact and so gain time, strength and freedom of movement.

As regards the form of the surrender, I was able to state that it had been approved by Kesselring, whose name was esteemed by the troops.

It was a tragic moment, this utter defeat and imminent capitulation after six years of fighting—tragic even for those of us who had long seen it coming.

I had already talked briefly with the two divisional commanders still under my command. They entirely understood the reasons for this development, for with the exception of the newly arrived units their formations no longer possessed any fighting value and would have disintegrated at the first assault.

After my address to the officers I went for my usual walk. On returning I learned that I was to head a mission to General Mark Clark, now commander of the 15th Army Group, concerning execution of the instrument of surrender. Accompanied by one or two persons I drove to the army corps H.Q. at Bolzano, where I was given the details.

As I already knew, the negotiations had started several weeks earlier, and evidently SS *Obergruppenführer* Wolff had been the driving force. He had secured the agreement of Himmler, Kesselring and von Vietinghoff to negotiate with the enemy, and it was while the discussions were in progress that the enemy's offensive had started, ending in the total defeat of our troops on the Po. Consequently the plenipotentiary Lieut.-Colonel von Schweinitz had been unable to negotiate anything less than total surrender and one or two formal concessions, such as the temporary retention of side-arms by officers.

Schweinitz had signed with the reservation that approval must be secured from his own C.-in-C. Kesselring had withheld his approval for total surrender of the army group. Yet it had become known that Himmler himself had entered into negotiations with the Swedish Count

Bernadotte, probably without the knowledge of Hitler. Evidently Kesselring had tried to evade the issue. He could claim that those to whom he had delegated his powers had greatly exceeded their authority. For that reason he had on May 1st ordered von Vietinghoff to be replaced as C.-in-C. of the army group by Schulz. On May 2nd there was utter confusion at army group H.Q. Schulz and his C.O.S., Wenzel, had been put under temporary arrest by the already deposed C.O.S., Röttiger, his own C.-in-C., having already departed. The officers were later released. The commanders of the 10th and 14th Armies accepted the agreement as a *fait accompli*.

In the end this was also the attitude of Schulz. For technical reasons the capitulation had to be announced before Kesselring's agreement was forthcoming, and it was only on the morning of May 2nd that Wolff could obtain it from the field-marshal after a two hours' telephone conversation.

I realised how much the death of Hitler had facilitated these developments, for Kesselring would not otherwise have given his consent. There would probably have been considereable opposition among large sections of the troops to an independent surrender by this army group. Even so, there were enquiries from the troops as to whether the laying down of arms had the approval of Admiral Dönitz, whom Hitler had nominated as his successor. It was a question dictated by conscience, which could not be answered, since the admiral's attitude and his decrees were not precisely known. He had spoken of cessation of hostilities against the Western powers provided this did not directly assist the Bolsheviks! This indicated that he was still thinking in terms of the old idea of being able to split the victorious powers at the eleventh hour before the inescapable capitulation.

We still had to face the possibility that individual commanders might encourage their units to go down fighting, thereby escaping the odium of laying down arms, and ending the struggle with a theatrical gesture. There would of course be only a minority ready to fight to the last cartridge while the mass of the troops were being taken into captivity. On the western front there had been many examples of this kind of débâcle. It would have been in line with Hitler's directive never to capitulate, and yet it could not have changed anything in regard to total capitulation.

May 3rd, 1945. In the morning I attended the negotiations between General Wolff and Dr. Angelis, leader of the South Tyrol Liberation Committee. The latter demanded the complete transfer of the administration to himself as representative of the Italian government. Wolff opposed this on the grounds that the Allies were taking over all control. While these discussions were proceeding on the balcony of the villa, Bolzano was surrounded by liberation troops. From the town we could hear the noise of firing between German troops and the Tyrolese freedom fighters, which claimed some dozens of casualties on both sides. My headquarters sent me a message that a British colonel had arrived there to fetch me. I invited him to come to Bolzano, where we gave him lunch. He was very correct and pleasant.

On the previous evening, when my nomination as leader of the surrender mission was intimated to General Mark Clark, he had ordered the U.S. 10 Alpine Division to send a general and a British colonel with an escort to collect me. These two officers had lost their way owing to the rising by the liberation troops at Rovereto, and only the colonel had reached Bolzano. It was he who accompanied me back to my corps headquarters, where the American General Ruffner had meanwhile arrived. Before a large fireplace in the comfortable winter billet I played the host for the last time by offering them the traditional cup of tea.

At 8 p.m. we moved off. I was accompanied by Lieut.-Colonel von Schweinitz, who had conducted the surrender negotiations at Caserta, and by Wolff's representatives, S.S. *Standartenführer* Dollmann, also by Lieutenant Zöllner, Captain von Cramm and the requisite subordinate personnel.

We found the village of Orli in the hands of liberation troops. Just before reaching Riva we encountered so extensive an obstruction that we had to continue on foot for a short distance. American soldiers were posted at the scene of the recent explosion, and they carried our baggage over the rubble. After some hot coffee we climbed into amphibious vehicles which soon plunged into Lake Garda, whose waters were agitated by a storm. Until dusk we headed into heavy seas parallel to the eastern road, which could not be used because of demolitions in the tunnels. About 9 p.m. we reached the battle H.Q. of the U.S. 10 Alpine Division and were transferred to other vehicles. The divisional commander, General Hay, escorted me in his large Packard, and we exchanged our impressions of past fighting, in which his division had been my most dangerous opponent. It was this division that had achieved the breakthrough that separated my corps from LI Corps. After all this time it was strange to be driving in a column showing bright headlamps. On reaching Verona we entered a tent for supper. The officers accompanying me were frozen after getting a soaking on Lake Garda and continuing the long journey in open cars. Snow still lay in the valley of the Adige. In Verona we spent the night at the well-known Hotel Colomba D'Oro.

May 4th, 1945. After a good English type of breakfast, for which we had to thank a British liaison officer with the 15th Army Group, Mr. John Profumo, we flew to Florence. Here we were received in General Mark Clark's headquarters according to a prescribed protocol. The victors received the vanquished formally and without ill-feeling, and provided hospitality. Shortly after our arrival I was told to report alone to the general. A kindly American officer had previously briefed me with a suggested form of words to use when reporting to the C.-in-C. Although it was no more than a suggestion, it included a reference to the fact that I had been authorised by my own superior commander to receive General Clark's orders for the surrender of Army Group C. I suppose that this formula could be regarded as meeting me half way inasmuch as it made no mention of unconditional surrender. But unfortunately this revived false hopes among the Germans. At the earlier discussions between the negotiators at Caserta there had still been talk of honourable concessions such as the retention of side-arms. If those negotiations in March had led to a surrender, it would have been a sensational event, but now the surrender was no different from the capitulation of the other army groups which found themselves unable to continue the fight. Moreover, in the first days of May the Allied radio broadcasts left us in no doubt that there was no alternative to unconditional surrender.

When I reported to General Clark he was standing in his tent under the Stars and Stripes flag, and at his side were the commanders of the U.S. 5th and the British 8th Army and of the Allied air forces.

I could not escape the impression that the Allied officers found this a painful scene. I had to respect them as opponents, whereas they could see in me only a representative of the Hitler régime. How could they know that this setting evoked in me little of the bitterness that they themselves felt? For me it marked the end of twelve years of spiritual servitude as well as a very personal turning-point in life, whatever my eventual fate might be. The long narrow face of the Allied C.-in-C., with the wide open, intelligent eyes of the soldier, made a very sympathetic impression on me. This impression was strengthened in the course of the afternoon, when in a long discussion alone with him I spoke frankly about the technical difficulties of the surrender. Prior to this discussion there had been a last combined session of my full mission and the staff of the army group, to which numerous press officials were admitted. The chair was taken by General Gruenther, Chief of Staff of the army group. He introduced his collaborators and with the aid of a map explained in which areas it was proposed to accommodate the German troops. In this context there was talk of co-operation between individual command posts of the Allied and German army groups, whereupon I asked to speak. I said that my C.-in-C. wanted to comply faithfully with the terms of surrender, but that this would not be possible so long as the activities of the so-called liberation troops led to clashes of arms with German troops. But since the communications links had largely broken down, the German command could exert only limited control over its own troops.

I referred to this problem again in my discussion with Mark Clark, and he at once agreed to help. He said that in any case the directives on which the liberation troops based their activities had been superseded through the conclusion of the negotiations for surrender. He had issued these directives—to occupy administrative buildings, take over German supply depots, disarm their guards, etc.—because he evidently hoped that the German army group would disintegrate before it laid down its arms. But in the last days of the fighting the liberation troops had made themselves surprisingly inconspicuous, and only became active after the capitulation. Mark Clark was prepared to admit that the German troops could not be expected to surrender their small arms as long as they were under threat from the guerrillas.

Yet during these days the whole process of handing over was seriously endangered. On May 3rd Allied air reconnaissance, as well as the officers who fetched us from the German-occupied area, had established that German vehicles of every kind were moving north from Trent towards the Brenner. That was an infringement of the terms of surrender, and the Allied 15th Army Group was threatening to operate its air forces against these movements. Furthermore, reports indicated that 1 Para. Corps had evidently not complied with the order to surrender, but was fighting on. We had always feared that something like this might happen.

All I could do was to give an assurance that the conduct of these troops ran counter to the honourable intentions of my C.-in-C. I could only assume that the guerrillas were preventing my C.-in-C. from exercising his authority. I therefore recommended that small mobile bodies of troops should be sent to re-establish order in the area still occupied by us, and to ensure communications with the German command posts. Unfortunately I could not get in direct touch with my army group, as the radio unit that had been allocated to me had not yet arrived. Indeed, it was soon learnt that it had been captured en route and was now in an American P.O.W. camp.

In accordance with instructions received before I started on the journey I pointed out that in the German view it would be dangerous to carry out the intention to bring the troops back to the region north of Bologna. We particularly wanted another solution. Both the troops and their officers were counting on an early discharge from the colours, and if they were now ordered south, this would precipitate a flight northwards of deserters. Yet such a break-up of the army group would be against the interest of Allies and Germans alike. And so I warned against the weakening of the authority of the German command that would result from troop movements of this kind, and suggested that they should be postponed until the authority of the Americans as the responsible power had been established beyond any doubt.

General Mark Clark did not close his ears to my arguments. His plan to move the German troops into the plain of the Po had been based on considerations of supplies, since stocks in the lower Alps would soon be exhausted. I, on the other hand, believed that the available motor transport facilities would be ample for supplying provisions to the troops from the plain, although I had no precise figures. I also pointed out that it would be more difficult to instal new camps in the fertile plain than in the mountainous lower Alps. Moreover, in the plain the Germans would find themselves among a hostile population. Unless thorough sanitary measures were instituted, accommodation in the low-lying camps could well lead to epidemics.

General Clark agreed to re-examine the whole question and to defer a decision. Meanwhile there was to be no mention of this subject to the German Press.

For the next few days negotiations were at a standstill, probably because the staff of the 15th Army Group were busy with questions unconnected with internment of the German troops. Meanwhile the Luftwaffe and the German Navy had sent representatives direct to the headquarters of the Allied C.-in-C. Mediterranean theatre of war. Although these representatives were subordinate to me, I had no control over them. On May 7th my mission was increased by twenty-two officers, all specialists. My small original mission had been accommodated in a tobacco factory; there were difficulties in housing the new arrivals. We were already prisoners, but received full American rations. I was given a small house to myself with three rooms and a bathroom.

Each day it became more apparent that we were no longer needed. A new organisation was created, different from that originally intended. Consequently on May 13th I was flown back to Bolzano, and returned to my old quarters at Matterolo where my staff was still intact.

On May 22nd I and my adjutant, Count von Cramm, were fetched from Matterolo and so I went into captivity as leader of the huge P.O.W. camp at Ghedi.

7

STRATEGIC CONTROVERSIES OF THE ALLIES

GREAT BRITAIN'S PLANNING ORGANISATION

When Winston Churchill became Prime Minister and Minister of Defence in 1940, he created his own instrument for planning the conduct of the war. The Chiefs of Staff were placed directly under the Minister of Defence, and this virtually eliminated the political heads of the three fighting services. Consequently the military experts in Great Britain acquired far greater influence over the formation of strategic aims than was the case in the other democracies. Between 1943 and 1945 the Chiefs of Staff were Brooke for the Army, Portal for the R.A.F. and Cunningham for the Navy. Their close cohesion enabled them to moderate a number of Churchill's more fantastic plans, and as the British historian John Ehrman put it, "Over several difficult years they exercised an influence such as no military committee in Britain had exercised before".*

The committee was bureaucratically overloaded and was therefore obstructed in individual cases despite its influence on the actual military planning. This planning occurred essentially at the level of the armed forces by a committee consisting of the heads of the operations divisions of the three services. Thus there was no need for the Chiefs of Staff to co-ordinate the departmental plans, for this had already been done by the subordinate committee. Churchill came into the picture by reason of his frequent direct contact with the planning committee, which thus assumed the funtions of the General Staffs of former times.

It seemed therefore that the military requirements of the three branches of the armed forces were properly co-ordinated. Yet there was a further organ possessing full authority and a qualified staff, by means of which the co-ordinated plans were put into operation. The functions of Lord Ismay were threefold. He was Secretary to the Minister of Defence, that is, to Churchill. But as the latter was also Prime Minister, Ismay's position was strengthened, since he had to assume some of the responsibilities of his Minister. He was also a member of the

---

* *History of Second World War—Grand Strategy, Vol.* VI, p. 327 (H.M.S.O., 1956).

Chiefs of Staff Committee, which he attended as Churchill's representative. His influence was actually greater than that of any Minister outside the Cabinet since he attended the meetings of the War Cabinet, which consisted of eight Ministers. He was the Military Deputy Secretary of the Cabinet, subordinate to its Secretary and co-equal with the Civil Deputy Secretary.

This was the organisation that served Churchill and was more or less at his personal disposal. His own authority grew from year to year. "His massive and uneven genius dominated the later, as earlier, stages of the war"*. "The committee system favoured the authority of a masterful Prime Minister; and within the military committees, the unique combination of his strategic grasp and his intimacy with the professional members . . . soon ensured that the mastery was achieved"†.

United States Planning Organisation

The American politico-military command structure differed considerably from that of Great Britain. According to the Constitution, the President was Commander-in-Chief of the armed forces, but in practice his influence was much smaller than Churchill's. Roosevelt possessed neither the military ambition of Churchill, nor, it seems, his genius. Consequently the American Joint Chiefs of Staff were allowed greater independence than their British counterparts. Moreover the authority of the Joint Chiefs of Staff was based on the Constitution. In the United States the President wields the highest executive authority, and is not responsible to any Cabinet. Hence if he so wished, he could give his Joint Chiefs of Staff full powers to prosecute the war without the need to consult or obtain authorisation from a Cabinet.

As C.-in-C. of the armed forces the President had his own Chief of Staff, a post that from 1943 was occupied by Admiral Leahy. He represented the President at the meetings of the Joint Chiefs of Staff without however being a member. This could have given him added authority, but he did not possess it to the same extent as Ismay in the British C.O.S. Committee. Leahy could not act as spokesman for the Joint Chiefs of Staff to the President or to other branches of the Executive, nor was he the man to augment his authority from personal motives. His was rather a more passive nature. Had it been otherwise, he would probably have come to grief. For it was Harry Hopkins who on behalf of the President wielded much greater influence over all the officers involved in the conduct of the war. He was more dynamic, more adaptable and industrious than Leahy. Yet since he

* *Ibid.* p. 333.
† *Ibid.* p. 334.

had no official status, his influence waned in proportion as the President's activity was reduced by his illness in 1944.

The most important figure in the "inner circle" was the Army Chief of Staff, General Marshall, of whom Eisenhower wrote that "he possessed . . . that ability to weigh calmly the conflicting factors in a problem and so reach a rock-like decision". And John Ehrman adds that he had "the entire confidence of the Army, the President and—perhaps his greatest achievement—of Congress". He was the ideal Chief of Staff, "who in the act of creating the largest military machine the United States had ever possessed, retained the traditional American distrust of militarism . . ."*

In the Joint Chiefs of Staff, Marshall really had only one colleague, namely Fleet Admiral King. The United States possessed no independent air force. True that the C.-in-C. of the Army Air Force had a seat on the committee, but he was subordinate to Marshall, which naturally simplified the latter's influence over strategic decisions. It also avoided friction, for in matters of air warfare the strategic interests of the Army and the Navy are usually at cross purposes.

THE LINKS BETWEEN THE TWO GENERAL STAFFS

Starting in March 1942, the Combined Chiefs of Staff worked from Washington, where the American Joint Chiefs of Staff were reinforced by representatives of the British Chiefs of Staff. The latter had already established a working relationship with the former. Until his death in 1944, Field-Marshal Sir John Dill, a former C.I.G.S., stood at the head of the liaison staff. He was a notable officer whom I had come to know personally as a true gentleman.

This arrangement marked the completion of a basic change in the Allied conduct of the war. The military executive council had become supranational. True that strategic decisions continued to rest with the political authorities in America and Great Britain. The statesmen either met each other personally, or occasionally allowed their ambassadors to represent them in making decisions, but this practice became ever less frequent. The statesmen made increasing use of the telephone. But since the Combined Chiefs of Staff met in Washington, that became the centre for political control. Anyone who has seen a liaison staff in operation at the G.H.Q. of an alliance between two powers will realise its limitations. The liaison staff is never as much involved in military planning as the team of the single dominant power. Yet the liaison staff shares in the responsibility by virtue of being in the organisation, even if it makes no decisions of its own

* *Ibid.* p. 343.

accord. It lacks that direct contact with its government that is available to the local authorities. Hence it must act diplomatically, present the divergent views of its own government and yet interpret to it the plans that were initiated by the dominant power.

Small wonder, then, that the Combined Chiefs of Staff Committee did not always function without friction. That this committee did not break down in the autumn of 1943 was only due, in the opinion of the British delegation, to the second Quebec Conference. One can understand the pessimism of the British delegation, for apart from the divergent strategic concepts, it was in a difficult position because of the growing preponderance of the United States as the centre of strategic planning. To a man of Churchill's calibre that in itself was a bitter reality, especially as he had to justify it before his own Cabinet, whereas the President of the United States bore sole responsibility as chief executive. In this capacity he was thus able to strengthen the position of his own military advisers in relation to the British, with the result that the primacy of the United States became even more marked.

It is questionable whether from the general political viewpoint this preponderance always served a useful purpose. The American historian William Hardy McNeill comments that "the Americans tended to separate military from political ends by an all but impassable barrier. Indeed, American generals often seemed to regard war as a game, after which, when it had been won or lost, the players would disperse and go home."* And John Ehrman writes: "The effects of such an attitude were particularly serious in Europe, whose problems were less well understood in Washington than those affecting the Far East, during the later stages of the war."† The end of the war provides an illustration of the waning influence of Great Britain. Ehrman states that in proportion as the campaigns in the Far East and Europe gained significance, so the Americans became less inclined to consult the Combined Chiefs of Staff. They regarded with growing and ill-concealed irritation the British attempts to interfere in a strategy that they regarded as a purely local matter.‡

FUNCTION OF SUPREME COMMANDERS IN THEATRES OF WAR

From 1943 onwards there was a growing tendency to leave the strategic conduct of operations to the Supreme Commanders in the various threatres of war. This was a natural result of the global character of the struggle. From now on the selection of the Supreme Com-

---

* *America, Britain and Russia. Their Co-operation and Conflict,* 1942–1946. (Royal Institute of Internal Affairs. 1953, p. 750.)
† Ehrman, Op. Cit. Vol. VI, p. 348.
‡ Ehrman, Op. Cit. (*Not* a verbatim quotation).

manders and their subordination to the overriding dictates of policy was a permanent function of the political heads.

It was a difficult problem to co-ordinate the strategy of the different theatres of war with the overall strategy. Decisions taken locally in the old-fashioned manner of conventional strategy were few and far between. The fact is that because of the inter-dependence of the overall conduct of the war there was little scope for individual Supreme Commanders to make strategic decisions.

In the old sense of strategy, a Supreme Commander was always in a position to plan and conduct a battle that could decide the issue of the whole war, but with widely separated theatres of war this was no longer feasible. The planning in any one area affected the overall planning and hence the planning in all other areas.

Where was the main effort to be concentrated? That decision would govern the allocation of forces and material to each theatre of war. In this respect the Allies were faced with a problem that never bothered the Germans: how much shipping to allocate to the Pacific, the Mediterranean and finally to preparations for the landings in France. All these were amphibious operations, and the total available shipping was limited.

Every local decision by a Supreme Commander was preceded by a conference with the higher authorities and was dependent on their approval.

In March 1942 the theatres of war were divided as follows on the suggestion of the President of the United States; the Pacific Ocean and China (Chiang Kai-shek) went to the United States; the remainder of Asia and the Mediterranean (later the Near East) went to Great Britain, while the Atlantic and the rest of Europe were shared between both Allies. Thus there were theatres of war, such as the last-named, where decisions had to be reached by the Combined Chiefs of Staff, whereas a theatre of war coming under only one power was controlled by the General Staff of that country. In the latter case the interests of the ally could only be safeguarded through the political intervention of the High Command. Such interventions were constantly necessary, since the strategy in one theatre of war had to be subordinated to the overall strategy.

Allied conduct of the war was further complicated by the fact that the British conception of the high command structure in a theatre of war differed from that of the Americans. The latter were like the Germans in giving the theatre Supreme Commander general directives and delegating to him extensive powers. An example of the strength and weakness of the American command structure is afforded by the conflict between the President and General MacArthur during the Korean conflict. The fact is that the political control of the American Supreme Commanders was not firmly rooted in the Constitution. As already mentioned, the President had delegated the authority for issuing orders to his Joint Chiefs of Staff, and in some cases they in turn delegated it to the Supreme Commander. Here was another source of potential conflict in regard to the Allied conduct of the war.

The British preferred a collective system, with the Supreme Commander as a kind of *primus inter pares*. Admittedly this system dated from the days of large amphibious operations when the Army C.-in-C. commanded a theatre of war while the sea and air forces merely acted in support of him. The system was also founded on the Constitution, for at the outbreak of war the professional heads of the three branches of the armed forces still came directly under their respective Ministers. That was changed by Churchill as a result of unfortunate experiences in the Norwegian campaign, but it remained valid for all sea areas. Even in 1943 the naval C.-in-C.s in the Atlantic, both British and American, came under their respective Navy Ministers, and were in no way subject to the authority of the Combined Chiefs of Staff. The three sectors of the American-controlled Pacific Ocean came under the supreme command of Admiral Nimitz, not under the Secretary of the Navy, but in this case under the Joint Chiefs of Staff.

There was also a special arrangement in regard to the command of the Allied bomber force that operated from England against Germany. The British Chief of the Air Staff was in charge of both British and American bomber fleets and was answerable for them to the Combined Chiefs of Staff in Washington. This gives some idea of the difficulties confronting an Allied "combined" staff. It had to allow for the rivalry of the separate armed forces and co-ordinate their efforts without offending national susceptibilities or public opinion in the two democracies; it had to cope with the divergent constitutional framework in the two countries, with the varying degree of authority that could be vested in the military officers of the Combined Chiefs of Staff and in the Commanders-in-Chief.

During the last two years of the war public opinion had to be considered more and more when selecting the Commanders-in-Chief. In Great Britain the man in the street had to resign himself to the transfer of the main power to the United States, a process that was made easier by Churchill's great prestige.

"The period of the main Allied offensive was also the period of the supreme command," says Ehrman.* This period started with the North African landings in November 1942, under the supreme command of Eisenhower. The British forces that had defeated the Axis in Libya joined up with the Americans in Tunisia, and Eisen-

---

* *Op. cit.*, Vol. V, p. 205.

hower remained the Supreme Commander, while Alexander became C.-in-C. of the Allied land forces. But in January 1944 the post of C.-in-C. Mediterranean was given to the British General Wilson. An American general was appointed as his deputy. The land forces and the control of their operations in Italy remained under General Alexander. At the same time the Combined Chiefs of Staff who were responsible for the overall strategy of the war arranged for the British Chiefs of Staff to assume responsibility for issuing the more detailed directives to the C.-in-C. Mediterranean. Thus the Mediterranean came entirely under British authority.

This was a political concession. The "Overlord" plan for the final defeat of Hitler's Germany had already been elaborated. The Americans considered that it required a unified supreme command. In the discussions in Cairo in November 1943, preparatory to the Teheran Conference, they even suggested a Supreme Commander for all Allied powers operating against Germany from the Atlantic and the Mediterranean, but Churchill and the British Chiefs of Staff raised objections which resulted in the compromise. "Overlord" was given an American Supreme Commander, while a British one, General Wilson, was chosen for the Mediterranean. The air forces operating from Italy against Germany were directly subordinated to the British Chief of the Air Staff in London. This had been done even before the "Overlord" undertaking, which was originally due to start in May, 1944.

At Teheran it was still being assumed that General Marshall would be the Supreme Commander for "Overlord", but the President decided on Eisenhower for this task. If all Allied troops fighting against Germany had been placed under a single unified supreme command, the prestige of Marshall would have justified his assuming such a command. But after the compromise reached with the British, this was no longer the case. Moreover the plan for "Overlord", which at first had been the subject of much argument, had now been so securely settled that in the President's view it no longer needed Marshall's prestige to see it through; indeed, as the leading military brain in Washington, he seemed indispensable for working out the overall strategy of the war. As Mr. Sherwood wrote, "It was one of the most difficult and one of the loneliest decisions Roosevelt ever had to make."*

The Strategic Decisions

Despite the wide powers given to the Combined Chiefs of Staff and the Supreme Commanders in the theatres of war, the big strategic

---

* Quoted in Ehrman, *Op cit.*, Vol. V, p. 201.

decisions remained in the hands of the political leaders. For them as for the military leaders there was close contact and co-operation between Washington and London, but contact with the Russians was slight. Historical sources attribute this to three principal reasons. The three powers had not of their own free choice become allies against Hitler. On the contrary, it was Hitler's attack on the Soviet Union that had forged the alliance. Secondly, Russia did not join in the war against Japan, with whom she had concluded a pact of neutrality. Lastly, and perhaps less obviously, the campaign in the East was conducted according to different rules from those prevailing in the West. The German invasion of Russia was followed by a set-back developing from the depth of the zone, and then by the Soviet Army's forward movement, whose tempo was determined by the laws governing the conduct of land battles. These laws did not really apply to Western strategy, and vice versa.

When the Germans started their offensive in the East, Churchill had initiated an exchange of telegrams with Stalin on similar lines to his discussions with Roosevelt, but the attempt to extend this contact came to nothing, and the negotiations were confined to questions of deliveries of supplies by the West to Russia. At first the Russians pressed for a "second front", but with their increasing successes the pressure for this slackened perceptibly.

At the preliminary talks in Cairo before the Teheran Conference the American Chiefs of Staff suggested forming a representative committe of the three or four powers. It was to meet on special occasions and, depending on the problems to be dealt with, there was always to be a representative from either Russia or China. This proposal was, however, struck off the agenda before the Teheran Conference opened.

The inadequate political contacts between the Western powers and the Soviet Union were reflected in the inadequate military contacts, which in turn aggravated the lack of political co-operation.

The broad Allied strategy in the Atlantic and European zone was based on three main principles. The Allies had to co-ordinate the Mediterranean and the northern European theatres of war. The decisive initial phase in all the major offensive campaigns of the Western powers consisted of amphibious operations. In each case the campaign was accompanied by an air offensive, which by 1943 had already become so effective that it might even have sufficed to defeat the Germans, who were already surrounded on all sides and under pressure from the East.

The close political contact of the Western powers at Teheran set the pattern for the rest of the war. The basis of the decisions at Teheran had already been reached at Casablanca in January 1943: control of the Atlantic, strategic bomber offensive, preparations for "Overlord" to be completed by May 1944, the offensive in Italy to eliminate the Italians from the Axis partnership and to tie down the German forces, the planning of a landing in the south of France as a diversion from "Overlord".

Since the two latter regional plans concern the course of the Italian campaign in which I was involved on the German side, I will here say a few words about them.

In the preliminary Cairo Conference the Allies were still not unanimous in their estimate of the importance of the Italian theatre of war. The Americans considered it as secondary after the landing in Sicily had been accomplished. They were disappointed at the rate of progress, especially as the defection of Italy on September 8th, 1943, led to no appreciable acceleration in the campaign.

Consequently the Americans wanted to invest "Overlord" with priority over all other plans, while the landing in the south of France, given the cover-name "Anvil", was to serve the same end. Troops from the Italian theatre of war were to be embarked and used directly in operation "Anvil".

Stalin agreed with this plan and hence opposed Churchill's proposal to initiate an offensive from Turkey. I shall revert to this later.

The American Army authorities wanted to build up forces at the enemy's weakest point, an idea that was in line with German strategic principles. Stalin himself rightly regarded the south of France as Germany's weakest spot.

These American plans caused Churchill much anxiety. He urged that the Italian offensive should be prosecuted without giving up troops for "Anvil", and wanted operations to be undertaken against the German-occupied Aegean Islands. He had a number of reasons for this. He was an advocate of the strategy of outflanking, which had already appealed to him in the First World War in the Gallipoli operations that he himself had sponsored. And now he missed no opportunity of trying to get Turkey to join the Allies, even if that meant sacrificing a small number of his own forces. Yet the strategic importance of Turkey became progressively smaller in proportion as the Russians advanced in the European theatre of war. Churchill wanted to penetrate into the Black Sea, thus shortening the supply line to Russia and giving her a helping hand. At the Allied conference the plan received short shrift, desirable as the accession of Turkey to the Allies might be.

Roosevelt and Stalin reacted much more strongly to Churchill's plan to round off the campaign in Italy before giving up any troops from that area. Churchill wanted at least the capture of Rome and the annihilation of the German forces south of the line Rimini-Pisa. For Great Britain the continuation of a successful offensive in Italy had become a matter of prestige. Churchill's main arguments centred on two points. He wanted to tie down German forces which would otherwise have been sent to France or the eastern front, and he considered that there was no point in withdrawing Allied divisions from Italy when landing-craft were not available for them in operations "Overlord" or "Anvil". Amphibious landings required two types of specially constructed vessels—the L.S.I. for landing infantry and the L.S.T. for landing tanks. He wanted to retain at least sufficient landing-craft in the Italian theatre of war as were needed for the Anzio landing, which he hoped would result in the early capture of Rome.

At the Cairo meeting Churchill had pleaded that while "Overlord" "remained top of the bill . . . this operation should not be such a tyrant as to rule out every other activity in the Mediterranean; for example, a little flexibilty in the employment of landing-craft ought to be conceded".*

My own part in the Italian operations was affected by the major strategic concepts as represented by Churchill's demands at Cairo, when he made the point that since the successful landing and assembly of troops in Italy in September, the war in the Mediterranean had taken an unhappy turn. Progress had been extremely slow, even when allowance was made for the bad weather.

In his fight for a strategy that would be worthy of the British national prestige, Churchill found that neither Roosevelt in Cairo nor Stalin at Teheran were on his side. Roosevelt was unwilling to sanction postponement of the date for "Overlord", which would have been necessary if Churchill's plans had been accepted. The date, originally planned for May 1944, was to be adhered to.

Stalin associated himself with this view. According to Churchill, Stalin regarded "Overlord" as a very important operation which should be supported by a landing in the south of France. Stalin would prefer defensive tactics in Italy and the renunciation of the capture of Rome if that would allow the landing of some ten divisions in the south of France. The "Overlord" operation would follow two months later, and the two invasion forces would then join up.†

Stalin's reasoning was derived from his experience of the Russian campaign, where his strategy was built up on pincer thrusts from two directions, of which Stalingrad was the classic example.

The controversy was not made any easier by the unsuccessful attempt to break through on the Cassino front in January 1944. This was the first of four such attempts, and only the last was successful. The three failures in January, February and March did not improve Churchill's position, for Roosevelt and Stalin saw in them the confirmation of their fears that the Allies were needlessly wasting their

* Winston Churchill, *The Second World War*, Vol. V. p. 295.
† Churchill, *Ibid*, Vol. V, p. 314.

strength with heavy losses on the Cassino front. After the Anzio landing, which at first made no progress beyond the bridgehead, Churchill found himself in an even more difficult position. On April 14th he sent the following telegram to Roosevelt: "I am very glad at what has happened in Italy. It seems to me that we have both succeeded in gaining what we sought. The only thing now lacking is victory".*

The Controversies

The controversies between the Allies after the breakthrough at Cassino in May 1944 arose because General Mark Clark did not turn with sufficient vigour against the German bridgehead at Valmontone to annihilate the German 10th Army. Instead he directed the main body of his troops towards Rome. Churchill considered it "very unfortunate" that the Germans had reached Valmontone before the Americans and were thus able to withdraw their 10th Army.†

Churchill urged Alexander to undertake a vigorous pursuit so as to cut off and destroy the German army group while it was still south of the line Pisa-Rimini, and this conformed to the wishes of the Combined Chiefs of Staff. On June 14th they directed Wilson and Alexander to do just this, and ordered that no forces were to be withdrawn from the Italian theatre of war if they were indispensable for that purpose.

The many setbacks of the Allies in the Cassino battles and the frustration of their plan to destroy the German army group after the May breakthrough in many respects prejudiced their designs in Central Europe, even if they anticipated an early victory after France had been invaded.

The immediate consequence of the delays on the Italian front was that operation "Anvil" started too late. It should have preceded "Overlord" or at least have occurred simultaneously, in which case it would have attracted the German reserves and thus facilitated the main landings in Normandy. That indeed is the object of all secondary offensive operations, whether they originate on land or from the sea. Yet the Normandy landings succeeded. The British official history of the war confirms my view that the weakness of the German defences was partly attributable to the fact that Rommel got his way over Field-Marshal von Rundstedt. In this context Ehrman writes: "The German Army lay dispersed along the coast, ignorant of the area of assault and undecided as to its own intentions . . . Rommel, who suspected that the Allies' air supremacy would prevent the rapid movement of a general

* Churchill, Vol. V, p. 454.
† Ibid, p. 536.

reserve, favoured a powerful and rigid obstruction, based on strongly fortified positions, along the whole of the threatened coastline, which would pin the enemy to the beaches for long enough to reinforce the sector of assault from reserves held well forward. . . . The enemy's reactions were clogged and slow, in marked contrast to his reactions to the earlier Allied landings in Italy."*

Allied controversies over "Anvil" reached a climax at the end of June 1944, when there would still have been a purpose in landing on the south coast of France. Churchill still opposed such a landing. On the 28th he sent a memorandum to Roosevelt, whose opening sentence reads: "The deadlock between our Chiefs of Staff raises most serious issues. Our first wish is to help General Eisenhower in the most speedy and effective manner. But we do not think this necessarily involves the complete ruin of all our great affairs in the Mediterranean, and we take it hard that this should be demanded of us."†

Churchill had a further motive in wishing to maintain large numbers of British troops in Italy. It was not merely that British prestige would increase if the German army group were defeated in a theatre of war under a British Commander-in-Chief. His plans went further; he wanted to advance through the Lubliana gap, establish contact with the Jugoslav partisans and so directly threaten the southern flank of the German positions. In addition he wanted to co-ordinate his movements with those of the Red Army, but this could only occur if he kept his forces undiminished, for he had to create reserves and to reckon with further German resistance. Wilson supported Alexander. Once again the differences of opinion were between one nation and the other. The influence of the United States caused "Anvil" to take place on the grounds that a further supply port was needed in France. Roosevelt considered that Alexander's plan to advance north-east-wards would involve major supply problems on the land route. Because of their higher material standards, supply problems were more impor-tant to the Americans than to other European armies, and similarly more important to the latter than to the Russians. Roosevelt also foresaw political friction in the event of an offensive from the region of Istria and Trieste, especially as the Russians were then advancing westwards. After August 1944 the Western powers' offensive was already being regarded as competing with the Soviet Union. "In June the two main campaigns directly helped each other: in August, the campaign in the West could be seen as a rival to that in the East. The very success of the 'Second Front', which at first was so welcome, might later be held to lead to complications in Central Europe."‡

---

* Ehrman, Vol. V., pp. 337–338.
† Ehrman, Vol. V., p. 352.
‡ Ehrman, Vol. V., p. 368.

It was not until August that operation "Dragoon" (the later name for "Anvil") was launched in the south of France. The landing forces met with only slight opposition and may have tied down some German forces. Yet the original purpose had not been achieved, while the British front in Italy had, of course, been weakened. German resistance in the Bologna area in the winter of 1944/45 could not have been so effective if several Allied divisions had not been withdrawn. Yet by August 1944, Hitler's Germany was already virtually defeated, so that these Allied operational plans had lost much of their significance. When it is merely a question of the final liquidation of a defeated and disorganised opponent, then operational mistakes can be perpetrated without the disastrous results that would occur, for instance, in a big battle. By August 26th Allied G.H.Q. was able to report that "the power of the German forces in the West has been shaken. Paris is again in French possession, and the Allied armies are streaming east towards the Rhine".

The continuous controversy conducted by letter, telegram and personal exchanges between Eisenhower and Montgomery during the Allied offensive only shows that they could afford to indulge in this luxury. According to German ideas it would have been preferable to adopt Montgomery's plan of massing troops in the north for an attack on the Ruhr and an advance on Berlin. Such an operation would have assumed the character of a pursuit, with the opportunity which that could provide of increasing the speed in order to prevent the enemy from halting or even offering any kind of resistance. Eisenhower, however, considered that for the safety of his troops it was best to launch a simultaneous attack with Bradley's army group south of the Ardennes towards the Saar Consequently no main axis of attack was formed, and the retreating German troops could not be overtaken.

The events that now followed showed clearly that Italy had become a secondary theatre of war. Only towards the end did it again play a political part, inasmuch as negotiations for a capitulation were initiated in January 1945 in Switzerland and at Caserta. When the Soviet government heard about this, it reacted strongly to the failure to invite any Soviet authority to attend the negotiations, and Molotov retorted sharply to the Western powers' attempt to compose the quarrel: " . . . In this instance the Soviet government sees not a misunderstanding but something worse. . . . In Berne for two weeks behind the backs of the Soviet Union, which is bearing the brunt of the war against Germany, negotiations have been going on between representatives of German Military Command on the one hand and representatives of the American and English Command on the other. Soviet government consider this completely impermissible and insist on its statement (i.e., for the cessation of these negotiations) which was sent out in my letter of March 16th".*

This broad outline of the Allies' strategic controversies is given to illustrate my point. In my view the Germans in the West suffered as great a defeat after the Normandy landings as they had experienced eighteen months earlier at the battle of Stalingrad. Any normal German government would have offered to capitulate after Stalingrad or at the latest after the Normandy landings. But Hitler could not get over his defeat, and so the war dragged on, the German people shedding their blood with nothing to show for it but a series of withdrawals in the east and the west. Nor did the Ardennes offensive produce any change in the final phase, although it delayed the Allied advance and caused the Germans 70,000 casualties, according to Allied sources.

One very young divisional commander, whom I visited at the front on December 17th, 1944, was still completely steeped in Hitler's outlook. Beaming with joy, he maintained that Germany was about to achieve a second victory over the West, similar to that of 1940! Even though Hitler's optimism might find an echo in this general, I was well aware that the Ardennes offensive was nothing more than the last spurt of a mortally wounded combatant.

The idea that Germany could capitulate to the Western powers alone was, of course, ridiculous. The Russian and Anglo-American armies would inevitably effect a junction. This occurred slowly and, understandably, with some conflict of interest, but there were also peaceable agreements. The military lines reached by the victorious powers could not have any political meaning. If any political consequences resulted from these positions, this was due to the primacy of political over military policy with both the Eastern and the Western Allies. At this stage there was already clear evidence of Russia's power politics and expansionism. Yet in the west the Combined Chiefs of Staff were still using the language of military guidance in their directives to Eisenhower while the Soviet Union was planning the subjugation of the Russian-occupied areas, which they were not prepared to give up. The significance of this was appreciated by Churchill— possibly without full realisation of the possibilities—when he wrote to Roosevelt that he had little doubt that the Soviet leaders were surprised and alarmed at the speed of advance of the Western Allies. He suggested that it was all the more important to effect a junction with the Russian forces as far east as possible, and if the circumstances permitted, to march into Berlin. And he returned to this theme in a message to the President on April 1st 1945: "If (the Russian armies) also take Berlin, will not their impression that they have been the

* Letter from Molotov to British Ambassador on 22nd March, 1945, quoted in Ehrman, Vol. VI., p. 124.

overwhelming contributor to one common victory be unduly imprinted in their minds, and may this not lead them into a mood whch will raise grave and formidable difficulties in the future?"*

Stalin sent a telegram to Eisenhower stating that he was in agreement with the latter's attack objectives of Dresden and Regensburg, and adding: ". . . . Berlin has lost its former strategic importance. The Soviet High Command therefore plans to allot secondary forces in the direction of Berlin".†

To reproach the Russians for these developments would be tantamount to a lack of judgment. To them it must have seemed quite reasonable that they should have priority in presenting their demands to the defeated Germans. Hitler had attacked their land after despicably breaking his word, and for years they had borne the greatest sacrifices. The Soviet government felt that it owed its people a fair reward for their victory.

To-day the greater part of the German people again forms part of the Western world, and it is tragic that this part is powerless to help the oppressed minority to gain its freedom and powerless to liberate the satellite peoples, whom Hitler's war has left under Soviet domination.

It was the British Prime Minister who saw the situation most clearly. Yet in view of what we now know it is of no particular significance whether in 1945 the Allies had advanced from Italy through the Lubliana gap to Vienna, whether they had landed a month or two earlier or later in Normandy and the south of France, or whether they had adopted Montgomery's proposal for an isolated thrust across the Rhine instead of advancing on a broad front as Eisenhower decided to do. Prior to their Normandy landings the Allies had contributed fewer forces to the overthrow of Hitler than the Soviet Union. It is the particular tragedy of myself as a German commander in Italy that in accordance with my duty I achieved a successful resistance, especially at Cassino. For the slow progress made here by the Allies diminished the political significance of their war effort against Germany. Hitler having been defeated in the East, the South and the West, the strategic deliberations of the Western Allies after the Normandy landings could no longer have any real significance for the overall strategy of the war. Now the urgency centred on a new task, namely, to win the peace while the armies were assembling for the final liquidation of the defeated enemy. This created the German illusion that by a reversion of policy Germany could join the Western Allies against the Soviet Union. But the Germans were soon to learn other-

* Churchill, *The Second World War*, Vol. VI., p. 407.
† Ehrman, Vol. VI., p. 142.

wise. Some of their statesmen and army leaders even hoped that the death of Roosevelt on April 12th, 1945, would herald a turn of fate similar to that which befell Frederick the Great on the death of the Empress Elizabeth on January 5th, 1762. But Roosevelt's death could change nothing in the march of events. Already at the start of the century Germany had failed to opt for or ally herself with the West. Now history was heading for the clash of the big power blocs in Central Europe, while Roosevelt's policy survived only as a figment of Western optimism.

8

CAUSES OF THE DEFEAT OF HITLER'S GERMANY

Future historians will not be much better informed as to the causes of the defeat of Hitler's Germany than those of us who as senior commanders of the Wehrmacht bore regional responsibilities in the war. It is now only a question of assessing the relative importance of the many factors that contributed to the defeat.

Basically the defeat sprang from the general political developments. The era is past when world history was shaped and made in Europe; and Germany as the heartland of Europe was most affected by the change. Always attuned to Central Europe, she was the last to appreciate that these nations had to opt either for the East or for the West. As long ago as the beginning of the nineteenth century Alexis de Toqueville saw that there could only be two world powers—America and Russia. Germany was still in the process of establishing national unity by means of wars, and so she remained aloof from developments in the outer world, isolating herself in the Bismarck era by declining to choose between Russia and the West, which was at that time represented mainly by Great Britain. The Prussian leaders were so busy defending German unity that they could not devote themselves to any colonial enterprises. This was the beginning of the "encirclement complex".

The big world powers came to terms with each other at Germany's expense. In both world wars Germany either consciously or unwittingly provoked this development. In its origin, development and outcome, the Second World War bears a remarkable similarity to the First. On both occasions German governments exacted external political dependence from the small eastern border states, which served as buffers against the Russian Colossus. In both cases she came to terms with Russia, the great Euro-Asian power. And in both cases Germany believed that she was championing the Western powers to such an extent that she could count on their neutrality. But in both cases the German governments were fooling themselves; the Western powers sided with Russia in order to defeat Germany. And in both cases the

German governments were wrong in hoping that at least the United States would remain outside the conflict.

Compared with this striking parallelism it is of minor importance that Germany happened to have different allies in the two wars. Historically significant is the fact that on both occasions she miscalculated her own strength and waged war against an almost worldwide coalition.

The catastrophe resulting from the second war was the bigger one. The political changes in Germany had undermined her strength before the war ever started, a process that continued while it was in progress. Like nearly all dictatorships, that of Germany was short-lived. The healthy internal political strife which brings leaders to the top was replaced by the graveyard stillness of a dominant police state. All dictatorships suffer from a dearth of leaders capable of assuming the succession. Being police states, they can for a time produce an apparently well-functioning executive and use all kinds of threats to maintain an excessively rigid discipline, but the bow becomes overstretched. Moreover in Germany the dictator was psychopathic and his collaborators equally so, none with the requisite qualifications of education, intelligence or sense of responsibility. The latter were certainly credulous, and seemed loyal without being so.

The sickness of the régime seemed also to infect the leaders of the Wehrmacht. Abroad it was generally supposed that the Wehrmacht provided the real support for Hitler, and it will never be easy to dispel that illusion. In time of war the armed forces of any country must represent its government. The Wehrmacht was even held responsible for the First World War, for Prussia had been the military state *par excellence*.

I myself had no roots in the Prussian tradition, but as a higher commander in the Wehrmacht I came to realise its potency, It is worth discussing this question in the light of the collapse of Hitler's Germany.

The Hitler régime was no offshoot of Prussian militarism. Prussianism east of the Elbe—which alone is the genuine type—was always averse to the régime, if not hostile to it. Moreover, many other officers supported those who had been brought up in the Prussian tradition. For all these it was odious to find themselves under the patronage of a leader with proletarian tendencies, and they were percipient enough to realise clearly the dangers of the course Hitler was taking in foreign policy. Among the many who opposed him were Fritsch, Beck, Hammerstein, Witzleben, Hoepner, Halder and Heinrich Stülpnagel. Nobody was more implicated in the plot of July 20th, 1944, than the Junkers from east of the Elbe, with whom the Prussian officers' corps had always had close historical ties.

These traditional Prussian officers found themselves faced with tragedy when they were called upon to fight a war which they never really believed they could win. They had not wanted war, but had been brought up and trained for it. They bore no political responsibility. It is just as unreasonable to charge them with such responsibility as it was in the Wilhelmine era to allow them so much scope.

In the Germany of Wilhelm II nationalistic tendencies were already getting the upper hand. The All-German Union, the *Flottenverein* and other organisations were the means of influencing not only public opinion, but the Imperial government itself, so that neither it nor Parliament was entirely master of its own decisions. These associations and the ideas they represented flourished throughout Germany, particularly in the industrialised and bourgeois western part, less in the agrarian eastern regions of the Junkers. To some extent they were the precursors of Nazism; like it, they fought for "supra-state" powers, and had no sense of diplomacy, compromise or association between the peoples of different countries. By their nature they had nothing in common with the West. That such a man as Ludendorff could belong to these circles may deceive those who are not acquainted with the nature of the German General Staff. Although he was the most prominent and dynamic staff officer of the First World War, he was not a typical product of the General Staff.

Under Hitler, conforming to the nature of the dictatorship, the most able people gradually departed and were increasingly replaced by second-rate characters. In the place of that calm deliberation and shrewd intelligence which once were the hallmark of the Prussian General Staff, the dictatorship preferred a mental attitude that had nothing to do with intelligence, namely an unshakable faith in the wisdom and superhuman importance of the Führer, and a belief in final victory notwithstanding the most damning defeats. Intelligence came to be regarded as a hindrance in the development of qualities of leadership. Army leaders had either to believe in the myth to which the German people had succumbed, or at least pretend to do so.

Even if one makes allowance for the part played by the Prussian officers' corps before and during the war and within the political system, there remains a measure of purely military responsibility for the defeat. In every country the armed forces are a part of the people, and cannot be considered apart from the history of that people. This is especially true of the Prussian Army, which left so strong an imprint on the history of the Prussian state and hence on the Germany of the Wilhelmine era.

A feature of both wars was that Germany, chiefly a land power, was fighting a coalition of sea powers. Her naval forces were of small account compared with those of her opponents. The Prussian General Staff was unfamiliar with maritime concepts, for these were something outside its traditions. Naturally, some of the best brains were very worried about the position. But the people failed to appreciate the limitations of the country's resources. They remembered Sedan and Königgratz, the great battle of Tannenberg, and the Schlieffen Plan. They believed that even though their relative strength was unfavourable, gifted leadership would make it possible to achieve a decisive victory, an illusion that was shared by the General Staff.

In the First World War Germany succumbed to the strangulation of her imports from overseas, while in the second she went under due to the cumulative effect of the Russian reserves of manpower and the material resources of the United States, which came from overseas. Whoever controls the sea routes dominates the sources of raw materials and hence the supply of armaments.

Underestimating the influence of modern maritime warfare is a corollary of overestimating the value of acquiring territory. The latter is indeed more important in a modern war than it was in the days when a short, decisive battle could terminate a war. But the acquisition of territory meant nothing if it did not also lead to the domination of the contiguous sea area. Because of the excessive importance attached to the acquisition of territory, the danger to the coasts of the occupied territories was under-rated. The advantage of combined operations by all three branches of the armed forces operating from seaward as against purely land defences was already obvious, and post-war technical developments have merely emphasised this advantage.

Looking at the war from this point of view, it becomes clear that the German achievements on land, which seemed so important in the early part of it, were illusory. They were due partly to surprise, and partly to the skilled use of a new technique, the assembly of powerful armoured forces in divisions and armies. To these forces can be ascribed the lightning successes in Poland and France, also in Russia up to 1941. The countries under attack were psychologically and operationally unprepared for resistance. Their grave territorial losses made it seem that they were totally defeated, but the reality was otherwise. Above all, the Axis powers lacked the forces to dominate the acquired territories. The enemy in the East had more and more men at his disposal, and before long he could throw in hordes of tanks that had been turned out in mass production. And the Soviet authorities took armoured tactics a stage further by combining masses of tanks with masses of infantry. Hence under certain conditions they could easily (and especially at night) over-run the German armoured units which were inadequately supported by infantry. Such a combination of men and tanks was never a feature of the fighting in the West, where on the other hand the Allies fully exploited the sea as an "assembly area". I have already described how these tactics succeeded against the weak German coastal defences.

It is often asked why, after the definite turn of the tide at Stalingrad,

El Alamein and Tunisia, the Allies did not apply the German tactics of concentrating masses of armour to achieve a rapid victory. It took the Russians a further two-and-a-half-years of bitter fighting to penetrate westwards. And the same sort of thing occurred in Italy. After the German defeat in North Africa and the collapse of Italy, the Allies should have continued the fight in the form of a pursuit. Even during the German agony of 1944, the Allies could not see their way to over-running the defeated and exhausted German forces and thrusting with armoured spearheads across the Rhine into the heart of Germany. The fact is that the tactics applied by the Germans in the period of their invasions had become ineffective. Armour had at last met its opponent in armour.

The years of fighting that still lay ahead in both East and West never produced sufficiently deep penetrations by the Allies to finish off their opponent's armies, which over and over again reverted to the old line tactics of mutual support. For this purpose the Germans kept a greater or smaller number of tanks in readiness behind the front, according to the nature of the terrain. Whenever the enemy threatened an armoured breakthrough, they would launch these tanks against his spearheads, so preventing him from exploiting his initial success. The tactics of raids and swift *blitzkrieg* strokes were a thing of the past. Despite their weakness in infantry, the numerous and rapidly mobile units could always keep in close touch and could therefore be manoeuvred according to the old line tactics.

It was this contrast between the original German methods and the later Allied tactics that engendered the legend that, given equal conditions, the German leadership was unbeatable. This was a fatal error, especially for the Germans themselves, who refused to realise that they had long since lost the war. For a long time the General Staff toyed with the idea of regaining the initiative through extensive disengaging movements, but Hitler's dilettantism in military affairs won the day. Moreover the General Staff itself failed to realise that the times were past when a war could be won by large outflanking battles, or that control of the seas, a stronger coalition and increasing war potential mattered much more than a dozen good Army leaders. The achievments of a commander-in-chief in the field depend on the extent of his resources and the moral and material efforts that his nation is capable of.

Clausewitz showed convincingly and logically that political superiority, acquired through a country's foreign policy, is an essential element of war. No longer can European nations fight each other while neighbouring countries remain neutral. To-day a great power's foreign policy can only be a policy of coalition, and this involves accepting certain limitations of national sovereignty, a fact of which the German leaders in both world wars were still completely unaware. A large

part of war strategy is nothing more than the continuation of peace-
time foreign policy.

Apart from the available material assets before and, above all,
during the course of a war, a country's war potential also depends
on less tangible factors, such as the skill of the commander in the
field and the morale of his troops. Yet however excellent these qualities
may be, they cannot provide a substitute for resources in men and
materials. The commander with the strongest battalions is in a
position to make the boldest decisions. But even if he wins, his victory
remains dependent on the statesman who has been conducting the
foreign policy while the fighting was in progress. He is advised by
the economic experts, who thus enable him to judge the war potential
at any stage of the war. It is this potential that determines the prospect
of further victories. In modern war several of these are needed at
sea, on land and in the air before final success is achieved.

The morale of the troops is also very dependent on material
resources. If the troops are well fed and clothed, they will fight all
the better, and success or failure on the battlefield will also govern
the state of their morale. Nor can the optimism that propaganda
tries to instill be a substitute for the clear insight of the intellect.
The morale of the soldiers of the Allies was all the higher because
of their confidence in victory.

One of Hitler's basic errors was to imagine that only the Germans
were fighting for an idea. It is true that most of them felt convinced
they were doing this, however vague the idea that was put before
them. Yet presumably the Russians were at least as sure that they
were fighting for an ideal, and they had the added incentive of resisting
the unprovoked German invasion of their country. Even if the
Russians had not been such convinced Bolsheviks, the call to defend
their fatherland would have united them. But our Western opponents
were fighting for personal liberty, a concept that the Germans had
never envisaged as the driving force of their own national history.

Germany's opponents thus had no common ideals, since the
Russians did not subscribe to personal freedom. With them as with
Hitler's Germany priority was given to state planning at the expense
of the individual and his family. With them the resulting order of
things counted for more than the principles of freedom. But it was
a questionable order, for it dispensed with the best elements of the
population, and abolished criticism and collective responsibility for
policy. Twelve years of Nazi domination gave the Germans a full
measure of that experience. The collapse of Hitler's Germany could
not surprise them.

The question of responsibility for this state of affairs must be
faced. In the span of one generation the German leaders condemned
themselves politically by repeating the fatal mistake of a war on two

fronts. A dictatorship so poorly endowed with qualities of leadership as that of Hitler is the antithesis of that democratic structure which is essential for the co-ordination of the whole nation's resources. Let there be no confusion in this matter. Quite apart from Hitler's catastrophic management of the state and of the war, it is obvious that even with a different and free government Germany could not have won *either* world war, having regard to her initial situation. In each case the total resources of her opponents, who dominated the sea, were so superior to her own that in the long run her land campaigns were bound to be ineffective, however skilfully managed. Moreover, in the Second World War the basic strategic concepts of Germany's opponents were of a higher quality from the outset, just as their conduct of affairs was superior throughout the war.

The causes of the German catastrophe were not just political and military, but also psychological. The Hitler movement acquired great impetus through the economic depression of the post-war period, with its ever-increasing unemployment which also threatened the survival of the manufacturers. To all of them Hitler promised revolutionary improvements, and on assuming power he seemed to fulfil his promise.

The method of surmounting the crisis by economic measures provided the opportunity for building up nationalism. After the loss of a war this policy of nationalism was in itself very questionable. That it could not be checked after the war indicates a lack of political sense. The German National Party came under the control of Hugenberg, who was involved in big business enterprises. He personified the decline of the old Prussian conservatism in face of the capitalistic and fanatically nationalistic middle class, which he rallied in his "Harzburger Front". The idea of helping the little man and of larding this help with nationalistic emotions was particularly ingenious, for at that time it met the aspirations of the mass of the people. It was an idea that Hitler exploited in the internal political struggle, winning the people over to his side. Although he failed to gain a majority of votes in the free elections before his accession to power, it can be assumed that ultimately he would have accomplished this by using the appropriate propaganda to exploit his real or imagined successes.

The coupling of the national and the socialist concepts was politically ingenious, but not a proper basis for a philosophy in the old meaning of *Weltanschauung*. With people whose spiritual life is no longer based on religion, political movements easily assume a para-religious character. The National Socialists aimed to replace the traditional religion by a pseudo-philosophy. In the preceding decades the influence of Nietzsche had been strong, although his philosophy was too abstruse for the ordinary citizen, who was more ready to adopt the flattering idea of racial exclusiveness. Here the normal pride in social origin was discarded for a mystical theory of descent, which embraced everyone, turning them into "master-men".

Any dictatorship is characterised by an absence of internal political struggle and the consolidation of its own power. The peace in internal politics satisfied the German citizen, who was thereby freed from all responsibility for decisions. The golden era of political unity had dawned with the forthright definition of objectives—or so it seemed. At first even those more intelligent people who saw the weaknesses tended to prefer firm leadership to the parliamentary criss-cross of the excessively doctrinaire Weimar Constitution with its system of elections by proportional representation. They spoke of the "storm-tossed ship, in which the helmsman had taken a firmer grasp of the tiller".

Hitler's successes seemed to speak in his favour. Evidently he had solved the most pressing European problem—unemployment. He built magnificent roads and revived the economy by starting an armaments industry, the construction of barracks and conscription. Nobody explained to the people that most of this programme involved unproductive labour whose output would not contribute to the wealth of the country since none of it could be exported. Yet the economy could only survive if there were an exchange of exports and imports. Ostensibly the state's purchasing power increased, for it printed money that could be spent. This created a new class of consumers and gave the internal economy a lift. But what would happen once the roads, the schools and the sports stadiums had been built and the Army equipped with the latest weapons? If Hitler had not from the outset been aware of the deceptiveness of his economic policy, he certainly became so in the course of time. Six months before the war started he addressed the Army leaders in the Kroll Opera House, explaining that a people without space—meaning with insufficient means of sustenance—must conquer fresh territory and new markets, neither of which could be attained by peaceful means.

Dictatorships are incapable of attracting new blood of any quality. In contrast to Mussolini's system of constantly changing his men, Hitler stuck to his associates of the early days of the political struggle. But he must have felt instinctively that they lacked experience in every sphere of policy. After assuming power he was clever enough to retain for the time being experienced non-party experts in the more important Ministries—in the Foreign Ministry, in Finance and War. At first he had no other choice, since his earliest Cabinet was a coalition. Cabinet discussions were abolished as far as the big political decisions were concerned. As there was no scope for the free play of democratic politics, an effort was made to ensure the advent of new blood by creating special schools, academies and so-called teutonic orders, which were run by the party apparatus. Although it was not admitted, this meant that nominations to the offices of state were made through the party and administrative machinery. Even this system might have worked rather better if the nominations had not been made on the basis of faith in the system, to the exclusion of other qualities such as common sense, industry and courage. The selectors took no account of intelligence; indeed they repudiated it. The Nazi concept of faith allowed no latitude in political preferences, and required acceptance of a prescribed attitude towards all historical events—an attitude that was to undergo many changes. It also required ackowledgment of the party's *Weltanschauung* and banned all criticism of persons or arrangements.

Hitler's administrative system gave a livelihood and a position to large numbers of officials. It was the boast of the party functionaries that they tackled affairs without respect for bureaucratic inhibitions. Many of the party Ministers followed this precept, and at first it brought a breath of fresh air into the administration. But before long it became apparent that the thoroughness, the methodical processes of officialism and hence bureaucracy itself could not be dispensed with. The lack of these led to disastrous confusion, as when officials eager to assume new responsibilities exceeded their authority and had to be shielded. It was a situation in which everyone gave orders and built up his own organisation regardless of encroachments on other spheres of activity. It was worst in the key posts, where a number of Hitler's old comrades-in-arms had been busy for years, men who could no longer be regarded as entirely normal. It is idle to debate whether their failure, corruption and criminal dealings were due to mental or moral shortcomings—the one defect goes with the other.

Germany's internal degeneration was concealed to the outside world by a magnificent façade, of which the Olympic Games of 1936 are one example. Another highlight was provided by the brilliantly organised "Party days," which met the need for mystical spectacles, parade-ground displays and community experience. Participation in the life of the state involved strenuous days of minutely organised assemblies, where people could "look the Führer in the eye" and hear the same vulgar speeches over and over again. The overpowering effect of those speechs will always remain a puzzle to any intelligent person. It is a well-known publicity stunt to work on the mind through reiteration, yet it remains inexplicable that the people did not tire of these unvarying phrases, in which all opponents were always insulted, all supporters praised, and nothing was contributed towards solving the really urgent political problems.

Yet one must admit that the people believed Nazism would bring them material as well as social benefits. The old stratum of leaders had been dethroned. Ostensibly these men were not to be persecuted, but were to be asked to associate themselves with the new order if they wished to do so, and this was only too often the case. It helped them to rise to positions of authority. Yet those who acquired such positions regarded themselves not as representatives of a formerly deprived class, but as convened leaders of the people, hitherto suppressed by the wicked parties of the Left.

There was no longer any place for members of the established upper level who possessed a conscience and a moral background. The rift was unbridgeable between this new philosophy of life and the simple manifestation of chivalry that is natural to all communities in every era. The systematic brutality towards those who were defenceless or held different beliefs or belonged to racial minorities was an affront to any genuine ethos.

Germany's relations with other states must be viewed in the light of her internal constitution under Hitler. He thought it right to adopt the same methods in foreign policy and in Europe as he applied in his fight aganst his internal enemies. It is certain that initially he wanted to avoid a war against the West, and maybe he hoped to avoid any war. But his economic policy drove him into it, and his confidence rested on the new and modern equipment of the Wehrmacht.

Naturally the methods that led to his improbable success in internal politics could not be effective in the realm of foreign policy, but this did not shake his belief in himself and his mission, which was encouraged by his Foreign Minister, the somewhat limited Ribbentrop. Hitler accepted his faulty estimate of the internal resources, reserves and war potential of the Anglo-Saxon countries. And as Hitler lacked all experience of the world, he mistook the calm of the Anglo-Saxons, their readiness to negotiate, their riches and their democracy for signs of weakness. He completely failed to understand the sources of strength of a free democracy, and thought of the countries of the British Empire as subdued vassals waiting to shake off the hateful yoke. The difficulties with Ireland seemed to justify his assessment, and he likened them to those of the Hapsburg Empire and its minority peoples. The granting of Home Rule to this small and economically dependent part of the British family of nations was beyond his comprehension, nor did he appreciate the art and wisdom of governing with a loose rein. It is the tragedy of revolutions that their originators usually spring from a milieu where the art of government is not understood.

Hitler's personal hostility towards Russia was genuine enough. It was based to some extent on envy of a not very dissimilar system which in many respects could boast of major successes. He wanted to show up the difference between his national fanaticism and Bolshevism. Yet his aggression against Russia was sure to fire that country with a fervent nationalism, if indeed it was ever short of that emotion.

In Germany there was much talk of tension between the Army and the party; the relationship between them fluctuated. The sudden introduction of universal service provided Hitler with the opportunity to broaden the basis for recruitment of officers to include every class of society. Consequently the political outlook of the whole people was reflected in the officers' corps, at first only in the lower ranks and later in the more exalted positions of command.

When Hitler first assumed office, the senior officers of the armed forces, who had never been selected on a democratic basis, were in sharp contrast to the rest of the community. In the 100,000-man Army created by von Seeckt, the senior officers came from the old Prussian circle or were steeped in its traditions. I have already referred to the incompatability of the real Prussianism with National Socialism. Inasmuch as these officers sprang from the class of landowners east of the Elbe, or came from old officer families related to them, the background of independent authority in which they had been reared would hardly encourage them to accept the new servility that had become so fashionable. Their outlook was monarchical and Christian-Protestant.

Yet when Hitler came to power there was already a number of generals to whom the leap into this new world presented no insuperable difficulty. By origin they were not so closely linked with the Prussian concept; several of them displayed the same mentality that had already brought Ludenorff into contact with Hitler.

After Hitler's accession General Baron von Fritsch was regarded as the leader of the opposition generals. It was his misfortune to be C.-in-C. of the Army at a time when the régime's first measures in the Army and among the people showed the way things would go. Consequently all those who still hoped that these unfortunate changes could be controlled pinned their hopes on von Fritsch. Yet the stage had already been reached when those who did not meekly submit found themselves powerless. The machinery of the state became an instrument of suppression, and anyone opposing it was destroyed socially, economically and frequently even physically. These events were a sorrowful burden to von Fritsch. His mother came from the Bodelschwingh family, whence he acquired his deep religious feeling. He was respected above all by the older officers. But he had as little chance as his successors of changing the fate of Germany. All men of his nature found themselves both militarily and humanly on a thorny path. At the risk of their lives they stuck to their posts hoping that their influence and personal example might help to avert a further deterioration.

The generals opposing Hitler have been reproached for their lack of enterprise, but this is not justified. In time of war there was rapid advancement for the younger officers, who though still drawn from the Prussian-educated officer corps, had closer ties with the régime—whether through ambition or mere blindness—than the Army commanders. In addition to the generals who aped Ludendorff, some others of a new type became more or less identified with the régime. Hitler dealt with the generals exactly as he had dealt with the politicians. With instinctive cunning he at first hesitated to replace the independently-minded older professionals by more compliant and personally acceptable types. It became easier to do this later, when he could pin the blame for a series of defeats on the older Army leaders who had always been reluctant to bow to his will. The history of war affords many examples of capable commanders suffering the consequences of a defeat for which they personally were blameless.

It is natural that in seeking the causes of the defeat the generals and General Staff officers should hold Hitler responsible, for he had assumed the supreme command and had also constantly interfered in details. The art of strategy is inborn and only too rare. It demands a healthy understanding of humanity and a knowledge of history. There is no need to wonder whether Hitler and his advisers possessed these qualities. His immediate advisers in the O.K.W. enjoyed no standing in Army circles. The respected Chiefs of Staff of the Army who had come from the excellent school of the old General Staff all came to grief. The first ended as a victim of the July 20th plot; the second finished up in a concentration camp; the third, selected by Hitler himself, was dismissed from the Army with ignominy, and the fourth, also picked by Hitler, withdrew from the task under the pressure of events.

It is not to be supposed that a different choice of army leaders would have allowed the war to be won. Certainly many a battle would have ended differently. But the military defeat was already implicit in the antecedent political defeat, which had provoked a coalition of all the great powers against Hitler's Germany. Even if the impossible had occurred and Germany had won, it is unthinkable that the defeated powers would have submitted for any length of time to a system of this character. The final outcome would have been no different.

After the First World War certain irresponsible politicians and historians succeeded in disguising the true causes of the total defeat. People clung to the illusion of an Army "undefeated in the field", the fable of the wicked Social Democrats who dealt this Army "a stab in the back", the nonsense of the completely exhausted enemy who could have been defeated in the shortest time "if only we had held on".

As for the Second World War, having considered the historical, political and military reasons for the defeat, there remains a most puzzling question: why did a large part of the German people place

their future in the hands of a man like Hitler? How did it come about
that a man who had so little to contribute could enlist such a huge
following? What was there in his personality that impressed so many
people? How did he manage to avoid being compromised by his
nearest friends and collaborators even before he assumed office? And
if an effective opposition was impossible, how could so many Germans
shut their eyes to all these wretched aberrations and crimes?

9

CAPTIVITY

THE CAMPS IN ITALY

On May 22nd, 1945, I was taken to the Ghedi prisoner-of-war camp to be leader of the camp. Ghedi is a large aerodrome in the plain of the Po. 100,000 men were under canvas—as many as I had commanded in the Cassino battles. Here I had no executive authority, only the responsibility. I felt it to be my duty to visit the officers, still in their existing divisional units, to prepare them for the big changes ahead. It was not merely a change from fighting to impotence, from a service rank to a number, but a change from being a soldier of a country that had kept the world in terror for twelve years to being a prisoner shut off from his family, his people and the outside world.

My talks in the camp were received mostly in silence and with indifference, for I had nothing to offer my audience that could please them. I had to accustom myself to the facial expressions of the officers who listened incredulously or regarded me as an opportunist. They hardly concealed their disappointment and bitterness towards the former authorities and also towards us generals. Many felt that we had misled them, had withheld the truth, had involved them in hopeless battles, and had sustained their morale by resorting to lies.

How gladly I would have spoken some comforting words to these thousands of officers! But that would have meant more lies. No, I was now free to dispense with lies. I explained frankly that all of us had lost our rights, that there was no point in lodging complaints, that for the time being there was no hope of communicating with our families and no right of appeal to officers of the custodian powers. However, it was already something that we were no longer subjected to the Nazi régime, although my audience did not yet know how to use this freedom.

Within a few weeks I was "discredited". The writer Klaus Mann published an article in the American Army newspaper *Stars and Stripes* in which he alleged that the man in command at Gehdi camp was not the authorised American commander of an A.A. brigade, but the German general. So the Chief of Staff to this American

340

general sent for me to say that I was "redundant" here and would be transferred to another P.O.W. camp. After a lengthy drive I was set down in the open country. They had intended to take me to an officers' camp at Modena, but when I arrived it was not yet in being, so I was attached to a German company, whose war-time rest-camp had been turned into a P.O.W. camp simply by surrounding it with barbed wire. Here I was given an excessively large tent, where I passed many a day in complete loneliness. The few German officers were still too obsessed with the difference in rank between themselves and me, their "Commanding General", and I had no desire to bore them with "enlightening talks".

Eventually I was taken to an officers' P.O.W. camp at Modena, where I found people with the same views as myself, in particular a staff officer from the Abwehr, a former collaborator of Admiral Canaris, so that there was some inducement for conversation. Here were started the discussion groups that sprang up everywhere in the further course of our captivity.

Before long I and a group of other generals were taken by truck to a camp at Aversa, north of Naples. At a certain point on our journey an Italian general announced: "We are now crossing the border." I was curious to know which border he meant, and on asking him, received the reply that it was the one between the Kingdom of the Two Sicilies and the rest of Italy. Southern Italians have a habit of ascribing all their misfortunes to the expulsion of the Bourbons, which occurred with the consent of the House of Savoy. Indeed it was only the fall of the Bourbons that enabled Savoy to win the crown of all Italy. This reminded me of Bismarck's action in driving the Guelphs and the Landgraves of Hesse-Cassel from their thrones, and of his speech about the mills of God grinding slow.

Passing Cassino, we saw the deeply scarred battlefield, now at peace. The new camp confirmed my fear that any change would be for the worse. The generals' camp was just one of many barracks; these were enclosed by a barbed-wire fence running only six feet clear of the outer buildings, a barrier that nobody would be allowed to pass for many months. So we tried to pass the days usefully by learning languages, reading and holding group discussions. For the sake of peace we abstained from political arguments. Since American officers were never accessible, we could make no requests. An order had been issued that every German officer had to salute every Allied officer, and the latter was forbidden to return the salute, "Thereby giving expression to his contempt for the Wehrmacht." That was the first reaction on discovering the horrors of the concentration camps! The Allies would not believe that the German generals had nothing to do with these things. In practice many American officers ignored the prohibition on returning salutes.

The generals made the best of things, and with a few minor exceptions life proceeded peaceably. One of the generals was due for an Allied investigation, and he asked me to assist him with my knowledge of languages in the event of a trial. I consented, but had to warn him that I was unsuitable for his defence because of my lack of juridical training.

In the late summer of 1945 the majority of us, that is, all who had no charges pending, were suddenly entrained and sent north. For my own comfort I still had a rubber bathtub, some tea and a spirit-lamp. On the Brenner I had a bath between the rail-tracks as water was available, then shared my tea with a friend.

At Heilbronn we detrained and continued wearily on foot for two kilometres to the new camp. We had not enough strength to drag our luggage along with us, and were threatened by our escorts. I left my trunk standing and felt dispossessed. Seeing our plight, a little girl of ten or twelve burst into tears. There were several dozen of us, and on arival we were ushered into a large tent which let the rain in. After some days we were moved to the prison at Hall. Here we were put by twos into cells which we could not leave. Shortly afterwards I was collected alone and delivered to the prison at Heidelberg. It was a bitter though brief interlude—lacking fresh air, with no comrades, and no reasons given. Within a few days I was taken to an airport. Here a tiny two-seater aircraft was waiting to take me to Italy, where the case against General Dostler that I have already mentioned was due to begin. The pilot did not know his way and had insufficient fuel to do the journey in one hop. I suggested flying through the Burgundy Gap to the Rhone Valley, where we refuelled. Then we flew to Marseilles, where my officer escort invited me to a simple evening meal, of which I was in much need.

The pilot doubted whether the fuel would suffice for the flight across the sea, but in that case it would certainly be inadequate for a flight along the coast. So we flew direct over Corsica to Rome. We arrived at twilight and circled the city several times as my escort wanted to get an idea of it, and I had to explain what was what. Owing to the bad light our landing was not too smooth.

The next day we continued south in good weather, but somehow landed at the wrong aerodrome, where nobody came to fetch me. While waiting I had quite a conversation with the pilot. He said he was pleasantly surprised by the greater cleanliness in Germany, which reminded him of the United States; he found that of all Europeans the Germans were most like the Americans. Evidently he knew little about our politics.

I was taken to another part of the camp at Aversa where General Dostler was still accommodated. I shared my quarters in one of the smaller barracks with Dostler's army commander, who had been retained there as a witness. A young lieutenant also lived with us. He had been punished with extended captivity because he had vigorously protested at the seizure of his personal belongings.

THE FIRST TRIAL OF AN OFFICER

I knew Dostler and esteemed him as a good comrade. I could only speak to him when counsel designated for his defence, the American Colonel Wolfe, wanted to consult him, which was often enough. The colonel took his job seriously, even if he usually seemed pressed for time. He inspired us with confidence.

We were moved to Rome for the trial. This meant a deterioration for me. since we were housed in *Ciné-Citta,* the Roman Hollywood, in solitary confinement and without any reading matter. As an authority on conditions in the Wehrmacht I was treated in the same way as the accused. Under the circumstances I would have preferred to share the company of Dostler.

Each morning we were driven through Rome to the Law Courts in a prison-van, its siren screeching continuously. The trial had attracted many spectators, mostly war-reporters and other journalists of both sexes. In the intervals of the trial we went over the proceedings in our own circle, which included the two American defence counsel and members of our guard. They were pleased whenever the examination seemed to favour Dostler.

The proceedings opened with the defence contesting the competence of the court, on the ground that Dostler was no criminal but a captive officer who could not be tried by an *ad hoc* court of generals, but only by a court-martial. Counsel for the defence argued that the court had not even been summoned by the theatre C.-in-C., Sir Harold Alexander, but by an American general subordinate to him. After withdrawing for lengthy deliberations the court rejected this plea.

The chief prosecutor, Major Frederick W. Roche, then explained the incident that led to the charge. In March 1944 a so-called commando unit of fifteen men had put to sea from Bastia with orders to blow up a tunnel between Genoa and La Spezia which the Allied air force had failed to destroy. The unit was composed of American soldiers of Italian origin. It was captured by Italian troops who were guarding the tunnel. By order of Dostler, who was the corps commander in this coastal sector, the fifteen men were shot.

The execution of these men conformed to the Führer's order of October 18th, 1942, whereby any saboteurs or commandos captured behind the lines were to be shot. Dostler had acted in accordance with this order and, as he maintained, in compliance with a further order received from his own army commander.

Like many of Hitler's orders, this one doubtless constituted an infringement of international law. There have always been soldiers in uniform who perpetrated acts of sabotage behind the lines. This activity constituted part of the fighting and was not criminal. The army commander, summoned as a witness, denied having given such an order. Dostler's Chief of Staff would have been an important witness for the defence, since he could have enlightened the court as to whether the order was indeed issued from a higher authority—that is, from the army group or the army. But strangely enough the Chief of Staff could not be found, although it later transpired that he was still in the big P.O.W. camp at Rimini.

Only once during the trial did I succeed in silencing the prosecutor, much to the satisfaction of the defendant. This was when I pointed out that an Allied battalion commander in North Africa had allegedly ordered a commando unit to kill any prisoners falling into its hands. There was a good reason for this order: a commando unit has always to remain concealed, and cannot afford to burden itself with prisoners. I therefore thought it quite possible that Hitler's order had been issued as a reprisal for this incident, which could be admissible in international law, and that the accused general could well have come to that conclusion without being sure of his facts.

But the prosecutor kept a few trump cards up his sleeve, which aggravated Dostler's case. The Abwehr officers who interrogated the prisoners had appealed directly to the army group commander to postpone the execution so that the men could be further interrogated. In other words, their execution ran counter to German interests. The Germans wanted to find out whether or not the enemy intended to make a fresh landing in the rear of the fighting front. The interrogation of these men might well be of the greatest importance.

It was further established that prior to the execution a delegation from the S.D. had arrived to collect the prisoners, but Dostler had ostensibly refused to comply. Was he still hoping to save them? That would have been out of the question once they had fallen into the hands of the S.D. In the end the prosecutor declared that the army group had been a few hours too late in ordering the postponement of the execution.

Counsel for the defence pleaded on behalf of Dostler that he was an honourable officer, who under such circumstances was bound to obey orders, and that this applied to all officers, whether they belonged to Hitler's Germany or to the United States of America.

I shall always remember the defending counsel's solemn affirmation to the judges: "There is no clause in the laws of the United States that would condemn this officer. If nevertheless you do so, it would have been better that we had not won this war."

The trial ended on October 12th, 1945, with Dostler's sentence to death by shooting. He and I were kept apart. Some time later I was taken, handcuffed to a pleasant young officer, to Dostler's camp. But first I was subjected to a physical search that verged on maltreatment. I was then shown into Dostler's cell, which he shared with a Catholic priest. He was his usual self, cheerful and relaxed, explaining that he only wanted to thank me for my friendship and good offices and to bid me farewell, as he was due to be shot next morning.

Too moved to speak, I stood there a while looking him in the face, this comrade with smiling eyes who in adversity had become my friend.

From his quarters Dostler could witness the rehearsal of the firing-squad. At his execution he declined to be blindfolded and died with these words on his lips: "My soul in God's keeping, my life for the Fatherland."

IN BRITISH CUSTODY

Together with Dostler's army commander I was taken back to the camp at Aversa, where we spent some weeks before being moved, suddenly as usual, to a British camp at Afragola near Naples.

Here life began with a shock. On the evening of the first day we were put into a special tent containing one or two members of the Parachute Rifle Division. Like them we had to surrender our trousers at night. A young German officer offered me a sleeping-berth on a table to avoid having to lie on the bare ground. The next day my request to see the camp commandant was immediately granted. I complained that we were being treated like particularly dangerous and criminal officers, and reminded him that at the trial in Rome we had only been called as expert witnesses. The commandant promised to make immediate enquiries, and within a few hours we were transfered to the normal officers' camp. Each of us was given a tent to himself, but this had disadvantages too, for the weather had turned bitterly cold. On fine days we could sit in the sun, but at night we shivered. In rainy weather the nights were warmer, the days cheerless. Yet I was content to be by myself. The camp contained very few older officers. Strangely enough the only S.S. officer had been appointed camp-leader. He was correct and polite, which was in keeping with the conduct that had been enjoined on all S.S. officers. They were very punctilious in such matters, for they regarded themselves as the élite of the Wehrmacht.

The weeks passed slowly, until I began to think that they would turn into years. We did not yet realise how fortunate we were to have fallen into the hands of the Western powers; many of our poor comrades in Soviet captivity were not to be released for twelve years. Intellectual interests were almost completely lacking in our camp. I became lonely and so entered a phase that officer prisoners in Russia must have found far more exacting. I stayed in this camp for three months in all, during which time I fell ill with enteritis and was put in the camp hospital. The complaint vanished almost overnight when I slept on a mattress again instead of the camp-bed that had been provided in the tent. I was visited daily by a British sergeant, presumably by order of the commandant, and he was full of kindness and sympathy.

On one occasion I was collected by a sentry and taken to one of the camp gates. Until then we never had any contact with the outside world or communication by mail, so that I was all the more surprised to be suddenly confronted by dear friends. At the gate were the Bishop of Veroli and my friend the Marchese Campanari with his daughter. They brought me cakes, a gift from the Benedictine nuns of Veroli.

There was a big change in February 1946. My two former army commanders, von Vietinghoff and Lemelsen, were transferred from the large officers' camp at Rimini to Afragola. Spending a night with us, they remarked how utterly primitive the conditions were compared with Rimini. Early the next morning we were summoned to the private quarters of the commandant. He did not allow us to sit down, and himself remained standing for two hours until the plane detailed for our transportation was ready to leave. His manner was polite and correct. Eventually we boarded the Junkers plane, where we sat on benches facing one another. I was happy to be with old comrades again, but gradually the conversation flagged and we all relapsed into gloomy thoughts of the future.

Fortunately I was unaware that at this time my nineteen-year-old daughter was travelling the hard way across the whole of Italy to Taranto. She was in a Red Cross truck, having set out from South Tyrol in an attempt to find and comfort me. On her return journey she reached the west coast and the camp at Afragola twenty-four hours after I had left by plane.

During the flight I did not conjure up any better hopes for the second, and probably longer, period of captivity that was in store for me in Great Britain. Two world wars had changed the destiny of both our nations. I had last stayed in England when the last landmarks of the nineteenth century were rapidly disappearing, and the country had since been transformed.

In London we were taken in a prison-van to the Central District Cage in Kensington. Here we were not badly treated, but the food was as usual inadequate. We were told to produce written comments on certain atrocities alleged to have occurred in our district while fighting the partisans. I was able to prove that during my period in command I had refused to implement directives from higher authorities regarding summary executions. In my view these so-called judg-

ments were not only illegal, but likely to provoke serious mis-
demeanours.

THE CAMP AT BRIDGEND

After a week or two we were moved to the P.O.W. camp for high-
ranking officers at Bridgend in South Wales, on the Bristol Channel.
The inmates ranged from Field-Marshals—Brauchitsch, Manstein,
Rundstedt—to Nazi Labour Force commanders with the equivalent
rank of general. In a sense these captives reflected the reaction of
the German people to the collapse of the Hitler régime and to the
lost war. The officers split themselves into three groups. The first,
which I joined, aimed at drawing up a balance-sheet, clearing-up
obscurities and coming to conclusions. Its members were long-standing
opponents of the régime, whose attitude towards it had been clear
to everyone long before the collapse. Membership of this group
was not an easy matter for those inmates of the camp who had
waited until after the collapse before criticising the Hitler régime;
they would not admit that its shortcomings had been previously
discernible. A number of generals in this category nevertheless
found their way into the group, but many others refrained from
joining it for the reasons given. The latter were far more numerous,
and they probably reflected the attitude of the average German
in his own country. Lastly, the third group consisted of die-hard
followers of Hitler, who understandably kept away from any
discussions on the subject.

A conflict existed between the first group and the other two.
The third in particular regarded any settlement of the account
with the Hitler régime as an undignified and grovelling method of
winning the favour of the custodian power. Many found it repellant to
welcome the speakers, mostly emigrants from Germany, who had been
sent to the camp to join in our discussions. The speakers were
listened to, but there was no discussion with them, on the excuse
that the prisoners were bitter because of what they regarded as
their unjustified detention.

All of us suffered through the deprivation of our freedom and
even more because of uncertainty over the fate of our families. Many
of us feared that we would be summoned to appear at the War
Crimes trials in Nuremburg. One or two were in fact sent there later.

In my opinion these professional military officers could not be said
to constitute a special category of "outlawed" Hitlerite generals.
They were but the representatives of our misguided and pitiable
people. Naturally I was least interested in the third group, the
majority of whom had been poorly educated. Much more of a problem were those in the second group who had resolutely refused
to believe anything bad about the régime. But at least they now

admitted these "bad things", and that was a way to salvation. I tried to deal honestly with the arguments of these men who "did not know", and there were many of them. I soon discovered that they had indeed known far less than I and my friends. That we were not so ignorant was certainly due to the fact that for years all the opponents of the régime had been like a secret order whose members could easily recognise each other and spoke freely about everything among themselves. I also discovered that the cases of betrayal of such men through careless speech or through informers were far fewer than I had imagined. Hitler's followers did not so easily unearth his opponents, who took the precaution of carefully disguising their attitude in one way or another. The opponents naturally knew more about the atrocities, but never the full extent of them.

Hence it could be said with some reason that the more knowledgeable opponents of Hitler had been more to blame than his ignorant followers. Yet far from solving the problem, this made it all the more difficult.

I was compelled to admit that other nations, such as the French, the Spaniards and the South American Spaniards had sometimes flourished under dictatorships which allowed no political freedom. So why not the Germans, particularly in the circumstances of economic decline after the first war under a feeble Weimar democracy? However desirable it might be to understand the mentality of those who "did not know", the gulf between them and us remained unbridgeable.

For instance, they never experienced any revulsion at the speeches of the deceased dictator, nor felt estranged by his fanatical rantings, which left not the smallest scope for impartial discussion. They remained unmoved when he uttered all those threats—against other nations, against the more liberal-minded citizens, against defenceless and intimidated Jews. They had not demurred at the pretensions to power of the thick-skinned party officials who ruled over them. If they did not sigh for political freedom, did they not miss the freedom of the arts and of the intellect, or suffer from the lack of taste of the party? To me it will always remain inexplicable that educated men failed to perceive the suicidal nature of the party's twelve-year fight against justice. The want of revolutionary liberating movements in Germany was reflected in the individual citizen's indifference to taking a share in shaping the history of the nation. Instead he cultivated an excessive respect for authority as represented by the executive. Despite its numerous repellent features, many saw in the Hitler régime only a strong executive which had discarded all pretence of representing the people which had "at last" dispensed with the multitude of opinions, the debates, the criticism of and parliamentary interference in the machinery of government. That is precisely what the German citizen wanted, for he had never felt politically at ease with the Weimar democracy. In this respect the average Army general had been like all other citizens except that he embodied these weaknesses to a higher degree. Authority and obedience were basic to his profession, and in the course of centuries he had come to judge a government by its capacity "to give orders and be obeyed". To that extent the generals of Germany were not really different from those of other nations, with the possible exception of the British and the Americans. What was different in Germany was that the people always tended to adopt the political views of the military. Consequently the political attitude of their senior military officers had a considerable influence on the nation on which they were dependent for their livelihood.

But this basic attitude did not necessarily have to result in National Socialism. Many generals who were against Hitler did not reject a dictatorship as long as the men at the top were "competent and sensible", by which they meant experts in the different branches of government. That naturally applied with special force to their own profession of arms. Hitler's amateur interference in strategic matters provided them with an argument against all civilian intervention in military affairs. They failed to appreciate that the incompetence of the statesmen in matters of strategy had itself contributed to a decline in the strategic art. Without the fertile soil of politics there can be no genuine strategy. It had been thus since Schlieffen, and continued so up to the time of Ludendorff's pretension to power and his inability to see strategic problems in a political setting.

A not altogether unjustified reproach was levelled at the generals because their opposition to the régime developed only as a result of their belief that they would have avoided Hitler's mistakes and might therefore have won the war. This kind of false comparison with Hitler, which related only to his lack of competence, was damaging to the German position both during and after the war. There were other opponents who, while attributing the defeat to Hitler's incompetence, had no understanding of the need for the statesman's political control of the military, and who nevertheless objected to the régime on moral grounds. This was particularly applicable to the tradition-bound Prussian officers, with their marked Lutheran outlook. In nearly every case it can be shown that those generals who fully backed Hitler had no roots in the old Prussian-Lutheran soil. This again reflected the condition of the entire nation; those men whose roots were in Christianity did not hesitate to develop an attitude of resistance to Hitler, irrespective of whether they were Catholic or Protestant. The Prussian generals were all Protestant. Catholicism, being a supra-national religion, immunised its adherents in another way, since their ties with fellow Catholics in other lands were irreconcilable with and would have been destroyed by a fanatical National Socialism that had developed its own philosophy of life.

In this situation the Prussians also turned their thoughts to a monarchy. They seized on an idea of Churchill's that Hitlerism might have been avoided if Germany had remained a monarchy. There is something in this idea, but it has its dangers. It springs from the concept that the people have a need to look up to some mystically elevated personality. Yet that concept prevents the growth of democracy in the sense of a liberal constitution. Moreover if a monarch is to safeguard the modern constitutional state, he must rely on a Parliament, in whose name his sovereignty is exercised to promulgate the laws. If the duties of the monarch are so conceived, it is immaterial whether he or an elected President stands at the head of the true democracy. This is borne out by the monarchies that still exist.

In Germany even the genuine opponents of the Hitler régime were at fault in allowing the executives to decide the form of the constitution. That had been the practice in the constitutional monarchy, and it resulted in the impotence of a people which had but little parliamentary control over the Ministers. The Germans had never experienced full political freedom. This backwardness was the breeding-ground for a submissiveness without which Hitler's dictatorship would never have been possible.

It was considerations of this nature that gave me a feeling of profound compassion for many of my comrades. They had never witnessed the greater power of a democracy as I had done in my youth. Such a democracy rejects any mystical cult of the leader, but relies on reaching common-sense decisions through the unceasing and uninhibited interplay of men's minds.

After some months I was asked to take over the functions of Press officer, which enabled me to see almost all the British weeklies and some of the daily papers. In my weekly reports I tried to outline the current political developments, and through a selection of Press commentaries I was able to exert a certain amount of educational influence. I felt it my duty to explain to those of my comrades who were less versed in languages how profoundly we had been defeated and how the civilised world had become estranged from our Fatherland. Nor did I conceal from my audience that one of the first to subscribe to the relief of the hungry population of Germany was the Jewish publisher Gollancz. There were many opportunities of inconspicuously encouraging the small circle of men of good will towards "the way back"—back to the normality of civil and civic life, back to a respect for essential moral standards, back to law and order—for this was the only possible basis for the new life of our own nation within the community of nations.

END OF THE ROAD—HOMECOMING

As a prisoner-of-war one was a mere number, but as Press officer one tried prudently to enlighten one's comrades. I also had a third contact with life. At Bridgend we had two successive commandants, both carefully selected, both personifying the British gentleman—polite, sympathetic and courteous, in short, disarming towards many an inmate.

Eventually I and one or two other prisoners obtained permission to walk out of the camp without escort in the morning, work throughout the day on one of the neighbouring estates, and return for the evening meal. Only those who have experienced captivity can appreciate what this change meant to me. The principal material benefit of this concession was that the owner of the estate supplied us with a large sandwich by way of additional mid-day nourishment. The hot soup that we normally had in the camp at noon was saved for our evening meal. For the first time in eighteen months we had enough to eat!

The large park was dominated by the residence. Usually we worked at a leisurely pace in the garden with the head gardener and his assistant. We started with three prisoners, but two of them gave up, so that I alone was left. Not until then did my real "freedom" begin, for now I could arrange my work and movements with the head gardener at my own discretion. During the day I lived, as it were, on the estate, although I never entered the owner's house. Saturdays were the best, when work stopped at noon and I never returned to the camp, but went for long walks along the lonely coast. Here I was more solitary than on the estate, and enjoyed it.

My squire was silent and reserved—even towards his countrymen and guests, as I could observe from my place of work. He owned a dozen or more large farms. He neither rode a horse nor hunted, but occasionally worked in the woods. His wife was young and pretty, with dark hair and blue eyes. She was probably breaking the rules when she occasionally entered into a conversation with me or brought me a piece of cake, for which I was most appreciative. When her mother or brothers were there on a visit, we chatted among each other as though we had all been invited to spend the week-end. Sometimes she would give me leave of absence for the whole day when there was a meet in the neighbourhood. She and her two adolescent daughters would be there, and I of course had to get permission from the camp commandant to attend it. He never refused, knowing about my enthusiasm for hunting.

It is true that the sport was not of the first order, which made it all the easier for me to follow the pack on foot or by getting a lift in a car. Occasionally a member of the hunt would express regret that "they" had not yet got me mounted! This countryside, which merged with the sand-dunes, contained few obstacles. On one occasion I captured a memorable impression of the time-honoured English setting when some twenty couple of hounds tore towards me in full cry followed by the scattered field, all against a background of the blue Atlantic waves.

On Sundays too we were given more liberty. We could attend the church service of our choice, and after going to Mass I visited one or other of the twenty-four sects in order to get an impression of them. On the whole they were more brotherly towards us than the established churches. The first to appear in the camp were the Plymouth Brethren, who are probably the least tied to church concepts. They brought along cakes and coffee and held forth at table on religious subjects. The Anglicans, Baptists and Methodists were moderate; their visits were not for the purpose of "converting" us. Those among us who did not belong to any Church were invariably anti-clerical. Our Lutherans had their own German priest in the camp. It happened that my comrades were dissatisfied with him, and I, being of another creed, was invited to give my opinion of him. I felt honoured at this manifestation of confidence in me. I interceded on behalf of the priest, but they continued to shun him. Thereafter he often visited me in my cell.

The Protestant prisoners did not easily accommodate themselves to the Church of England, for they thought that its services were too Catholic. Yet our parish was by no means High Church. Among us Germans the Church of England is often mistakenly described as "High Church".

I could not help admiring the sects, which were held together by a sense of brotherliness. They had no long tradition of divine service, no ancient theology and no clearly defined or inflexible doctrine, yet they maintained their faith.

Within the camp there was no rift between the various religious denominations. As everywhere in post-war Germany, so also in this camp the reconciliation between the confessions became closer in proportion as the Christians clung to their faith. The great danger that all had so recently experienced convinced people of the need to stand together. Although the compulsion of the state was a thing of the past, we were still troubled at the lack of integrity that had led to the German catastrophe.

Despite all the philanthropic concessions, captivity remained a heavy imposition. I was not allowed to send P. more than a few lines each month, not enough to advise her on the administration of our property, or even to give counsel on the children, who would soon be of marriageable age. Despite her many friends, P. was loneliest in Göttingen whenever she most needed some guidance. I at least had the satisfaction of knowing that the British were being helpful to her. They knew who we were. The British commandant in Göttingen visited her soon after the occupation; his wife exchanged provisions with her, so that both were able to relieve the monotony of their fare. By dealing in antiques, P. was able to keep her head above water. Her former passion for collecting things now bore fruit. It all started when she gave advice to the deserving poor who did not realise the value of their small collections and were in danger of selling them for a song. She helped these people to put a proper price to their transactions with the enthusiastic American collectors.

When St. John's, my old College at Oxford, heard of my captivity they at once offered to arrange for my son to come and visit me. However, the bureaucratic machinery was so slow that in the meantime I was repatriated. But my son was invited all the same, and the President of the College befriended him. Thirty-five years earlier he and I had been in College together as undergraduates, and had kept up our friendship. I often recalled those happy days. Reclining on the huge lawn of St. John's, I used to admire the Tudor façade that had appealed to me before ever I set foot in Oxford. I used to get great pleasure out of my frequent dinners in the Senior Common Room, where a dinner jacket is *de rigueur*. At the end of the meal we stood over a glass of port for the centuries-old toast of "The Church and the King", which was given by the Senior Tutor.

In the camp we were also visited "collectively" by the distinguished military writer, Captain B. H. Liddell Hart, who was so well-disposed towards the Germans, and with whom I have since developed a friendship that is not merely professional. Several times I have enjoyed the hospitality of his home, and he was on a visit to me in Germany when the Korean War broke out.

Finally I was visited at Bridgend by my old friend from the Oxford days, Kurt Hahn. The founder of Salem, he had since been compelled to emigrate and had opened the well-known school at Gordonstoun in Scotland. He suggested that after my release I should work in one of his schools. Thus I could hope not to remain idle for too long.

At last the day came when on return to the camp in the evening the sentry congratulated us on our impending discharge. Some time elapsed before we packed our kit-bags, like emigrants. With melancholy thoughts I left my old overcoat on the bed of my cell. It had been with me in many a battle and was worn to a thread. On May 13th and 14th we drove via Oxford and Newmarket, where horseracing had taken place ever since the Stuarts, saw in the distance the many church spires of Cambridge, and arrived at the dispersal camp at Bury St. Edmunds. The next day we embarked at Harwich for the Hook of Holland, which again stirred memories of thirty-five years earlier. The sea was rough and dotted with medium-sized yachts taking part in a regatta. They dominated the scene as they fought, widely scattered, against a strong wind. I sat alone, contemplating the sea and the storm-tossed boats. What a change it would be, after ten years of strictly military life and captivity, to learn to stand again on one's feet, to earn a living in the open market so as to provide for the family, to come to terms with one's new surroundings. It was hardly to be expected that the German people would receive their generals back with open arms. They would more likely (and rightly) reproach us for not realising the situation and for doing nothing to put an end to the war.

I also had to realise that the great majority of our officers had long since returned to their homes, that the debates on the Army's relations with Hitler had been going on for some time and that the dubious case of the pro-Hitler generals had been exposed and was a matter of public knowledge.

Finally I could not picture the sort of home to which I would be returning, for my house, which had formerly contained my small family and one or two servants, was now occupied by seventeen people with varying pretensions. They had gradually taken possession of all the rooms and the bathroom, leaving my wife with one room to herself. The knowledge of all this clouded the prospect of my reunion with P. and of my new liberty.

At the Hook of Holland we were well catered for in an officers' mess that had evidently been equipped for the British, then travelled on to Munsterlager, where we arrived on May 16th. The formalities of discharge were brief. The British commandant at Bridgend had accompanied us throughout our homeward journey and ensured that everything went smoothly. On the 18th he drove me and two colleagues as far as Hanover, where we parted on the friendliest terms. I took the next train to Göttingen, which I reached in the middle of the night.

On the deserted street I could see a solitary figure, apparently also homeward-bound. So I addressed him: "We'll soon be home now!" to which he answered: "Things are not the same there as they used to be." He was probably alluding to a broken marriage. That, too, is part of the German tragedy.

The kit-bag seemed heavy as I continued alone through the darkness on that long, gently rising road. I wondered how I would summon P. without rousing all the others. Then I was at the "Hohe Weg". Very quietly I stepped into the garden behind the house and gave the low whistle that was our special signal. P. appeared on the veranda.

BIOGRAPHICAL NOTES

Baade, General: Commander of 90 Panzer Grenadier Division. His last command was a Panzer Corps on the western front, killed in air attack, 8.5.1945.

Beck, Ludwig, Colonel-General: Born 1880, served in World War I as a General Staff Officer. In 1933 became Chief of the *Truppenamt*, and in 1935 Chief of the Army General Staff. In August, 1938, he opposed Hitler's war plans during the Sudeten crisis, and retired. In World War II he was at the head of the German resistance to Hitler, and when the plot to kill him on 20th July, 1944, failed, he committed suicide.

von Bohme, Colonel: Chief of Staff to General Heinrich von Stülpnagel.

von Brauchitsch, Walter, Field Marshal: Born 1881, died 1948. Succeeded Fritsch in 1938 as C.-in-C. of the Army, and conducted the campaigns against Poland, France, Jugoslavia, Greece and Russia. Retired in December, 1941, when Hitler assumed the title of C.-in-C. of the Army.

Canaris, Wilhelm, Admiral: Born 1887. In 1935 became head of the German military Secret Service. During World War II he collaborated with Colonel-General Beck in secret resistance to Hitler. In February, 1944, he was dismissed, and after the 20th July was arrested and hanged at Flossenburg concentration camp on 9th April, 1945.

Fellgiebel, General: Head of Army Communications. After Count von Stauffenberg's attempted assassination of Hitler on 20th July, 1944, he helped him to make his escape, and was accused of being involved in the plot.

von Fritsch, Werner, Colonel-General: Born 1880. Between 1935 and 1938 was C.-in-C. of the Army. Tried on a trumped-up charge of homosexuality and acquitted, he sacrificed his life while fighting in the front line against Warsaw in 1939.

Geyr von Schweppenburg, General: Born 1886. From 1933 to 1937 was German military attaché in London, Brussels and The Hague. In the war he was the Commander of armoured forces in the west and Inspector of armour at Army G.H.Q. In 1951 the English version of his book was published under the title "The Critical Years."

Guderian, Colonel-General: Born 1888, died 1954. Was instrumental in building up German armoured forces. During W.W.II he commanded a Panzer Army, but was relieved in December, 1941, and in 1943 was appointed Inspector of Armoured Forces. After the 20th July, 1944, Hitler made him Chief of the Army General Staff.

Hahn, Kurt: Born 1886. Founder of the educational establishment at Salem, of which he was head from 1920 to 1933. The following year he came to England, where he founded the school at Gordonstoun.

Halder, Colonel-General: Born 1884. Until 1942 was Chief of the Army General Staff. After the July, 1944, plot he was arrested, and at the end of the war was liberated from a concentration camp.

von Hammerstein-Equord, Count, Colonel-General: Born 1878, died 1943. In 1934 he resigned from his post as C.-in-C. of the Army. In 1939 he became an Army Corps Commander in the West. He was one of the most active opponents of Hitler in the resistance movement.

Heidrich, General: Commander of the 1st Paratroop Division.

Hoepner, Erich, Colonel-General: Born 1886. In 1938, during the Sudenten crisis, he was already involved in the plans of Beck and Witzleben for a *coup d'état*. In the war he commanded an Army Corps, and on the eastern front, a Panzer Army. In 1942 he was ordered by Hitler to give up his command, and later was condemned to death for participating in the conspiracy of July, 1944.

Hohenlohe, Prince Hubert: Assistant Adjutant on the German Liaison Staff with the Italian Armistice Commission.

Hoth, Colonel-General: Commander of the 4th Panzer Army up to the Stalingrad crisis in 1942.

Hube, Colonel-General: Commander of XIV Panzer Corps in Sicily, and later in Italy.

Keitel, Wilhelm, Field-Marshal: Born 1882, executed at Nüremburg on 16th October, 1946. Chief of Staff of the O.K.W. (Supreme Command of the Armed Forces). In June, 1940, he conducted the Armistice negotiations at Compiègne and on 8th May, 1945, had to sign the instrument of surrender in Berlin.

Kesselring, Albert, Field-Marshal: Born 1885, died 1951. In 1936/37 was Chief of Staff of the Luftwaffe. In W.W.II he commanded Air Fleets 1 and 2 in Poland and France and in the campaign against Russia. During 1943/5 was C.-in-C. South in the Italian campaign. In May, 1947, was sentenced to death by a British Military tribunal, the sentence being commuted to life imprisonment, but he was released in 1952.

von Mackensen, Colonel-General: Commander of 14th Army in Italy.

von Manstein, Field-Marshal: Born 1887. Was a career officer from 1905 to 1945. His last command (1942-44) was as C.-in-C. of the Southern Army Group on the eastern front.

Olbricht, Friedrich, General: Born 1888. As Head of the Army Administrative Services (Allgemeines Heeresamt) he was a member of the military resistance to Hitler, and was summarily executed on the evening of 20th July, 1944.

Oster, Hans, General: Born 1887. Was an active member of the resistance within the Secret Service (Abwehr), and was murdered by the Gestapo on 9th April, 1945, at the concentration camp at Flossenburg.

Paulus, Friedrich, Field-Marshal: Born 1890, died 1957. Was C.-in-C. of the 6th Army when it was forced to capitulate at Stalingrad on 31st January, 1943.

Rommel, Erwin, Field-Marshal: Born 1891, committed suicide on 14th October, 1944. In 1940 he took command of the German African-Corps, and later he commanded Army Group B in northern France up to 17th July, 1944.

von Rundstedt, Gerst, Field-Marshal: Born 1875, died 1953. Was relieved of his Army Group Command in 1941 by Hitler's order, but in the following year was made C.-in-C. West. Was again relieved in 1944, but soon re-instated as C.-in-C. West.

Schmidt von Altenstadt, Colonel: Chief of Staff of XIV Panzer Corps.

von Stauffenberg, Count: Born 1907, executed on 20th July, 1944. He made the unsuccessful attempt on Hitler's life.

von Vietinghoff-Scheel, Colonel-General: C.-in-C. of the 10th Army in Italy.

Warlimont, Walter, General: Deputy Chief of the Operations Staff in O.K.W. Author of a book on the O.K.W. covering the war years, published in 1962.

Westphal, Siegfried; Cavalry General: Born 1902. Between 1932 and 1935 was in the War Academy in Berlin. In 1942 was C.O.S. to the German-Italian Armoured Forces in Africa. In the last two years of W.W.II he was successively C.O.S. to the Army Group in Italy and to the C.-in-C. West.

von Witzleben, Erich, Field Marshal: Born 1891, executed on 9th August, 1944, in Berlin. In 1938 he was already planning with Halder to arrest Hitler, but the negotiations at Munich precluded concerted action. As the leading participant in the plot of 20th July, 1944, he was condemned to death by the "People's Tribunal".

Wolff, Obergruppenführer in the S.S.: On 8th March, 1945, he started secret negotiations in Switzerland for the capitulation of German forces in Italy.

INDEX